HIGH MAGIC & LOW CUNNING:
BATTLE SCENES FOR FIVE ICONS

A 13TH AGE ADVENTURE

BY CAL MOORE

Pelgrane

Press

13TH AGE IS A FANTASY ROLEPLAYING GAME BY
ROB HEINSOO, JONATHAN TWEET,
LEE MOYER, & AARON McCONNELL

FIRE OPAL

www.fireopalmedia.com and **www.pelgranepress.com**

CREDITS

PUBLISHER
Simon Rogers

ASSISTANT PUBLISHER
Cathriona Tobin

AUTHOR
Cal Moore

DEVELOPER, EDITOR, AND ART DIRECTOR
Rob Heinsoo

COVER
Patricia Smith

ARTWORK
Rich Longmore, Patricia Smith

CARTOGRAPHERS
Pär Lindström (The Three), Gill Pearce (Archmage), Ralf Schemmann (High Druid, Orc Lord, Prince of Shadows)

MAP WRANGLER
Simon Rogers

ICON AND MONSTER TILES
Lee Moyer, Aaron McConnell

LAYOUT
Aileen E. Miles

PLAYTESTERS
Matt Adelsperger, Kate Irwin, Doug Jacobson, Sarah Keortge, Marc Weddle, Steve Robinson, Allison Shinkle, Joe Smith, Emi Tanji, Rich Williams, Steve Ellis, Cat Tobin, Dave, Steve Dempsey, Mark Fulford, George Thaw, Jay Godden, Christopher Godden, John Scott, Beth Lewis, Joanna Piancastelli, Simon Hibbs, Roland Rogers, Whit Mattson, Josef Castiel, Stephen Hoffman, Matt Hoffman, Candace Koller, Jacob Fleming, Víctor Andrade, Aaron Pérez, Sebastian Pérez, Luis Gallardo, Carlos Negrete, Laura Elisa Jiménez, Sean Nokes, Jeremy Bednarski, Cory Milligan, Mike Fuller, Christopher Duncan, Kevin Elmore, Stephan Pfuetze, Brendon Hays, John Edwards, Robert Dempsey, Crystal Elmore, Matthew Parmeter, Steven Cagle, Samuel D Frazier II, Robert Dorgan, William Ansell, Chad Brown, Jonathan Duhrkoop, Vincent Foley, Edward Kim, David Stenkampf, Kristofer Wade, Jeff Hewartson, Will Holden, Derek Storey, Jackson Martin, Larissa Black, Terry laForge III, Wayne Ergang, Andrew Sturman, Duncan Sellars, Glenn Jones, Linda Streatfield, Jacqlyn Edge, Stefanos Anastasiadis, David Brandt, Felipe Bouroncle, David Brandt, Chris Collier, Miah Collier, Rick Lewis, David Aldridge, Yannis Choupas, Sigurd Kirkevold Næss, Mikko Kivelä, Joseph Norris, Max Renner

TABLE OF

Contents

Introduction

This book contains battles for *13th Age* GMs looking for both inspiration and for something solid to run in a hurry. The battle scenes work well when you don't have anything prepared for a session, or when story-guide dice indicate a specific icon is in play and you're not sure where to go with it, or when you need to fulfill a complication (or an advantage in some cases) from icon relationships. Each set of battles is keyed to a particular icon, pitting the PCs against NPCs and enemies that are linked to that icon, or fall under that icon's influence.

This book covers five icons: the Archmage, High Druid, Orc Lord, Prince of Shadows, and the Three. We designed a set of battles for each icon in each tier, giving you three total sets of battles to work with per icon, 15 in this book). Since these are iconic battles, each one is designed to be **more challenging than a normal battle** (about 25% more difficult) so be warned. Some are double-strength battles, making them very difficult. If your players and their PCs are less battle-focused, you might need to reduce the enemies they face or give them larger benefits for icon advantages.

Each scene in a set of battles has a storyline that links it to the battles that come after, with the intent that a GM could take the PCs from one full heal-up to the next using only the battles in the set, but with room for GMs to expand upon the stories to fill multiple sessions of gameplay as needed. Or a GM can use only a battle or two that works with their current storyline, spreading them out as needed.

The book includes multiple ideas on how to get the PCs into the battle scene story, and possible outcomes that result from their actions, but we expect GMs and players to have more creative and personal solutions to form the "connective tissue" between battle scenes and group-created adventures.

The battle scenes contain a mix of existing enemies from the core rulebook, *13th Age Bestiary*, and *13 True Ways*, as well as plenty of new monsters to challenge the PCs. There's a scattering of magic items inside too, some new and some from the core books or the *Book of Loot*.

When you decide to use one of these battle scenes, we suggest giving it at least one read-through so you get the basic premise of the story and don't miss any of the fun details, especially the various terrain challenges that pop up in many battles. A read-through will help whether you play it straight or adapt the scenes to fit your group and current storylines.

Structure of the Scenes

Each set of battle scenes contains the following sections.

Level Range

The suggested level range for PCs facing the battle scene to have a challenging and fun battle. If the PCs' level is higher or lower, you'll need to adjust the enemy stats accordingly. Generally the scenes are keyed to groups of between 4 and 6 PCs.

Introduction

This is the setup for the battle scenes to give you a sense of the story.

Story Openings

We provide a handful of possible ways the PCs get involved with the battle scenes. We fully expect GMs and players to be more creative and use connections that fit what's going on in their current campaign, but these are some default options using the icons.

Alternate Icons

Just because the battle scenes are keyed to a specific icon doesn't mean you can't rekey them to another icon to fit better into your campaign. This short section gives tips for possible conversions.

Overview

This section outlines the framework of the battle scenes to help you understand the plot. It's no substitute for reading the full scene, but it gets you started figuring out how to work the scene into your game.

Battles (2 to 4)

Each set of battle scenes contains between two and four battles (some will be double-strength fights). Each battle has the following sections.

Map: The map shows the terrain features, cover and the starting positions of the PCs and their foes. The map labels show the rough position of monsters and some terrain features. Monster positions are approximate because battles use different numbers of monsters based on the number and level of the PCs. You can download full color version of the maps, and a version without the creature tokens from the Pelgrane Press website, or get the complete set, printed out, in *The High Magic & Low Cunning Map Folio*.

Flavor Text: This text describes the scene for the PCs and can either be read aloud to set the stage or used as extra detail to describe the setting as you like.

Location Description: This section provides more detail on the scene location and general setup of the battle, including notes about detecting enemies, ambushes, and NPC motivations.

Terrain & Traps: Every battle scene contains terrain that the PCs and their enemies will interact with. Some also include obstacles, challenges, and traps that will test them as well. Note that not all DCs conform to the standard 15/20/25 etc. suggestion in the core book; we adjust those DCs up or down at times to fit a scene. Whenever text asks for checks, assume it's a skill check that can apply backgrounds, even if we've only referred to it as a check that involves a particular ability score. It's always fun to work backgrounds into the game, and the math of the skill checks assumes it.

Monsters & Monster Chart: A description of the enemies in the battle, additional motivations, and starting locations. The monster chart outlines how many enemies to throw at PCs depending on their level and their number (assuming between four and six). There's also a subheading that lists "Additional Reinforcements" you can add to make the battle even more difficult if your group is full of pros or everyone is rolling crits. It's up to you how those forces fit into the story.

Tactics: What basic tactics the monsters will employ against the PCs. We assume you'll run them how you want, and they'll react to the PCs' actions, but we provide the monsters' default options for you to play off of.

Loot: The main valuables the monsters have, including magic items. We chose not to provide lists of mundane but interesting items the monsters might also have, leaving that to you to flesh out (and often create new adventures out of).

Icons: Most of the time we're positive that the GM and players will come up with amazing, creative uses for the PCs' icon advantages before and during the battle that are way better than anything we can provide. But we did want to leave some suggestions just in case; use or adapt them as you will. The advantages we list are connected to subsets of icons, but that's only a guideline since not every game will use all of the icons. Really, an advantage with any icon could be used to change the story and help the PCs out if the GM is okay with it.

Stats: The monster stat blocks.

Next Steps: When the battle is over, this section helps set up the next battle, or describes some outcomes after the final battle in the set. Again, we expect you and your players to come up with their own interesting possibilities, but these are defaults.

Story Endings

This section offers possible outcomes from the battle scenes based on the story opening used in the setup. It accounts for both successes and failures (such as when the PCs are forced to flee or fail in some way to resolve the story). When you create your own story openings, you probably won't be able to use our suggestions except as inspiration.

Battle Scene Connections

Some people might want to go directly from one battle scene to another instead of letting the game wander off into fully GM-created territory. This section helps with that, offering suggestions for battle scenes the current set of battles could link to, in addition to slight changes to the story that might help set up those connections.

Battle scenes for the five icons in this book are no problem, but the text also refers to battle scenes for the other eight icons that have not been published yet. We thought about taking these references out, but we've opted to keep the references to things that haven't been published yet so that the book will be most useful in the long run.

Get Battling!

I hope you enjoy the stories contained within these battle scenes and get hours of gaming out of them. Many of the scenes are based on battles I designed for my weekly gaming group over the last fifteen years, including the first *13th Age* campaign I ran soon after Rob and Jonathan introduced me to the system during design. We hope these battle scenes help spur memorable campaigns and help forge mighty heroes.

I'd like to thank the players who helped me iron out the kinks, especially the guys in the Thursday night group for humoring me by participating in playtests. I must also thank my wife Julie for not only putting up with me while I wrote the book, but also her support as she would say each night at dinner, "Tell me about the adventures you wrote today."

Thank you.
—Cal Moore
November 2014

Archmage:
Moz's Magnificent Mess

Level Range: 2–3

Introduction

The themes of *Moz's Magnificent Mess* are humorous magic gone awry, dangerous constructs, and an unhappy magic item. The best setting for this group would be a semi-rural location near a village or small town, close enough to the Archmage's bureaucracy to have help arrive quickly.

Background: Moz the Magnificent is a gnome wizard of middling skill except when it comes to creating magical messes. He likes to experiment with animation and transmutation magic. Not long ago Moz acquired an orb of transmutation, a sphere filled with chaotic magic that he believed would allow him to make new discoveries in his research and unlock new power.

The problem was that Moz and the orb didn't get along very well, and Moz didn't ward the laboratory in his tower the way he should have. Deciding it had enough of Moz, the orb devised a way to walk out of the tower by adjusting the magical programming of one of Moz's simple gargoyle construct helpers, but not before leaving the gnome some animated furniture and other annoying magical problems to deal with.

Now the orb, carried by the construct, has escaped the tower and is making its way across the countryside, seeking a better situation. Wherever it goes, the magic leaking from the orb affects its surroundings, causing trouble by transforming creatures and bringing objects to problematic life.

Moz the Magnificent

You could play this set of battle scenes straight, but Moz is waiting to be played for laughs. He's a wizard with some power and thus takes himself seriously, but he also refers to himself as "Moz the Magnificent," so there's that.

We suggest hamming it up a bit with this NPC, as long as the party takes the threat of the rampaging orb seriously enough to track it down. In addition, a wizard PC in the group may have heard some stories of Moz from school, or from other wizards. Those stories involved some magical mishap perpetrated by the great Moz going horribly wrong, but Moz managed to avoid expulsion thanks to having some powerful family member within the Archmage's organization (perhaps even a Superior).

Moz generally has a positive outlook on life and isn't mean-spirited, though he might be a bit petulant with PCs who don't take him seriously. He also will remind any PCs with connections to the Archmage that they are expected to help. He will also offer magical bribes to keep this incident quiet (things like self-buttoning shirts, a wizard hat that wipes your face during a rainstorm, and similar oddities will be his initial offers). He'll have at least one true magic item for a group that helps him.

Moz has asked the Archmage's people for help with a "delicate magical situation" without going into too much detail on the nature of that situation. Wizards associated with the Archmage frequently use this phrase as a euphemism for a problem they can't handle alone, so the PCs have probably heard the phrase before. Once the PCs show up, Moz will put them on the trail of the wayward orb so they can return it to him. Of course, if they could help him get his laboratory settled first, that would be most excellent. There's a hat rack and some cutlery that have it out for him, and probably more items than that Moz didn't see before he slammed the door and ran.

Moz's Magnificent Mess Story Openings

- **Discretion Among Peers:** One or more PCs with a positive or conflicted relationship with the Archmage receives orders from the bureaucracy to help a fellow wizard in their vicinity, a gnome named Moz. That request/order reminds the PC that the Archmage's reputation is involved, no matter what the situation Moz has created (this isn't his first request for aid over the years), so best to follow through.

- **The Doll Summons:** A strange visitor suddenly shows up before the PCs. It's a small, wooden doll of a boy moving under its own power. The toy speaks to the PCs, claiming to be sent by a nearby wizard named Moz who needs the help of heroes such as them. The doll says help offered will be rewarded with wizardly favors or magical items. The PCs can follow the doll back to the tower.

- **The Light Show:** While traveling nearby, the PCs see glowing lights in the distance and hear a few small explosions. Drawn in by the oddity of it, they soon see a squat tower whose narrow upper floor windows glow with green light and occasional crackles of energy. Suddenly a gnome in robes runs out the door to the tower and then turns and throws himself against it. Something slams it partially open once, twice, and then relents. Seeing the PCs, the gnome, who calls himself Moz, asks for assistance. He offers them a reward for their help.

- **An Opportunity for Leverage:** A PC with a conflicted or negative relationship with the Archmage hears about a situation with a wizard that the Archmage's people can't immediately deal with. A gnome wizard named Moz has asked for help with a magical incident. The PCs have a couple days before any "official" help arrives, and the PC knows that Moz, while a bit of a fool, also has certain connections. The group could help him keep the incident quiet in exchange for certain information or help.

Alternate Icons

 Elf Queen: Moz could be the cousin of someone important at the Elven Court, and he asks for help from the servants of that icon instead. It could be an opportunity to help the Queen avoid some bad PR, or to use it against her.

 The Three (Blue): Moz could instead be a kobold sorcerer with a personality flaw for playing with things he doesn't understand. The escaped orb could be something the Mistress (the Blue) has requested be sent to her. Or it could be that Moz can't afford for word to get out about the orb's loss, which will put a bad light on the Blue and thus ensure his destruction by his peers. Technically, he's also an envoy of the Blue and thus considered a citizen of the Empire, and not just some kobold to kill.

Moz's Magnificent Mess Overview

Once the PCs pay a visit to Moz, whether by chance or at the request of the Archmage's allies or enemies, they will learn about the missing orb of transmutation. Depending on why they're there, they may negotiate with Moz for a reward.

Before the PCs rush off into the surrounding lands to search for the orb, however, Moz asks them to solve another problem because he needs to access his laboratory. Before the orb left, it caused some of the equipment and objects in his lab to animate,

and they've been trying to kill him ever since. Battle 1 involves dealing with those animated objects. Once that's done, Moz will give them a way to track and safely store the orb.

Once on the orb's trail, the PCs will encounter a band of goblins that have come into contact with the orb's power and now have a new god to worship. The orb managed to animate a scarecrow at the edge of a farmer's field, which ran off into the nearby woods after the orb. Battle 2 sees the PCs facing the goblins and their Straw King in a double-strength fight.

When the PCs finally catch up with the orb and its construct bearer, the orb's magic will be in full force as it tries to avoid returning to Moz, who the orb considers unworthy (also an imbecile). To that end, its transmutation magic helps it turn some nearby insects into giant versions of themselves that will attack the PCs. In Battle 3, the PCs must overcome those enemies and defeat the construct to regain the orb.

GM, feel free to expand upon these battles by including battles with another group seeking the orb, additional goblin threats, and other enemies created by the chaotic transmutation magic of the orb.

The battles outlined here can take place over a few hours or days, depending on the setting. Since the Archmage is in play, the enemies presented here are magical constructs, animated objects, and other creatures warped by magic. The locations should have a sense of strong (and sometimes humorous) magic, abnormal oddities, and magic power gone awry.

See story endings after the final battle for options on what happens after the PCs finish the last battle.

BATTLE 1: THE ANIMATED LABORATORY

The lower story of the tower seems normal enough—a storage area for various provisions for Moz as well as common equipment and a simple kitchen and dining table. But the sound of repeated banging is coming from beyond the door at the top of the stairs. Readying yourselves, you throw open the door to a chaotic mess. Of course, you figure the place isn't normally all that tidy, but now there is overturned furniture, broken glass all over the ground, smashed clay pot shards strewn everywhere, and a large patch of something green and sticky stuck to the ceiling slowly dropping chunks. The racket stopped as you opened the door, however, and nothing seems to be moving. In one corner, a small goblin-faced gargoyle statue has a broom in each hand, almost as if it were readying to clean the place.

LOCATION DESCRIPTION

When the PCs initially enter the laboratory in the upper level of Moz's tower, the animated objects there will stop moving and seem completely inanimate. Of course, it's a ruse. The barely-intelligent items will wait for most of the PCs to enter the lab before coming to life and attacking. The furniture isn't so much malevolent as it is animated, chaotic, and destructive. When the orb fled, it imparted a bit of its fear of captivity upon the objects it infused with magic, and so the items will act out—they don't want to be sorted, organized, or contained.

The tower chamber is 80 feet in diameter and open, without partition or inner wall. On one side, there's a small bed, a fireplace with hearth tools nearby, a pair of cushioned armchairs and a small table that's been flipped sideways, and a bookshelf with all of its books spilled upon the ground in front of it in a heap.

On the other side are a number of low tables that once held many glass vials and containers, now mostly shattered and fallen upon the ground as sharp shards. Numerous shelves of pottery holding various components now have their contents spilled over the floor and tables as well. The gargoyle with the brooms stands nearby, looking like it's there to clean up the mess.

Stuck to the 15-foot-high ceiling in the center of the tower are the clumps of green material slowly dripping clods to the ground. They were some swamp plants Moz had gathered and was trying to grow in bins on the opposite wall. The stone bins still have a bit of dirt in them. Last but not least is a low hat rack impaled by a number of small blades and other sharp implements leaning against the wall near the door.

TERRAIN & TRAPS

Random Animated Objects: There's still a good amount of chaotic magic flowing through the laboratory. Once the PCs have entered the lab, or at least one enters and remains for more than a short time, or the PCs begin attacking things in the room for the heck of it, random animated objects in the room will start hurling themselves at the PCs or attacking as befits them and the door will slam shut. At the start of each round when the escalation die advances, make the following attack against one random PC in the lab.

Escalation	Effect
1:	**Hurled component jar +6 vs. AC**—5 damage.
2:	**Ball of fire +6 vs. PD (1d2 nearby enemies in a group)**—4 fire damage (generated by fireplace).
3:	**Sudden darkness**—All current light sources (even magical ones) in the area fade until the start of the next round; PCs take a −4 penalty to attacks until someone creates light again.
4:	**Wet clump +7 vs. PD**—The target is dazed until the end of its next turn as a clump of goopy dirt hits them in the face

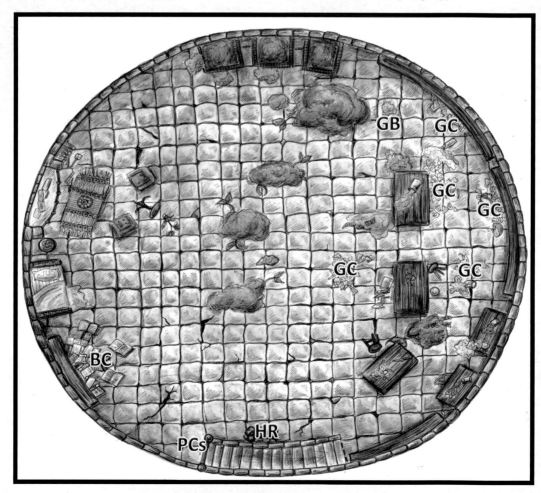

5: **Spray of glass shards +6 vs. PD (1d3 enemies)**—3 damage

6: **Armchair slam +6 vs. AC**—7 damage as a chair rams the target

Glass Shards: Anyone moving in the right side of the tower (from the door) will have to be wary of glass shards in the area. They can move carefully and must succeed on a DC 10 Dexterity check or lose their move action. Or they can move normally but take 1d4 damage from broken glass shards that jump upward of their own accord to find weak points in boots and armor.

Narrow windows: If the PCs avoid the door and want to try to climb the outer tower to see through the windows (there are six of them each 6 inches wide), they must succeed on a DC 15 Strength check or fall for 2d6 damage. If they do, they'll see the gargoyle smacking a table with one broom (the banging sound).

Monsters

The laboratory holds four different enemies: a gargoyle broomsweeper, the knife-embedded hat rack, a bookbound construct, and a group of small glassling constructs.

Each construct has limited intelligence and looks like normal debris, except for the gargoyle, which was one of two constructs Moz used to help him with experiments and to clean up. This gargoyle has taken its cleaning duties a bit far with the brooms.

The oak hat rack will expel the blades and tools stuck in it with deadly accuracy. The bookbound construct consists of a pile of heavy books that turns into a small whirlwind of destruction. The glassling constructs form out of the broken glass shards in the area, slicing and dicing any flesh they contact.

Additional Reinforcements: If you want to challenge the PCs more, add 1d3 x 4 wibbles (*Bestiary*, page 223) that show up following the trail of incompetent spellcasting.

Tactics

None of the constructs has more than a basic intelligence, so each will attack the nearest creature, or the creature to attack it last.

If the PCs choose to leave the lab, the constructs will try to follow, but no further than the door exiting the tower. While not intelligent, they have a sort of magical cunning, so the glassling constructs, for example, might slide down the chimney chute to the lower level, or the bookbound construct might send a version of itself (half hp) that is formed from ripped pages that will fit under the door.

Loot

Most of the equipment in the lab has been ruined, but there are a few components, a gem or crystal or two, and tools that might

bring a total of 100 gp if sold, though Moz won't like that. The main reward could come from Moz when the orb is returned (see Battle 3).

Icons

A PC that has relationship advantages with the Archmage, Elf Queen, Diabolist, Priestess, or maybe the Great Gold Wyrm might use one or more of them to negate the magic within a construct (sort of like an exorcism) to remove that enemy from battle. Along with the advantage, the PC would need to make a skill check. They automatically negate the construct for one round, but it will last longer depending on the roll: DC 20 for 1d3 + 1 rounds, and DC 25 for the rest of the battle.

Any PC could also use one or more advantages to do the same with the random animated terrain objects, but the DCs are easier: DC 15 for 1d3 + 1 rounds, and DC 20 for the rest of the battle.

#/Level of PCs	Gargoyle Broomsweeper (GB)	Knife-embedded Hat Rack (HR)	Bookbound Construct (BC)	Glassling Construct Mook (GC)
4 x 2nd level	1	1	0	4 (1 mob)
5 x 2nd level	1	1	1	2 (1 mob)
6 x 2nd level	1	1	1	5 (1 mob)
4 x 3rd level	1	1	1	5 (1 mob)
5 x 3rd level	1	1	1	11 (2 mobs)
6 x 3rd level*	1	1	2	10 (2 mobs)

Gargoyle Broomsweeper

This goblin-faced gargoyle bears a wire-brush broom in each hand. It's only funny until the broom's mutant hooks are covered with your blood.

4th level troop [CONSTRUCT]
Initiative: +4

Hooked wirebrush broom +9 vs. AC (2 attacks)—6 damage
First natural 11+ each turn: The gargoyle can make a *bite* attack this turn as a free action.

[Special trigger] Bite +8 vs. AC—4 damage, and the gargoyle gets a good taste of blood. It gains a +4 attack bonus against the target it most recently bit.

Flight: It's rocky, and the landings aren't pretty.

Nastier Specials

Rocky hide: The gargoyle has *resist damage 12+* against attacks targeting AC.

AC	23	
PD	20	**HP 48**
MD	13	

Knife-embedded Hat Rack

The blades and sharp tools stuck in the oak hat rack quiver and vibrate as the thing spins around to face you.

3rd level archer [CONSTRUCT]
Initiative: +6

Piercing hat hooks +5 vs. AC—4 damage

R: Expelled blades +8 vs. AC—8 damage
Largest blades last: On a hit, the target also takes extra damage equal to the escalation die.

Self-propelled blades: When the hat rack is staggered, roll two d20 for each attack and take the best result as blades that miss spin around and fly back at the target.

AC	18	
PD	15	**HP 44**
MD	12	

Bookbound Construct

It doesn't look like much until a heavy, wood-cover-bound tome swings up and smashes you in the face.

Double-strength 2nd level troop [CONSTRUCT]
Initiative: +4
Vulnerability: fire

Double-book slam +7 vs. AC (2 attacks)—6 damage
Escalation die is odd: On a hit, the target takes 3 ongoing damage from bad paper cuts.
Escalation die is even: On a hit, the target is dazed until the end of its next turn from having an open book plastered across its face.

Swirling books: Each round, the first attacker to hit the construct with a weapon attack must roll a save. On a failure, the construct takes 6 less damage.

AC	16	
PD	15	**HP 60**
MD	11	

Glassling Construct

Shards of broken vials, glassware, and alchemical equipment swirl together with a high-pitched squelch of glass on glass, as the bits launch forth toward you.

3rd level mook [CONSTRUCT]
Initiative: +8

Slicing glass +7 vs. AC—6 damage
Natural 16+: A vial or glass component still has an alchemical substance in it that explodes when it contacts air. The target rolls a save; on a failure, it takes 1d4 x the escalation die cold, fire, acid, or poison damage (GM's choice).

Death shatter: When the glassling construct drops to 0 hp, it shatters and makes a *shattering impact* attack.
Shattering impact +7 vs. PD (each enemy engaged with it)—3 ongoing damage from many small bleeding wounds.

AC	18	
PD	18	**HP 11 (mook)**
MD	11	

Mook: Kill one glassling shard mook for every 11 damage you deal to the mob.

Next Steps

Once the animated furniture has been taken care of, Moz will enter the laboratory, crying out as he examines all of the damage and berating the PCs for making it worse if you think you can get away with that for a moment. Despite grumbling, he's clearly happy to be able to return. Once the PCs are ready, he will rummage through the equipment until he collects a small clear crystal lens and a black pouch embroidered with runes in gold stitching.

The lens lets whoever looks through it see a trail of magical silvery light that follows the orb's course, allowing them to track the item. The pouch is designed to contain the orb's chaotic magic. Once the PCs set out after the orb, go to **Battle 2: The Straw King.**

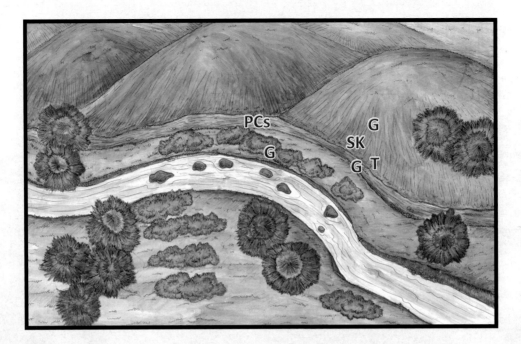

BATTLE 2: THE STRAW KING

The orb's trail leads you away from the tower and past small copses of woods, along animal trails, and through farmers' fields of crops. Then it diverts into a larger, darker wood and follows a slow-moving stream into the deeper hollows. The sunlight is sparse and the shadows getting long when you hear hoots and calls coming from a small ridge to your left, and then more from the bushes to your right. There's movement ahead and you see a tall, gaunt figure come out from behind a large tree; it looks like it's only made of sticks and oversized clothing, until its burning purple eyes rest their gaze upon you. Some goblins emerge alongside it, smiling. One goblin female says, "You die now! The Straw King says so!"

LOCATION DESCRIPTION

The orb of transmutation and its gargoyle handler moved away from the tower and passed through the fields of some farmers. One of those fields held a scarecrow that was animated by the magic of the orb as it passed. The scarecrow followed the orb into the nearby woods where it encountered a band of goblins raiding in the area. At first, the goblins tried to dispatch the thing, but after it snapped the necks of two of their raiders, they began to worship the construct, naming it the "Straw King."

The Straw King can no longer sense the trail of the orb, so it has settled within the wood. One of the goblins, a runecaster named Tassra Zoi, used a ritual to assert a small amount of control over the construct and can now set it upon the band's enemies.

As the PCs enter the goblin's ambush point, Tassra Zoi will order the Straw King to attack while she and her band attack them (see **Terrain & Traps**). This is a double-strength battle.

TERRAIN & TRAPS

Small Ridge: The ridgeline to the left rises to about 30 feet above the level of the trail. It has a steep slope that requires two move actions to ascend even though the goblins at the top are nearby. A PC can attempt to climb it as a single move action with a successful DC 15 Strength or Dexterity skill check.

Stream & Large Stones: The stream is 25 feet wide and slow moving, with holes as deep as 8 feet. Moving through the water without falling completely in and ending that move action requires a successful DC 10 Strength or Constitution check (not a skill check this time).

There are also a handful of large stones that jut up just above the water scattered around the stream. A PC can try to jump to any of them with a successful DC 13 Strength check. Failure means a plunge into the stream. Goblins may attempt to reach PCs on a rock and get swept downstream (far away) if they fail a save. The Straw King won't go near the water (if it ends up there, it must succeed on a save each round while submerged or take 10 damage).

Shrubs, Bushes, & Trees: Between the stream and the PCs are some small shrubs, ferns, and other foliage where the goblins are hiding. The area can be used by PCs for concealment too. There are a handful of small fir trees ahead of the group, as well as some behind. The trunks are 2 to 3 feet in diameter and can provide light cover if you desire. Climbing one requires no check since they have plenty of low branches.

MONSTERS

The Straw King looks like an 8-foot tall scarecrow with stick legs and arms that end in wicked wooden claws. It wears a straw farmer's hat and has a canvas head stuffed with straw, but eyes that were painted with purple berry juice now glow with eldritch, chaotic energy.

Tassra Zoi leads this band, known as the Bloody Eyes. Tassra is a runecaster, a type of goblin spellslinger that uses rune magic to harm enemies and invigorate allies. Her *rune of pain & strength* imprints itself on an enemy's flesh and provides a damage benefit to allies until it fades. She starts the battle well behind the Straw King and other goblins, far away.

The rest of the band consists of goblin raiders who can either attack at range or in melee.

Additional Reinforcements: If you want to challenge the PCs more, add a barbarous bugbear to the battle as an extra guard for Tassra Zoi.

#/Level of PCs	Straw King (SK)	Tassra Zoi, Runecaster (T)	Goblin Raider (G)
4 x 2nd level	1	1	4
5 x 2nd level	1	1	6
6 x 2nd level	1	1*	8
4 x 3rd level	1	1	8
5 x 3rd level	1**	1*	9
6 x 3rd level*	1**	2***	11

* Tassra Zoi will use her nastier special.

** Increase Straw King by one level: +1 initiative, attacks, and all defenses, *stickclaws* deals 16 damage, *eyes of fear and loathing* deals 12 damage and 5 ongoing, and increase hp to 136.

*** Tassra has a sister named Tsolla also with the band. Same stats.

TACTICS

Potential Ambush: If you use all the read-aloud text at the start of The Straw King, there's no ambush, the goblins have announced themselves with atypical bravado, buoyed by their new god. Roll initiative normally.

If the PCs (or the players!) are cocky and in great shape for combat and you want to make this tough battle even harder, keep the goblins quiet until the shooting has started. To run this as an ambush, have each PC roll a DC 15 Wisdom check. If more than half fail, the goblins gain surprise and two of the raiders will make ranged attacks before initiative is rolled. If the PCs had an advanced scout, then only that PC rolls the check and the scout's success or failure determines if there's an ambush.

The Straw King starts nearby the PCs, just in front of Tassra. Tassra will direct the scarecrow toward the most dangerous looking melee types. It will make an *eyes of fear and loathing* attack, then move in for melee, continuing to attack the same enemy throughout the battle until that enemy drops or Tassra orders it to attack another.

Tassra is cunning and will focus her own magic on enemy healers, or any ranged attackers using fire attacks. She hasn't become a raid leader for nothing! If things are going badly (the Straw King is down and she's under 10 hp), Tassra will try to escape into the woods.

The goblins' tactics are simple. Ranged attackers use short bows from the ridge on unengaged targets first, then enemies fighting the Straw King second. Those in melee gang up on one or two PCs, especially anyone using fire.

If you want to make the fight a little easier, consider changing out half the goblin raiders for goblin scum, with each one being worth three (2nd level) or four scum.

LOOT

The goblins have had some success in raiding and have a total of 80 gp in coins and loose jewelry divided among the raiders, in addition to many peculiar odds and ends.

Tassra kept the best stuff for herself, including a pair of silver and garnet earrings worth 40 gp.

When destroyed, the Straw King could be only sticks and straw, nothing more than the original materials. Or for a different story, consider putting something special inside the scarecrow's remains, something the chaotic magic spawned there. It could be a magic item, but even more interesting might be a 'treasure map' to the next adventure made out of enchanted beetles, the beating crystal heart of someone the PCs haven't met yet, or the Straw King's gem-like eyes infused with chaotic magic that an NPC necromancer or villain needs for a ritual and will soon come to the PCs to buy/steal/acquire.

Icons

A PC that has relationship advantages with the Archmage, Diabolist, Elf Queen, Prince, Priestess, or maybe the Emperor or High Druid could use one or more of them to hinder or confuse the Straw King. The scarecrow could lose an attack, or if the PC breaks Tassra Zoi's ritual, the Straw King might attack random creatures in the battle each turn instead.

Any PC could use one or more advantages to put doubt into the goblins, making them think the Straw King will kill them or that they should avoid that PC or flee the battle (with enough advantages).

Straw King

It rises to its full seven-foot height and glares at you with purple eyes filled with the sight of your own terror.

Double-strength 4th level spoiler [CONSTRUCT]
Initiative: +8
Vulnerability: fire

Ripping stickclaws +9 vs. AC (2 attacks)—12 damage
Natural 2–6: The Straw King gains a +2 bonus to its next attack this battle.
Miss: 4 damage.

C: Eyes of fear and loathing +8 vs. MD (1d4 nearby enemies)—8 psychic damage, and 5 ongoing psychic damage
Each failed save: The target moves away from the Straw King as a free action, taking opportunity attacks, if any.
Limited use: 1/battle, but the Straw King regains the ability when it's staggered.

Made of sticks and straw: The Straw King has *resist weapon damage 14+* against attacks using piercing or bashing weapons (arrows/bolts, spears, hammers, maces, etc.)

AC	19	
PD	13	**HP 100**
MD	18	

Tassra Zoi, Goblin Runecaster

The goblin female holds up a chicken-leg wand in her rune-tattooed hands and a green rune of magic energy flares in the air before you.

4th level caster [HUMANOID]
Initiative: +6

Obsidian knife +8 vs. AC—11 damage

R: Rune of pain & strength +9 vs. PD—5 damage, and 5 ongoing damage
First failed save: The target takes 2 extra damage from the attacks of Tassra Roi's goblin allies until the start of its next turn.

R: Rune of vulnerability & deadliness +9 vs. MD (one nearby or far away enemy)—10 damage, and until the end of its next turn, if the target moves closer to Tassra Roi, it's vulnerable until the start of its next turn.

Natural odd hit: The target is more vulnerable than normal and any natural roll of 16+ against it is a critical hit.

Rune of escape: Once per battle as a quick action, Tassra Zoi can pop free from all enemies.

Nastier Specials

R: Rune of death & succor +8 vs. PD (one nearby dying enemy)—The target immediately fails a death save, and Tassra Zoi heals 10 hp. If the target would die due to this effect, it can roll a normal save to cancel this effect.

AC	21	
PD	13	**HP 51**
MD	17	

Goblin Raiders

What you thought was red war paint is really bloody tears streaking its face from small, sharpened pieces of straw holding its eyelids open.

2nd level troop [HUMANOID]
Initiative: +6

Scavenged hand axe or shortsword +6 vs. AC—8 damage
Natural even hit: The goblin can pop free from the target after the attack.

R: Shortbow +7 vs. AC—5 damage
Eyes wide open: Skill checks to hide from the goblin take a −2 penalty.

Shifty bugger: Goblins gains a +5 bonus to disengage checks.

AC	17	
PD	14	**HP 30**
MD	10	

Additional Reinforcements

Barbarous Bugbear

4th level wrecker [HUMANOID]
Initiative: +12 (see *ferocious start*)

Warclub +9 vs. AC—11 damage
Natural even hit or miss: Each enemy engaged with the barbarous bugbear takes 1d8 damage.

R: Throwing axe +8 vs. AC—10 damage
Limited use: 2/battle.

Ferocious start: Until the barbarous bugbear is staggered or the escalation die is 2+, it acts twice per round. Roll initiative once at +12. It takes its second turn when the initiative count is seven less (minimum 1).

AC	18	
PD	17	**HP 51**
MD	16	

NEXT STEPS

After experiencing the goblins' spontaneous cult worship of the Straw King, the PCs should realize how dangerous the escaped orb truly is. The trail leads away through the woods but is still easy to follow.

After a quick rest and a bit of a chase, the PCs will finally catch up to the orb of transmutation and its handler at the ruins of a magical research station from the 1st Age, but the orb doesn't want to go back to its original master. See **Battle 3: Defiant Orb.**

BATTLE 3: DEFIANT ORB

You leave behind the dark woods of the goblins and enter into a grassy vale with light tree covering. The trail leads to the center of the valley, where some old ruins wait. Near a small pond, a black stone obelisk bearing Imperial runes rises high into the air and crumbling walls from some previous age show that this place was once important. Insects buzz around the area and the wind dies down as you see a demon-faced gargoyle waiting by the obelisk; it holds a large purple stone orb in one hand. As you draw near, the orb flashes with magical energy that leaps to the obelisk, and with flaring runes the whole area is suddenly bathed in a purple glow. The sound of buzzing insects grows much louder and something stirs in the sand at your feet.

LOCATION DESCRIPTION

Thanks to the obelisk, a magic amplifier used during the Wizard King's reign, the orb is able to transmute living creatures instead of only inanimate objects. It doesn't wish to return to Moz, and so it, the gargoyle carrying it, and some new allies in the form of giant wasps and giant scorpions will battle the PCs. The scorpions grow near the obelisk, and the wasps do the same near the ruins.

In addition, the orb will create terrain effects at the start of each round to hinder its pursuers (see **Terrain & Traps**). Although this is a normal battle, the mix of enemies and terrain effects is designed to lock the PCs down, possibly making it a longer battle.

The site, a former magical research station for the Wizard King's mages, provides a perfect backdrop for weird magical effects, and the obelisk can be used by the orb or the PCs to achieve interesting effects via icon advantages or creative ingenuity.

The area is generally open sandy ground, except for the obelisk and a scattering of ruined stone walls, foundations, and similar structures scattered here and there. The PCs begin the battle far away from the orb and gargoyle but nearby the other enemies.

TERRAIN & TRAPS

Orb-Obelisk Effect: At the beginning of each round before any creature acts, the orb flares with purple energy, which spreads to the obelisk. One or more runes on that spire light up and a random magical effect occurs (roll a d6).

1: **Sinkhole:** The sand and dirt part, and one random PC starts to sink in. That PC must roll an immediate save; on a failure, they are stuck until the end of their next turn.

2: **Ray of Invigoration:** Choose one random living creature (not the gargoyle) in the battle. It must roll a save. On a success, it gains 10 temporary hp. On a failure, it must spend its next standard action releasing harmless beams of colored energy as it becomes overfilled with light.

3: **Anti-gravity:** Choose a random PC. That creature flies up into the air 10 feet and is stuck in place in midair until the end of its next turn unless it has a means to propel itself.

4: **Improved Insight:** Choose one random creature in the battle. For its next attack this battle, it can roll an additional d20 and take the best result.

5: **Psychic Interference:** Choose one random PC. For that character's next attack this battle, it must roll an additional d20 and take the worst result.

6: **Something weird and random:** Something strange happens. It could be a mechanical effect of the GM's choice, or story one. For example, all the PCs' magic item quirks trigger and

remain in effect until their next full heal-up; or the psychic image of a wizard from the 1st Age manifests and asks for help in powering down an ancient magical power lattice that has kept her soul trapped for ages; or take something one of the players said offhand and have it interfere with the battle in some small way. GMs, have fun.

Ruined walls: There are a scattering of ruins around the area. Most are low walls or foundations 2 to 4 feet in height and easily bypassed. Two partial walls to an ancient structure form a corner 8 feet high with a standing 4-foot diameter pillar next to it that's 10 feet high and another beyond it that's toppled. Climbing to the top of either wall forming the corner is a DC 12 Dexterity or Strength check. Leaping from there to the top of the standing pillar is a DC 15 check. The scorpions won't be able to attack enemies on the top of the walls or pillar (but can reach anyone on the toppled pillar).

Pond: The pond is filled with reeds and water lilies. It's 10 feet deep near the center and muddy near the edges. The giant wasps won't attack anyone submerged in the water.

Obelisk: The obelisk is 30 feet high and 6 feet wide on each side, forming a pyramid point at the top. Various runes of empire and civilization, plus a few of magic, are inscribed upon it, though many are faded. Climbing the semi-smooth surfaces is difficult and requires a successful DC 20 Strength check; failure results in a fall for 2d6 damage.

Monsters

The orb is in the gargoyle's hand, and they both start the battle by the obelisk. The gargoyle is under the orb's control. If the orb is separated from it somehow, the gargoyle will stop attacking (though a 6 result on the orb-obelisk terrain table could bring it back under the orb's control) and begin reverting to its worker-drone origins. If the orb is somehow destroyed, there will be a big magical explosion, the enemies will lose their magic/revert, and the event should cause a major story shift somehow.

The transmuted giant scorpions will fan out in front of the gargoyle and attack (or intercept) anyone in that direction, fighting to the death.

The transmuted giant wasps are very mobile and will buzz in from the side, looking to attack and poison the closest enemies, especially ones that are stuck from a sinkhole or anti-gravity effect.

Additional Reinforcements: If you want to challenge the PCs more, add one or two wolf spiders (core rulebook, page 206) to the battle that also get enlarged from normal versions in the area.

#/Level of PCs	Orb & Gargoyle (G)	Giant Scorpion (S)	Giant Wasp (W)
4 x 2nd level	1	1	1
5 x 2nd level	1	2	1
6 x 2nd level	1	3	1
4 x 3rd level	1	2	2
5 x 3rd level	1	3	2
6 x 3rd level*	1	4	3

Tactics

The gargoyle will stay close to the obelisk so the orb can use it to create terrain effects (the orb must be nearby the obelisk for the terrain effects to work). It will use its *claw* attack in melee, but will try to disengage after so the *orb blast* attack doesn't provoke opportunity attacks.

The giant scorpions will grab and strike whoever is closest, intercepting any PC that comes toward the gargoyle.

The giant wasps are very mobile and will swarm one enemy at a time until another attacker damages one, which will then peel off and attack that PC.

Between the scorpions and wasps, there will be plenty of lingering poison damage which could add up. If the PCs have a good amount of poison protection, feel free to add an extra wasp or scorpion to the battle.

Loot

There is little of obvious value at this site, although the poison from such large venomous creatures could bring some coin if harvested correctly (DC 15 Intelligence check per creature, assuming someone has a vial or sealable container). The venom from each creature will bring 40 gp.

In addition, returning the orb to Moz may come with a reward in coin (300 gp) or magic items (a few colorful but useless items), plus a *+1 oil*, an *elemental oil* (*Book of Loot*), and a *potion of invisibility* (as the 5th level wizard spell).

KEEPING THE ORB

Some players might decide to not return the orb of transmutation, instead keeping it for themselves. Besides the story ramifications with the Archmage, there's one other problem: the orb has lost a lot of the chaotic magic that was running through it, especially during the final battle where the obelisk nearly drained it dry.

If the PCs go this route, the PC who takes it gains an arcane implement, a *+1 orb of transmutation (recharge 16+):* One nearby ally gains the effect of your choice: +1 to AC and PD until the end of the battle from hardened skin; OR that ally's attacks deal extra damage equal to the target's level due to increased size or strength. Quirk: Is overcome by strong desire to add chaos to a situation.

Icons

A PC that has relationship advantages with the Archmage, Diabolist, Elf Queen, High Druid, Lich King, or maybe the Three could use one or more of them to counteract a terrain effect from the obelisk, or to have an effect instead target one of that PC's enemies on a roll of 1, 3, or 5 thanks to ancient knowledge of such obelisks.

A PC with one or more advantages with any icon could use them to try to convince the orb to stand down and join with the group instead of returning to Moz. In this case, the advantage(s) opens the door and social skill checks and roleplaying are required to convince the orb to stand down (use DCs of 15 to 20 depending on how convincing the story is; the orb speaks telepathically). Additional advantages all with the same icon also might remove the need for any skill checks as the orb chooses to embrace and support that icon through the PC. In this case, the orb will soon try to move from the PC to more powerful members of that icon's organization (climbing the ladder). There's a good chance too that Moz sends more heroes to retrieve the orb, or that enemy icons send agents to retrieve the powerful implement.

ORB-ANIMATED GARGOYLE

This gargoyle looks like any other, except for the purple energy exuding from a crystal sphere in its hand that matches the color of the light spilling from the creature's eyes to become a glowing purple demon-mask.

Double-strength 3rd level spoiler [CONSTRUCT]
Initiative: +5

Claw +9 vs. AC—11 damage
Natural 11+: The gargoyle can make a *horn spike* attack as a free action this turn.

[Special trigger] **Horn spike +8 vs. AC**—5 damage, and the target is dazed until the end of its next turn

R: Orb blast +8 vs. PD (1d3 nearby or far away enemies)—5 damage, and the target loses its next move action.

Transmutating orb: As a standard action, the gargoyle can make a *claw* attack and an *orb blast* attack.

Rocky hide: The gargoyle has *resist damage 12+* against attacks targeting AC.

AC 21
PD 16   HP 82
MD 15

TRANSMUTED GIANT SCORPION

In a matter of seconds it grew from a small, nasty pest into a large, very nasty threat.

2nd level wrecker [BEAST]
Initiative: +7

Pincer +7 vs. PD—2 damage, and the scorpion gains a +2 attack bonus against the same target this turn with its *stinger* attack
Limited use: 2/round, each requiring a quick action. (Hitting the same target twice with *pincer* gives the *stinger* attack a +4 bonus.)

Stinger +7 vs. AC—5 damage, and 3 ongoing poison damage

AC 17
PD 16   HP 31
MD 11

TRANSMUTATED GIANT WASP

These things are mean when they're small; when they get this big, they're worse.

3rd level spoiler [BEAST]
Initiative: +7

Venomous sting +8 vs. PD—5 damage, and 5 ongoing poison damage
Escalation die is 1, 3, 5: The save for the ongoing poison is hard (16+).

Flight: Giants wasps are good fliers and can hover, though they aren't as quick as normal-sized versions.

AC 17
PD 16   HP 31
MD 11

NEXT STEPS

It depends on whether the PCs choose to return the orb to Moz or not.

Moz's Magnificent Mess Story Endings

Here are outcomes for each story opening, detailing what success or failure might mean.

If the PCs did face all three battles, remember to give them a full heal-up.

Discretion Among Peers

Success: Moz gets his orb back, the collateral damage was limited, and the Archmage's reputation avoids another blemish. All is well. In fact, Moz is so thankful to keep the orb's loss under wraps, he gives the PC in charge a useful magic item or set of one-shot items (see Loot).

Failure: The job is botched and the orb escapes. Before too long, it finds its way into a dwarven statuary shop and things get ugly. The Archmage's people are furious and probably call in some "real" help for that one, unless they decide that the PCs need to make amends. Later, there are rumors that Moz is now working as a scribe loaned out to some paladins of the Great Gold Wyrm in the Red Wastes.

The Doll Summons

Success: As with Discretion Among Peers.

Failure: Not only does the orb get away, but the PCs also learn that Moz's extensive doll collection was also animated and is now running amok in the nearby village of Thornik with each one saying, "I am Moz" repeatedly as it causes mischief. Moz had hoped to recover the orb and use it to summon the dolls back.

The Light Show

Success: Moz thanks the PCs for their help, knowing he'd be in deep with the Archmage's people if they discovered this happened AGAIN. Not only does he spread the word of how capable the PCs are (each gains a 6 with the Archmage until their next full heal-up), but he also reveals the location of an old Wizard King vault nearby he's been meaning to explore for the last year that should be full of loot.

Failure: The orb and its magic are just too much for the PCs and it escapes. The problem is, a group of Lich King followers are on the trail of the orb and now believe the PCs know where it's hidden. They ambush the heroes at the next possible opportunity, turning a normal battle into a double-strength one.

An Opportunity for Leverage

Success: If the PC doesn't choose to keep the orb, in Moz they gain another ally in the Archmage's service, one who now owes them a major favor.

Failure: The Archmage's people show up early and are waiting in force for the PCs when they return with the orb. The PCs need to hand it over or they'll have a triple-strength battle on their hands. Or if they choose to keep the orb, a huntsman wizard and his pack of hound constructs will get onto their trail, tracking them down to reclaim the orb.

Battle Scene Connections

The stories from this set of battle scenes can lead to scenes that will appear in later Battle Scenes books:

 The King's Tribute (Dwarf King): Either the orb, or the item that Moz gives to the PCs, is the item that was stolen from Lord Silveraxe.

 A Pixie Problem (Elf Queen): Tizilla steals the orb from the PCs (either before they return it, or after they decide to keep it).

 The Secret Crypt (Lich King): Moz points the PCs toward a "vault full of magic" that happens to be the Secret Vault. Either they find it thanks to his directions, or they get close when the story opening kicks in.

ARCHMAGE: THE LIGHTNING STATION

LEVEL RANGE: 5–6

The themes of this set of battles is dealing with weather magic, navigating overworld dangers, and facing those who would see the Archmage's public works destroyed. The setting for this set of battles could be nearly any location that rain-filled storm clouds blow through, such as mountain a pass or a gap in the Sea Wall that protects the Dragon Empire from the Iron Sea.

The Archmage has many projects in place to support the smooth-operation of the empire, especially projects related to maintaining the weather. His wards and weather stations help make it rain when and where it's needed and prevents catastrophic storms. This type of control requires the Archmage to install many weather stations scattered through the overworld. Of course the High Druid hates these stations and the chains the Archmage puts on natural storms.

Lately, weather in the area you've chosen for action has become erratic. One of the Archmage's storm stations in charge of gathering lightning has fallen along with the cloud it perches upon. The fallen cloud, the weather station, and the cloud giants charged by the Archmage to keep the weather station operational, have crashed on top of a nearby mountain or high hill. The Archmage's hired cloud giants might have been able to handle matters, but they've now been raided by gnoll reavers in a stolen airship who are seeking the weather technology for the icon they serve (probably the Diabolist). While fighting off the attackers, the cloud giants can't work on restoring the station, and their cloudbreak is slowly disintegrating. If they delay liftoff much longer, the station will be stranded permanently.

The PCs must traverse the strange terrain of the cloudbreak, then deal with the gnolls and a demon-fevered cloud giant who are battling at the station.

THE LIGHTNING STATION STORY OPENINGS

- **Emergency Response Team:** One or more PCs with a positive or conflicted relationship with the Archmage are asked or ordered to travel to a location nearby to solve an issue with one of the great wizard's weather stations. The

AIR TRAVEL

Usually, overworld adventures slot easily into the epic tier, but having a piece of the overworld come to the PCs is a good way to introduce them to it!

If, on the other hand, your PCs are already capable of low-level extended flight through ritual magic, an airship, or other means, feel free to have the cloudbreak be slowly but erratically sinking to the ground rather than already crashed. Or perhaps it already hit the land, skidded and popped back into the air a few times, and has lost most of its momentum. If the PCs don't hurry, the weather station will come to a final stop upon the land.

station has gone dark and fallen from the overworld, and no one is sure why. The PCs must travel there and help the cloud giant caretakers get it functioning again.

- **Storm Warning:** PCs with a positive relationship with one of the heroic or ambiguous icons are contacted about a dire problem in the area. Many local villages and settlements have been exposed to horrible lightning storms and tornadoes that are destroying buildings and killing people. The storms will soon reach even more populated areas. This seems to be happening because one of the Archmage's weather stations has fallen from the overworld. The PCs need to go there and see if they can help the caretakers get it aloft again. In this case, the PCs might or might not learn that the caretakers are cloud giants.
- **Claiming the Prize:** One or more PCs with negative or conflicted relationships with the Archmage are contacted by enemies of that icon, or agents of another icon. One of the great wizard's weather stations has fallen from the overworld, making it a ripe target for anyone who can get there before his people find a way to get it back into the skies. Acquiring the magic and technology the Archmage uses to control weather would be a major blow against him. The PCs must try to take the station, or at least learn its secrets.

ALTERNATE ICONS

If your campaign centers on someone other than the Archmage, here are alternative storylines to adapt.

 Emperor: The station has fallen and the Archmage asks the Emperor for help because he doesn't have any of his people in the vicinity. The battles should work about the same, although the Emperor's people might want to learn more about the station (covertly). Also, the cloud giants have no agreement with the Emperor, so the PCs may be seen as invaders (or at least intruders) by them.

 The Three: The station is instead an experiment by the Blue, who has dabbled in harnessing storms to power her citywide rituals. Clearly something has gone wrong. Rather than cloud giants, the station's caretakers are probably djinn. The PCs could be traveling to the cloudbreak to help, or to put the place fully out of commission while its defenses are down. This works particularly well if you have a shades-of-gray campaign where the Three are accomplishing good things ("Just helping with Imperial weather control") at the same time that they're powering up some potentially nasty ritual.

High Druid: What do you call a fallen weather station? A good start. Finish the job and make sure this piece of Archmage-garbage stays out of commission.

Icons in Play

Characters that have relationships (and story-guide advantages) with the Archmage, Emperor, Diabolist, the Three, and perhaps the High Druid should be able to shine in these battle scenes. Moreso than PCs with other icon relationships, feel free to give such PCs extra knowledge about the opposition, make checks to pull off fun actions the players might suggest, and use their advantages to particularly good effect, such as negating or bypassing some of the advantages or abilities of the enemies.

The Lightning Station Overview

The PCs travel to the downed station's location, where the cloudbreak is hung up on a mountainside or similar high snag. The cloudbreak is slowly dissolving the longer it remains in the lower world as the winds tear off pieces. A large island of stone containing a fortress or large building of some sort is visible from the mountain, attached to the back of the cloudbreak.

The PCs must first make their way to the station, traversing through a plain of lightning rods—magical metal posts stuck into the cloudstuff that absorb lightning strikes. The rods function thanks to the lightning elementals trapped within them, but now some of those elementals are loose, and random lightning discharges spark through the area.

Beyond the lightning fields lies an unexpected complication. Plowed into the far side of the cloudbreak is a gnoll reaver airship. And the gnolls are attacking the cloud giant weather station. The PCs must deal with the gnolls, while trying to reach the giants. The only problem is that the gnolls have poisoned their weapons and a cloud giant thane has lost his mind to demon fever, attacking anyone he sees as a threat.

GM, feel free to expand upon these battles by including battles with other groups who have traveled to the station to gain its secrets, local monsters that have wandered onto the cloudbreak, or additional battles with gnolls or cloud giants.

The battles outlined here can take place over minutes or hours, depending on how extensive you'd like the cloudbreak to be. Since the Archmage is in play, the enemies presented here are elementals and creatures of the overworld, plus some gnoll reavers for variety. The setting should be flavored with otherworldly magic, odd cloud structures, and the foulness of demon-worshiping gnolls.

See story endings after the final battle for options on what happens after the PCs finish the last battle.

BATTLE I: THE LIGHTNING FIELDS

The cloudstuff is solid yet queasily spongy as you walk across it. In places, there are sinkholes, possibly through the bottom of the cloud. In other spots, chunks of stone rise out of the clouds, apparently supported by misty vapor. You're moving toward the weather station on the far end of the cloud, but to get there you must pass through a large open plain of cloudstuff, that's dotted with numerous large metallic spikes protruding from the denser cloud material. Each spike is covered in silver runes that glow with energy. It must be a part of the weather magic system the Archmage uses.

Location Description

The four rows of spikes stretching away from the PCs in the direction of the weather station are actually lightning rods that store storm energy. Each spike is 10 feet high, and they are spaced 30 feet from each other over the course of 390 feet, with 20 feet between rows.

As the PCs move through this lightning field, some of the wards on the spikes will sputter and fail, releasing lightning elementals. The creatures were trapped by the wards to help in the process of pulling in lightning from storms and transmitting the energy to the weather station.

The elementals will shimmer between jagged lightning forms and the rough shape of creatures that have wandered near their wards, probably cloud giants and aurochs. No matter their current outline, each elemental fights the same, but feel free to make the players think they see other patterns.

Terrain & Traps

There are additional dangers in this double-strength battle. As the spikes continue to fail, they release their stored energy each round, sending lightning forking around the battlefield, harming the PCs and disintegrating areas of cloudstuff.

Lightning Rod (Spikes) Trap: The rods are about 10 feet tall with their lower ends buried in cloudstuff. Each is covered in silver warding runes that keep a lightning elemental trapped inside and helps with the transfer of storm energy.

Each time the escalation die advances, make the following attack at the start of the round.

C: Forked lightning strike +10 vs. PD (one random PC)—20 lightning damage

Natural even roll: Make another *lightning strike* attack against a random PC that hasn't been targeted by a *forked lightning strike* this turn.

The rods also make a *forked lighting strike* attack against any creature that touches them, but a natural even roll won't generate another attack.

Cloud Hole: GM, feel free to add a small 10 x 10 sinkhole in the cloudstuff each time the rods make a *forked lightning* strike with a natural odd attack roll. The sinkholes will appear on open ground,

not below a rod. When a sinkhole appears, roll a d6. On a 1 or 2, it appears below a random PC. That PC must roll a save; on a failure they fall in and are stuck (save ends) in the cloudy vapors. Sinkholes that don't appear below PCs can leave openings that go all the way through the cloud if the GM prefers, though creatures maneuvered or thrown into them should get a chance to save to avoid leaving the cloud. Luckily, the cloudbreak is near land, so any PCs that falls through only takes 5d10 damage, but they're out of the battle unless they can fly back up. (Two sinkholes marked as S on map already.)

Cloudstuff: It's solid but spongy. Anyone falling upon it takes only half damage. Spellcasters could possibly shape the stuff into semi-solid forms that last a turn or two with a DC 20 check.

Monsters

The lightning elementals lurch out of each lighting rod with a crackle of energy. They aren't overly happy to have been trapped for so long, and choose to take it out on the PCs. Each elemental flickers between its lightning form and the rough outline of a giant or auroch, or another creature of the GM's choice.

Additional Reinforcements: If you want to challenge the PCs more, include one or two clay golems (core rulebook, page 231) that are programmed to repair damaged lighting rods. They are immune to the lightning and looks like small cloud giant engineers. They will interpret the PCs as the cause of the elementals escaping. Plausible.

#/Level of PCs	Lightning Elemental (E)
4 x 5th level	6
5 x 5th level	8
6 x 5th level	9
4 x 6th level	9
5 x 6th level	12
6 x 6th level	14

Tactics

The elementals attack the closest PCs, but will favor those wearing metal armor. If faced with multiple enemies with metal, they react to whoever struck them last, attacking back.

Loot

None, although preserved cloudstuff or fragments from a lightning rod could have some value to the right people.

Icons

A PC that has relationship advantages with the Archmage, Lich King, Elf Queen, the Three, or maybe the Priestess or High Druid could use one or more of them to affect the lightning rods that release the elementals, weakening the monsters in some way, or forcing them back into the rods and repairing the wards. Any actions that actually remove the monsters from play thanks to advantages probably require at least one DC 20 Intelligence or Wisdom check per enemy, with greater success the higher the roll (so a roll of 18 might stun an elemental for a round or two, while a 27 would remove it completely from the battle).

Lightning Elemental

Webs of lightning repeatedly streak in all directions, outlining the form of the creature and then dissipating. Each flash happens so fast, it leaves the thing's image burned into your eyes.

7th level spoiler [ELEMENTAL]
Initiative: +14

Lightning zap +12 vs. AC—20 lightning damage
Natural odd hit: The target is dazed until the end of its next turn.
Metal affinity: The attack gains a +1 bonus against an enemy wearing metal armor or wielding a metal weapon.

R: Lightning strike +12 vs. PD (one nearby enemy or a far away enemy at –2 atk)—24 lightning damage
Metal affinity: The attack gains a +1 bonus against an enemy wearing metal armor or wielding a metal weapon.

Flight: Lightning elementals zip from place to place about half-as-quick as lightning, hovering above the ground to avoid being grounded.

Lightning storm transformation: Roll a d8 at the start of each of the lightning elemental's turns. If you roll less than or equal to the escalation die, it shifts into lightning storm form until the end of the battle. While in this form it gains the following improved attack (and you stop rolling *lightning storm transformation* checks):

C: Storm strike +12 vs. PD (up to 2 nearby enemies)—20 lightning damage
Natural even roll: The elemental can include an additional target in the attack (requires attack roll) that hasn't been hit by *storm strike* this turn, but the attack only deals half damage.
Metal affinity: The attack gains a +1 bonus against an enemy wearing metal armor or wielding a metal weapon.

Resist lightning and thunder 16+: When a lightning or thunder attack targets this creature, the attacker must roll a natural 16+ on the attack roll or it only deals half damage.

AC	22	
PD	22	**HP 100**
MD	15	

Next Steps

After putting an end to the elementals and passing through the lightning field, the PCs move up a ridge of cloudstuff to get a full view of the weather station, but they see something unexpected.

The station is under siege. A large airship has plowed into the side of the cloudbreak, and half the ship hangs out over the void. Large and heavily armored gnolls are lumbering out of the ship, and others are already fighting cloud giants in front of the station.

For the moment, the attackers and defenders haven't noticed the PCs. Once the PCs decide to join the fight, go to **Battle 2: A Giant Gnoll Problem.**

BATTLE 2: A GIANT GNOLL PROBLEM

Ahead and slightly below your position on the ridge of cloudstuff a battle is in full swing. At the end of a short bridge of stone just in front of the large weather station door, a female cloud giant with a morningstar and a male cloud giant with a sword are fending off a small horde of gnoll reavers. At the back of the grouped gnolls, a few massive gnolls with bows seem to be directing the attack. Suddenly the giant with the morningstar screams out as an arrow pierces her cheek. She staggers for a moment, then frothing at the mouth, spins and bashes in the head of the second cloud giant in a fit of rage! There are giants and gnolls fighting in scattered clumps all around, but the gnolls facing the crazed giant are the ones who have noticed you as they howl in triumph. Maybe they're howling too soon....

Location Description

The gnoll reavers saw a target of opportunity, and after a poor landing, are assaulting the weather station. A few of the cloud giants emerged to fight off the reavers before they could enter the station. The problem is, the cloud giant thane was poisoned with demon fever by a fiendfletch arrow strike and now sees only enemies to attack, including her fellow giants and the PCs.

The PCs start far away from the battle, at the top of a ridge of cloudstuff. There's a gentle slope that stretches 100 feet to a natural channel in the cloud. The reaver airship is crashed onto the cloudbreak on the PCs' side of the channel. The weather station is on the far side, with a 40 foot long, 20 foot wide stone bridge across the channel. The cloud giant stands in the middle of the bridge, far away (or farther).

Some of the reavers are looking in the PCs' direction. Have them each roll a DC 20 Dexterity check if they choose to try to remain out of sight. At least half must succeed. If seen, a group of reavers will move toward them, while more mooks try to bring down the giant.

This is a double-strength battle, even though it's only modeling the portion of the battle that the cloud giant defenders aren't taking care of.

If your PCs are hostile to the weather station and its defenders, they may want to keep that secret for awhile. If not, feel free to make things even harder.

Terrain & Traps

Channel: The channel is 40 feet deep with roiling cloud material at the bottom. Anyone who falls into it takes no damage, but is stuck (hard save ends, 16+) in the grasping vapors (a magical defense enacted by the giants). Climbing up or down the sides of the channel requires a successful DC 20 Strength check, but avoiding the vapors (and the stuck effect) to get to the far side is difficult and will require some sort of dicey move (making the roll allows movement to one side or the other).

Stone Bridge: The bridge is slightly arched and stable. Anyone going off the side falls into the channel. As a dying action, the cloud giant could try to shatter the bridge, sending everyone on it into the channel.

Reaver Airship: The front of the demonic airship looks damaged, as if it had rammed into a stony portion of the cloud instead of landing properly. It uses oars instead of sails to magically propel it (with the help of levitation magic). Currently, half of the ship is hanging over the edge of the cloud precariously.

At the GM's option, there could be a number of human, elven, and dwarven slaves chained in place to the oars, some of whom might be related to icons or organizations the PCs are familiar with. If you decide to use the human sacrifice option (see the *What to do with the Airship* sidebar, page 28), the slaves may cry out that the gnolls are killing them one by one to power the ship.

Gnolls will pursue PCs that board the ship, or additional gnoll mooks might come up from below. In this case, the ship will creak and tilt and has a 25% each round of onboard combat of tipping and going over the side (GM, if this happens, give the PCs a round to save prisoners or get off while it's slowly sliding into the void).

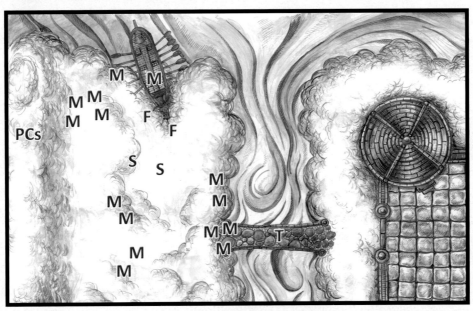

Monsters

The gnoll reavers seek both new slaves for their ship, and whatever magic they can find at the station to serve them. They are demon-worshipers that support the Diabolist, even if they might not be directly working for her on this raid. Believing the giant thane to now be the lesser threat, the gnolls will focus their attention on the PCs. There are gnoll shredders, fiendfletches, and reaver mooks. The leaders of these reavers are the fiendfletches.

The cloud giant thane is momentarily insane with demon fever rage. She will kill a few gnoll mooks and then turn her attention on everyone else. It is possible to cleanse her of the fever, but it will take an icon advantage or two at the least, along with a successful skill check. If she regains her senses, she'll stop attacking PCs if they don't attack her.

Additional Reinforcements: If you want to challenge the PCs more, add one or two hezrou demons to the fight. They traveled with the gnolls on the reaver airship.

#/Level of PCs	Cloud Giant Thane (T)	Gnoll Shredder (S)	Gnoll Fiendfletch (F)	Gnoll Reaver Mook (M)
4 x 5th level	1	1	1	20 (2 mobs)
5 x 5th level	1	2	2	16 (2 mobs)
6 x 5th level	1	3	3	13 (1 mob)
4 x 6th level	1	3	2	20 (2 mobs)
5 x 6th level	1	4	3	25 (2 mobs)
6 x 6th level	1	5	4	30 (3 mobs)

Tactics

The fevered cloud giant thane will smash a pair of gnoll mooks (not part of battle) engaged with her during her first turn, then direct her attention to the other gnolls and PCs, seeing both as enemies. She will hurl chunks of cloudstuff given form by her will at nearby enemies (*chains and shrapnel*), or wade in with her *morningstar*. At the start of each of the giant's turns, roll a d6. On a 6 she will target gnolls that turn, otherwise it's the PCs (unless only engaged with gnolls).

The reavers swarm one or two PCs while the shredders block anyone trying to reach the fiendfletches, who pepper everyone with arrows.

Icons

A PC that has relationship advantages with the Archmage, Priestess, Diabolist, GGW, Crusader, or maybe the Elf Queen could use one or more of them to find a way to heal the giant thane; in that case, once the thane drops to 50 hp or less, she recovers her senses.

Cloud Giant Thane

Huge 7th level wrecker [GIANT]
Initiative: +11

Cloud-forged morningstar +12 vs. AC—60 damage
Natural even hit: The target loses any *flight* abilities and can't gain *flight* in any way (save ends).
Natural odd hit or miss: The thane can make a *chains and shrapnel* attack as a free action.

C: Chains and shrapnel +12 vs. AC (1d4 random nearby creatures)—20 damage

Strike with advantage: A cloud giant gains a +4 attack bonus against any enemy taking ongoing damage or that has an ongoing condition (dazed, for instance).

AC	22	
PD	21	**HP 290**
MD	21	

Gnoll Shredder

Gnoll shredders love close-in fighting and viciously strike down enemies that try to flee. They also know to keep their heads down when the fiendfletch bows begin to creak with the sound of death.

7th level blocker [HUMANOID]
Initiative: +9

Diabolical axe +12 vs. AC—25 damage, and one of the shredder's allies engaged with the target can pop free

Battle lock: Gnoll shredders gain a +2 bonus to opportunity attacks, and enemies take a –8 penalty to disengage checks against them.

Legion fighting: When the escalation die increases, if there are more gnolls in the battle than their enemies, one gnoll shredder in the battle can make a melee attack as a free action.

Nastier Specials

Spoiling strike: When the shredder hits with an opportunity attack, it can make a *spoiling strike* attack against that enemy as a free action.

Spoiling strike +17 vs. PD (one enemy it hits with an opportunity attack)—The target loses the rest of its actions that turn (and stops moving if it was moving).

Vicious in-fighting: When an enemy would pop free from the shredder, it must roll a disengage check as a free action instead. If it fails, the shredder can make a *diabolical axe* attack against that enemy as a free action.

AC	27	
PD	19	**HP 95**
MD	15	

GNOLL FIENDFLETCH

Pack bloodlust has been harnessed into disciplined ranks of archers.

7th level archer [HUMANOID]
Initiative: +11

Infernal mace +12 vs. AC—18 damage
Natural 16+: The fiendfletch can make a disengage check as a free action this turn after the attack.

R: Hellbent bow +13 vs. AC (one nearby or far away enemy)—30 damage
Natural 16+: The target is dazed until the end of its next turn as it suffers debilitating pain from a hellish arrow.

Close-quarters archery: While making a ranged attack, the fiendfletch gains a +4 bonus to AC against opportunity attacks.

Nastier Specials

Duck and cover: While the fiendfletch has at least one blocker, troop, or wrecker ally (like a shredder) between it and an enemy, it gains a +4 bonus to all defenses against ranged and close-quarters attacks from that enemy.

Possession arrows: When the fiendfletch rolls a natural 16+ with a *hellbent bow* attack and hits, the target is confused (save ends) instead of dazed (something like this must have happened to the giant...).

AC	23	
PD	19	**HP 75**
MD	15	

GNOLL REAVER

A serious contestant in the 'eat ripped-out entrails while fighting other enemies' category of the competition.

5th level mook [HUMANOID]
Initiative: +8

Scavenged axe or flail +9 vs. AC—10 damage
Natural 16+: The gnoll bites the target for 5 extra damage.

R: Javelin +10 vs. AC—8 damage

Reaver swarm: The reaver gains a +1 bonus to damage for each additional reaver engaged with the target (max +5).

AC	21	
PD	18	**HP 20 (mook)**
MD	14	

Mook: Kill one gnoll reaver mook for every 20 damage you deal to the mob.

ADDITIONAL REINFORCEMENTS

HEZROU (TOAD DEMON)

Large 7th level troop [DEMON]
Initiative: +11

Meaty, clawed hands +12 vs. AC (2 attacks)—28 damage
Any hit: The demon can grab the target if it isn't already grabbing a creature. The grabbed foe can't move except to teleport, pop free, or attempt to disengage, and disengage attempts take a –5 penalty unless the creature hit the hezrou with an attack that turn.
    The hezrou gains a +4 attack bonus against any enemy it is grabbing.

Demonic stench: While engaged with this creature, enemies with 84 hp or fewer are dazed (–4 attack) and do not add the escalation die to their attacks.

AC	22	
PD	16	**HP 210**
MD	20	

NEXT STEPS & LOOT

Once these gnolls are defeated, and the thane has been put out of her misery, restrained, or cured, the surviving cloud giant warriors will mop up the remaining gnolls, while other cloud giants emerge from the station to determine the PCs' intentions. This group is in the employ of the Archmage, so they are somewhat accustomed to dealing with small folk. They will be thankful the PCs took care of the reavers and offer them food, refreshment, and lodging if the PCs were sent to help them. They'll also be happy to let the PCs loot the gnolls' ship, or do what they want with it.

The gnolls have a few treasure chests of raided valuables in the airship, including 6000 sp, 270 gp, 30 pp, and three champion tier *healing potions*.

What to Do With the Airship?

There are at least three ways to handle the airship if the PCs win out and keep it from going over the side. Either it's too damaged to fly again and they simply loot it and save any slaves; or it's really not all that badly damaged and the PCs now have an airship (welcome to champion tier!); or they could have an airship if they wanted it, but it turns out that it's a horribly demonic airship that has to be powered by daily human sacrifices.

Any option that involves keeping the ship is going to require crew. Or slaves. Or sacrifices. Complications, certainly.

If you plan on having a lot of overworld adventures in epic tier, you could wait until everyone has forgotten about the ship, then bring it back as a gift, prize, or maguffin in some future adventure. Perhaps the giants or other servants of the Archmage will repair the airship and give it to the PCs as a boon when they reach epic tier. Hopefully they'll notice the human sacrifice problem and fix it. Or maybe it's going to be a joint operation with the Crusader.

Even if the crazed thane was killed, the cloud giants might reward the PCs with a *+2 glass breastplate (recharge 11+):* You generate a pulse of lightning that deals 2 x your level lightning damage to each enemy engaged with you and pops it free from you. You also have *resist lightning 16+.* Quirk: Frequently spasms while talking. The armor could be light or heavy.

Hostility?: In the outlier situation in which the PCs are set on destroying the station, you can decide how tough you want the cloud giant defenders to be. The station itself only holds a few sleeping chambers, a workshop, and a tower filled with machinery the Archmage uses for weather control.

Liftoff: Without the pressure of being under attack, the giants soon figure out how to get the cloudbreak launched back into the overworld. That's the PCs' cue for departure, if they haven't already dealt with the ship and slaves and scooted off the cloud.

The Lightning Station Story Endings

Here are outcomes for each story opening, detailing what success or failure might mean.

If the PCs did face both battles, remember to give them a full heal-up. That's probably important if the next step is fighting the cloud giants....

Emergency Response Team

Success: The PCs win through to the station and defeat the gnoll reavers. Given time, the cloud giant technicians manage to get the weather station back into the overworld and reconnected to the weather wards. Each PC gains a 6 with the Archmage that lasts until they use it or level up.

Failure: The cloudbreak with the weather station finally breaks apart upon the mountain top. The station becomes an outpost for gnoll reavers, and the weather in the region becomes much harsher, affecting crops and the rest of the Empire's wards. Word of the PCs' failure gets out. Each PC must reroll the next two 6s they gain with a heroic icon.

Storm Warning

Success: As with Emergency Response Team, except each PC gains a 6 with any one of their icons.

Failure: The PCs fail to restore the weather station and the surrounding lands get hammered by continuous bad weather. The balance of power in the area shifts to the High Druid, or one of the ambiguous icons.

Claiming the Prize

Success: The PCs get to the station, defeat the enemies trying to take it, and overpower the caretakers, allowing them to steal the secrets of weather wards, plus some magical equipment and diagrams of the machinery. The Archmage takes a hit, and one of the other icons (perhaps the Blue) prospers. Each PC gains a 6 with one of their icons that lasts until they use it or level up. But they're now on the short list as enemies of the Archmage, gaining a 1 point negative relationship with that icon until they level up.

Failure: The PCs fail to take the station and the Archmage's people get it back up and running. The Archmage's power in the region grows too. Each PC must reroll the next 5 or 6 they get with the Archmage and one icon of their choice.

Battle Scene Connections

The stories from this set of battle scenes can lead to adventures in this and other Battle Scenes books:

 Mad Wizard's Loot (Prince of Shadows, page 129): The Prince's people discover that the PCs are good at dealing with weird and powerful magic after their successes with the lightning station. Their people contact or blackmail the PCs into visiting the vault.

 The Lich's Spire (Lich King): The cloud giants inform the PCs that the station malfunctioned after a burst of necrotic energy slammed into it. The energy came from a wizard's tower in a nearby forest. As representatives of the Archmage, they ask the PCs to find out who's interfering with the empire's weather.

 Zephalarius' Nightmares (Great Gold Wyrm): The cloud giants are at a loss on how to get the lightning station aloft. They suspect the dragons will have to help while they simply maintain the cloudbreak. The cloud giant's surviving leader sends the PCs to the lair of the gold dragon Zephalarius to ask for his help.

ARCHMAGE:
†HE OVERWORLD VAVL†

LEVEL RANGE: 9–10

The themes of this set of battles are traversing overworld terrain, ancient dark magic, and the Archmage's secrets. The setting is a hidden vault in the overworld, but the PCs can start on the land if they have access to the overworld (like a nice portal created by the Archmage's people).

After the Wizard King perished (or so it was thought), the first Archmage began the work of undoing much of the dark magic that he had put in place. Some of this involved gathering powerful magical artifacts crafted from dark magic and hiding them away until the world was ready for them (or was about to end and needed some extra firepower). The Overworld Vault is one such place where these items were hidden.

Kept safe for ages through the power of the first Archmage and many of those who followed after, the vault remained a repository of those early artifacts, though over the ages some Archmages removed certain items for personal use or to do some world saving. In fact, there's only one major artifact left: the *Staff of Chaos*.

That's now an issue because the outer wards on the vault just went down with a ringing sound like a champagne glass struck with a dagger, a sound heard by anyone with magical sense anywhere near the overworld. While the vault still has magical guardians, its best defense was the outer ward that hid the dome from detection. Now many of the powerful entities in the overworld know that something interesting just popped to light. They'll investigate.

In truth, someone nasty already knew about the vault. A group of devils in the service of one of the icons (or perhaps free agents, depending on the campaign story and how you've made use of *Chapter 5: Deviltry* in *13 True Ways*) performed a ritual to bring the ward down. Now they are trying to access and search the vault for the staff for their own use.

The PCs must claim the staff first.

†HE OVERWORLD VAVL† STORY OPEΠIΠGS

- **Time to Save the World:** One or more PCs with a positive or conflicted relationship with the Archmage are told/asked/

GE††IΠG †O †HE OVERWORLD

It might be that the PCs are already traveling the overworld as part of their epic adventures. If not, there are plenty of ways to get there from the worlds below—airships, portals, climbing the Cathedral, riding a dragon, and more. Use whatever method works best for the group.

bribed to travel to the overworld vault and collect the *Staff of Chaos* to keep it out of unsafe hands. They are the Archmage's closest or most available operatives in the area. The outer ward is down, but there will be magical guardians (though what they might be is unclear since the current Archmage never visited the vault).

- **Thwarting the Magic Police:** One or more PCs with a negative or conflicted relationship with the Archmage learns that one of his powerful vaults in the overworld has just been revealed. The wards came down for some reason. Those vaults hold all sorts of wonderful magic from the First Age, and that magic needs to be shared with the world, or at least in their hands.

- **Help the Archmage Help the Empire:** The PCs are contacted by one of the icons associated with the Empire (Emperor, Priestess, Crusader, Great Gold Wyrm, or maybe even the Lich King or the Blue in the right story). One of the Archmage's overworld vaults has been revealed, and many are seeking the prizes within. Most who do so aren't friends of the empire, and so the PCs must travel there first and claim whatever artifacts of powerful, ancient magic the vault holds.

ALTERΠATE ÍCOΠS

Lich King: The story isn't too tough to tell from the other side. One of the Lich King's old vaults has now been revealed, and the PCs must reclaim or protect the staff. Feel free to change some of the enemy guardians to undead if it's a vault the Lich King created.

The Prince: The Prince found a way to bring down the ward, but he has other business to take care of (like taking something REALLY valuable from the Archmage while the icon is busy dealing with the vault), so the PCs are sent in to grab the prize.

Icons in Play

Characters that have relationships (and story-guide advantages) with the Archmage, Emperor, Lich King, and maybe the Diabolist or whichever icon the devils are tied to should be able to shine in these battle scenes. Moreso than PCs with other icon relationships, feel free to give such PCs extra knowledge about the opposition, make checks to pull off fun actions the players might suggest, and use their advantages to particularly good effect, such as negating or bypassing some of the advantages or abilities of the enemies.

The Overworld Vault Overview

The PCs travel to the edge of the vault in the overworld. The vault is within a dome of magic force that was previously concealed from all. Entrance to the dome is gained via a magical gate within a panoramic mural upon one face of the dome. The mural shows a scene of storm giants and frost giants facing necromancers and undead monstrosities. In Battle 1, some of the giants in the mural peel off it and come to life to defend the vault. As the PCs finish up and open the gateway to the interior of the dome, an airship flies past, beating them inside.

As the PCs travel inside the dome through a long canyon valley full of rich soil, the ground rumbles and then a huge overworld worm attacks in Battle 2. While the PCs fight, they see flashes of lightning on the horizon from the devils in the airship battling other guardians.

In Battle 3, after visiting a few structures in the valley that prove to be empty sites that once contained dangerous artifacts, the PCs finally discover the one with the staff. It's a wide, squat tower of green stone columns with a stairway up the outside. As they reach the top, they see the staff stuck at the center of the tower, but just then the airship of devils arrives to also claim the prize.

GM, feel free to expand upon these battles by including battles with other competing artifact hunters, guardians at installations with now-missing artifacts, and other enemies that makes sense for the site.

The battles outlined here can take place over minutes or hours, once the PCs reach the vault. Since the Archmage is in play, the enemies presented here are magical guardians, epic monsters held in magical stasis, and powerful adversaries (devils) who also want the artifact.

See story endings after the final battle for options on what happens after the PCs finish the last battle.

Battle 1: The Hidden Gate

Getting to the overworld was the easy part. Finding the location of the vault by following the aetheric currents of the magic of the now-fallen ward was more difficult. Now you stand before a tall wall that forms one pane of the huge force dome protecting the vault. It is the only place on the outside of the dome that's different from the rest. The pane is opaque, and upon it are images of a group of storm and frost giants fighting against a horde of undead led by powerful necromancers. As you study the mural for a clue to how to open the dome, there's a flare of light. Some storm giants "peel" off the mural, followed by a group of frost giants, and expand to full size. One of the storm giants yells, "Protect the vault!

Location Description

The dome sits within an area of land resting upon and formed from cloudstuff. The area the PCs are in is relatively flat, but pools of cloudstuff bubble up here and there all around. Besides the dome panes that curve away from the area, there is little cover, but that could change.

For those with the will, the raw cloudstuff can be formed into simple terrain: small hills, boulders, walls, etc. So there may be cover if any of the PCs create it.

If not, it's just an open area with various-sized pools of cloudstuff.

TERRAIN & TRAPS

Force Dome: The dome rises many hundreds of feet up to its apex and covers a lot of ground. At the bottom, each pane of force that forms the dome is roughly 80 x 80 with only a slight curve inward. The panes are effectively impenetrable, unless the gate is opened. An exceptional PC might be able to scale a pane, and then higher up the dome, but it will require a successful DC 35 Strength or Dexterity check.

Cloud Pool: There are five pools of different sizes in the area around the mural. Any PC that enters a pool gets mired in cloudstuff and becomes stuck (save ends).

It's possibly to shape the cloudstuff into terrain. It flows out of a pool and coagulates into temporary reality for a time as directed by the will of the creator. It can't be made to fall on or crush an enemy, but it can form cover or possibly a temporary prison. The possibilities are only limited by imagination and force of will, and more will is required for larger objects.

A PC can attempt to shape the cloudstuff as a move action. It's a DC 25 Intelligence check (or perhaps Charisma in some cases) to form one shape and make it temporarily real for a simple piece of terrain. Higher rolls on the check will result in larger effects.

Mural: The giant guardians "peel" off the mural to defend the vault. Once they drop to 0 hp, they dematerialize and reappear back on the mural.

Once the PCs have time to study the mural, the clue to the entrance is a small detail on one of the necromancers fighting the giants (the figure glows slightly). Taking the necromancer's staff and pulling it makes it act like a lever that comes out of the 2D mural toward the PCs into 3D and causes the entire pane to shimmer and fade momentarily.

Or if you choose, GM, make opening the door a more difficult puzzle that your players will enjoy: it could have runes, talking 2D characters, or whatever you want. Make checks to notice details or deal with 2D characters DC 25.

MONSTERS

The storm giants are clad in ancient silver chainmail armor and vaporous silvery clothing. They wield bows made of lightning and huge greatswords.

The pale blue-skinned frost giants have ice-white beards. They wield blue-ice axes and wear heavy fur armor.

Additional Reinforcements: If you want to challenge the PCs more, add an advanced ice sorceress (*Bestiary*, page 77) to

the battle. Increase her to level 10, adding +3 to her initiative, attacks, and defenses. Her *staff* attack now deals 40 damage and 40 cold damage, and *winter wind* deals 115 cold damage.

TACTICS

The frost giants engage the nearest foes while the storm giants try to stay back using their bows. They plant their swords in the ground next to them for when they have to switch to melee, and if they wish to return to ranged attacks, their bows fly to their hands on currents of lightning.

If the PCs create terrain, the storm giants might use their limited flight to take advantage of it too.

LOOT

None.

ICONS

A PC that has relationship advantages with the Archmage, Diabolist, Elf Queen, High Druid, Lich King, Priestess, or the Three could use one or more of them to craft cloudstuff terrain without a check, or to enhance what they do craft.

A PC that has relationship advantages with any icon could use one or more of them to help open the gate through the pane, if you decide to challenge the PCs with a puzzle to open it.

#/Level of PCs	Storm Giant (S)	Frost Giant Adventurer (F)
4 x 9th level	1	4
5 x 9th level	2	3
6 x 9th level	2	5
4 x 10th level	2	4
5 x 10th level	3	4
6 x 10th level	4	3

Storm Giant

Storm giants don't bother hating those trapped in the world beneath the clouds. They just don't think enough of them to care much whether they live or die. "Let the lightning sort out the small fry" pretty much sums up their live-and-let-lightning-strikes-determine-who-else-lives philosophy.

Huge 10th level archer [GIANT]
Initiative: +16

Truly enormous greataxe +15 vs. AC—120 damage
 Natural even hit or miss: The giant can make a *lightning bolt* attack against a random nearby enemy as a free action.
 Miss: 40 damage OR the giant can make a *release the thunder* attack as a free action.

R: Giant longbow +14 vs. AC (2 attacks vs. nearby or far away enemies)—60 damage
 Natural even hit: The giant can make a *lightning bolt* attack against a random enemy that is nearby the target of the *longbow* attack.

[Special trigger] C: Lightning bolt +15 vs. PD (one random nearby enemy)—2d6 x 10 lightning damage
 Miss: Half damage.

[Special trigger] C: Release the thunder +15 vs. PD (all nearby creatures)—1d10 thunder damage per *building thunder* point (see below).

 Miss: Half damage.

Building thunder: Keep count of the number of times the storm giant uses its *lightning bolt* attack during the battle. Add that number to the escalation die to get the current building thunder value.

Skystep: A storm giant can use its standard action to walk or run through the air, using move actions to continue. If the storm giant makes a standard action attack, it settles back to the ground below it without falling.

Storm born: The storm giant has *resist thunder 16+* and *resist lightning 16+*.

AC	26	
PD	24	**HP 650**
MD	22	

Frost Giant Adventurer

Often the first into the fray, the frost giant adventurer scatters its foes like fifteen pins. Yes, giants play with fifteen pins. And they're a lot bigger than your dwarven ten-pins.

Large 8th level spoiler [GIANT]
Initiative: +13
Vulnerability: fire

Overlarge club +13 vs. AC (one nearby enemy or one enemy engaged with giant)—75 damage
 Natural even hit: The target loses its next move action, and if it's engaged with the giant, it pops free.

Ancient cold: While battling one or more frost giants, there is only a 50% chance that the escalation die increases at the start of the round.

Blood of the niefelheim: When an enemy the frost giant adventurer is engaged with scores a critical hit against the giant, that enemy is hampered (hard save ends, 16+).

Resist cold 16+: When a cold attack targets this creature, the attacker must roll a natural 16+ on the attack roll or it only deals half damage.

AC	24	
PD	23	**HP 280**
MD	18	

Next Steps

Once the giants are defeated, they fade back to the mural but won't animate again. Now the PCs must figure out how to open the gate. It can be easy, using a bit of study and lore to touch the slightly glowing staff of a necromancer figure in the mural to pull a lever which opens the pane. Or it can be a puzzle in itself that the GM's devises.

In either case, the moment the pane disappears, there will be a blast of wind and heat as a large longship-like airship held aloft by rings of fire suddenly appears (cloaked or perhaps descending from on high) and zooms overhead into the breach. The PCs perhaps get a glimpse of a devilish face if you want to foreshadow the final battle, but it might be better to reveal only the sight of rowing oars and sound of a cracking whip followed by screams.

Once the PCs pass through the pane, go to **Battle 2: Wormhollow Canyon.**

Battle 2: Wormhollow Canyon

Beyond the gate into the vault you find oddly familiar terrain. You're in a box canyon formed from dry, reddish rock and earth with gravel covering the ground. It looks like any of a thousand canyons from the world below. The airship that passed overhead is now out of sight far ahead, but you move as quickly as you dare. The canyon begins to widen, and the rocky ground turns to soft soil and low vegetation. That's when the first tremor hits, nearly knocking a few of you off your feet. All is quiet for a moment, and then the ground shakes and explodes upward as a huge, segmented, silver-gray worm blasts half out of the soil. Its top lands with a slam that shakes the ground, knocking a chunk of canyon wall down, and a swarm of giant gold-shelled insects speeds toward you from the swarm around the worm's great silver-toothed maw.

Location Description

The canyon is 120 feet across and much longer, eventually bending out of sight about a quarter mile ahead. There is very little cover except for a large boulder and chunk of stone that fell out of the canyon wall when the worm emerged.

The creature is an overworld worm, basically an ancient purple worm flavored (and colored) for the overworld; in all aspects, it's the same as the *Bestiary* monster. It's joined by a few mobs of lightning beetles that are stronger than normal due to being in the overworld, where their lightning is enhanced.

Terrain & Traps

Cliff Walls: The cliffs rise nearly 80 feet, and the rock is rough and crumbly, but relatively easy to climb. The problem is, the worm is so big, the PCs need to climb at least 40 feet to get out of

its range. And it can tunnel into the soil around the base or slam against the ground to cause the cliffsides to tremble and break away, potentially dropping a PC back to the ground.

Climbing the cliffs requires a successful DC 20 Strength check for each move action (about 30 feet). Hanging on when the cliffs shake or crumble away requires a DC 25 Strength check. Anyone who falls takes 1d12 damage per 20 feet.

Boulder & Stone Chunks: The boulder is big enough to at least slow the worm down. A PC using it for cover could get a +2 bonus to AC and PD from a generous GM. It's oddly shaped, so climbing to the top of the 13-foot chunk of stone requires a successful DC 18 Strength check.

Dicey moves to leap from the stone to the worm's back aren't easy, requiring a DC 25 Dexterity check.

Furrows & Wormhole: It's easiest to have the worm stay in its hole and extend itself to lash out at enemies, but if all PCs move away from it, it will burrow toward them, creating a 20-foot deep furrow through the soil. Any PCs attempting to cross or escape from a furrow must roll a DC 20 Strength check.

The wormhole descends 50 feet before curving away and collapsing, so any PC entering the hole will fall and take 3d12 damage unless they roll a DC 25 Dexterity check. There's probably a good chance the hole collapses around them too.

Monsters

The overworld worm is huge, mean, and hungry. It was kept in stasis in a hollow below the canyon until someone passed overhead without phrasing the proper warding words. It won't leave the canyon area, however, due to the magical control still exerted upon it.

The lightning beetles are gold-winged, silver-bodied beetles with mandibles that spark with lightning at each wingbeat.

Additional Reinforcements: If you want to challenge the PCs more, there are two overworld worms, but the second one is only a purple worm (8th level) advanced to 9th level (+1 to initiative, attacks, and defenses; +35 damage on *maw* attack).

#/Level of PCs	Overworld Worm (W)	Lightning Beetle Mook (B)
4 x 9th level	1	7 (1 mob)
5 x 9th level	1	16 (3 mobs)
6 x 9th level	1	23 (4 mobs)
4 x 10th level	1*	20 (4 mobs)
5 x 10th level	1*	17 (3 mobs)**
6 x 10th level	1*	22 (4 mobs)**

* The worm can use its nastier special.

** The lightning beetles are double strength: their *mouthparts* attacks deals 32 damage, *lightning zap* deals 70 lightning damage, and they have 100 hp.

Tactics

The worm's goal is simple: it wishes to consume all creatures traversing the canyon. To that end, it attacks the nearest enemy, or whichever enemies last hurt it.

The beetles fly out from their host, seeking warm flesh. They also act as scouts for the worm thanks to a symbiotic and telepathic connection to it. They will swarm any enemies not being directly attacked by the worm. Feel free to include a few of them that are not part of the normal monster totals inside the worm's gullet, waiting for new food.

Loot

There is treasure inside the worm from past victims, including 1000 sp of ancient design inside a sealed glass chalice that hasn't dissolved, and a coffer made of some dark metal embedded in the worm's stomach wall and protected from the acid there. It holds a *dwarven mug* (core book page 295) with a velvet pouch inside containing five 200 gp rubies.

Icons

A PC that has relationship advantages with the Archmage, Crusader, Dwarf King, High Druid, Prince, or the Three could use one or more of them to know a trick to escaping from a worm's gullet (look for a certain structure that will expel them out a gland, or do something that causes the worm to regurgitate early, for example).

Overworld Worm

Maybe it's angry about living in the overworld instead of the deep underworld, or maybe it's just angry.

Huge 12th level wrecker [BEAST]
Initiative: +17

Devouring maw +18 vs. PD—100 damage
Natural even hit: The target is swallowed whole if it's smaller than the worm (see below).
Miss: Half damage.

Tail sting +18 vs. AC (up to 2 random nearby enemies)—40 damage, and 40 ongoing poison damage
Miss: 20 damage.

Prodigious thrash +18 vs. AC (1d4 random nearby enemies)—50 damage
Miss: Half damage.
Natural 1–2: The worm and any creatures it has swallowed take 8d6 damage (but it still deals miss damage on a 2).
Limited use: The worm can make this attack as a free action if it has one enemy swallowed or less after using its standard action during its turn.

Swallow whole: While a creature is swallowed whole, it takes 10d12 acid damage at the start of its turn and is stuck, hampered, and unable to attack or affect anything outside the worm's stomach (and vice-versa). Most teleport abilities don't work because you're hampered *and* you can't see the location out of the worm you want to teleport to. There are two ways out.

Cut your way out: Deal 80 damage to the worm with a single attack and you can cut your way out. All edged or bladed weapons are reduced to d6 damage dice (at most) inside the worm's gullet, so good luck. At least you'll be damaging the worm attacking it from within.

Get upchucked: While the worm is staggered, you can use a standard action to try and crawl out of its mouth. Roll a hard save (16+); on a success, the worm vomits you out and spits you somewhere nearby. The worm also vomits out all creatures it has swallowed when it drops to 0 hp.

Burrow: As the standard monster ability (*13th Age* core rulebook, page 200), but with a +5 bonus to the check.

Nastier Specials

Resist most energy damage 16+: Overworld worms generate weird energy resistances thanks to overworld radiation and their odd diets. Roll a d8 twice, in secret, to determine what energy types the worm is not resistant to. The PCs probably have to find out what energy works best against the worm the hard way, though you might have mercy and allow a DC 35 Wisdom skill check to figure out what energy types work against the worm.
1: acid; **2:** cold; **3:** fire; **4:** lightning; **5:** thunder; **6:** holy; **7:** negative energy; **8:** poison.

AC	27	
PD	25	**HP 1200**
MD	21	

GOLDEN-WINGED LIGHTNING BEETLE

10th level mook [BEAST]
Initiative: +16

Mouthparts +14 vs. AC—16 damage
Natural even hit or miss: The target also takes 10 lightning damage.

R: Lightning zap +14 vs. PD (one nearby enemy not engaged with an overworld worm or lightning beetle)—35 lightning damage
Natural even hit or miss: The target takes 10 extra lightning damage.

Flight: The beetles fly badly, usually just enough to get back to the worm when they've been shaken off from their hiding spots in its segments.

Scaredy bugs: Whenever one or more golden-winged lightning beetles drop to 0 hp, roll a d6. If you roll less than or equal to the number of beetles that were destroyed by that attack, all beetles in that mob stop fighting, using all their actions during their next turn to disengage and fly away.

AC	29	
PD	24	**HP 50 (mook)**
MD	19	

Mook: Kill one lightning beetle mook for every 50 damage you deal to the mob.

NEXT STEPS

As the PCs take a quick rest after facing the overworld worm they will hear some booms and see flashes of lightning in the sky in the direction they are traveling. (The devils on the airship are breaking into one of the many locations in the vault while trying to find the staff, but the PCs won't know that yet.)

Once the PCs are ready to continue, the canyon ends after about a quarter mile. It opens to a mostly circular valley (like the depression of a ball in a blanket) with a flat grass-covered plain in the center. The valley holds numerous small towers and structures that once held powerful artifacts. The PCs will be able to quickly determine which ones are empty and unguarded as they search the area. They might see more energy flashes near the far rim of the valley from the airship and devils too, if you like, without getting much detail.

After a few minutes of searching, the PCs will see a spire created from multiple smaller columns of dull green stone (similar to jade) rising in a close bundle. Column stairs ascend the outside edge and energy flares off the surface of the tower, indicating that it is attuned to a magical source. When they are ready, go to **Battle 3: The Staff of Chaos.**

Battle 3: The Staff of Chaos

You begin the ascent up the hundred-foot tall tower of green stone columns. The terrain is so odd it could only have once been cloudstuff. Those attuned to arcane magic can sense the energy fields rolling across the tower. As you crest the top, you see a single green column rising a few feet higher than the others near the center of the tower, and standing upright from it is a staff made of dark metal that crackles with energy. The surface between you and the staff is flat, but there are many small holes and pockets created by the columns that could be treacherous. Suddenly, there's a crackling sound and a whoosh as an airship rises up from behind the far side of the tower. As it passes over, a handful of figures leap down. Some look insectoid, but other larger ones are have horns and wield barbed forks—devils!

Location Description

The top of this tower of stone columns is roughly 140 feet in diameter, with each group on an opposite edge 70 feet away from the staff (far away). The many pockmarks and holes created by the construction makes it hard to move across easily.

The devils are here for the staff, and they were the ones who figured out how to bring down the outer ward that was hiding the vault initially. There are greater ice devils leading the group with horned devil shock troops following their orders.

In addition, the airship climbs into the air about 60 feet and hovers there. During the battle, the ice devil captain will direct the fire rings that help keep the craft aloft to send rays of fire down upon the PCs to harry them.

While the staff is simply sticking up out of a column, it's not unprotected, which the first creature to try to take it will quickly realize.

This is a double-strength battle, and actually a little tougher than that due to the airship attack.

Terrain & Traps

Uneven Footing: Any PC moving across the tower's surface normally (not flying, teleporting, or using other special movement) must roll a DC 20 Dexterity check; on a failure, it only moves half as far as it wants with that move action due to the poor footing. The horned devils' feet are too big for the holes and each ice devil creates a layer of ice where it walks that keeps this from happening.

Falling Off Tower: If any creature falls off the tower, it takes 4d12 damage and must spend a full round climbing or getting back to the top of the stairs.

Staff of Chaos: When a creature physically tries to grab the staff (a quick action), defensive energies keeping the staff in check flare forth. That creature must roll a hard save (16+); on a failure, a forcestorm erupts automatically dealing 50 force damage to the creature taking the staff, as well as making the following attack:

Forcestorm +20 vs. PD (each nearby creature)—4d10 force damage.

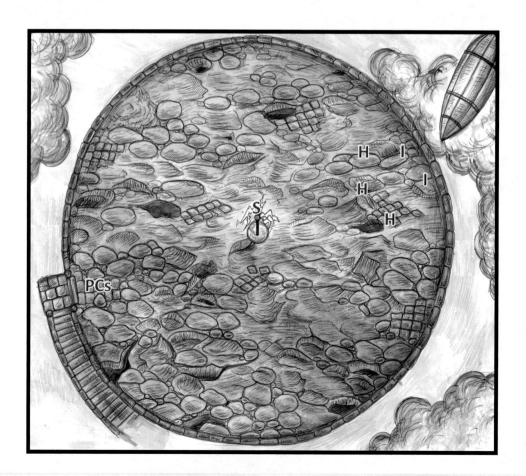

Once a creature has the staff in hand, chaotic energy within the staff infuses the holder. That creature's next attack deals double damage. The staff is then dormant until it can be attuned.

Airship Attack: At the start of each round beginning on the second round, the airship captain directs a *ray of fire* attack against one random PC.

> **Ray of fire +15 vs. PD (one random nearby or far away PC)**—3d20 fire damage.

Monsters

The greater ice devils lead this group of artifact hunters. They want the staff for some diabolical plan. Each devil stands about 7 feet high and looks like an ice-blue insectoid humanoid with four arms using a large glaive. Ice coats their bodies and the area around them where they move, radiating cold.

The horned devils stand nearly 10 feet and are very thick and muscular, with long, prehensile tails covered with sharp ridges. They look exactly like you would expect a devil to look, including the vicious barbed fork and sharp horns.

Additional Reinforcements: If you want to challenge the PCs more, the airship is crewed by 2d8 devil rowers with no devil's due ability who will join the battle. (Their stat block below uses the orc great fang cadre from the core *13th Age* book as a base, but they don't have bows and use various weapons or body spikes.)

#/Level of PCs	Greater Ice Devil (I)	Horned Devil (H)
4 x 9th level	2	2
5 x 9th level	2	3
6 x 9th level	2	4
4 x 10th level	2	3
5 x 10th level	3	4
6 x 10th level	3	5

Tactics

Although the greater ice devils are leaders, they lead from the front and will engage the PCs in melee to try to lock them down with ice then move away, buying time for their horned devil allies to take the staff. They will quickly identify the PCs who are the greatest threat and direct their troops to gang up on that character.

The horned devils will attack PCs who are stuck, trying to take advantage of the ice devil's *shattering counsel*, though one may hang back to use its ranged attacks in support of the others.

If a devil grabs the staff first, don't forget to have the staff damage the devil and all nearby. Then feel free to change the battle by having the airship drop down on one edge of the tower so that the devil with the staff can move toward it at full speed. The devil should take a full round to reach the edge, then can move aboard during its next turn. Perhaps at that point, the battle flows onto the ship. The captain and crew are busy flying it, so they won't get involved initially.

Remember to apply the *devil's due* ability of each devil when the PCs attack, giving the PCs the choice to use the escalation die or not each time they attack. Also, each devil has the same special ability, *devilish resilience*, shown at the start of the stat blocks.

Loot

The devils have nothing of value on them, and they will turn to smoke after death. If the PCs manage to capture the airship, that might be a prize, or you could keep things simple and invoke the devils' smoking-exit termination clause.

The real prize here is the *Staff of Chaos*. If recovered and turned over to the Archmage or another icon the PCs are working for, they should be awarded with at least one true magic item in addition to other favors (see the story endings on page 39 for examples). If a PC chooses to keep the staff, treat it as an epic *+3 Staff of the Overworld* (*Book of Loot*, page 8), but since it's an artifact, also give it a second champion-tier power that makes sense for your game, probably something to do with chaotic magic—like rolls on the chaos mage weirdness table anytime the user casts a daily spell.

Icons

A PC that has relationship advantages with the Archmage, Crusader, Diabolist, GGW, or an icon that these devils have aligned with could use one or more advantage to identify the devils and their powers, or to cancel devil's due effects for a round.

A PC that has relationship advantages with the Archmage, Elf Queen, Lich King, or the Three could use one or more of them to disrupt the airship's fire attack for 1d2 rounds by channeling the chaotic magic of the staff or magically warding it toward the ship.

All Devils

Note, each devil has the following devilish special ability:
Devilish resilience: The devil gains a +4 bonus to saves.

Greater Ice Devil (Gelugon)

When you get close to an ice devil, it becomes apparent that its size is partly an illusion thanks to layers of supernatural ice. Of course, when you get that close to an ice devil, you're probably busy getting trapped in ice and seeing your screaming face reflected in the devil's hundred compound eyes.

13th level leader [DEVIL]
Initiative: +17

Wicked glaive +18 vs. AC (2 attacks)—40 damage
Natural even hit: As a free action, one of the ice devil's nearby allies of its level or lower can make a basic attack as the ice devil sets the battlefield. That attack only deals half damage.
Natural odd hit: The target is stuck (save ends).
Miss: 18 damage.

Devil's due (Rime): When you choose to add the escalation die to an attack against an ice devil, you are stuck (save ends).

Shattering counsel: When a lower level nearby ally of the ice devil attacks a creature that's stuck, the crit range of that attack expands by the escalation die.

Resist cold 13+: When a cold attack targets this creature, the attacker must roll a natural 13+ on the attack roll or it only deals half damage.

AC	28	
PD	26	HP 414
MD	26	

Horned Devil (Cornugon)

Horned devils are experts in inflicting pain, and they enjoy learning the weaknesses of each new enemy. Typically, one wields a trident-like two-pronged fork. When these devils stab you with their forks, they can taste your mortality, and you can feel it.

Large 12th level troop [DEVIL]
Initiative: +15

Barbed fork +17 vs. AC—150 damage, and until the end of the battle against the target, the devil gains a +1 bonus to attacks and its crit range expands by 1 (cumulative)
Natural even hit: The horned devil can make a *slicing tail* attack against a different target as a free action.
Natural even miss: The horned devil can make a *slicing tail* attack as a free action.

Slicing tail +17 vs. PD—35 ongoing damage from a bleeding wound

R: Flaming dart +17 vs. AC—60 damage, and 30 fire damage
Natural 16+: The target also takes 30 ongoing fire damage.

Devil's due (Weakness): When you choose to add the escalation die to an attack against a horned devil, you are weakened until the end of your next turn after you make the attack.

Flight: Horned devils are clumsy but determined fliers.

Resist fire 13+: When a fire attack targets this creature, the attacker must roll a natural 13+ on the attack roll or it only deals half damage.

AC	28	
PD	26	HP 700
MD	26	

Additional Reinforcements

Devil Rowers

10th level mook [DEVIL]
Initiative: +13

Weapon or spike +15 vs. AC—25 damage
Natural 11+: The rower can make a second *weapon or spike* attack (no more) as a free action.
Dangerous mooks: The crit range of melee attacks by rower mooks expands by 3 until half the mob has dropped.

AC	27	
PD	25	HP 50 (mook)
MD	21	

Mook: Kill one devil rower mook for every 50 damage you deal to the mob.

Next Steps

As the battle ends, the airship most likely speeds off to report the devils' failure. The PCs recover the *Staff of Chaos*, and either hand it over to an icon or choose to keep it themselves. Keeping the staff might have further consequences, such as having more devils come after it, or servants of the icon who wanted it in the first place.

If the PCs hand the staff over to the Archmage, he's probably going to replace it with another less destructive magic item, and possibly another one or two champion-tier items. Other benefits and favors depend on the story opening.

The staff could also be a key piece to a larger plot or threat that is in the works involving the Archmage or another icon.

Taking the Airship

Most likely, the airship flies off when the devils are defeated on the tower below. But if the PCs have some way to reach it, or put some icon advantages to good use, they might be able to board the airship. Most of the heavies dropped down, so they'll have a chance. Run another battle using one normal ice devil, a barbed devil, and a pile of mooks who are the rowers—humanoids who've signed themselves over to the devils' power.

If the PCs win out, they now have a working airship in which to zip around the overworld. Or you turn it to smoke at a time of your convenience. Whichever makes you happy.

The Overworld Vault Story Endings

Here are outcomes for each story opening, detailing what success or failure might mean.

If the PCs did face all three battles, remember to give them a full heal-up.

Time to Save the World

Success: The PCs recover the staff and thwart the devils' plans. The Archmage is very interested to know who was after the staff, too. He's so thankful, he rewards the PCs from his personal treasury. Each PC also gains a 6 with the Archmage that lasts until they use it.

Failure: The PCs fail to get the staff, losing it to the devils. It's part of a larger plot by them that will make things worse for everyone, probably something that the PCs will now need to go fix. But their failure has lost them face with the Archmage's bureaucracy. The next time the PCs roll icon dice (with all icons), any 6s become 5s, and the complications could be something involving pressure or tension caused by the Archmage.

Thwarting the Magic Police

Success: The PCs find the vault, defeat its guardians, and beat a group of devils to the only real prize in the place, the *Staff of Chaos*. Yeah team! Now they have the staff, but the Archmage's people are searching for them, and they keep feeling like someone else is watching them too (the devils). It's only a matter of time before one group or the other strikes.

Failure: The PCs falter in their attempt to claim even one artifact. Not only do they come up empty, but those allies they have who are linked to the Archmage doubt them. Each 6 the PCs get for the Archmage the next time they roll icon dice is a 5 instead.

Help the Archmage Help the Empire

Success: The PCs search the overworld vault but only come up with one true artifact, the *Staff of Chaos*. Still, it's a powerful item, and good that it's not in the hands of the empire's enemies. In fact, it would look nice in the hands of the icon who contacted the PCs. The PCs are well-rewarded for it, of course. Each PC gains a 6 with that icon that lasts until they use it, and one of them gains a new epic-tier magic item from the icon.

Failure: The empire's enemies now have the *Staff of Chaos*, and that's bad. In fact, the empire's power decreases in the region as the icon (or devil) who has the staff gains in power. Now they have to find a way to get the staff back from the enemy, and that can get epically messy.

Battle Scene Connections

The stories from this set of battle scenes can lead to at least one other scene in a future book:

 Games of Power (Emperor): Besides the artifact, there's one other item: a scrollcase with a letter in it. The letter indicates that a certain powerful Imperial family, House Ivrhea, placed the artifact here for a contact. It also suggests that they are traitors to the empire and that proof can be found at the Ivrhea estate. The Emperor should probably know of this fact to see if there's any truth of it. The fact that it was found in the overworld vault should count for something.

HIGH DRUID: THE WILD SACRIFICE

LEVEL RANGE: 4–5

Note, this set of battle scenes is a little different from the others because there's a direct continuation of the story at champion tier and again at epic tier for GMs who want to thread together a larger story. The three sets of battle scenes don't have to be linked. They play fine as separate instances, but if you want a longer plot line, it's there.

The themes of this set of battles are investigation into a blasphemous murder, fighting wild beasts and civilized monsters, and dealing with tensions between the Empire and the Wild. This set of battle scenes works best in a semi-wild environment where the edge of the Imperial frontier meets wilderness.

Background: A half-elf druid named Kalel Blackmane has been murdered. And not only murdered, but apparently killed as part of a sacrificial ritual. Kalel was a druid of some power who kept watch over an area of wilderness where frontier folk of the Empire have started to expand their holdings. There have been many disputes and much tension between the folk of the wild and the frontier settlers in the region, but Kalel had managed to keep the peace between the sides.

As a representative of the High Druid, Kalel was an outspoken advocate for the wild denizens, and often came into conflict with the frontier folk. But he also had friends among the frontier folk living in the nearby village of Thorn. His murder has stirred tensions, and large-scale violence could break out in the region anytime, especially if one group or the other is found responsible. But the details of his murder raise questions about whether this may be something even darker than a political assassination.

In truth, the turmoil from Kalel's death is only a secondary benefit for the murderer. The druid was murdered and sacrificed to claim both his soul and his power as part of a larger ritual meant to weaken the High Druid's influence in the area and to increase the power of his killer, a weretiger sorcerer-assassin named Tianthe Vang, and her master.

The weretiger's involvement plays into a larger storyline involving multiple icons and factions in the champion and epic tier adventures for the High Druid.

THE WILD SACRIFICE STORY OPENINGS

- **The Call of the Wild:** A PC with a positive or conflicted relationship with the High Druid is asked or told to travel immediately to the nearby village of Thorn. A druid there has been murdered and the PCs need to discover who did it and why, and then take appropriate measures for justice (or vengeance).
- **The Emperor's Representative:** A PC with a positive or conflicted relationship with the Emperor is instructed to travel immediately to the nearby frontier village of Thorn. A druid was murdered there and tensions are high, so the PCs need to discover who was behind it to protect the villagers from the folk of the wild, who are blaming everyone in the village.
- **Wrong Turns:** The PCs take the left path out of the village of Thorn instead of the right one, and it lands them into a mess. They walk onto the scene of a recent grisly murder and are asked by the victim's friend to help find the murderer.
- **A Perfect Opportunity:** A PC with a conflicted or negative relationship with the High Druid or Emperor, or a positive relationship with the Orc Lord or Diabolist, is told to travel immediately to the nearby village of Thorn. Tensions are high between the wild folk and frontier folk of the Empire after the murder of a druid, and there may be an opportunity to further their icon's interests. The PC is asked to get in good with the locals by finding the murderer and bringing them to justice.

ALTERNATE ICONS

Elf Queen/Dwarf King: Replace the druid with an elf or dwarf ambassador, and either leave the werewolves as they are or change to another lycanthrope and it should work as long as you change the location/setting slightly. Either an elven village on the edge of human lands of the Empire, or a dwarf camp that's an island within Empire-controlled lands.

ICONS IN PLAY

Characters that have relationships (and story-guide advantages) with the High Druid, Emperor, Orc Lord, Elf Queen, and possibly with the Diabolist or Prince of Shadows, should be able to shine in these battle scenes. Moreso than PCs with other icon relationships, feel free to give such PCs extra knowledge about the opposition, make checks to pull off fun actions the players might suggest, and use their advantages to particularly good effect, such as negating or bypassing some of the advantages or abilities of the enemies.

 The Three (the Blue): You could also have an envoy of the Blue get murdered on the edge of Drakkenhall lands, or a location where humanoid monsters hold sway, creating tension with the Empire.

SACRIFICE OVERVIEW

The PCs start the first scene investigating the druid's death with the help of an NPC named Moira Llarn, an herbalist from Thorn who was Kalel's friend. In Battle 1, most of the clues, along with Moira's details on the local situation, lead the PCs to a camp of half-orc werewolf woodsman who won't be happy to see the PCs. Making matters worse, a mob from Thorn led by an former Imperial legionnaire shows up seeking vengeance for Kalel's death, and they begin attacking the PCs in addition to the werewolves. Unless the PCs are quick to defuse the situation, they'll be in the middle of a double-strength battle since the werewolves will think the PCs are part of an ambush.

After the battle, investigation and an unexpected ally will reveal that the werewolves weren't responsible for the druid's death. A new clue leads the PCs into the wilds, toward the lair of the murderer. For Battle 2, the group stumbles across the hunting grounds of a bulette and its young, and a manticore that takes advantage of the fight to stoop for lunch.

Finally, in Battle 3 the group enters the lair of Tianthe, a weretiger sorceress who sacrificed and killed the druid to gain his power and stir tensions in the region. Even if Tianthe and her allies are defeated, the victory isn't complete. Clues reveal that the druid's soul and power were taken as part of the sacrificial murder, and she gave an item holding them to another master as part of a larger plot. That master's identity isn't clear.

GM, feel free to expand upon these battles by including more interactions with NPCs as part of the investigation, additional battles in the wilderness while traveling to Tianthe's lair, meetings with interested third parties, and more.

The battles outlined here can take place over a few hours, days, or even weeks, depending on the setting. Since the High Druid is in play, the enemies presented here are beasts and those living in the wilds or on the edge of the wilderness. The locations should be flavored with natural settings and nature gone wild.

See story endings after the final battle for options on what happens after the PCs finish the last battle.

INVESTIGATING A MURDER

You enter a glade to see a body covered by blankets. It lies on the ground amid four small piles of stones set at each cardinal point and stacked into a pyramid shape. A human woman in simple clothing who is sitting nearby and crying looks up at your approach.

INITIAL INVESTIGATION

Depending on the story opening used, Moira the herbalist will either be expecting them (the Emperor's or High Druid's folk summoned them) and the body has been preserved here for some hours or a day or two. Or the murder is recent and Moira just found Kalel's body and covered it (they stumble upon the scene).

No matter which opening you use, Moira is here to explain what she found, answer their questions, and ask them to find Kalel's killer. The only difference will be whether she was expecting them or not.

Moira can relate the following information about Kalel:

- Kalel Blackmane was a druid who lived in the area. He tried to fight for the rights of the wild folk while managing the expansion of the Empire in the area.
- Her name is Moira Llarn, an herbalist who lives in the nearby village of Thorn. She was Kalel's friend.
- She was supposed to meet Kalel here and discovered his body. Something horrible was done to it, more than just killing him (see below).

- Kalel had enemies in the area. He was constantly thwarting Imperial efforts to expand into the wild lands beyond the village, and so he had few friends within the Empire. But he also had enemies among the wild folk, because he made concessions.
- She believes a group of woodsmen from the wilds killed him, and performed an old ritual upon his body as a sign to others not to help the Empire. She believes this because one of the woodsmen, a half-orc named Pogral, swore he'd kill the druid yesterday in front of people in Thorn when Kalel agreed to open up some areas to Imperial logging.
- The woodsmen stay at a camp not far from here (she can give directions). There's something "off" about them more than the fact that they like to live alone in the woods, but she's not sure what.

In addition, the PCs can learn the following information by investigating the site.

- Kalel's throat has been shredded and his body lies in a dried pool of his own blood (DC 18 Intelligence check to notice the wounds look like those of animal teeth). But also, something happened to his flesh; it's shriveled and dried-up, almost like a prune or raisin.
- The area has been muddied up with blood and various footprints. There are definitely signs of booted feet (some small), but also a partial set of prints that look like those of a giant wolf (an intentional clue placed by the murderer).
- The four sets of stones exude a sense of magic and power. Any ritual caster will know that the murder was actually a sacrifice as part of a ritual (DC 15 Wisdom check for anyone else to note this, with failure meaning they add some other incorrect information).
- Any PC with a magical background that tries to scan the area using their magic senses will note that a powerful ritual

Moira Llarn

Moira is a human woman in her mid-forties with auburn hair, pale skin, and piercing green eyes. She carries a number of small pouches upon her for her herbal craft.

Play her as being sad, angry, upset, and alternatingly forlorn and furious about Kalel's death. She will push hard for the PCs to "talk to" the half-orc woodsmen. She's also the one who will rouse the Thorn mob, being unsure if the PCs will follow through (and other reasons). If possible, play her as highly intelligent with a deep inner strength. If questioned about her past, she'll just say that she once lived in Axis, but not go into details.

Moira has a larger role in the story, which will come to light in the epic battle scenes for the High Druid.

occurred there. If they succeed on a DC 15 check, they'll also realize that the ritual involved claiming the druid's magic and soul.

At this point, the players might want to go talk to people in Thorn (a small village) or try other things to learn more about the murder. Feel free to roll with it, but the investigation should keep pointing back toward the woodsmen and Pogral's threat of killing Kalel. Moira will also encourage the PCs to visit the woodsmen to see if they admit to it and to find out what they did to the druid.

Once the PCs choose that course, move on the **Battle 1: Wolves Among Us**.

BATTLE I: WOLVES AMONG US

Moira's directions are clear and a short while later you see the woodsmen's camp ahead, light smoke swirling around a set of animal hide tents set near each other. A group of half-orcs are sitting around a small campfire on log stools, talking and drinking. One of them turns partially toward you, deeply sucks in air through flaring nostrils, and then spits on the ground.

LOCATION DESCRIPTION

The camp is set up in a flat glade of dirt and grass 100 feet long and 60 feet wide, and is encircled by a foliage line of young trees and small bushes. The area outside the camp is lightly forested with a lot of open area, but also plenty of logs and bushes to hide behind. The camp consists of a circle of log seats around a small fire near a large stack of firewood, 3 medium-sized tents set up beyond the fire, various tools of the woodcraft trade (saws, axes, etc.) scattered around a simple wood plank table on the right, and some stores of ale and water beside the table.

Unless the PCs are attempting to be stealthy, the half-orc woodsman/werewolf just picked up the PCs' scent. If they are trying to be stealthy, have each PC roll a DC 18 check (Dex or Int). If any of them fail, the werewolves detect them.

If the half-orcs don't detect the PCs, they will continue to banter and drink for a few minutes until one of them goes to relieve himself (they're all male). At that point, he'll gain their scent if they haven't acted. Their conversations during this time indicate nothing more than a rough group of woodsmen.

If the PCs don't try to remain hidden or anyone fails the roll, the sniffing half-orc will growl a warning almost like a beast and the others will quickly leap up and spread out to face the PCs.

Pogral is the largest of the group and he'll step forward, demanding to know who the PCs are and why they are there, intruding upon the camp. The woodsmen are not happy to see strangers. The PCs have a brief moment to keep the werewolves from immediately attacking. It will take quick talking, and/or a DC 20 Charisma check or an icon advantage to open a dialogue with Pogral. Otherwise the half-orc werewolves assume they're being hunted and will try to strike first.

If the PCs get the half-orcs talking, Pogral will tell the PCs to leave or "pay the price." If the PCs tell him of Kalel's murder, Pogral will shrug and say that it was bound to happen sometime the way Kalel was selling out (by working with the Imperials). The werewolf woodsmen are spoiling for a fight (and fresh meat), however, so any insults (real or perceived) or threats will set them off, and they'll shift into hybrid form and attack immediately. Delicate words and actions will be required to avoid that.

Even if the PCs manage to avoid a fight and get Pogral talking, the half-orcs won't own up to the murder (they've killed plenty of folk in the area, but not Kalel). They won't have much else to say except for telling the PCs to leave. At that point, however, there will be yells from around the camp as a mob of humans and half-elves led by a former Imperial legionnaire named Kyros Vaughn attack with yells of *"Kill the murderers. Vengeance for Kalel!"*

When the villagers attack, the werewolves will shift into hybrid form and attack the PCs, assuming that the heroes were part of an ambush ploy. If the PCs are already fighting the werewolves, this surprise attack happens at the start of the second round of battle instead.

This is a double-strength battle, but if the PCs can convince the mob to not attack them, it will be easier.

TERRAIN & TRAPS

Surrounding Foliage: Outside the camp the terrain is fairly open and easy to move through, but there are small trees and light vegetation that can be used for concealment.

Tents, Firewood, & Casks: The tents block line of sight and possibly could provide light cover. The three ale casks are small and could be thrown with a DC 12 Strength check for 1d6 x level damage plus dazed (save ends). The pile of firewood is stacked, 5 feet long and 3 feet high, and might provide an opportunity for a dicey move (DC 15).

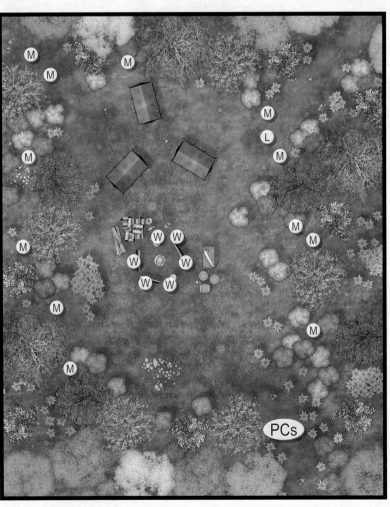

Fire & Logs: The fire isn't big, but it and the logs could be an impediment to movement through the area for any creature trying something dicey (DC 12). Any creature that ends its turn in the fire takes 1d8 fire damage.

Monsters

The half-orc werewolves are a band of brigands that settled this area half a year ago to look for opportunities and to hunt. They've killed both wild folk and villagers in that time. Kalel was aware of their true nature and torn on whether to cleanse the pack or not, which was another reason they didn't' like him.

Following their wolf instincts, they will break up into pairs or threes to attack enemies, focusing first on the PCs since the Thorn mob will attack from the fringes.

The mob of frontier folk from Thorn assembled when they found out about Kalel's death and they assumed that the woodsmen did it because of Pogral's threat. The woodsmen have also caused other trouble, so it didn't take long for the villagers to organize this group (actually Moira did it) to go after the half-orcs. They are led by a human warrior, Kyros Vaughn, a former legionnaire.

The mob was unaware that they were attacking lycanthropes, however. If the PCs were talking with the half-orc werewolves and you want to add some flavor to the scene, add a few extra villagers to the battle who run off screaming when the half-orcs first shift into hybrid form.

Additional Reinforcements: If you want to challenge the PCs more, include a centaur ranger (*Bestiary*, page 35) with the mob who's taken on the village as his tribe.

#/Level of PCs	Half-orc Werewolf (W)	Former Legionnaire (L)	Thorn Mob Mook (M)
4 x 4th level	6	1	12 (1 mob)
5 x 4th level	8	1	15 (2 mobs)
6 x 4th level	9*	1	20 (2 mobs)
4 x 5th level	7**	1	20 (2 mobs)
5 x 5th level	9**	2***	18 (2 mobs)
6 x 5th level	10**	3***	22 (2 mobs)

* The werewolves use their nastier special.

** Each werewolf is double-strength: increase its *bite* attack to 28 damage and its hp to 100, and it uses its nastier special.

*** The second former legionnaire is named Falia, and the third is Kamfort.

Tactics

The werewolves will attack in groups to take advantage of their *pack attack*. If you want, you could make Pogral slightly tougher by giving him +8 hp and a +1 attack bonus. Note, remember to increase the *bestial fury* damage if the PCs are 5th level.

As they attack in hybrid form, some of the werewolves will growl out about how they didn't kill Kalel, but now the PCs will suffer the same fate for involving themselves in something that's none of their business, which should reinforce the fact that they weren't behind the murder. As they fight, the bloodlust will take them, so only the last werewolf will consider fleeing in wolf form once it's staggered.

The Thorn mob mooks will split their ranged attacks between werewolves and PCs (roll a d6 for each attack, with 1–3 meaning a mook targets a PC), because they assume the PCs are allies of the werewolves. Kyros will use both his javelins then enter melee combat.

If any of the PCs try to convince the mob otherwise (a standard action), doing so will require two DC 15 Strength (intimidation) or Charisma (diplomacy) checks, or the use of icon advantages. Success means Kyros and the mooks begin only targeting werewolves (GM, instead of rolling an attack for each mook against the werewolves, feel free to assume one in three manage to hit).

Loot

The werewolves have a few valuables stored in the tents from past kills, including 50 gp, two small wood sculptures (a wolf and a tiger) of elven make worth 20 gp each, and an assortment of cheap trinkets worth another 25 gp.

The mob members didn't bring valuables with them other than low-quality weapons.

See also next steps for clues about the murder.

Icons

A PC that has relationship advantages with the High Druid, Emperor, Lich King, Priestess, or maybe the Elf Queen could use one or more of them to help convince the mob that they aren't with the werewolves, giving the group one automatic success instead of a check for each advantage used (and maybe a story about a similar misunderstanding in the past).

Half-orc Werewolf

This beast is thicker and heavier than others of its kind, with powerful jaws designed for tearing flesh.

4th level troop [BEAST]
Initiative: +11

Ravening bite +7 vs. AC—14 damage
  Miss: The werewolf gains a +2 attack bonus (cumulative) to *ravening bite* attacks until the end of the battle.

Bestial fury (hybrid form only): Werewolves gain a bonus to damage equal to the escalation die (champion: double the die; epic: quadruple the die).

Pack attack: When the werewolf attacks a creature that is engaged with one of its allies, the target is vulnerable to that attack.

Unnatural vigor (hybrid or animal form only): When the werewolf is not staggered at the start of its turn, it heals 8 hp.

Nastier Specials

Sustaining blood: When the werewolf hits with a *ravening bite* attack, it heals 5 hp.

AC	18	
PD	16	**HP 50**
MD	20	

Kyros Vaughn, Legionnaire

The man has only one good eye, but he fights with the experience of many battles.

5th level wrecker [HUMANOID]
Initiative: +7

Well-honed gladius +9 vs. AC—16 damage
Natural roll is above target's Wisdom: The target is weakened (save ends) as Kyros uses a veteran maneuver.
Miss: 4 damage.

R: Javelin +9 vs. AC—18 damage
Limited use: 2/battle.

The confidence of experience: Kyros gains 8 temporary hp at the end of his turn if he hit with an attack that turn.

AC	21	
PD	18	**HP 61**
MD	15	

Thorn Mob

These frontier villagers are used to fighting for everything they have in life.

4th level mook [HUMANOID]
Initiative: +5

Axe, spear, or long knife +8 vs. AC—6 damage

R: Bow, hand axe, or javelin +9 vs. AC—6 damage

Capture the murderers! (group ability): For every four mooks in the mob, one of them can make a single *hooked net* attack each battle.
[Group ability] **C: Hooked net +8 vs. PD (one nearby enemy)**—The target is stuck (hard save ends, 16+). A stuck creature can spend a standard action during its turn to make the save normal.

AC	20	
PD	17	**HP 14 (mook)**
MD	13	

Mook: Kill one Thorn mob mook for every 14 damage you deal to the mob.

Additional Reinforcements

Centaur Ranger

6th level archer [HUMANOID]
Initiative: +13

Twin scimitars +10 vs. AC (2 attacks)—10 damage

R: Longbow +11 vs. AC—20 damage
Natural even hit: The centaur ranger can take an additional move action this turn.
Natural 16+: The centaur ranger can make a second (but not a third) *longbow* attack this turn as a free action.

Moving combatant: The centaur ranger gains a +4 AC bonus against opportunity attacks and only takes half damage from opportunity attacks that hit it. When an enemy makes an opportunity attack against it and misses, that enemy takes 10 damage from a counter-attack.

Terrain familiarity: Once each round when the escalation die is odd, the centaur ranger can make use of the area's terrain to its advantage as a free action. It can choose either to gain a +2 attack bonus for its attacks that turn, or to gain a +2 bonus to all defenses against the next attack that targets it by using a flashy or tricky maneuver (leaping off a rock over an enemy, stirring up a hornet's nest near an attacker, etc.). The target of its attack or a creature attacking it when it attempts this stunt rolls a normal save; on a success, the bonus is negated.

AC	22	
PD	20	**HP 85**
MD	16	

Next Steps

Once the werewolves are defeated, the mob will be easier to talk to and convince that the PCs aren't also lycanthropes. If any PC attempts to do so, remaining villagers will call a halt to hostilities. Otherwise, the villagers will flee after one more round. If the PCs get the frontier folk to stop fighting, the villagers will express regret about attacking the PCs but explain how they couldn't be sure. They will also explain how they are sure the woodsmen killed Kalel, especially considering that they were evil shapeshifters. The only evidence, however, was the threat Pogral made openly against the druid.

There's a major problem with that theory, however, which will emerge once the battle ends. An owl will swoop in and then shift form into that of a female wood elf druid named **Silverleaf**. Saddened by the news of Kalel's death, she will relate that she was his apprentice and that he asked her to track the werewolf pack to keep tabs on them. The previous day (when the murder occurred) the pack was hunting miles away and couldn't have done it.

With this information, the PCs will have to seek other answers. Feel free to reward creative efforts with the information below, but if no one in the group suggests anything, Silverleaf will go speak with the animals near the murder site. There she learns that the murderer was a dark-skinned human woman. The only such woman in the region that Silverleaf knows of is Tianthe, a grim woman who lives with a small clan of reclusive gnomes in a set of caves near Thorbal Peak. She also reveals that the druid not only died, but lost his soul and his power to the killer if the PCs haven't already learned of it.

When the PCs are ready to track down Tianthe, Silverleaf can provide directions (she has to arrange Kalel's burial so she won't join them). On the trip to Thorbal Peak, however, the PCs will run into some other trouble. See **Battle 2: From Above & Below.**

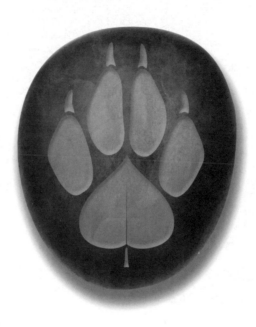

BATTLE 2: FROM ABOVE & BELOW

The trail to Thorbal Peak takes you along a ridge of low hills through the wild lands. Toward sunset you enter a hollow filled with apple trees that seems scenic and serene. Until you see the first toppled tree, and then another, each overturned with the roots jutting out of the ground amid a pile of dirt. When the ground begins to tremble under you, you notice the furrows and small hills of dirt scattered all over the orchard. The rumbling is getting worse too.

LOCATION DESCRIPTION

The apple orchard happens to be the current feeding ground for a green bulette and its young, who have managed to consume most of the animal life in the area except for the PCs and one other predator—a manticore who's been trailing the creatures waiting for an opportunity to grab one of the young calves. But the PCs will make a nice meal for it as well.

The orchard is open territory with groups of 20-foot tall apple trees (no fruit currently) scattered here and there, and grass growing from the rich soil in between. A handful of large oak tree stumps, 8 to 10 feet in diameter, are mixed in among the small hills and furrows that riddle the ground.

The bulette and its calves have sensed the PCs' movement and are moving in for the kill. The manticore is flying among the clouds watching, but it will descend to strike once the combat with the bulettes begins.

TERRAIN & TRAPS

Stumps & Trees: The stumps provide some protection from the bulettes, who can't easily pass through the roots under them. Anyone on a stump gains a +2 bonus to AC and PD against bulette attacks. As a move action, however, the green bulette can pass by a stump and give it a nudge to try to knock off prey for her young. Anyone on the stump must roll a DC 18 Dexterity check or get knocked off.

The apple trees are too small to provide protection from the bulettes, who will knock them over as part of an attack. They do provide some cover from the manticore's ranged attacks, however. Anyone hiding under a tree gains a +2 bonus to AC against the manticore's *volley of tail spikes* attack.

Furrows, Pits, & Dirt Piles: The ground is riddled with furrows, dirt piles, and also hidden pits that the bulettes have dug beneath the soil. Each time a PC moves more than a few feet from their current location, they must roll an immediate easy save (6+). On a failure, that PC stops moving short of their destination due to the difficult terrain. Anyone who rolls a natural 1 is instead stuck (save ends) when they fall into a dirt hole buried to the waist.

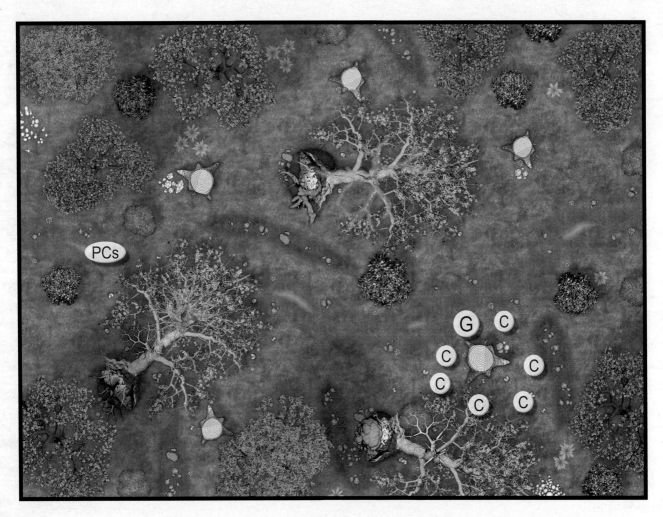

Monsters

The green bulette and her calves are hungry and will pursue moving food at all costs. The mother carries a small hillock upon her back as she moves through the rich soil. The calves are about one-third of her size. If there is a second bulette, it's the other parent.

The manticore is a cunning hunter and understands the common tongue, which it may use to thwart PCs' strategies if they don't think it understands them. It will flee if reduced to 15 hp or less. It could also be convinced to take a dead calf and leave the battle if a PC puts some effort into it (either using an advantage while bringing up ancient Imperial laws, or with a successful DC 25 Charisma check as a standard action).

Additional Reinforcements: If you want to challenge the PCs more, make it a mated pair of manticores.

#/Level of PCs	Green Bulette (G)	Bulette Calf mook (C)	Manticore
4 x 4th level	1	5 (1 mob)	1*
5 x 4th level	1	5 (1 mob)	1**
6 x 4th level	1	5 (1 mob)	1
4 x 5th level	1	7 (1 mob)****	1
5 x 5th level	2	7 (1 mob)****	1***
6 x 5th level	2	12 (1 mob)****	1***

* The manticore doesn't enter the battle until the start of the 4th round, or once the bulettes all drop to 0 hp.

** The manticore doesn't enter the battle until the start of the 3rd round, or once the bulettes all drop to 0 hp.

*** The manticore enters the battle on the first round.

**** The calves are double-strength mooks with 30 hp that deal 12 damage with the maw (16 automatic).

Tactics

At the start of the battle, the green bulette will pick a target, preferably one on open ground, and make a *charging maw* attack against it. The calves will be trailing in their mother's wake and then at least half will attack the same target, trying to take advantage of vulnerability from the *maw* attack. After that, the bulettes will attack more randomly against whoever is engaged with them or closest to them.

As noted in **Terrain & Traps**, the green bulette will attempt to nudge prey off of stumps if that is its only option.

Starting on the second round, the manticore will fly lower and attack with its *volley of tail spikes*, gaining a +2 attack bonus that round for surprise (GM, you could give each target a chance to spot it with a DC 15 Wisdom check to avoid the attack bonus).

Then it will enter melee, using it *jaws* against a poisoned enemy, or using its *paws* otherwise.

Once staggered, it will disengage to return to the air and rain death with its spikes again.

Loot

The manticore is actually wearing an ancient golden medallion with the Imperial crest upon it on a gold chain; it's worth 150 gp.

The bulettes have little of value, although if someone wished to cut into the mother's stomach, there's 30 gp in coins and two 50 gp pearls that haven't passed through yet from a previous kill. Bulette claws are considered valuable in some places and could bring a total of 100 gp for anyone willing to collect them.

Icons

A PC that has relationship advantages with the High Druid, Emperor, Orc Lord, the Three, or maybe the Elf Queen could use one or more of them to convince the manticore to leave with a bulette calf meal, but not until at least the start of the fourth round (humanoids are so much tastier).

Green Bulette

This bulette adorns its rough-textured outer shell with soil and plants as it rises from the soil. It appears to be only a shrub-covered knoll or grassy hillock until it launches out of the ground..

Large 5th level wrecker [BEAST]
Initiative: +12

Charging maw +12 vs. AC—30 damage
 Natural even miss: The target pops free from all enemies engaged with it and is vulnerable to all attacks (save ends).
 Leaping bite: The green bulette gains a +3 bonus to attack and damage with its first attack each battle.

Into the earth: The first time each round an attack hits the bulette, it can choose to hunker down as a free action. If it does, it gains a +3 bonus to AC and PD until the start of its next turn. Force attacks and opportunity attacks don't trigger this ability. If the green bulette hunkers down while it's moving (for example, from a readied action), its movement ends that turn.

Blood-frenzy escalator: While at least one creature in the battle is staggered or unconscious, the bulette gains a bonus to its attacks and damage equal to the escalation die but can't use *into the earth*. Creatures that have no blood (constructs, oozes, plant creatures, etc.) don't trigger this ability.

Occasional burrower: Like all bulettes, the green bulette can burrow. While above ground, it prefers to move slowly on the surface and rely on its plant- and soil-covered shell to stay hidden until it attacks.

AC	19	
PD	17	**HP 92**
MD	13	

BULETTE CALF

They aren't as big as the mother, but those jaws could still bite a man in half.

4th level mook [BEAST]
Initiative: +8

Snapping maw +8 vs. AC—6 damage
  Natural 16+: The target is grabbed if the calf isn't already grabbing a creature. If the bulette is grabbing a creature at the start of its turn, that creature automatically takes 8 damage from its *maw* attack as a standard action.

Weak burrower: Bulette calves can dig through soil and loose dirt reasonably well, but they often need a larger adult to break up the tougher soil first.

AC	18	
PD	17	**HP 15 (mook)**
MD	12	

Mook: Kill one bulette calf mook for every 15 damage you deal to the mob.

MANTICORE

Ages ago, a drunk or insane Emperor granted manticores hunting rights that might arguably include humans in certain ill-defined portions of the badlands. The fact that everyone in the 13th Age acts like that treaty never existed drives manticores freaking crazy. And they're pretty crazy to begin with.

Large 6th level archer [BEAST]
Initiative: +13

Battering paws +11 vs. AC (2 attacks)—20 damage
  Natural 16+: The manticore can make a single *volley of tail spikes* attack (one attack roll) against a different target as a free action.

Crushing leonine jaws +11 vs. AC—30 damage; OR 50 damage against a creature taking ongoing poison damage

C: Volley of tail spikes +13 vs. AC (1d3 nearby or far away enemies in a group)—5 ongoing poison damage (hard save ends, 16+)

Flight: Manticores are poor fliers in tight spaces, but out in the open, they are more capable.

Poison reservoirs: Each time the manticore uses its *volley of tail spikes* attack, it takes 1d6 damage, or 2d6 damage if it is staggered.

AC	22	
PD	20	**HP 182**
MD	16	

NEXT STEPS

Once the PCs defeat the bulettes and manticore, they can continue their journey to Thorbal Peak. See **Battle 3: Tianthe's Lair.** If the PCs managed to befriend the manticore (by using multiple advantages), it might be able to shed some light on Tianthe, namely that she and her pack of gnomes are shapeshifters, and that she recently had a powerful visitor who arrived as a cloud of smoke.

BATTLE 3: TIANTHE'S LAIR

Thanks to Silverleaf's directions, you reach what must be Thorbal Peak and begin making your way around the base of the tall hill. You soon find Tianthe's lair, a grouping of three cave openings, one of which is about thirty feet up a cliff and to the right. You don't see or hear anything moving around outside the caves, but there are signs that someone has been living here recently.

LOCATION DESCRIPTION

The cave system consists of a large, multi-tiered cavern plus three small side caverns all connected to it. Two of the cave entrances lead into the main cave (one on ground level and the higher one up a cliff), and the third on ground level enters a side cave.

The main cave is 70 feet deep, 60 feet across, and has a wide upper ledge on the right 15 feet off the ground with terraced natural steps leading to it on one side. The ceiling is 40 feet high. Each side cavern is irregularly shaped and roughly 25 feet in diameter, with one of them holding a natural pool that drains away into the stone floor. The smell of rotting flesh/carrion fills the entire area.

Tianthe Vang, a female weretiger sorceress lairs here, along with a band of vampiric gnomes who are also werebobcat

CONVERSING WITH TIANTHE

Assured that she and her allies will end the PCs, Tianthe doesn't mind taunting them and also revealing some information as she plays with her kill. Have her relate how she tricked Kalel into going to the site of his murder, a special place where the ley line energy was right for her to perform the *Ritual of Taking* that allowed her to steal his soul and his druidic power. She'll go on about how she savored his power during the transfer, so much so that she's considering doing the same to any druid PCs (or other spellcasters).

Before she drops, feel free to have her mention how it's a shame really, that she had to give Kalel's soul to her master, since it was so intoxicating, but now that she knows the ritual, she'll be able to take such power for herself.

lycanthropes. Tianthe holds power over Stulin, the vampires' gnome leader, in the form of direct oaths and also a favor from the Lich King that keeps the vampires from messing with her. They serve her in limited ways and she protects them during daylight hours.

Assume the PCs approach during twilight, before the gnomes are fully awake. If they choose to wait until dark, they will see

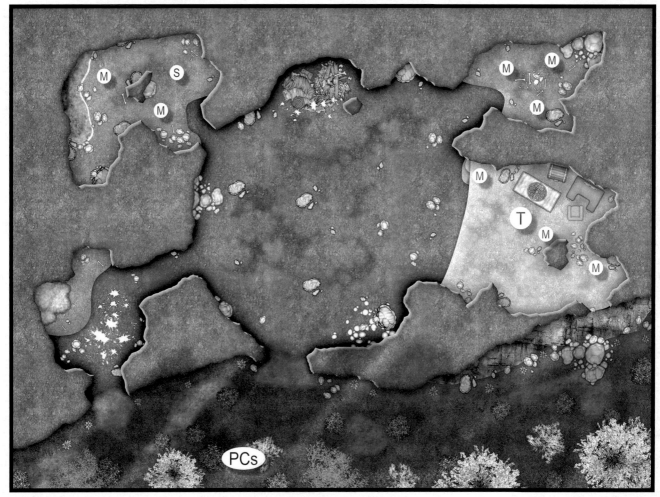

activity as the gnomes emerge from the cave and go about semi-normal camp business until they're ready to hunt later that night. If the PCs enter the caves immediately, Tianthe will be lounging on the upper tier of the main cavern, while the gnomes rise from their slumber in the two darker side caves.

Unless the PCs come storming in ready to fight, Tianthe will talk to PCs when they enter the cavern to learn why they've come (hidden and speaking from the shadows above) while she waits for the gnomes to rouse. She'll play a game of cat and mouse with them if they mention Kalel's murder, testing to see how much they know. Eventually, she'll tire of the game, telling them that her master wouldn't want any loose ends as she attacks.

For one possible view of what things look like as the fight gets started, see the cover. As you can see, Tianthe uses magic to keep herself richly dressed and comfortable, even in the cave that's otherwise befouled by her minions.

Terrain & Traps

Main Cave Tiers: The upper section of the main cave is a 20 x 30 ledge that's 15 feet high. The stone is rough but perfectly vertical and requires a DC 15 Strength check to climb to the top. There are two steps, however, on one side of the ledge that make scaling it easier, but noticing them in the dark cave without additional light requires a DC 12 Wisdom check. One of the gnomes will also be guarding the top, ready to knock PCs back off the edge.

The cave leading in from outside is 10 feet above the upper ledge. The monsters have no issues leaping up to it.

Sunlight: If the PCs manage to expose a gnome vampire to the sunlight, that gnome is dazed until the end of its next turn and will take 2d8 fire damage if it ends its turn in the light.

Monsters

Tianthe Vang is a weretiger, but before contracting lycanthropy, she was also an accomplished sorcerer. She has combined her talents to become an assassin who hires out her services. As described in the epic battle scenes for the High Druid, her master is a rakshasa named Vooram who is collecting druidic souls and power for a large ritual to influence the area (and gain in his personal power). Being a weretiger, she had a strange bond with the rakshasa. Tianthe will refer to her master, but never reveal his true nature, even under pain of death. She works for him out of fear and longing for the sorcerous power he has promised her.

Being a mercenary of sorts, Tianthe isn't above fleeing and leaving the gnomes to their fate if she has a chance. In her tiger form, she can outrun most PCs in the wilds. She could easily become a recurring villain who hunts the PCs after they disrupt her plans, if you like.

Stulin is the master vampire of this pack of gnomes. They were bobcat lycanthropes first, and then he managed to infect them with vampirism (the curses/diseases didn't counteract each other in the gnome physiology for some reason). They begin the battle in the two side caves not connected to the outside, or on the ledge near the steps out of sight from below, or you could set the scene dramatically like the cover!

The vampire mooks will die easily with normal weapon attacks. Stulin might require stronger measures, depending on how you handle vampiric death in your game.

Additional Reinforcements: If you want to challenge the PCs more, add a second werebobcat vampire, Stulin's consort Vema (same stats as Stulin).

#/Level of PCs	Tianthe Vang (T)	Stulin, Vampire (S)	Vampire Werebobcat Mook (M)
4 x 4th level	1	0*	5 (1 mob)
5 x 4th level	1	1	4 (1 mob)
6 x 4th level	1	1	10 (1 mob)
4 x 4th level	1	1**	7 (1 mob)**
5 x 5th level	1	1**	13 (2 mobs)**
6 x 5th level	1***	1**	15 (2 mobs)**

* Include Stulin if the PCs had an easier first battle because they convinced the mob to fight with them against the werewolves.

** Make Stulin and each mook a double-strength monster: Stulin has 136 hp and his *bite* attack deals 30 damage. Each mook has 24 hp and its *claws and fangs* attack deals 10 damage.

*** Make Tianthe triple strength: she has 244 hp, she gains a third *claws and fangs* attack, the *chaos pulse* can target up to 2 enemies for 30 damage (or 20 and 10 ongoing), and *shadowforce blast* deals 20 damage.

Tactics

Tianthe will lash out with a *shadowforce blast* first, then use *chaos pulse* until the PCs come to her on the ledge. She'll move back away from the ledge every other turn to get out of sight of ranged attacks from below. Once an enemy does come to her, she's very capable of dealing out melee damage in her hybrid form with her *claws and bite* attack.

Stulin and his vampire-weres will engage the PCs with melee attacks, looking for blood. The animal aspects of the lycanthropes make their *bite* attacks more vicious than normal. They will avoid the areas of the cave near the entrance where any sunlight might be filtering in through the hanging moss over the entrance.

Loot

The vampires have acquired a few odds and ends in their time, though now they mostly only care about leeching the blood out of their next meal. There's a scattering of coins and other small valuables from past victims on the ground worth 90 gp.

Upon the ledge, Tianthe has set up a small stone chair and table with a small mirror hung on one wall. Next to it is a small wooden chest. In it she keeps a few treasures, including 200 gp in gold and jade jewelry, 150 gp in loose coinage, six 50 gp rubies, a *potion of sleep* (imbiber must roll a hard save; on fail, they slumber without waking for 1d4 hours) and a magic item appropriate for one of the PCs (default would be a *+1 circlet of approachability*, *13th Age* core rulebook, page 290).

Finally, there is a scrollcase with a note inside instructing Tianthe where to procure a number of rare components for the *Ritual of Taking*, as well as an expectation of immediate delivery. It is signed only with the letter V.

Icons

A PC that has relationship advantages with the High Druid, Archmage, Elf Queen, Emperor, or Priestess could use one or more of them to momentarily force one of the lycanthropes to revert to humanoid form for a round or two (or for the battle for a mook). They could also use an advantage to possibly replicate the energy of the sun somehow as part of a spell, causing harm to all nearby vampires (perhaps adding 2d8 fire damage) as a standard action.

Tianthe Vang, Weretiger Sorceress

Power seethes around and through this ebony-skinned woman. She eyes you like a piece of meat, and sniffs the air likes she's tasting your soul. And then she shifts into something more fierce.

Large 6th level caster [BEAST]
Initiative: +9

Claws and fangs +11 vs. AC (2 attacks)—18 damage

R: Chaos pulse +11 vs. PD—40 damage of the GM's choice (fire, thunder, or lightning)
Natural even hit: The target instead takes 30 damage of the chosen energy type, and 10 ongoing damage of that type.

C: Shadowforce blast +9 vs. PD (1d3 nearby enemies)—13 damage, and the target must roll a save; on a failure, it becomes shadowy and phases out of sync with the world until the start of Tianthe's next turn. While shadowy, the target can't attack or be attacked, but is still aware of what is going on around it. If the target drops to 0 hp or below from this damage, it must begin making last gasp saves, with the fourth failure meaning its soul remains in the land of shadow.
Limited use: 2/battle, but she regains one use if she drops an enemy to 0 hp or below with the attack.

Bestial fury (hybrid form only): Tianthe gains a bonus to damage equal to double the escalation die.

Unnatural vigor (hybrid or animal form only): When the weretiger is not staggered at the start of its turn, it heals 24 hp.

AC	21	
PD	18	**HP 166**
MD	20	

Stulin, Werebobcat Vampire

This cat-gnome has dead black eyes and a deep blood-hunger.

5th level spoiler [UNDEAD]
Initiative: +10

Bloodsucking bite +10 vs. AC—15 damage
Natural 12+: The target is dazed until the end of its next turn from blood loss.
Natural 14+: As above, and the target takes 3 ongoing damage (hard save ends both, 16+). Stulin gains 6 temporary hp.
Natural 16+: As above, except the target is weakened instead of dazed, and Stulin can pop free from the target and move as a free action.

Bestial fury (hybrid form only): This werebobcat gains a bonus to damage equal to double the escalation.

Mistform killer: Twice per battle as a move action, Stulin can change his form to mist, pop free of all enemies, and move before reforming again. When he drops to 0 hp, his form turns to mist and he drifts away unless slain somehow.

Unnatural vigor: Until he drops to 0 hp, Stulin heals 3 hp at the start of each of his turns, or 1 hp if in gnome form.

AC	22	
PD	17	**HP 68**
MD	16	

WEREBOBCAT VAMPIRE SPAWN

Small, almost cute, yet vicious to the core.

4th level mook [UNDEAD]
Initiative: +7

Claws and fangs +9 vs. AC—5 damage
Natural 16+: The target takes 5 ongoing damage and the mob gains 5 temporary hit points as the spawn sinks its fangs in.

Bestial fury (hybrid form only): These werebobcats gain a bonus to damage equal to the escalation die.

Unnatural vigor (hybrid or animal form only): The werebobcat vampire spawn mob heals 5 hp at the start of each round (this might mean a dropped mook rejoins the fight, or a new mook enters the battle).

AC	19	
PD	16	**HP 12 (mook)**
MD	15	

Mook: Kill one werebobcat vampire spawn mook for every 12 damage you deal to the mob.

NEXT STEPS

While the PCs have discovered who murdered the druid Kalel, they will only partially know why. The note in the scrollcase will provide some of the answer: that the druid's death was part of something known as the *Ritual of Taking*. But it also leaves open the question of who is the mysterious "V" that put Tianthe up to it. Since Kalel's soul and power, which Tianthe stole, are not in her lair in any form that the PCs will be able to determine, her master must now have it. What that means isn't clear.

More information on the purpose of the ritual is waiting for the PCs to discover in the champion- and epic-tier battle scenes. You can either throw some other adventures at the PCs before returning to this story line, or if the PCs were 5th level when they faced Tianthe, continue on with the next part of the story.

✝ HE WILD SACRIFICE STORY ENDINGS

Here are outcomes for each story opening, detailing what success or failure might mean.

If the PCs did face all three battles, remember to give them a full heal-up.

THE CALL OF THE WILD

Success: You successfully find Kalel's murderer, the weretiger-sorceress Tianthe, and bring her to justice (or take vengeance on her). Although there seems to be a larger plot going on, at least you removed one enemy of the High Druid from the world. In thanks, one of the High Druid's servants delivers a gift (a magic item) to the PC sent to investigate.

Failure: Tianthe gets away with murder. Whether she faced the PCs, or heard about their inquiries only, she and her master are now aware of them and begin to throw distractions at them, making life generally more difficult. Also, if the PCs move on to the champion-tier battle scenes, they will face extra enemies in the first battle.

THE EMPEROR'S REPRESENTATIVE

Success: You discover the druid Kalel's murderer to be a weretiger-sorceress named Tianthe and bring her to justice, one way or another. The truth of who murdered the druid quells the anger of the wild folk in the area, who disavow Tianthe as one of their own and realize she was not in league with any of the villagers. Tensions die down, and in recognition for their service, each PC gains a 6 with the Emperor until they use it or level up.

Failure: The PCs let the weretiger woman named Tianthe get away with the murder, and without any proof of her involvement, the wild folk take it out on the Thorn villagers. With their attack on the half-orc woodsmen, the PCs are seen as Imperial toadies and a group of wild folk will approach them and demand they leave; failure to do so results in a battle. The Emperor's reputation takes a blow in the region.

WRONG TURNS

Success: The PCs manage to trace the murder to Tianthe and bring her to justice. The people of Thorn and the wild folk in the area are grateful that the truth was discovered before it caused further violence between them, and now realize there might be an outside threat trying to harm both groups (and the icons they support). Each PC can gain a 6 with either the High Druid or the Emperor that lasts until used or the next full heal-up.

Failure: Not only do the PCs fail to help Moira find Kalel's killer, but some from Thorn and also those among the wild folk believe the PCs were behind the killing, especially after the battle with the werewolves and villagers. The next two times the PCs roll icon relationship dice, any 6s with the High Druid or Emperor are 5s instead.

BATTLE SCENE CONNECTIONS

The stories from this set of battle scenes can lead to other scenes:

 Corrupted Nature (High Druid, page 54): The three Druid scenes are naturally linked. While the PCs are in the area after Kalel's murder, another druid, Mother Bark, gets kidnapped.

 A Pit of Vipers (The Three, page 153): The Vipers' lair is in the area, away from civilization, and the PCs stumble across kobolds, or are enlisted to test the lair's defenses.

 The Lich's Spire (Lich King): The village of Dheirone and the spire are on the far edge of the wood that Thorn borders, but still only a few days' travel away. Their contacts instruct them to visit the tower and/or put an end to Cornellion.

High Druid: Corrupted Nature

LEVEL RANGE: 5–6

Shortly after the druid Kalel Blackmane was killed as part of ritual murder, another powerful druid in the area has disappeared. In this case, it's the female gnome druid known as Mother Bark. She makes her home in a hollow among the roots of a cluster of elm trees near the Olander homesteads about twenty miles from the village of Thorn, though she roams the area widely in her duties as a druid.

Mother Bark has been abducted by a group of weretigers and has been taken to a site of elemental energy in the wilderness where she'll be sacrificed as part of a ritual to gain her power and unlock an elemental node. Luckily, the abduction was sloppy. One of the Olander cousins, a human ranger named Storry Olander, witnessed the attack on the druid. Unable to overpower Mother Bark's attackers on his own, he followed them and sent word via his animal companion to druid acolytes serving Mother Bark once he discerned the kidnappers' likely destination: Raven's Spire, a place of power deep within Vinerock Gorge.

The druid acolytes are still new to their power and not up to fighting weretigers, so they seek help in recovering Mother Bark. Unfortunately, Storry Olander ran into trouble while trailing the kidnappers, only too late discovering that the wilderness in the area around Raven's Spire has become corrupted and deadly thanks to a rakshasa warrior working for an even greater master.

Corrupted Nature Story Openings

If you played through The Wild Sacrifice, you may have plenty of story hooks to choose from already. If not, consider these.

- **The High Druid's Summons:** A PC with a positive or conflicted relationship with the High Druid is asked to travel into the wilds near the Olander homesteads along the frontier not far from the village of Thorn. Druids have been targeted by someone in the area, and a gnome druid named Mother Bark has been kidnapped. Servants near the homestead can provide more information.
- **The Druid's Wisdom:** The PCs are seeking knowledge about a cure to some disease, ancient lore about the area, where to find special natural components in the region, or something similar from a powerful druid named Mother Bark. When they arrive at her home, druid acolytes tell them she isn't there because she's been taken. If the PCs can help retrieve her, the druids will happily work to provide whatever they seek.
- **A Different Vision of the Wild:** A PC with a conflicted or negative relationship with the High Druid is seeking out a powerful druid named Mother Bark. The gnome woman is thought to be the best contender to replace the high druid at the next druidic moot, and the PC believes she is the best way for them to get back into the fold, or at least to shake things up in the High Druid's version of natural order. The only problem is that Mother Bark is missing. According to her acolytes, she was kidnapped, but they know where she's being taken thanks to a local ranger who's tracking the abductors. If the PCs save her, she will surely favor them in all future dealings.
- **What Backwoods Hole Is This?:** The PCs wander into a small group of homesteads along the frontier. The place is the home of the Olander family, a group of thirty or so human frontier folk. While asking directions to someplace more interesting, a group of local druid acolytes approaches the PCs. Their superior, Mother Bark, has been kidnapped by some weretigers for some foul and evil purpose. They want to know what it would take to get the PCs to help recover her. They know where she's being taken thanks to one of the Olanders who's tracking the kidnappers.

Alternate Icons

 Priestess: Mother Bark could be a priestess of a nature god who is considered to be one of the borderline Gods of Light. The abduction is reported to the Priestess' people, who either seek help directly or pass the information on to a divine servant that contacts the PCs.

 Elf Queen: Perhaps Mother Bark is actually a dryad who will die if kept away from her elm tree for more than a few days. The Olander homestead and/or acolytes could be a small vale of fey creatures who ask the PCs for help in exchange for fey gifts or other knowledge.

Icons in Play

Characters that have relationships (and story-guide advantages) with the High Druid, Elf Queen, Priestess, and maybe the Lich King (corruption) or Diabolist (ritual sacrifice) should be able to shine in some of the upcoming battle scenes. Moreso than PCs with other icon relationships, feel free to give such PCs extra knowledge about the opposition, make checks to pull off fun actions the players might suggest, and use their advantages to particularly good effect, such as negating or bypassing some of the advantages or abilities of the enemies.

CORRUPTED NATURE OVERVIEW

The PCs meet the druid acolytes and learn about Mother Bark's disappearance and the fact that a ranger has tracked her abductors' path. They believe she is being taken to Raven's Spire, a powerful site of elemental energy two days' travel away. They provide directions, or possibly an animal guide to show the PCs the way.

As the PCs begin the track through the wilderness, they begin to realize something is not right in the area. Then combat proves the point when rabid beasts fouled by corruption attack them in Battle 1.

The closer the PCs get to Raven's Spire, the more corrupted the wilderness becomes, troubled by sickly animals and perversions of nature. Soon the PCs reach Vinerock Gorge, a long canyon cutting through the area. They must get to the other side, but to avoid losing time, they will need to use vine swings or ropes to cross, which is a problem since the gorge is filled with poisonous mists from the elemental node in the area. Battle 2 involves an attack by corrupted treants and giant wasp spirits that attack while the PCs swing across.

Finally, after getting across the gorge, the PCs make their way beside it toward Raven's Spire. The spire rises above the ridgeline, but there's a flat rocky area where the elemental node leaks poisonous mist into the gorge. In Battle 3, the PCs try to stop the weretigers and their leader—Xantip Nos, a rakshasa who has orchestrated the kidnapping—from sacrificing Mother Bark. Unfortunately, they're going to be too late, but that won't become apparent until the corrupted body of the druid rises to attack as well.

GM, feel free to expand upon these battles by including more battles in the wilds with corrupted creatures, strange NPCs from the wilds who might be able to point them in the right direction, or other dangers from the gorge or spire.

The battles outlined here can take place over a few days or only hours depending on the how the GM wants to pace them. Since the High Druid is in play, the enemies presented here are corrupted beasts and other warped creatures created by the corruption of the *Ritual of Taking* and perversion of the elemental node. The locations should be flavored with natural settings made horrible by the corruption in the area.

See story endings after the final battle for options on what happens after the PCs finish the last battle.

BATTLE 1: CORRUPTED BEASTS

You're following a trail through the wilderness to Raven's Spire that the druids said would take you there quickly. The trail wends its way through a copse of tall sycamore trees and dark elm trees that form a thick canopy above. The ground around the trees is

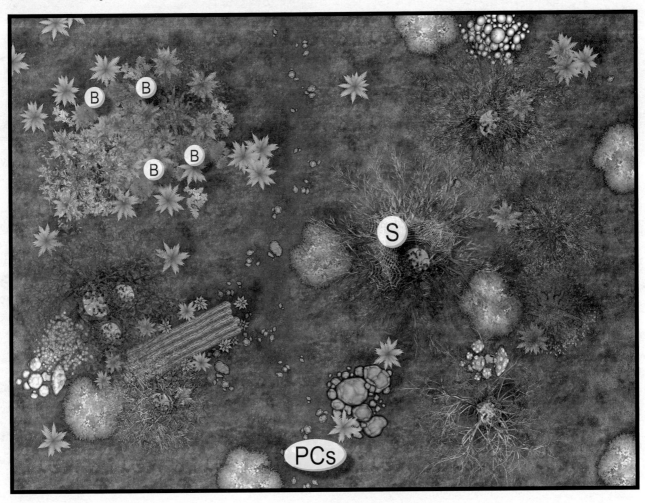

flat and open except for the occasional fallen log, pile of dead branches, or patch of small shrubs and you're traveling fast. Dark shadows here and there limit visibility in places, and it's from one such pool of shadow that you begin to hear grunting noises off to your left. Something large is breathing heavily there. You've heard lots of big animals before, but this is weird-sounding.

Location Description

There are two dangers lurking in the trees and shadows of this place: corrupted dire boars among the shadows, and corrupted giant web spiders in the trees. The spiders are more cunning and will wait to attack unwary prey, while the boars simply charge in anger from their pain and fury.

The path moves through a few large clumps of trees and there's a patch of ferns ahead coiled in shadows from which the sounds are coming. The terrain is mostly open and easy to navigate. Both the boars and spiders above begin the battle nearby, though the spiders are hidden.

Terrain & Traps

Sycamores & Elms: The trees on the left are sycamores that rise 60 to 80 feet and have trunks 3 to 5 feet in diameter. Climbing them up to about 30 feet isn't difficult (DC 15 Strength check), but they thin out beyond that (add +3 to DC for every additional 15 feet).

The dark elm trees on the right are shorter at 40 to 60 feet, but wider with a thick canopy of branches. The trunks are 2 to 4 feet in diameter and the lowest branches are 15 feet off the ground, requiring a DC 20 Strength check to climb them.

Fighting from the branches of either type requires a check at the end of a PC's turn to avoid falling (or taking a −2 attack penalty next turn).

The spiders are hidden among the upper branches of the elm trees. Any PC looking in the canopy or climbing a tree can roll a DC 25 Wisdom check to notice a spider in the trees.

Log Pile: There is one pile of logs 5 feet high and 15 feet long that is big enough to slow the charge of a corrupted boar (it will go around, possibly losing an attack). The log pile can also provide cover to a small PC or someone lying behind the logs.

Monsters

The corrupted dire boars are grubbing in the shadows among the ferns when they pick up the PCs' scent. Their brains are addled by the corruption that has spread out from the elemental node, and they attack immediately.

The spiders are in the trees. The corruption has spread upward less quickly, but they have consumed corrupted beasts and become corrupted themselves. If any PCs consumed the flesh of these creatures, they may become corrupted in some way as well.

Additional Reinforcements: If you want to challenge the PCs more, include a hive of 2d6 corrupted lokkris mooks (see stats) nearby that are roused by the fighting and enter the battle.

#/Level of PCs	Corrupted Dire Boar (B)	Corrupted Giant Spider (S)
4 x 5th level	2	1
5 x 5th level	3	1
6 x 5th level	2*	2
4 x 6th level	2	2
5 x 6th level	3*	2
6 x 6th level	4*	2

* The boars use their nastier special.

Tactics

The boars attack by charging out of the shadows and engaging the nearest enemies. They react to the last damage dealt to them. The spiders will wait to go until the end of the round, trying to silently drop down behind or above a single PC isolated from the others. If the spiders haven't been detected yet, allow that PC a DC 25 Wisdom check. On a failure, the spider gains a +2 attack bonus with its first attack due to stealth.

Loot

The beasts have nothing of value, though spider poison might have some value if extracted (but it's corrupted too). There might also be a webbed up humanoid meal hanging in the trees that has some valuables, if you like.

Icons

A PC that has relationship advantages with the High Druid, Elf Queen, Diabolist, or maybe the Archmage or Priestess could use one or more of them to identify and counter the corruption in a beast, keeping it from attacking for 1d2 rounds or negating any spread of corruption.

CORRUPTION TABLE

For each group of creatures, roll on the following corruption table to see what form their corruption takes:

d4 Roll	Corruption Effect
1	On a natural odd hit, some of the corruption rubs off on the target (save ends). While corrupted, the target is vulnerable and corrupted creatures seek to attack it first. If the target fails to save by the end of the battle, it is corrupted in some way (GM, decide what that means).
2	A natural 16+ attack roll also weakens the target (save ends). If the effect would already weaken it, the effect is hard save ends (16+) instead.
3	The corrupted creature has 20% more hit points but takes a −2 penalty to all defenses.
4	Any PC staggered by a corrupted creature's attack must roll a save. On a failure, that PC is tainted by corruption and takes a −1 penalty to attacks, checks, and saves (non-cumulative) until cured (or the elemental node is cleansed). GM, decide what that requires.

CORRUPTED DIRE BOAR

Dire boars are vicious to start with. The corruption running through this one makes it really scary.

Large 5th level troop [BEAST]
Initiative: +6

Battle-hardened tusks +13 vs. AC—22 damage
  Natural 16+: The dire boar can make a *bash* attack against a different target as a free action.
  Miss: See *Carnage.*

[Special trigger] Bash +10 vs. PD—The target is weakened (−4 to attacks and defenses) until the end of the boar's next turn

Bestial durability: When an enemy's attack has an effect on the dire boar other than damage, the boar can roll an immediate hard save (16+); on a success, it negates that effect.

Carnage (dire feature): The dire animal's attacks that miss deal damage equal to its level. When staggered, its missed attacks deal damage equal to double its level.

Last stand: The boar doesn't die until it reaches −60 hp. While at 0 hp or below but more than −60 hp, it must roll a normal save at the end of each of its turns; on a failure it dies. (Fighting dire boars always presents a choice for the PCs: pile on damage to drop it to −60 hp, or trust the save roll to go their way.)

One random corruption feature: Use the corruption table to add a corruption feature to the boar.

Nastier Specials

Furious streak: When the dire boar can make a *bash* attack, if it isn't engaged with a different enemy, as a free action it can pop free of the enemy engaged with it and move to a nearby enemy to make that *bash* attack.

AC	18	
PD	16	HP 180
MD	12	

CORRUPTED GIANT WEB SPIDER

You see a sickly green haze coating this huge spider's many eyes as it moves to collect you.

Large 6th level blocker [BEAST]
Initiative: +6 (but they'll go at end of round)

Bite +11 vs. AC—30 damage, and 10 ongoing poison damage
  Natural even hit: The target also takes 3d6 ongoing poison damage if it's dazed or stuck.

C: Web +11 vs. PD (up to 2 nearby enemies in a group)—9 damage, and the target is dazed until the end of the spider's next turn
  Natural 16+: The target is also stuck until the end of the spider's next turn.

One random corruption feature: Use the corruption table to add a corruption feature to the spider.

Wall-crawler: A giant web spider can climb on ceilings and walls as easily as it moves on the ground.

AC	24	
PD	20	HP 168
MD	16	

Additional Reinforcements

Lokkris

6th level mook [beast]

Initiative: +16

Stingers on each leg +11 vs. AC—8 damage, and 5 ongoing poison damage

Lays eggs in your eyes!: Each time the lokkris hits with the attack, the crit range for all lokkris against that target expands by 1 until the end of the battle.

Flight: Lokkris are quick darting fliers that move with an angry buzzing sound.

Wall-crawler: A lokkris can climb on ceilings and walls as easily as it moves on the ground.

AC	**22**	
PD	21	**HP 23 (mook)**
MD	14	

Mook: Kill one lokkris mook for every 23 damage you deal to the mob.

Next Steps

Even during the confusion of the battle, it should be clear that these beasts were corrupted. Their flesh is sickly, they have splotches or withered limbs, and perhaps open sores. Also, anyone in tune with the wilderness should sense a wrongness emanating from the beasts and from the direction the PCs are traveling.

After a quick rest and a few more hours of travel, the PCs come to a large gorge whose bottom is lost in mist. It's not clear how long it will take to go around, but if the PCs consider it one of them should realize that the gorge goes on for miles and miles. Luckily, the trail ends at a place where long vines dangle from huge trees along the edge of the gorge, allowing PCs to swing from one side to the other. Ropes are also strung across the gap, though they dip into the mist. Once the PCs decide to cross, see **Battle 2: Vinerock Gorge.**

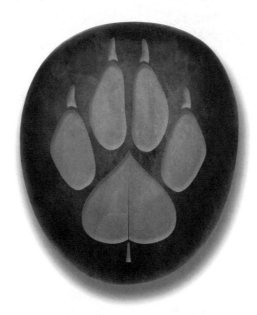

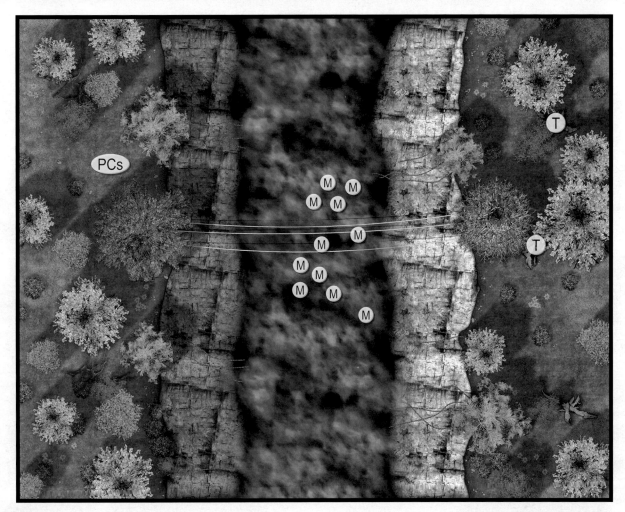

BATTLE 2: VINEROCK GORGE

The trail you've been following ends at a long gorge perhaps two hundred feet across. Heavy mist hangs below you, slowly spiraling. It seems to have an unnatural green sheen. You have no idea how deep the gorge is, and it goes out of sight both directions. Going around would take hours you don't have—it's either down and back up, or across. Luckily, across might be an option since there are long creeping vines hanging from tall blackwood trees along both edges of the gorge and multiple ropes are stretched across the gap between the trees, though the mist envelops them from time to time.

LOCATION DESCRIPTION

Unless they have a means of flying, crossing the gorge by vine or rope is the only real option for the PCs if they want to have a chance to reach the druid in time (going around would take hours). The far side is more than far away too, so normal magical teleportation won't work until the PCs are half way across at least. That leaves the two options, swinging across and climbing across, unless they want to try to climb down into the gorge and back up the other side, all within the mist.

Swinging across risks a long fall, or perhaps missing the far vine to swing back to a starting point. Climbing across is safer, but risks being exposed to the mist.

Whatever the choice, as the PCs cross and reach the far side, more corrupted creatures will attack them. Waiting at the far side of the gorge are a group of treants that have become addled by the corruption leaking from the elemental node. They have fallen under the control of Xantip Nos, the rakshasa that has defiled the node, and they now guard the approach. In addition, a group of flying wasp spirits will rise out of the mists to attack those moving across.

There's also one more grisly sight, since the ranger who was tracking the kidnapped druid met his end here. Storry Olander is impaled upon the branches of one of the treants, a look of surprise still on his face.

TERRAIN & TRAPS

Vine Swing: The vines hang far enough for a PC to climb to a high branch on their side and swing down and out, trying to grab a vine on the far side. Once they grab the second vine, they can slide down it to the ground on the far side of the gorge. It takes two move actions to do this.

Transferring from one vine to another requires a DC 25 Dexterity check. Failure means the PC must use another move action to try again, unless the check fails by 5 or more, in which case they fall (see Vinerock Gorge below) unless the PCs figure out an ingenious way to prevent it, of course.

Climbing Across the Ropes: Climbing along the ropes is safer (especially for those tying themselves on), but it takes longer. It requires four move actions to move to the other side this way. If a PC isn't tied on and tries going over more quickly (like walking a rope or trying some other maneuver that doesn't involve wrapping arms and legs around a rope while hanging upside down), it takes two move actions and requires a DC 20 Dexterity check. Failure by 5 or more results in a fall (see Vinerock Gorge below).

The problem with using the ropes is that the mist envelops them from time to time, and it's poisonous. For each move action spent moving across, the PC must roll one save. Each failure means the mist envelops them (see below).

Vinerock Gorge: The gorge descends 300 feet from the PCs' location along the edge of the gorge. The mist prevents normal visibility beyond about 20 feet. Anyone falling into the gorge has a long way down, but luckily there are more ropes strung across the gap.

When someone falls into the gorge, they will only fall about 30 feet before striking one of these ropes. At that point, the creature takes 4d8 damage and rolls an easy save (6+). On a success, they catch the rope and stop falling. On a failure, they fall again and hit another rope, taking damage and saving again. They get three total saves before the final long fall of 200 feet into a wide stream at the bottom and 8d10 more damage.

When a PC falls and catches a rope, they must either return to their side or move to the far side. Doing so requires between one and three move actions, depending on how far across they were and which side they are moving toward. Each move requires a successful DC 15 Strength check or they hang in place. Time spent on the ropes climbing is automatically in the mist.

Climbing from the sides of the gorge back up to the edge out of the mists is a full round action, but only requires a DC 15 Strength check. Anyone who falls to the bottom and survives will have to spend the rest of the battle climbing back up if they survive the fall and the poisonous mist.

Poisonous Mist: The mist filling the gorge has been tainted by the corrupted elemental node, and the vapors are noxious. At the end of each turn a PC spends in the mist, they take 10 poison damage unless they don't breathe, aren't living, or have a way to block the vapors. This includes PCs hanging from ropes or climbing up the sides of the gorge.

Monsters

The corrupted treants are waiting on the far side of the gorge, but are partially hidden among the other trees there (though they

Fighting While Swinging and Climbing

Fighting monsters while hanging from ropes and vines is difficult. You can ignore that fact to keep things moving quickly and not impose any penalties. Or, if you like, use this rule for PCs fighting in precarious positions.

When a PC takes damage from an attack while on a rope or vine, they must roll a DC 15 Dexterity check. On a failure, they lose their next move action. On a natural 1, they fall, unless tied on.

aren't as tall) and they won't be obvious to those on the far side. A PC halfway across could roll a DC 20 Wisdom check to examine the far side of the gorge. On a success, they spot the human ranger Storry Olander spitted on a branch of a low tree (a treant).

There's also a second group of enemies hidden within the mists—wasp spirits. Once one PC has moved to the far side, a high-pitched humming sound will begin, and then a group of wasp spirits will rise out of the mists to attack anyone on the ropes or swinging. The spirits look like dog-sized wasps that are semi-corporeal but faded without color. They were giant wasps that were killed by the noxious mist in their hive, but the elemental magic preserved a remnant of them.

Additional Reinforcements: If you want to challenge the PCs more, make one mob of wasp spirits double strength.

#/Level of PCs	Corrupted Treant (T)	Wasp Spirit Mook (M)
4 x 5th level	2	10 (1 mob)
5 x 5th level	2	16 (2 mobs)
6 x 5th level	3	15 (2 mobs)
4 x 6th level	3	13 (2 mobs)
5 x 6th level	2*	15 (2 mobs)
6 x 6th level	3*	10 (1 mob)

* Each treant is double strength: it gains two *grasping branches* attacks, and it has 202 hp.

Tactics

Once the first PC reaches the far side of the gorge, the treants will move to attack as the wasps rise from the mist. The treants' goal is simple, smash or jab any living thing that comes across the gorge.

Note that the mechanics of crossing the gorge are likely to split the party, so that one or two PCs arrive at the other side first. If the group is taking a lot of damage from poison or if brittle party members who aren't going to survive long on their own are way ahead of the rest of the PCs, you could easily adjust the battle by placing only one of the treants near the edge. The others could be farther away, moving towards the edge at the same time that the rest of the PCs are getting across the gorge.

The wasp spirits emerge from the mist and attack anyone on the ropes and vines first, then on the edges of the gorge if there aren't any other targets.

Loot

Storry still has a pouch with 50 gp in it on his corpse. His quiver holds two *+2 keen arrows.*

Icons

A PC that has relationship advantages with the High Druid, Elf Queen, the Three, the GGW, or maybe the Prince or Orc Lord could use one or more of them to improve their chance of making checks on the ropes or vines by +5 per advantage, or possibly succeeds automatically. They could also use one to guarantee a successful save on a fall.

A PC that has relationship advantages with the High Druid, Elf Queen, Diabolist, or maybe the Archmage or Priestess could use one or more of them to identify and counter the corruption in a treant, keeping it from attacking for 1d2 rounds, or making a mob of insect spirits attack themselves for a round.

CORRUPTED TREANT

This living tree is covered in green splotches of mold that have rotted its core.

7th level spoiler [PLANT]
Initiative: +6
Vulnerability: fire

Grasping branches +12 vs. AC—14 damage, and the treant grabs the target. When the treant starts its turn grabbing an enemy, it can make a *twist and snap* attack against that target as a standard action that turn.

[Special trigger] **Twist and snap +16 (includes +4 grab bonus) vs. PD**—42 damage

Fire fire fire!: When the treant takes 15 or more fire damage from a single attack, it releases all grabbed creatures.

Hardwood resistance: This creature has *resist damage 12+* to all damage except fire damage and melee weapon damage, which damages it normally.

TREANT CORRUPTION

To represent the corruption in the treants, you can either use their nastier special, or roll on the corruption table from the last battle and give the treants one of those effects.

Nastier Specials

Toxic haze: The treant exudes a toxic cloud of pollen. When an enemy engages the treant or starts its turn engaged with the treant, it takes 4 poison damage.

AC	25	
PD	23	**HP 101**
MD	17	

WASP SPIRIT

They're the pests of the spiritworld that still exist in this world.

6th level mook [BEAST]
Initiative: +12

Corrupted sting +11 vs. AC—6 damage, and 5 poison damage
Natural 16+: The target is weakened as the poison and corruption within the spirit affects them.

Flight: Wasp spirits are perfect fliers that can hover and dart mid-air.

Semi-corporeal: Wasp spirits don't take miss damage.

AC	21	
PD	19	**HP 20 (mook)**
MD	18	

Mook: Kill one wasp spirit mook for every 20 damage you deal to the mob.

NEXT STEPS

The PCs can take a quick rest after the gorge battle. An obvious trail on that side of the gorge leads along it toward Raven's Spire a few miles distant. When the PCs are ready, go to **Battle 3: The Sacrifice of Mother Bark.**

BATTLE 3: THE SACRIFICE OF MOTHER BARK

Raven's Spire is now in view, a small peak extending upward near the end of the gorge ridge. The trail you've been following switchbacks up a stone cliff before entering a flat plain of weathered brown rock overshadowed by the peak. Large and ancient stone disks piled in columns are stacked all around the outer edges of the area, and in the center is huge obsidian sphere that seems to be slowly rotating as mist pours from it and runs across the plain and into the gorge. Directly in front of it is a raised wooden X-shaped platform planted into the ground. An old gnome woman in tattered druidic clothing hangs from it on bindings. There's a lot of blood streaking her clothes and a circle of strange runes painted on the ground around her, but you can see some movement as she turns her head and opens a hand. A few feline humanoids pace the area near her.

Location Description

The plain is roughly 150 feet in diameter though not perfectly round. The stacked stone columns encircle it and each rises 20 feet. The sphere is 15 feet in diameter and looks to be floating and rotating in an oval depression in the rock that seems designed for it; there's a greenish-silver glow at the bottom between sphere and ground where the mist pours away from it.

The sphere is an elemental node that is producing the poison mist as a byproduct of the ritual recently enacted here by the rakshasa warrior Xantip Nos. The ritual is already completed, and Mother Bark's soul and magic has been stripped from her flesh, stored in a receptacle, and delivered to Xantip's master Vooram. The thing the PCs see moving on the wooden support is now a corruption wight, but they might not realize that at first.

In addition to the two weretigers near the sphere, there are others slinking around the node or watching the area from hidden vantages. The rakshasa Xantip is also in the area, hidden among the noxious mist, which doesn't bother him. Finally, the corrupted wight Mother Bark is held in place by vines, but it can release itself and leap down to attack whenever it wishes.

Between the magic of the sphere and the enemies arrayed here, this is a double-strength battle.

Terrain & Traps

Stacked Stones: The stone columns themselves are normal, but each has been marked with warding runes. If anyone crosses the perimeter of the plain (think lines of invisible energy connecting each column to the next around it) or touches a column, a pulse of green light will flare across the area as a warning.

Detecting the ward requires a DC 25 check using a magical background. Removing a ward is easier, requiring only a DC 20 check to disable it and bypass the column without warning the enemies.

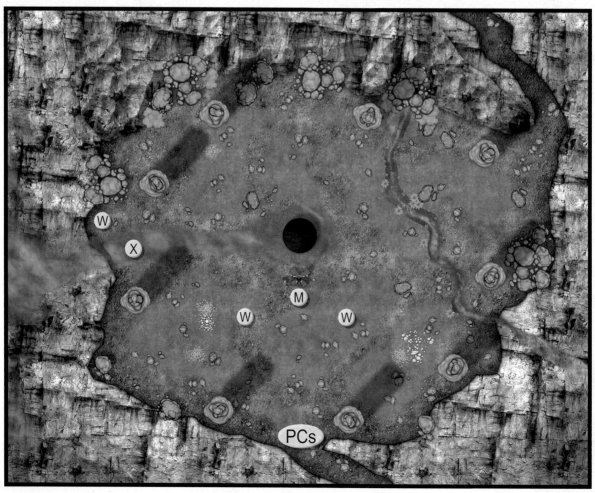

It is possible to push over a stone stack, but they are heavy. Doing so requires a successful DC 30 Strength check or some sort of magical force. Enemies under the column can roll a save to avoid damage; on a failure they take 5d10 damage.

Elemental Node: The rotating sphere is filled with powerful elemental magic. It's currently expelling the residue of an unnatural ritual Xantip performed to remove Mother Bark's soul and power from her—the poisonous mist.

It is possible to manipulate the energy of the node to your own advantage, but a PC must first attune to it as a standard action. Doing so requires a DC 25 check (using magical backgrounds), with failure resulting in the loss of a recovery (or damage equal to a recovery roll). Once that happens, how the magic is used is up to the PC, but here are a few options:

- DC 20: As a quick action, create an expulsion of mist that covers the area nearby the node for one round, concealing all creatures within it.
- DC 20: As a free action, gain a sensory input into how the node was used to remove Mother Bark's power and spirit from her flesh. It also reveals that she is dead and now a creature of corruption.
- DC 25: Tap into the elemental energy of the node to power a spell as a quick action. A daily spell becomes recharge 16+ instead. On a failure, the spell takes a −4 penalty to hit or is limited in some other way for non-attack spells.
- DC 30: As a quick action, have a vision related to the High Druid about some other story element for that PC, or see a withered old man (Vooram shapechanged) watching them from a strange chamber of black glass. The man's face seems to shift for a moment, revealing fangs and glowing eyes. Each PC can only access a vision once. Failure results in being weakened (save ends).

Wooden Cross: The X-shaped cross has two "legs" sunk into the stone of the plain. It's 12 feet high at the top of each "arm." The gnome woman hangs in the center by vines growing from the wood (not ropes). The corruption wight can free itself whenever it wishes.

Poisonous Mist: Unless you want it to, the mist pouring off the node isn't thick enough to cause harm (it flows down to pool in the gorge). It does waft across the plain toward the gorge and provides concealment for creatures within it.

Monsters

Xantip Nos: Xantip is a rakshasa warrior, part of a caste that serves the whims of the more powerful rakshasa casters. He orchestrated the kidnapping of Mother Bark and performed the *Ritual of Taking* to steal the druid's power and spirit for his master. The ritual was completed before the PCs arrived, and he and his weretiger servants are now preparing plans to unleash the corruption wight as part of a new scheme. During this battle, he will appear as a balding and wiry old human man who laughs cruelly unless somehow forced to change shape.

Xantip serves Vooram, but if captured, he is willing to trade his knowledge of Vooram's location and the fact that his master is collecting the power and souls of druids to somehow dethrone the High Druid in exchange for his life. He will try to hold back the fact that he and Vooram are rakshasas, saying only that his master is a powerful wizard.

Weretigers: The weretigers are already in their hybrid form at the start of the battle. When they die, they revert to wood elves.

Mother Bark: The old gnome woman is now a corruption wight, but it won't be apparent from a distance. Once a PC gets closer, they will see that the gnome woman's skin is barklike and greenish, with blighted black spots covering it. When she opens her eyes, they show solid green pupils. If any PCs try to rescue her, she will remain still and seem dazed, only releasing herself from the cross when someone tries to cut her down. If the PCs simply attack without trying to save her, she joins the battle at the end of the round or during her initiative the following round.

Additional Reinforcements: If you want to challenge the PCs more, after the weretigers drop to 0 hp, have 1d3 of them rise again as warped beasts (*Bestiary*, page 70) that have been taken over by entities from another dimension that were able to cross over thanks to the corruption ritual.

#/Level of PCs	Xantip Nos, Rakshasa (X)	Weretiger (W)	Mother Bark, Corruption Wight (M)
4 x 5th level	1	3	1
5 x 5th level	1	4	1
6 x 5th level	1	5*	1*
4 x 6th level	1	4*	1*
5 x 6th level	1	6*	1*
6 x 6th level	1	8*	1*

* The enemies use their nastier specials.

Tactics

Unless the PCs disable the wards on the stacked stones, a warning will go off when someone moves onto the plain. The weretigers near the node will move toward them, while others hidden around the perimeter will approach from the periphery (possibly surprising PCs). They will choose their prey and quickly try to bring it down, each picking a different PC.

Xantip Nos begins the battle hidden within the mist pouring off the node. He will delay until after the weretigers go, unless he has been spotted and engaged. Then he will move to engage a spellcaster (druids first, then healers, then arcane spellcasters), knowing the danger they pose. He looks like a human monk using claw-strike attacks. He will try to escape if reduced below 20% of his hit points and most of his allies are slain. He doesn't shift into his natural form unless forced to, such as being hit by a crit once he's staggered, or some powerful magic effect that confuses him or makes him lose control momentarily.

The corruption wight will be drawn toward druids and divine casters, but will wait to see if anyone tries to free it first, possibly gaining a +2 bonus to its first attack due to surprise.

Loot

The weretigers have collected a few valuables as mercenaries and keep them in packs and satchels in a small hollow beneath an overhang just beyond the plain (no check if PCs search). There's a total of 650 gp in loot.

Xantip wears a pair of large gold and emerald earrings in his right ear; each is worth 300 gp. He also wears an onyx *ring of deception (recharge 11+):* Reroll one skill check made to bluff, lie, or misdirect someone. Quirk: Never tells the full truth.

Icons

A PC that has relationship advantages with the High Druid, Priestess, Lich King, or maybe the GGW or Archmage could use one or more of them to ward one PC from the corruption wight's touch that battle (it won't attack the chosen PC unless they attack it).

A PC that has relationship advantages with the High Druid, Archmage, Diabolist, Elf Queen, Lich King, Priestess, or maybe the Three could use one or more of them to attune to the elemental node without a roll, or gain a +10 bonus to a roll to use the node.

Xantip Nos, Rakshasa Warrior

"Beware the rakshasa's claws, but beware the thing's eyes more, for they hold only chaos and death."

Double-strength 7th level spoiler [HUMANOID]
Initiative: +14

Claws +12 vs. AC (2 attacks)—23 damage
First natural even hit each turn: The rakshasa can make a *stare into your soul* attack against the target as a free action.
Miss: 7 damage.

[Special trigger] C: Stare into your soul +12 vs. MD (one enemy engaged with it)—5 psychic damage, and the target can't use the escalation die (save ends). For each enemy unable to use the escalation die, the rakshasa warrior gains a +2 damage bonus to its *claws* attacks.

Shapechange: As a standard action, the rakshasa can change its form to that of any humanoid, or back to its own shape. Seeing through the shapechange requires a DC 25 skill check.

Whirling savagery: Twice per battle as a move action, the rakshasa warrior can pop free of all enemies and whirl away somewhere nearby. Each enemy engaged with it takes damage equal to 1d6 x the escalation die.

AC	23	
PD	22	**HP 205**
MD	18	

Weretiger

If you're not all that sane to begin with, lycanthropy can push you over the edge. And for wood elves, it's a long way down.

Large 6th level troop [BEAST]
Initiative: +11

Claws and bite +11 vs. AC—20 damage
First natural 11+ each turn: The weretiger can make a second *claws and bite* attack as a free action.
Second natural 11+ each turn: The weretiger can make a third *claws and bite* attack as a free action if the escalation die is 3+.

[Special trigger] Springing strike +11 vs. AC—25 damage
Limited use: When an enemy engages the weretiger, if weretiger isn't already engaged, it can make a *springing strike* attack against that enemy as an interrupt action before the attack.

Bestial fury (hybrid form only): These weretigers gain a bonus to damage equal to double the escalation die.

Unnatural vigor (hybrid or animal form only): When the weretiger is not staggered at the start of its turn, it heals 24 hp.

Nastier Specials

Stymie: When the weretiger hits with a *springing strike* attack, the target pops free from it and can't take any more actions that turn unless it succeeds on a save.

AC	20	
PD	18	**HP 180**
MD	22	

MOTHER BARK, CORRUPTION WIGHT

The gnome woman is gone. In her place is darkness, corruption, and a need to spread her contagion.

7th level spoiler [UNDEAD]
Initiative: +12
Vulnerability: holy

Corrupting touch +12 vs. AC—15 damage, and 10 ongoing negative energy damage
  Natural even hit: The ongoing damage is hard save ends (16+).
  Natural odd hit: The ongoing damage is easy save ends (6+).
  Natural even miss: The wight can make another *corrupting touch* attack with a −2 penalty. It can make extra attacks after missing this way a number of times equal to the escalation die (minimum 1).

C: Vomitus insect swarm +11 vs. AC (1d3 nearby enemies)—13 poison damage, and the target takes a −1 penalty to saves until the end of the battle (cumulative).
  Limited use: The wight can only use this attack the turn after hitting with *corrupting touch.*

Nastier Specials

Corruption spreader: When the corruption wight scores a critical hit against an enemy or drops an enemy to 0 hp or below, that creature becomes tainted with corruption that slowly grows inside it. It's up to the GM and player to decide what that means. If not cured, the corruption eventually kills its host and turns them into a corruption wight.

AC	23	
PD	20	**HP 100**
MD	16	

NEXT STEPS

If the PCs were creative, they may have learned more about the plot against the High Druid either from Xantip or through accessing the elemental node. Other options for revealing bits of the story might come from captured weretigers or even comments from Mother Bark in wight form. Or maybe the PCs remain in the dark after this set of battle scenes until the final confrontation in epic tier.

The epic tier battle scenes for the High Druid conclude the story of Voorham and the *Ritual of Taking* he's been using to weaken druidic forces in the region. It's for characters of level 7 or 8, so the PCs will most likely need to engage in further adventures before being drawn back into the rakshasa's web of intrigue, unless you really want to challenge them.

CORRUPTED NATURE STORY ENDINGS

Here are outcomes for each story opening, detailing what success or failure might mean.

If the PCs did face all three battles, remember to give them a full heal-up.

THE HIGH DRUID'S SUMMONS

Success: The PCs manage to track the kidnappers back to Raven's Spire and put an end to them, even if they couldn't save the druid. They also learned more about who and what is attacking the druids, and the fact that sacrificial rituals are being used to draw their power for someone. That information helps the High Druid's people figure out what is going on. For their help, each PC gains a 6 with the High Druid that lasts until they use it or level up.

Failure: Mother Bark perished and her kidnappers escaped. Worse, her murder is somehow linked to a new corruption growing in the wilds near Raven's Spire. The earth is crying out in pain and the druids must direct their resources to that fight instead of discovering who is targeting them. The next time the PCs are in an important battle, another corruption wight will show up to harass them for meddling.

THE DRUID'S WISDOM

Success: While the PCs were unable to save Mother Bark, they did avenge her by defeating those who abducted her (and perhaps gaining information about the larger plot). After performing their own ritual upon the body, the acolytes inform the PCs that her spirit has been trapped in the world, but if they can defeat the one who holds her, she will be able to reincarnate. The next two times the PCs roll icon dice for the High Druid, they can reroll each 5 once and take either result.

Failure: The PCs fail to recover Mother Bark or avenge her capture and death. The PCs eventually return to the Olander homestead to find the acolytes and frontier folk all murdered and many of them have become corrupted undead as well. Mother Bark has returned there to bring more creatures under her corruption.

A Different Vision of the Wild

Success: While the PCs were unable to save Mother Bark and their hopes to promote a rival to the High Druid are dashed, they do garner good will from others who believe there needs to be a change among the druids. Each PC can reroll any of the icon dice once the next time they roll dice, taking the new result.

Failure: Not only is Mother Bark dead, but the local druids now suspect the PCs were involved in her kidnapping and demise somehow. Each 6 the PCs roll with the High Druid is a 5 instead until they level up. Of course, on the other hand, mysterious magical messengers begin to show up, inquiring about their interest in helping enact a change that removes the druids from the equation completely.

What Backwards Hole Is This?

Success: The PCs are unable to save Mother Bark, but they can return her body to the Olanders and acolytes. The druids are thankful their leader was returned to them and her corrupted body not allowed to despoil the region the old gnome loved. They pay the PCs whatever was agreed upon, and provide three healing salves (champion tier *healing potion*) as well.

Failure: The acolytes are unhappy to learn of Mother Bark's fate, whether from the PCs upon their return or when she and some corrupted animals attack the homesteads. They are unwilling to pay the agreed upon price for a job not done. They may be willing to do so, however, if the PCs go back to the gorge and track down the corruption wight's lair and put an end to the thing once and for all.

Battle Scene Connections

The stories from this set of battle scenes can lead to scenes in this and other books:

 Danger in Darkwood (Elf Queen): When the PCs return to the Oleander homesteads, the druids there tell them that before she was taken, Mother Bark traveled deep into the wood to gain wisdom from an old hermit woman there. She came back scared; perhaps the hermit can shed light on what's going on.

 The Ritual of Taking (High Druid, page 67): The events around Mother Bark play directly into the larger plan by Vooram to steal the High Druid's power. The PCs are called back to Thorn based on the signs of where the corruption is greatest.

 The Lich's Spire (Lich King): Searching through Xantip's belongings reveals a map to a tower in the forest and a note that says, *"Come to the tower and we will discuss my participation in the plan. I can provide the ritual components."*

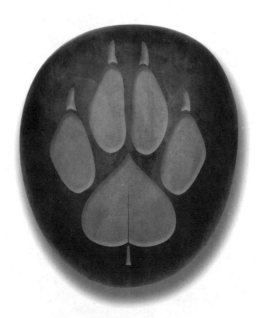

HIGH DRUID:
THE RITUAL OF TAKING

LEVEL RANGE: 7–8

This set of battle scenes is a little different from the others because its story is linked to the adventurer-tier and champion-tier battle scenes. If you opted against using the earlier adventures, or are just running an epic game, these battle scenes still work fine on their own.

The themes of this set of battles are rakshasa dark magic rituals and facing horrors of the forest created by corrupting magic. This set of battle scenes works best in a semi-wild environment where the edge of the Imperial frontier meets wilderness.

Before: Two druids have been ritualistically murdered in the vicinity of Thorn, a small frontier village. Kalel Blackmane was the first. Later, Mother Bark was sacrificed before the PCs could save her. In both cases, the murderers stole that druid's power and delivered it to their master before the PCs could intervene.

Now: That master, a rakshasa named Vooram, is collecting druidic power through a dark rite known as the *Ritual of Taking*. He only needs to perform one more sacrifice of one of the High Druid's followers to siphon away a large portion of the icon's divine power. And Vooram has chosen his third victim, the druid Lancaster Oakenleaf.

The only ones able to stop this heinous ritual are the PCs, who've come close before but have been too late. After their failure to save Mother Bark, they are probably on the trail of the one who claimed her power, keeping their eyes open and checking with contacts about who might be behind it all. Perhaps they've even resorted to divinations and other arcane or divine means.

They'll get their chance as another druid gets taken. The rakshasa Vooram, who has been posing as Kalel's friend and Thorn's herbalist, Moira Llarn, is ready to enact the ritual again. They must race through dark woods fouled by the rakshasa's corrupt and stolen nature powers, facing treants and animated trees. If they're quick, they'll interrupt the rakshasa as he is performing the *Ritual of Taking* one final time within a circle of stones on a druidic holy site. Vooram can't be allowed to complete the ritual, but the rakshasa's allies will try to stop the heroes as the ritual begins to empower the rakshasa.

THE RITUAL OF TAKING STORY OPENINGS

- **Caught in the Act:** One or more PCs with a positive or conflicted relationship with the High Druid are contacted by a dryad named Willow who summons them back to the frontier village of Thorn in the High Druid's name. Another druid has been kidnapped, Lancaster Oakenleaf, who the High Druid sent to investigate Kalel's death and only recently arrived. This time, however, Willow can provide quick transport via striding through trees miles apart to get the PCs right on the kidnappers' trail.

- **An Opportunity For Leverage:** One or more PCs with a conflicted or negative relationship with the High Druid hears from various sources connected to the icon that another kidnapping has taken place, again in the village of Thorn. This time it's a druid named Lancaster. Another icon connected to at least one of the PCs sees an opportunity to learn the *Ritual of Taking* from this mysterious kidnapper, possibly to be used at a future point if it's as powerful as suggested. The icon can also arrange for the PCs to arrive on the kidnapper's trail immediately. If they save Lancaster, he might be another ally when it comes time to remove the High Druid.

- **It Happened Again!:** The PCs are taking it easy back in the frontier village of Thorn when the cry goes up. Lancaster Oakenleaf, the druid sent by the High Druid to replace murdered Kalel, has been taken. These people have the worst druid luck. Considering how the last two were treated, the villagers plead with the heroes to go after the man and catch the kidnappers. A small group of forest creatures that served the druid will lead them into the forest after him.

ALTERNATE ICONS

 Diabolist: It could be Diabolist cultists led by Vooram that have taken Lancaster for some foul rite out in the woods. The demonic taint has infected the forest.

 Lich King: Agents of the Lich King have taken the druid, and they plan a foul ritual using old necromantic magic that will raise the spirits of those who've died in the forest, raising tensions with Emperor and High Druid. Flavor Vooram as a necromancer, or stat up a new archvillain.

ICONS IN PLAY

Characters that have relationships (and story-guide advantages) with the High Druid, Archmage, Emperor, Elf Queen, Lich King, or Priestess should be able to shine in these battle scenes. Moreso than PCs with other icon relationships, feel free to give such PCs extra knowledge about the opposition, make checks to pull off fun actions the players might suggest, and use their advantages to particularly good effect, such as negating or bypassing some of the advantages or abilities of the enemies.

THE RITUAL OF TAKING OVERVIEW

Through iconic help, the PCs are put on the still warm trail of Vooram's allies, who have captured Lancaster and are taking him into the woods to an old druidic stone circle where the rakshasa waits to perform the last *Ritual of Taking*. In Battle 1, the PCs are assaulted by dark treants called forth through Vooram's magic and the corrupted connection to the forest that the rakshasa stole from Kalel and Mother Bark.

The PCs push past the treant guardians and soon come to the stone circle, still on the heels of the kidnappers. Vooram has the druid bound to a central stone and is in mid-ritual when the PCs arrive. His weretiger allies will try to slow or stop the PCs while the rakshasa, now revealed as Moira, tries to complete the ritual. The dark power of corruption infects the local vegetation, which works against the PCs.

In a final double-strength showdown, Battle 3 reveals Vooram in his true form, along with his rakshasa guards. Powerful energies flow among the stones as the ritual ramps up, attacking the PCs as they face their enemies and try to save Lancaster from a horrible death.

BATTLE 1: BAD TREES

You're on the trail of those who kidnapped the druid Lancaster thanks to help from your allies. You can't be more than twenty minutes back, and you're closing. That's when a large tree branch falls onto the path just in front of you with a loud snap. Looking up, you don't see any enemies, until you realize that the trees themselves are swaying and moving toward you. The biggest oaks have wooden jaws that tear open in their trunks as they hum and creak with a song about eating bloody meat. Which is just wrong.

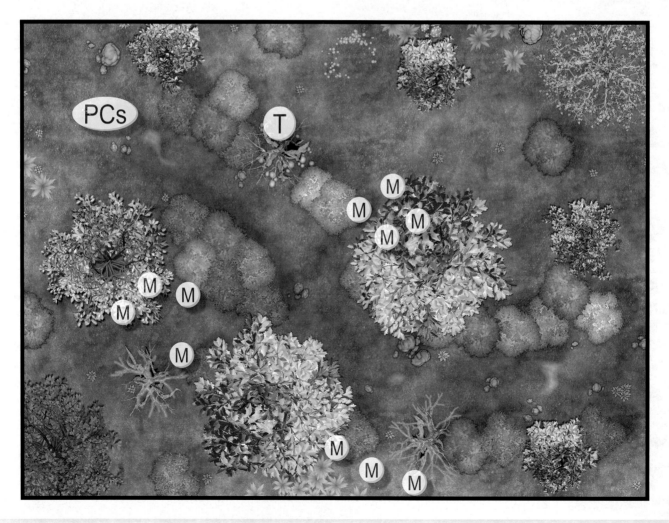

Location Description

The path winds through a lightly forested area of oak trees with a few patches of thorn bushes here and there. The path is roughly 8 feet wide and stretches about 80 feet in either direction before turning out of sight behind the trees.

Not all of the trees are normal. Some are treant titans who have been corrupted by Vooram's dark magic and the druidic magic he's absorbed so far. The treants believe they serve the wood and the Green Lady (High Druid) by stopping the PCs, and so they'll attack. Neither group will surprise the other since the trees are aware of the PCs but they give away their intent with the dropped branch. They are assisted by a young copse of awakened oaks.

Terrain & Traps

Oak Trees: There are three oak trees in the area that *aren't* monsters. A PC can try to climb one with a DC 25 Strength check (although not animated, they want to help the treants, so branches shift slightly, making climbing harder). Each is roughly 50 feet high. Any PC more than half way up that falls from the tree will take 2d12 damage.

Berry Bushes: The bushes provide concealment to PCs hiding among them. Any PC entering the bushes will have to deal with the thorns. Make the following attack against any non-plant creatures entering an area with the bushes.

Grasping thorns +15 vs. PD (one enemy going in the bushes)—The target is stuck (save ends).

Monsters

The oak treant titans stand around 30 feet tall at the tips of their branches, but the main bulk looks like a 18-foot stunted oak trunk. Eyes and a mouth open in the trunk and they groan as they fight. Those attuned to nature like a druid or someone with that type of background might notice a sickly green mold on the creature's bark flesh (the corruption of Vooram's magic).

The awakened oaks are normal trees that pull their roots out of the earth to lend aid. Only the younger trees do this, since the older ones' roots go too deep now.

Additional Reinforcements: If you want to challenge the PCs more, also have the earth itself attempt to kill the PCs. A wide maw of stones and roots opens in the ground due to the corruption in the land and tries to swallow them. Use the deep bulette stats (*Bestiary*, page 28) and ignore the *tunnel fighter* ability. The maw can move around and it can take damage. If you want, a natural 16+ could force last gasp saves as the target is sucked into the ground.

#/Level of PCs	Treant Titan (T)	Awakened Oak Mook (M)
4 x 7th level	1	5 (1 mob)
5 x 7th level	1	11 (1 mob)
6 x 7th level	1	17 (2 mobs)
4 x 8th level	2	10 (1 mob)
5 x 8th level	2	21 (2 mobs)
6 x 8th level	3	15 (2 mobs)

Tactics

Each treant titan attacks a separate enemy, while the awakened oaks spread out and lash at those grabbed by a treant or anyone they can reach. Remember that they gain a +4 bonus to attack grabbed enemies.

Loot

None.

Icons

A PC that has relationship advantages with the High Druid, Elf Queen, Orc Lord, or maybe Priestess (nature god) could use one or more of them to try to convince (or threaten) the treants to let them pass without further fighting because the PCs wish to help the druids not harm them. Using the advantage allows the PCs to roll a DC 25 Charisma check as standard action to convince some of the trees to stand down. It takes two successes to do so.

Treant Titan

It took the worst corruption magic to trick these titans into thinking they were working for the High Druid, but that's what Vooram has got.

Large 10th level spoiler [PLANT]
Initiative: +9
Vulnerability: fire

Grasping branches +15 vs. AC (2 attacks)—30 damage, and the treant grabs the target. When the treant starts its turn grabbing an enemy, it can make a *twist and snap* attack against that target as a standard action that turn.

[Special trigger] **Twist and snap +19 (includes +4 grab bonus) vs. PD**—80 damage, and the target is dazed (save ends). If the treant starts its turn grabbing a dazed enemy, it can make a *titanic rend* attack against that target as a standard action that turn.
Miss: 40 damage.

[Special trigger] **Titanic rend +19 (includes +4 grab bonus) vs. PD**—160 damage, and the treant titan can continue making *titanic rend* attacks against the target until it escapes the grab, at which point the treant will have to use a *grasping branches* attack against it again.
Miss: 60 damage.

Fire fire fire!: When the treant takes 35 or more fire damage from a single attack, it releases all grabbed creatures.

Hardwood resistance: This creature has *resist damage 18+* to all damage except fire damage and melee weapon damage, which damages it normally.

Nastier Specials

Coffin of living wood: When the treant titan hits with a *titanic rend* attack, the target is pulled into a hollow chamber within the treant. While grabbed by the treant this way, the target can't be the target of its allies' powers or spells.

Gauntlet of branches: Countless smaller branches whip through the air around the treant titan. When a creature engaged with the treant misses it with an attack, that creature takes 12 damage from the whipping branches.

AC	28	
PD	26	**HP 390**
MD	20	

Awakened Oak

If you listen, you can hear their battle song in their quickly swaying branches.... Hah, you stopped and listened! Now they're beating you to death!

8th level mook [PLANT]
Initiative: +9
Vulnerability: fire

Lashing branches +13 vs. AC—22 damage

Hardwood resistance: This creature has *resist damage 12+* to all damage except fire damage and melee weapon damage, which damages it normally.

AC	26	
PD	24	**HP 37 (mook)**
MD	17	

Mook: Kill one awakened oak mook for every 37 damage you deal to the mob.

Next Steps

The battle against the treants should only slow the PCs momentarily. As they continue on the path, they will see obvious signs of recent passage. Lancaster is doing what he can to make the land slow his kidnappers and provide a trail for pursuers, and it's working. Feel free to narrate how Lancaster's magic is gradually carving the path open behind him and leaving a small trail of newly sprouting oak leaves to mark the route, sprouting off plants that shouldn't have oak leaves.

The trail soon begins to climb through a low range of forested hills with a small river running down a series of small rapids to the left. Then the PCs break out of the trees to see a ridge ahead. The ridge pushes toward the river and actually juts out over the water below it. Steep cliffs from the river lead up to the top, where a circle of large stones planted into the ground tower over the area. Vooram and his allies are performing the *Ritual of Taking* there, but the PCs must get to him first. Go to **Battle 2: Taking the Causeway.**

BATTLE 2: TAKING THE CAUSEWAY

A trail branches away from the path up a causeway to the stone circle, some 300 feet away. There are figures up there, a struggling man that must be Lancaster bound to a stone with a human woman next to him chanting out in a powerful voice. Arcs of green lightning are beginning to move from stone to stone.

The only problem with reaching the druid, however, is the group of weretigers prowling around the base of the causeway. Before you can reach the stones, you'll need to deal with those guardians, since scaling the cliffs leading up to the top of the ridge looks like it would be difficult due to the writhing vines and vegetation covering the cliffs. In fact, the bushes and grass leading up the causeway are moving on their own too.

LOCATION DESCRIPTION

Unless the PCs are looking to split the party, they really need to deal with the weretigers first. Make it clear that getting above will take a while (as demonstrated by the rules in the Causeway section below) and that the figure still looks to be mid-ritual, so there's time to deal with the guards first.

The bottom of the causeway is open ground with the ramp beginning just behind the weretigers as it ascends. The PCs are at a junction where a side path from the track they were on leads up to the stones. Areas of low vegetation off the sides of the path are glowing with a dim greenish light and writhing as they seek flesh to grasp. A pair of standing stones form an semi-archway to the causeway.

Waiting for the PCs are a group of weretiger mercenaries that Vooram has employed. They are led by a weretiger captain.

TERRAIN & TRAPS

Grasping Bushes & Vines: Any PC going off the path will enter areas where the foliage is animated. When they do, they must roll a save; on a failure, they become stuck and lose the rest of their movement that turn. During their next turn, if they don't move back to safe ground, they must roll another save to keep moving through the vegetation.

The enchanted plants will also snake onto the path in places during the battle. At the start of each round when the escalation die is 1+, make the following attack against one random PC that isn't flying.

> **Grasping vines +15 vs. PD (one enemy)**—The target is stuck (save ends).
>
> *Each failed save:* The target takes 20 damage from squeezing vines.

Causeway: It's 300 feet up the causeway to the plain with the circle of stones from the bottom, so normal movement to it will take roughly four full rounds to get there. But each round PCs going up must also roll a save to avoid becoming stuck until the end of their turn from vegetation. Once the weretigers are

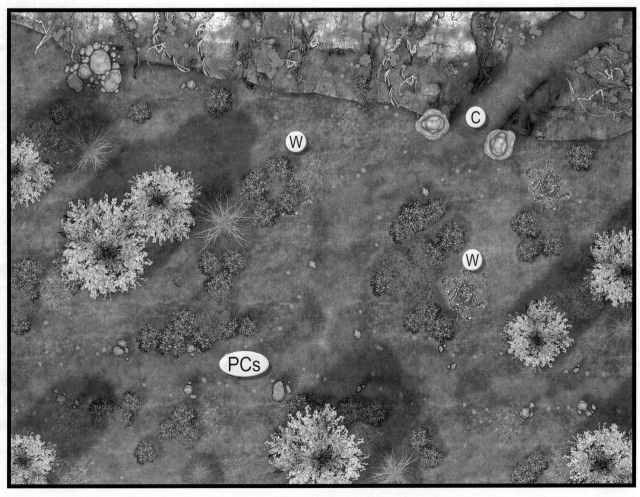

defeated, the vines die down a bit as Vooram becomes focused on the ritual, allowing the PCs to move upward freely as a group.

The start of the causeway is flanked by a pair of 20-foot high rough granite stones like those in the circle. Climbing one requires a successful DC 20 Strength check. The top is 4 feet wide.

Monsters

The weretigers are mercenaries who've been well paid by Vooram, both in coin and in evil intangible benefits, and they are dedicated to his plan to gain the High Druid's power. Once their captain falls, however, each will flee if reduced to under 40 hp.

Additional Reinforcements: If you want to challenge the PCs more, a pair of fallen lammasu (*Bestiary*, page 131) are working with Vooram. They provide overhead ranged support as the weretigers fight, but will try to fly off once reduced to 50 hp or fewer.

#/Level of PCs	Weretiger Captain (C)	Weretiger (W)
4 x 7th level	1	2
5 x 7th level	1	3
6 x 7th level	1	4
4 x 8th level	1	4**
5 x 8th level	2*	3**
6 x 8th level	2*	4**

* There's a second captain present, though by rank he's just a sergeant.

** Increase the weretigers to 8th level: increase their initiative, attacks, and defenses by +2, *claws and bite* deals 35 damage, *springing strike* deals 43 damage, and each has 280 hp.

Tactics

The captain, Riss, will attack a single enemy, while the others work in pairs to take down the others. They are smart enough to gang up on any leaders or healers facing them.

Loot

The weretigers carry their pay, which is in pouches on them (they will return to human form when the die or are captured). The rakshasa paid them 700 gp total in small diamonds.

Icons

A PC that has relationship advantages with the High Druid, Archmage, Diabolist, Elf Queen, or maybe the Lich King could use one or more of them to calm the effect of the ritual upon the foliage, getting it to stop grasping at the PCs for 1d3 rounds.

WERETIGER CAPTAIN

This man-tiger is big and quick. His scars tell a tale of survival and death.

Large 9th level troop [BEAST]
Initiative: +14

Claws and bite +14 vs. AC—50 damage
First natural 11+ each turn: The weretiger can make a second *claws and bite* attack as a free action.
Second natural 11+ each turn: The weretiger can make a third *claws and bite* attack as a free action if the escalation die is 3+.

[Special trigger] **Springing strike +14 vs. AC—60 damage**
Limited use: When an enemy engages the weretiger, if the weretiger isn't already engaged, it can make a *springing strike* attack against that enemy as an interrupt action before the attack.

Bestial fury (hybrid form only): The weretiger captain gains a bonus to damage equal to quadruple the escalation die.

Unnatural vigor (hybrid or animal form only): When the weretiger is not staggered at the start of its turn, it heals 30 hp.

Veteran mercenary: While the weretiger captain is staggered, the crit range of its attacks expands by an amount equal to the escalation die.

AC	24	
PD	23	**HP 360**
MD	22	

Weretiger

Weretigers sometimes lives among people, but they usually separate themselves socially from close association. They may be wanderers, drovers, sages, or assassins. The most famous belly dancer in Horizon is an elven weretiger, not that anyone has figured it yet.

Large 6th level troop [BEAST]
Initiative: +11

Claws and bite +11 vs. AC—20 damage

First natural 11+ each turn: The weretiger can make a second *claws and bite* attack as a free action.

Second natural 11+ each turn: The weretiger can make a third *claws and bite* attack as a free action if the escalation die is 3+.

[Special trigger] Springing strike +11 vs. AC—25 damage

Limited use: When an enemy engages the weretiger, if weretiger isn't already engaged, it can make a *springing strike* attack against that enemy as an interrupt action before the attack.

Bestial fury (hybrid form only): These weretigers gain a bonus to damage equal to double the escalation die.

Unnatural vigor (hybrid or animal form only): When the weretiger is not staggered at the start of its turn, it heals 24 hp.

Nastier Specials

Stymie: When the weretiger hits with a *springing strike* attack, the target pops free from it and can't take any more actions that turn unless it succeeds on a save.

AC	20	
PD	18	**HP 180**
MD	22	

Next Steps

Once the weretigers are defeated, the PCs can quickly move up the causeway to confront Vooram, who's taken the shape of Moira. The rakshasa is just finishing the *Ritual of Taking*, which will empower him greatly with divine druidic power.

Give the PCs a quick rest as they make their way up the causeway and ready themselves for the confrontation to come. See **Battle 3: Facing Vooram.**

Battle 3: Facing Vooram

You ascend the causeway toward the circle of stones that towers above the cliffs and river, each planted into the rock and rising nearly 20 feet in the air. A human woman chants out words of power and green energy arcs between the stones and down toward the man bound to a stone at the center. He screams through his gag with each arc. The woman is... familiar, one of the villagers, the herbalist known as Moira [who you met when she was mourning her friend Kalel's death, the first druidic murder]. Whatever foul ritual she's performing, it has to be stopped. She looks at you, then nods to the side. You see more tiger-men emerge from behind the stones. Only these tiger-striped humanoids are sleeker and their inky-black eyes reflect the green lightning of the ritual in stuttered flashing echoes—uh oh, they're rakshasas!

Location Description

The circle is 100 feet in diameter. Each stone is 10 feet wide, 4 feet thick, 20 feet high, and made of rough granite. Just beyond the stones is a narrow 4 to 8 foot ledge of earth and then cliffs that descend 80 to 100 feet down to the river. The vines and plants growing from the cliffs writhe and try to grab onto anyone climbing the cliffs.

In the center of the circle is another stone of similar but smaller dimensions lying flat on the ground, upon which Lancaster is bound by vines and gagged. Standing next to him is Vooram shapechanged as the herbalist Moira (an NPC from the adventurer-tier battle scene). The other rakshasa guards move out from behind the stones to stand between the PCs and the stone.

Vooram (Moira) has completed the active part of the ritual, now he only needs wait for the power to be taken from Lancaster and transferred to him (he must remain in the circle). Until that power transfers, he is free to fight (see the Ritual of Taking below).

In addition, the energy arcing between the stones and Lancaster is partially under Vooram's control and each round it will seek to attack one of the PCs.

Terrain & Traps

Standing Stones: The stones are made from granite and 20 feet high. They are wide enough for a PC to stand on top, but climbing them requires a successful DC 20 Strength check, and the arcing energy (below) will attack a PC on the stones instead of a random PC.

Cliffs & Vines: Anyone falling off the edge of the causeway must roll a save; on a success, they are caught by the writhing plants instead and stuck (save ends). Climbing back up requires a DC 25 Strength or Dexterity check.

Those falling all the way into the river take 4d12 damage and are probably out of the battle unless they have magic to get them back up the cliffs.

Anyone trying to climb along the cliffs to get around to the backside of the stones has to make a DC 25 check as above, and also roll a save each round or become stuck (save ends) from the vegetation.

Arcing Energy: The ritual has tapped into the ley line energy running through the stone circle. As it draws Lancaster's power (and through him some of the High Druid's as well), the corrupted magic flares and lashes out. Since Vooram's will is behind it, it won't attack him or his allies, instead targeting a random PC (or a PC on top of or in contact with a stone). At the end of each round, make the following attack.

Arcing strike +15 vs. PD (one random PC inside the stone circle)—The target gains 1d3 x 10 temporary hit points from life energy, but is also dazed (hard save ends, 16+).

Ritual of Taking & Lancaster: The ritual continues to draw energy from Lancaster during the battle even after Vooram stops his chanting to fight. At the start of the first round, the druid will fall unconscious. Unless he is removed fully from the circle (or slain), the ritual will continue to draw his lifeforce. At the start of the turn when the escalation die is 6+, the ritual transfers Lancaster's power to Vooram. At that point, if he hasn't shapechanged to his true form already, he will as the energy overwhelms his control. When this happens, all of his wounds heal (put him at max hp) and his attacks deal double damage every other round starting with that round. Lancaster will die.

Lancaster is unconscious and has 50 hp remaining. Any attack targeting him will hit automatically, but the ritual protects him from random attacks from the energy arcing and from the rakshasas. He is bound hand and foot, and removing each shackle is a move action.

Monsters

Vooram is a rakshasa mage who's currently shapechanged to look like Moira, revealing that he had planned it all from the start, picking out Kalel and manipulating the PCs. If he's hit by a critical attack, or when the ritual completes and he's filled with energy, feel free to have him shift to his true form involuntarily so the PCs know what they're truly dealing with. The rakshasa wears purple robes with green bands around it at neck, hem, and mid-line.

The rakshasa guards wield gold-handled curved sabers, wear armored vests and leggings of braided ogre mage hair, and have short purple and green caps signifying their loyalty to Vooram.

Each rakshasa has the humanoid-tiger features and backward hands indicative of their race.

Additional Reinforcements: If you want to challenge the PCs more, reduce the amount of time it takes to complete the ritual by a round or two. Or you could have one or two fallen lammasu working with Vooram (see stats). They rise up over the stones and attack from above.

#/Level of PCs	Vooram, Rakshasa Mage (V)*	Rakshasa Guard (G)
4 x 7th level	1	1
5 x 7th level	1	2
6 x 7th level	1	3
4 x 8th level	1	4
5 x 8th level	1	6
6 x 8th level	1	8

* This battle is easier if the ritual is stopped, and harder if not, since Vooram heals up.

Tactics

Vooram is overconfident and powerful. He'll seek to blast the PCs with green lightning and rend their minds while belittling them for how he was under their noses the whole time, and how the High Druid will soon be obsolete. He tries to avoid melee and will move around the circle, but always remain inside until the ritual is complete or fails. If any PC tries to remove Lancaster, Vooram will attack them and order the others to do so as well. If his ritual is ruined and he's under 100 hp, he'll try to flee, running to the edge of the circle and leaping into the river, then turning to smoke and drifting off.

The guards split into two groups, those who move to attack, and those who hold back to intercept anyone going for Vooram or the druid at first. They aren't above threatening to coup de grace an unconscious enemy if the PCs don't fall back, and following through on the threat just for fun.

Loot

The rakshasas all wear a ring of a different type of metal on each finger of their right hands: copper, silver, gold, and platinum. The four rings are worth 250 gp total per creature. Vooram's platinum ring is probably magical. As a default, use a *ring of resilience* (core rulebook, page 291), or pick a ring that fits your PCs, probably with a quirk that plays on the corruption angle.

Vooram also has a pouch of 600 gp in small diamonds for payments to the mercenaries.

Icons

A PC that has relationship advantages with the High Druid, Archmage, Diabolist, Elf Queen, Lich King, Priestess, or the Three could use one or more of them to delay the ritual by one round (per advantage). Another option would be to ward themselves from the arcing energy all battle, or stop the energy from arcing for 1d2 rounds.

A PC that has relationship advantages with any icon could use one or more of them to understand the ritual taking place, what it means to the High Druid, and how Lancaster needs to be in the circle and alive.

A PC that has relationship advantages with the High Druid could use one or more of them to make the vines and plants on the cliff stop writhing and coiling. They might also be able to siphon off some of the power the stones are drawing from the ley lines and ritual to do something "big" with the energy.

Vooram, Rakshasa Mage

"I have already won. You're simply too much of a worm to realize it. Now, prepare to scream."

Double-strength 11th level caster [HUMANOID]
Initiative: +16

Claws +16 vs. AC—80 damage, and 20 ongoing damage
  Miss: 50 damage
  Natural odd hit or miss: Vooram pops free from each enemy engaged with him as he spins away.

R: Corrupted lightning bolts +16 vs. PD (1d3 nearby enemies)—50 lightning damage, or 75 lightning damage against a staggered target
  Natural even hit: The rakshasa can make a *rend mind* attack as a free action.
  Miss: 30 lightning damage.

C: Rend mind +16 vs. MD (one nearby enemy)—25 psychic damage, and the target is confused until the end of the rakshasa's next turn

Filled with chaos and primal power: Once per day as an interrupt action when at attack would hit Vooram, he can roll a save. On a success, the attack instead targets one random creature in the battle other than Vooram.

Shapechange: As a standard action, the rakshasa can change its form to that of any humanoid, or back to its own shape. Seeing through the shapechange requires a DC 25 skill check.

Nastier Specials

Hasten fate: Once per day as a quick action, Vooram can advance the escalation die. When he does, his next attack that hits before the end of his next turn deals double damage.

AC	26	
PD	21	HP 530
MD	26	

Rakshasa Guard

It takes its frustration on not being its own master out on you in a deadly dance of claws and steel.

Double-strength 9th level troop [HUMANOID]
Initiative: +15

Saber +14 vs. AC (2 attacks)—35 damage
  Natural even hit or miss: The rakshasa can make a *claws* attack as a free action.

[Special trigger] Claws +13 vs. AC—20 damage

C: Dance of steel +13 vs. MD—5 psychic damage, and the target takes a −2 penalty to AC until the end of this turn as it watches the guard spin and slash its saber.
  Limited use: 1/round, as a quick action.

Shapechange: As a standard action, the rakshasa can change its form to that of any humanoid, or back to its own shape. Seeing through the shapechange requires a DC 25 skill check.

Whirling savagery: Twice per battle as a move action, the rakshasa guard can pop free of all enemies and whirl away somewhere nearby. Each enemy engaged with it takes damage equal to 1d6 x the escalation die.

AC	24	
PD	24	HP 340
MD	21	

Additional Reinforcements

Fallen Lammasu

Large 7th level wrecker [BEAST]
Initiative: +11

Fiery hoof +12 vs. AC—30 damage
  Natural even hit: The target takes 20 ongoing fire damage.
  Natural odd hit: The fallen lammasu can make a second *fiery hoof* attack (but not a third) as a free action.

R: Rain of hellfire +11 vs. PD (1d4 random nearby creatures)—20 fire damage
  Natural even hit against an ally: The target takes 10 ongoing fire damage instead of 20 fire damage, and until that ally saves against that damage, it adds the escalation die to its attacks.
  Natural even hit against an enemy: The target also takes 15 ongoing fire damage.

Blessing of hellfire: When the fallen lammasu fails a save against an effect created by an enemy, each enemy engaged with it takes 3d10 fire damage.

AC	22	
PD	16	HP 205
MD	21	

Next Steps

If the PCs defeated Vooram, removed Lancaster from the stone circle, or even killed Lancaster to stop the ritual, they achieve varying levels of victory. Some options might have to be explained to the High Druid or the High Druid's people, however. If Vooram escapes, he is a powerful enemy who is sure to seek revenge against the PCs for foiling his plot.

The Ritual of Taking Story Endings

Here are outcomes for each story opening, detailing what success or failure might mean. If the PCs took an unorthodox kill-the-prisoner route to victory, you'll want to adjust the success level.

  If the PCs did face all three battles, remember to give them a full heal-up.

Caught In The Act

Success: The PCs get to Lancaster in time to save him (or stop the ritual at least), possibly also killing the foul rakshasa who was behind the whole plan. In thanks, each PC gains two 6s with the High Druid that last until they use them.

Failure: The ritual is completed and the rakshasa Vooram now holds a portion of the High Druid's power, corrupting many forests and wilderness areas with that power. The High Druid's power in the region diminishes, and the Emperor's and Diabolist's increases. Each PC must reroll the next two non-villainous icon rolls they make that are 6s.

An Opportunity For Leverage

Success: The PCs thwart Vooram, learn the secret to the *Ritual of Taking*, and possibly even gain Lancaster as an ally against the High Druid, since he now realizes her power has diminished and she is vulnerable to such ploys. Each PC gains a 6 with one of their icons that lasts until they use it or level up.

Failure: The PCs fail to stop the ritual, or stop it but fail to capture Vooram and learn the ritual from him. Lancaster, if alive, is thankful for the save but unhelpful. The icon that put the PCs on the task isn't happy with them for such failures. They can't roll icon dice for that icon the next time they roll.

It Happened Again!

Success: Being the heroes they are, the PCs find the druid, stop the ritual, and possibly even kill the rakshasa behind it all. All in a day's work. In thanks, they are made honorary citizens of Thorn and provided free food and drink for a month; and don't turn up you noses, hi-falutin' PCs, the residents of Thorn go all out to make this reward mean something! The Emperor and the High Druid are also thankful to know who was behind it, and each PC gets a 6 with one of those icons that lasts until they use it or level up.

Failure: The PCs were Lancaster's only hope, and now he's dead, the rakshasa Vooram is really powerful, and he's pissed they tried to thwart his plans. The next time they PCs are in a battle, a rakshasa assassin will show up to make life difficult, possibly kidnapping one of them who strays from the group.

Battle Scene Connections

The stories from this set of battle scenes can lead to other scenes:

 Old Injuries Repaid (Orc Lord; page 101): After defeating Vooram, the PCs discover correspondence between him and someone who signs only, "your humble servant." It talks about a plan set in motion to kidnap the elven ambassador to Wreath, to disrupt the peace accords between Emperor and Elf Queen. It seems that there's more than pomp and circumstance behind the reaffirmation of the rituals, and the PCs must stop the kidnapping.

Hellhole Retrieval (Diabolist): Vooram had many plots going on, and one involved using his shapechanging abilities to regain a magical crown from a demon in a hellhole. A set of letters received from a cultist outlined the plan. Vooram was to perform the job in less than a week's time, in exchange for a powerful ritual that would allow him to take advantage of his newly gained power.

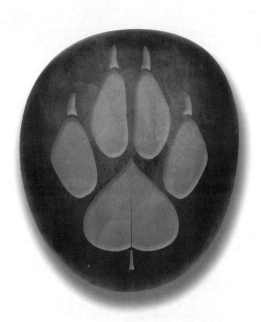

ORC LORD:
RAFTING RAZOREDGE GORGE

LEVEL RANGE: 1–2

The themes of this set of battles are fighting in a strange (and watery) environment, battling orcs, and the crazy things orcs will do to try to kill you. This set of battles works best in the wilds between points of civilization where orcs can prey upon travelers, and also where a river gorge makes sense.

The PCs have a problem: they need to get somewhere fast, faster than walking or even riding a horse will get them. There aren't any airships, amiable dragon mounts, or other flying options available either. And they're just not quite powerful enough to have access to reliable teleportation magic. So that leaves only one choice.

The heroes must take a boat or raft down the Razoredge River to get where they need to go, traveling through Razoredge Gorge in the process. And it's a dangerous place, infested by beasts and vicious humanoid raiders. They're going to be waiting for an easy meal, of course.

If that story doesn't work for the group, one of the other story openings might do the trick.

Whatever the reason, the PCs are at the small thorp of Waterwillow, where transport downriver just happens to be available.

RAFTING RAZOREDGE GORGE STORY OPENINGS

- **We Need to Get Downriver Quick:** The PCs need to be 80 miles downriver in two days to talk to a contact before that

person leaves, to claim a reward, to catch a ship heading to one of the Seven Cities, or for some similar need.

- **A Test of Courage:** Before a local half-orc spiritcaller will reveal the location of the dragon boneyard, cairns of the ancestors, or some other place the PCs need to find and only he knows, they must pass a test of courage. The old half-orc tells them they must survive a trip down Razoredge Gorge and then return to him.

- **Into the Raiders' Den:** The PCs have been hired to put a stop to orc raiders harrying merchants on the south road, or perhaps heard about a reward for doing so. But going into the Razoredge Hills directly would be suicide. There is another option that should take the orcs by surprise, that won't give them time to prepare, and that will lead right to the raiders' camp. A raid of the PCs' own traveling by boat down the river through Razoredge Gorge.

- **Guard the Silver Shipment:** A small dwarven mining consortium needs to get their silver downriver to meet a delivery to a well-known Imperial jeweler. If they do, they'll have the contract with her. The problem, of course, is that their last shipment was attacked in transit by orc raiders. This time, they want to guarantee its safety, and that's what they've hired the PCs to do.

ALTERNATE ICONS

Dwarf King: Orcs are still an enemy of the dwarves, so these battle scenes work as written if the dwarves have hired the PCs to guard a shipment, or it could also be a test of the PCs' skills to see if they're capable enough to assault an orc stronghold. If you take the Dwarf King's route, you might want to establish that the Gorge ends up running into the underworld.

Great Gold Wyrm, Priestess, or Prince of Shadows: Have the PCs carry a plague cure that needs to get to a town downriver. The orcs could be demon-touched humanoids that started the plague (GGW), or just bandits looking to steal the cure and ransom it to the town (Priestess or Prince).

ICONS IN PLAY

Characters that have relationships (and story-guide advantages) with the Orc Lord, Dwarf King, Elf Queen, and High Druid, should be able to shine in these battle scenes. Moreso than PCs with other icon relationships, feel free to give such PCs extra knowledge about the opposition, make checks to pull off fun actions the players might suggest, and use their advantages to particularly good effect, such as negating or bypassing some of the advantages or abilities of the enemies.

RAFTING RAZOREDGE GORGE OVERVIEW

During their raft trip, the PCs will face three battles against orcs and their allies.

Battle 1 is against orc archers on the ridges and a swarm of warriors and berserkers with nets who are looking to bash the PCs.

Battle 2 involves zip-lining orc kamikazes, and fighting a running battle while navigating some rapids.

Battle 3 is a double-strength fight, as the raft hits dead water right by the main camp of the Razoredge raiders. Orcs pour forth to claim their kills as the PCs fight to gain the shore.

GM, feel free to expand upon these battles by adding additional locations and enemies the PCs encounter during their trip. The battles outlined here can take place over a few hours or a day or two of travel if you prefer to stretch things out. Since the Orc Lord is in play, we suggest flavoring descriptions and battle scenes with touches of brutal wilderness savagery, and tough, nasty enemies living in dangerous terrain.

See story endings after the final battle for options on what happens after the PCs finish the last battle.

BATTLE 1: CATCH OF THE DAY

So far so good. You've got the hang of navigating the "raft" you're using to travel through Razoredge Gorge. You've been in the gorge for an hour now, seeing only the sharp-edged canyon walls that give the place its name. But things are too quiet.

LOCATION DESCRIPTION

The raft is actually two long, flat-bottomed boats tied and planked together at the middle. The surface area is 14 feet long and 10 feet across. With a lot of effort, someone could manage to cut and untie the lashings that bind the boats together, but that would create issues with stability and honestly wouldn't help the PCs get downriver at all. Treat cutting the raft in half as a bad idea with unpredictable consequences.

The boat is just swinging around a bend in the river where the canyon walls flatten out and the water slows. There's a large sandbar on the right that's 50 feet long and 15 feet wide, with lots of small, dry brush growing from it. On the far side, the river

is still at least 20 feet deep, but near the sandbar, it shallows to about 4 feet.

A group of orc raiders have staked this area out, waiting for the next set of fools to come downriver. A few archers are hidden on ledges along the canyon walls, sending signals to others waiting by the sand bar. The orcs there wait to trap any craft moving down the river, while the rest go hack them up.

Have each PC roll a DC 15 Wisdom check to notice the ambush. If more than half fail, the orcs surprise them (see Tactics). Otherwise, the heroes realize the truth as the net goes up.

Terrain & Traps

Net Across the River: The orcs at the sand bar have secured a bundle of ropes to the stone on the far side of the river, forming a thick net. It stretches across under the water. On their side, they've sunk a post into the sand as a brace. When the raft gets near, two of them will haul on the ropes and lift the net into the air, then tie off the ends to secure it.

If the PCs are surprised, they will have no chance to react to the net. Otherwise, have the net go in initiative order exactly halfway between when the first PC and the last goes (if there's an odd number of PCs, it goes right after the middle PC).

When it's the net's turn, the raft slams into it and stops. Any PC on the raft must roll a DC 18 check (probably Dex or Str) to avoid flying off the raft into the net and water. Those who fall off take 1d6 damage and are dazed until the end of their next turn. Roll a die to determine which side of the boat they are on: even is sandbar side, and odd is the deep water side.

Note, if any PC who acts before the net tries to slow the raft down, move the net down in initiative order by one PC for each PC that spends an action to do so (see raft).

Cutting the ropes to the net to free the raft is difficult because there are so many ropes, some underwater. It takes three DC 20 skill checks to do so; decide if that means the PCs flee the battle and have a campaign loss like warning drums relaying their approach, or whether they used good strategy to get past quickly.

Raft: While hung up in the net, the raft will be tilted slightly and water will be pushing at it and spraying over the sides as it turns sideways. Each turn while fighting on the raft, a creature must roll an easy saving throw (6+) at the start of its turn. On a failure, it takes a −2 penalty to attacks, defenses, and skill checks involving Strength or Dexterity until the start of its next turn.

PCs acting before the net in initiative order can use a standard and move action to row the raft toward the sandbank, or only a move action with a successful DC 10 Strength check. For each PC who does so, reduce the net below the next PC down in initiative order. If the net goes after all PCs, then the heroes successfully row the raft to the sandbank. (For example, for 5 PCs, the net normally goes after the third PC in initiative order. If two of the first three PCs spends actions to row and are successful, the raft will reach the shore.)

In the Water: PCs in the water might have a tough time of it. If they are on the sandbar side, they can stand and fight easily unless small. But if on the deep water side, they will get pushed into the net at the end of their turn unless they succeed on a DC 15 Strength, Constitution, or Dexterity check.

During their turn, a PC can use a move action and roll a DC 10 Strength check to try to swim to shallow water. On a failure, they lose their move and get pushed into the net. While pressed against the net they are weakened until they can move away from it. In addition, the constant chum created by the orcs means that a nasty breed of giant biting crawfish lives in the area.

The orcs who move into the water to attack have ropes tied around their waist to avoid being pulled into a net. If their rope is cut, they have to roll a normal save to swim away.

Any PCs who drop while in the water get one less death save than normal.

Biting Crayfish: When a creature ends its turn trapped against the net, it takes 8 damage from the biting crayfish. These creatures aren't a direct enemy with hit points, so there's nothing to attack unless you want there to be (let the players know they are a terrain obstacle rather than enemy).

Rocky ledge: The ledge is only 4 feet wide and is 25 feet off the river level. There is, however, a natural ramp leading from the sandbar to the ledge. Anyone who wants to climb to the ledge instead must succeed on a DC 12 Strength check. A creature that falls from the ledge takes 3d6 damage.

Attempting to bypass an orc on the ledge to get at one behind it is a dicey move that requires a DC 15 check in addition to a successful disengage, with failure resulting in a fall.

Monsters

The orcish archers are on the sandbar side of the river, up on the ledge. They are nearby, but moving to them along the ramp will take two move actions due to following the terrain.

There are a mix of orc bashers and berserkers hiding on the sandbar by the post. All wear rough hides and bear warpaint made from the red rock dust of the canyon in a wavy river sign.

Additional Reinforcements: If you want to challenge the PCs more, include a giant hungry crayfish that rises from the river depths (see stats).

#/Level of PCs	Orc Archer (A)	Orc Berserker (B)	Orc Basher Mook (M)
4 x 1st level	1	1	7 (1 mob)
5 x 1st level	2	1	6 (1 mob)
6 x 1st level	2	2	5 (1 mob)
4 x 2nd level	2	2	6 (1 mob)
5 x 2nd level	3	2	8 (1 mob)
6 x 2nd level	3	3	10 (2 mobs)

Tactics

The archers will fire upon the PCs as long as possible, targeting foes who aren't engaged with the others at first. If anyone comes up the ramp, the archer closest to that enemy will switch to melee, but any others behind it will continue to fire.

The bashers and berserkers will rush out to attack the PCs in the raft or thrown into the water on the sandbar side, hoping the water will delay the rest. They attack in pairs, or groups of three.

GOING MORE HIGH FANTASY WITH YOUR RAFT

You don't have to use a raft or boats constructed from wood. If it plays better, perhaps it's the carcass of some beast, the slowly deteriorating stalk of a giant mushroom, the lashed together floating bones of giants, a thousand small elven baskets tied together, or whatever else you desire (or the players suggest off-handedly). Whatever it is, consider the benefits and disadvantages it might offer the PCs, and make sure it will float in water... at least most of the way down the gorge.

If they are losing badly, the orcs might cut the net ropes tied to the post, hoping the raft and their enemies float away. Of course, PCs on the sand bar might choose to do the same (but see Net in Terrain & Tactics).

LOOT

The orc raiders of the Razoredge tribe have had a few victories with their unorthodox method of ambush. There is a total of 40 gp in various coins and trinkets among them, in addition to the usual odd fare of orc belongings.

One of the archers is carrying an adventurer-tier *lethal strike* arrow unknowingly (+1d10 damage on a hit). (Of if you're feeling nasty, you could hit one of the PCs with another randomly selected magic arrow in the fight to foreshadow this find.)

ICONS

A PC that has relationship advantages with the Orc Lord could use one or more of them to intimidate some of the basher mooks by announcing their "battle name" or their "tribe," convincing one or two to flee while still alive.

A PC that has relationship advantages with the Emperor or High Druid could use one or more of them to automatically succeed on any skill check involving the raft or navigating the water during the battle.

ORC BASHER

"Bash and brawl. Smash and crawl."

1st level mook [HUMANOID]
Initiative: +5

Spiked club +6 vs. AC—5 damage
Natural 1: The basher "accidentally" smashes another mook in its mob, if there's one also engaged with the target.

Bash and brawl: Orc bashers gain a +1 attack bonus with melee attacks for each *spiked club* attack that has hit the target that turn.

AC	16	
PD	16	HP 7 (mook)
MD	10	

Mook: Kill one orc basher mook for every 7 damage you deal to the mob.

ORCISH ARCHER

It takes patience to be a true archer. Orcs lack that. So they fire as many arrows as possible, hope for the worst, and work themselves toward a frenzy that demands the sword.

2nd level archer [HUMANOID]
Initiative: +5

Scimitar +6 vs. AC—6 damage

R: Short bow +6 vs. AC—7 damage
Natural 1–5: Reroll the attack against a random nearby creature. If the rerolled attack is also a natural 1–5, the orcish archer takes 3 damage from sheer agonized frustration, but it doesn't get to make another attack.

Final frenzy: When the escalation die is 3+, the orcish archer gains a +3 bonus to melee attacks and melee damage.

AC	18	
PD	17	HP 32
MD	11	

ORC BERSERKER

2nd level troop [HUMANOID]
Initiative: +5

Greataxe +7 vs. AC—8 damage
Dangerous: The crit range of attacks by orcs expands by 3 unless they are staggered.

Unstoppable: When an orc berserker drops to 0 hp, it does not immediately die. Ignore any damage in excess of 0 hp, roll 2d6, and give the berserker that many temporary hit points. No other healing can affect the berserker or give it more temporary hit points: when the temporary hp are gone, the berserker dies.

AC	16	
PD	15	HP 40
MD	13	

ADDITIONAL REINFORCEMENTS

GIANT CRAYFISH

2nd level wrecker [BEAST]
Initiative: +4

Snapping claws +7 vs. AC (2 attacks)—4 damage
Natural 16+: The crayfish grabs the target unless it's already grabbing two creatures. It deals automatic damage (4) with one claw to any creature it's grabbing during its turn instead of making an attack.

AC	18	
PD	15	HP 38
MD	11	

NEXT STEPS

Unless the raft ends up spilling downstream when the net is cut, the PCs should be able to get it to the sandbank safely and remove the net. The orcs have a small camp just up a gulley through the canyon ridge. It holds a few supplies, but looks like only a temporary camp.

After a quick rest, the PCs can continue down the river toward **Battle 2: Zip-lines and Wardrums**.

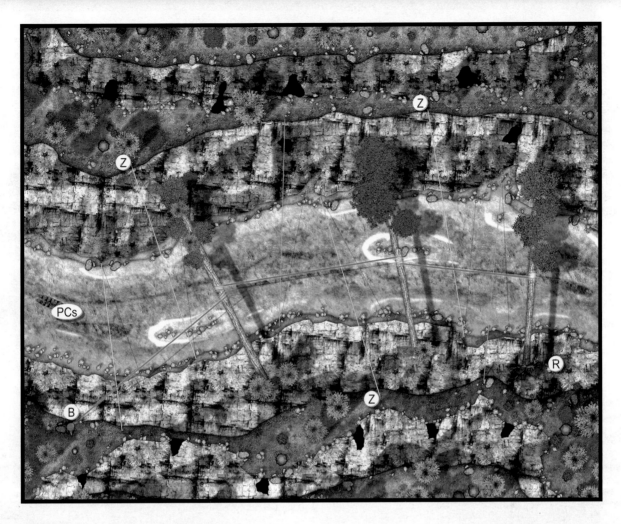

BATTLE 2: ZIP-LINES AND WARDRUMS

The river begins to pick up speed as the gorge narrows around you. The sharp, rocky cliffs are riddled with small caves and low bushes that could hide almost anything. Higher up the canyon walls, you see a ridge of large pine trees, some of which have fallen into the gorge and wedged. As you go under one large trunk, you see a rope extending away from it downstream to another similar log. That's when the drumming starts.

LOCATION DESCRIPTION

This battle happens as the raft travels downriver. The current is strong and trying to stop would probably result in flipping the raft.

The gorge narrows to between 30 and 60 feet wide through this stretch, with the canyon walls climbing as high as 150 feet up. The caves are occupied by many cave orcs, who act more like a terrain obstacle than monsters as they throw rocks down at the passing raft, staying out of open daylight.

The real danger comes from three places: the river should anyone end up in the drink, an orc battle screamer in a large mobile basket-cage overhead that keeps pace with the moving raft as it slides down a rope on a pulley-basket, and orc zip-liners that use zip-lines to land on the raft and attack.

Once the orc threat ends, they have one last parting gift for the PCs—a large boulder that will send them scrambling.

Note, there's a lot of moving parts to this battle, so it's a good idea to read through each of the Terrain & Traps sections a couple of times. Or, if you prefer, you can simplify it and just have the orcs zip-lining onto the raft without any other effects.

TERRAIN & TRAPS

Hurled Rocks from Cave Orcs: Once the battle screamer starts drumming, the cave orcs along the river gorge wake up and start hurling rocks at the raft. When the escalation die reaches 1, randomly choose two PCs at the start of each round and make the following attack against each:

Thrown rocks +7 vs. AC—5 damage

There's basically an unending supply of these cave orcs mooks, but the PCs can remove this threat each round by attacking them. Each one has the following stats: 7 hp; AC 15; PD 13; MD 11. If the PCs kill at least two during a round, the cave orcs don't make the two attacks during the next round as the PCs have cleared the way for the moment.

The Drummer's Basket: For the purposes of this running battle, there is only one battle screamer in a basket with a single stat block, but it's represented by multiple drummers. At the end of each round, the drummer's basket comes to the end of the rope it's sliding along, stopping at a log wedged in the canyon. But then a drummer in a new basket on the other side begins following the raft.

The PCs can attack the battle screamer directly (it remains nearby as they travel downriver), or they can try to attack the rope the basket-cage is sliding along. Doing so will take a well-aimed ranged attack, however, due to the moving raft and height of the rope. The rope has an AC and PD of 20, and an attack must hit and deal 5 damage to sever the line. When this happens, the drummer plunges with a scream into the river.

But it's not as easy as that since the drummers keep trailing the PCs until the battle screamer drops to 0 hp. The first time the line is severed, reduce the battle screamer to its staggered hit point value, or deal 8 damage to it if it's already staggered. The second time the line is severed, it dies if it has 8 hp or less. Otherwise, reduce it to 1 hp. When the battle screamer drops to 0 hp, or has its line severed a third time, it's dead (no more drummers). Remember that all the drummers use a single battle screamer stat block.

If the idea of multiple battle screamers using a single stat block just doesn't work for you, feel free to make it a single screamer who slides down a rope then transfers a new hook to the next line and keeps going. Boost the rope's HP to 10 and say the PCs have to do all that damage in one turn to sever the rope or it resets due to a new rope. If the rope is severed, the battle screamer falls and dies.

Zip-lines: The zip-lines the orcs use to drop onto the raft are secured ropes angled steeply downward across the gorge from one side or the other, allowing them to use a leather strap to slide down the line. PCs who want to watch for these zip-lines can try to attack them ahead of time to disrupt a zip-liner's attack. The last PC in initiative order, or anyone readying an action to attack a zip-line, can roll a DC 15 Wisdom check; success means they spot a line being used (there are many, not all are being used). A PC who spots a line in-use can make a ranged attack against it to sever the line (AC and PD of 17, since they are closer to the river, and 1 hp).

When a line is severed, if it's a normal hit, the orc still makes it to the raft, but lands badly and is dazed (save ends). On a crit, the orc falls short and misses this battle.

The River: Anyone that goes into the river will get pulled along with the raft as it travels downriver, but where the flat-bottomed boats go over the rocks, creatures tend to smash into them. While in the water, at the end of a creature's turn, it must roll a save; on a failure, it takes 6 damage and is dazed until the end of its next turn from being smashed and drowned.

Getting out of the river into the raft requires a DC 13 check, or DC 10 if an ally reserves a move action to help.

Creatures fighting while in the river take a −2 penalty to attacks, defenses, and skill checks, and might not be able to do some actions (GM's call).

The Raft: The raft is fairly stable and there's not a lot of high boulders sticking out of the river to cause trouble for those on board. If someone throws the raft into a spin, or separates the two boats, things get more dicey. Each creature fighting on the raft must roll an easy save (6+) at the start of its turn; on a failure, it takes a −2 penalty to attacks, defenses, and skill checks.

Monsters

The battle screamer in the basket trolley above starts things off, waking the cave orcs as it paces the raft from above.

The orc zip-liners wait on the canyon walls to zip down to the passing raft, where they will jump on and attack. Instead of weapons, they wear leather gauntlets set with bone barbs that they fight with; the gauntlets help them hang onto the strip of leather they use to zip-line down.

The boulder roller orc isn't a normal enemy with a stat block. Instead, it's an orc waiting at the end of the canyon who will tumble a boulder at the raft as it passes out of their territory (see **Tactics**).

Additional Reinforcements: If you want to challenge the PCs more, have an orc tusker (*Bestiary*, page 157) drop down onto the raft from a zip-line too.

#/Level of PCs	Battle Screamer* (B)	Orc Zip-liner (Z)	Boulder Roller Orc** (R)
4 x 1st level	1	3	1
5 x 1st level	1	4	1
6 x 1st level	1	5	1
4 x 2nd level	1	4	1
5 x 2nd level	1	5	2
6 x 2nd level	1	6	2

* One stat block, even though there are multiple "drummers."
** No stat block, see Tactics.

TACTICS

The orc battle screamer plays a skull drum as it slides along in its basket-cage above the PCs. Each time it hits with the drum attack, it will either let an orc ally make an attack, or make an extra check to get into the raft from the river as a move action. Even though it begins drumming to start the battle, it will go last in the round to give the zip-liners time to get on the raft.

The orc zip-liners use straightforward tactics. Each round two of them will zip down their line as a move action and land on the raft, then attack with their bone gauntlets (to the maximum number of zip-liners in the battle). If the PCs do something (besides shooting the line) to make it harder for the orcs to land on the raft that round, make it an easy save (6+) or the orc lands badly and is dazed until the end of its turn. The zip-liners will look for opportunities to knock foes into the river.

Boulder Roller Orc: Once the battle screamer and zip-liners have dropped to 0 hp and the battle seems over, this orc has a last surprise for the PCs. It doesn't have a stat block; what it does is roll a placed boulder off the cliff toward the raft. The boulder doesn't hit the raft, but it does make a big splash. Each PC must roll a save; on a failure, they get thrown in the river and battered by rapids over a few minutes until they can get back into the raft, losing one recovery. If you're feeling nice, you could allow a DC 20 Wisdom check for the PCs to see the boulder coming and gain a +4 bonus to the save.

If there is a second boulder roller orc listed for the battle, that boulder comes in just after the first. Anyone still on the raft must roll another save, or go into the river (so no PC can lose more than 1 recovery this way).

BATTLE/TERRAIN EFFECTS PER ROUND

Escalation die	Effect
0	Battle Screamer starts drumming, 2 zip-liners
1	Rocks, 2 zip-liners (or remainder)
2	Rocks, 2 zip-liners (or remainder)
3	Rocks, Boulder?
4	Rocks, Boulder?
5	Rocks, Boulder?
6+	Rocks, Boulder?
End of Battle	Boulder

LOOT

Most likely, the only loot the PCs can get will come from zip-liner corpse on the raft, unless you're feeling generous and the battle screamer just happens to float by. Each zip-liner wears a special badge of courage in the form of a small amber disc amulet showing crossed arms in gauntlets worth 25 gp each.

GETTING NASTY WITH BOULDERS

If you've got a group that can handle orcs with ease and shows no fear, one way to ratchet up the tension is to instead start boulders rolling at the end of each round once the escalation die reaches 3. That'll give the PCs incentive to end the battle quickly. Once all the orcs are defeated, roll one last boulder that round and be done.

PCs that fail their save and go in the water while a battle is still going on are floating along with the raft and can still get back on it as normal, but they still lose the recovery from a bad fall.

Icons

A PC that has relationship advantages with any icon could use one or more of them to help sever the drummer's line, giving a big bonus to the attack (+5) or not even requiring an attack with multiple advantages (yes, this is combat-related, but it seems like there could be many interesting stories why someone turns out to be a great shot in this situation).

A PC that has relationship advantages with the Orc Lord, Elf Queen, High Druid, or maybe the Archmage could use one or more of them to navigate the raft each turn as a standard action to avoid thrown rocks, or help them stay in the raft or get back in the raft without a roll.

ORC BATTLE SCREAMER

Some tribes have just enough culture to support pseudo-bards whose battle screams sound like marching hymns to orcish ears. They use skull drums and sharpened flutes made from the femurs of their enemies. You don't even want to know what they make bagpipes out of.

3rd level leader [HUMANOID]
Initiative: End of round

Sharpened flute or club-like drumstick +9 vs. AC—10 damage

Orcish Instruments: Choose ONE

R: Skull drum +7 vs. MD—8 damage, and as a free action, one nearby orc ally can move or make a basic attack (doesn't trigger special abilities)

R: Bone flute +7 vs. MD—8 damage, and one nearby orc ally deals +1d6 damage on a hit during its next turn

R: War bagpipes—1d3 nearby or far away enemies that can hear the bagpipes must immediately roll a normal save; on a failure, the target is hampered until the end of its next turn

AC	22	
PD	15	**HP 33**
MD	15	

ORC ZIP-LINER

With a yell, an orc whizzes towards you on a rope. You'd have to be crazy to try this! Yes.

1st level troop [HUMANOID]
Initiative: +5

Bone gauntlets +6 vs. AC (2 attacks)—2 damage
  Natural 18+: The target is knocked off-balance; it must make an easy save (6+) or fall into the river.

Zip-line specialist: This orc uses zip-lines to reach the battle. During the round the orc uses its zip-line, if it rolls a natural 20 with the attack, it knocks the target off-balance (and into the river).

AC	16	
PD	16	**HP 26**
MD	10	

NEXT STEPS

This battle should put fear of orcs into the PCs, preparing them for worse. After they catch their breath and take a quick rest, they'll be ready for the big showdown with the Razoredge Gorge orcs in **Battle 3: Razoredge Orc Camp.**

BATTLE 3: RAZOREDGE ORC CAMP

The steep canyon walls of the gorge seem to be behind you now as the river begins to slow and the cliffs flatten out. As you pass around a tight bend, the current spins you into calm water formed by a long sandbar and the raft hangs up on some bushes in the shallows. That would be fine, except for the surprised-looking orcs fishing in the shallows, and a full orc camp spread out behind them on a sandy tree-filled beach. With howls to the rest of their tribe, they lift their spears toward you.

LOCATION DESCRIPTION

The camp holds the leader of the Razoredge orcs, a shaman named Tok'rash Razorknife, and the warriors who follow him.

The main camp covers an area from the beach to some short cliffs surrounding it that are riddled with caves where many of the orcs sleep during the day. The beach is 90 feet wide and stretches back 60 to 70 feet to the cliffs (far away), which climb to a height of 60 feet, then slowly descend down the back side. A narrow ledge leads up the cliffs to the caves, and then on up over the top, switching back once on the right.

There are a few 80-foot tall beech trees scattered along the beach. A few tents of varying sizes are pitched on lines strung between some of the trees. There's also some ziplines from the caves on the cliffs down to branches on trees by the water.

Between the tents is a large fire pit with low, smoldering coals giving off heat and a little smoke. A small deer carcass hangs gutted from a tree branch not far from the fire.

TERRAIN & TRAPS

The Raft & the River: The raft is caught up on some short trees/bushes at the edge of the beach. It will take four move actions (any number of PCs) to free it enough to push back toward the slow current on the far side of the river.

The river where the raft is stuck is shallow (2 feet) and sandy, so footing isn't an issue. Anyone farther out needs to make a DC 10 Strength check to swim back to the shallows, otherwise they gain no ground as the current pushes them.

Fire: The fire pit is 4 feet in diameter, but the coals are almost dead. Anyone entering (or pushed into) the pit will take 1d6 fire damage, and the same amount if they end their turn there.

Beech Trees: The trees have low branches and are easy to climb. If a PC is interested in the trees or chooses to climb the ones by the beach, they will notice four zip lines connected back up to the ledges. Climbing a rope up to the ledges requires two move actions and a DC 15 Strength check, and they are weakened while doing so.

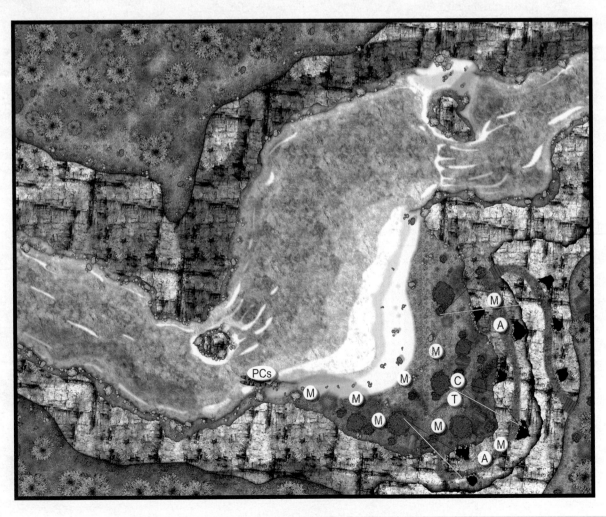

Any dicey moves while in the trees requires a DC 15 Dexterity check; on a failure, that creature falls and takes 2d6 damage.

Cliffs: Moving from the ground up the ledge to the switchback takes one move action, and a second move action to get to the top caves, or a PC can climb the zip lines (see trees above) or directly climb the cliffs with a DC 18 Strength check. Of course, the orcs will be coming to the PCs, mostly.

The ropes secured to the top ledge and tied to the lower branches of the beech trees close to the water allow the orcs there to zipline down with a leather strap. The Razoredge orc warriors on the ledge will try to slam into a PC standing at the edge of the beach or in the water near the trees.

Using the zipline to attack this way requires a move action and standard action. When one of the mooks tries it, use the following attack (and GM, feel free to let a natural 1 mean the orc slams into an ally or takes damage from plowing into the ground or a tree limb).

C: Zipline smash +7 vs. PD—8 damage, and the target is dazed (save ends); in addition, the orc takes 4 damage
Natural 18+: The orc times it perfectly and takes no damage.
Miss: The orc takes 1d8 damage and ends up in the river.

Monsters

Tok'rash the shaman will be in a tent toward the cliffs at the start of the battle and will emerge to kill the intruders and issue commands to the warriors.

Tok'rash has (somewhat) tamed a bear he unoriginally calls Claws. He has fed it on humanoid meat and trained it to attack anyone attacking him. Claws comes out of the tent with Tok'rash, lets out a roar, and stays close to the shaman. If there's a second bear, its name is, of course, Fang.

The orcish archers are scattered between the base of the cliffs and the cliff ledge. The Razoredge orc warriors are fishing in the shallows, scattered about the camp, and up on the cliffs waiting to swing down.

This is a double-strength battle, so there' are a lot of mooks. If you want to reduce the number of enemies, add an orc berserker and remove 4 mooks (1st level) or 3 mooks (2nd level). Also, if there's more than one mob, feel free to hold it back until the escalation die reaches 2 if you're worried this battle might overwhelm you or your players.

Additional Reinforcements: If you want to challenge the PCs more, have a heavy hitter, an ogre named Quarg (core rulebook, page 240) rush out of a tent to put a stop to all of the racket. If that feels a bit too much for the PCs, especially those at 1st level, make the ogre old and half-blind, with half the hit points of a normal ogre.

Tactics

Tok'rash will stay back, using his *battle curse* attack for as long as he can. Claws (and Fang) will stick close, intercepting any non-orc who tries to attack the shaman. If he has both bears, Tok'rash might send one of them to attack a nearby enemy who's causing trouble. While brave, the shaman didn't get to be leader by being overly stupid. He will use move actions to try to put interceptors between him and his enemies.

#/Level of PCs	Tok'rash (T)	Claws (C)	Orcish Archer (A)	Razoredge Orc Mook (M)
4 x 1st level	1	1	2	8 (1 mob)
5 x 1st level	1	1	3	11 (2 mobs)
6 x 1st level	1	2	4	9 (2 mobs)
4 x 2nd level	1	2	3	10 (2 mobs)
5 x 2nd level	1*	2	4	9 (2 mobs)
6 x 2nd level	1*	2**	4	15 (3 mobs)

* Make Tok'rash double strength: he has 72 hp, his *spear* attack deals 12 damage, and his curse deals 8 psychic damage.

** Give each bear a +1 attack bonus, and its *bite* attack deals 3 extra damage (9 total).

Half the archers will be on the cliff ledges, and half on the beach back by the tents at the foot of the cliff. They will try to stay mobile and use ranged attacks as much as possible, until engaged by two or more enemies.

The Razoredge orc mooks are scattered everywhere. At least three of them will be in the water with hunting spears, and at least two will be on the top ledge ready to swing down. The rest will emerge from the tents with howls, ganging up on the PCs as much as possible. They are smart enough to use basic tactics, but generally trust in their ferocity to see them through.

Loot

The Razoredge orcs have managed to do fairly well of late raiding river travelers and those in the surrounding lands. Scattered among the various orcs is a total of 200 gp in mixed coinage and small jewelry.

In Tok'rash's tent, there's a leather satchel holding 75 gp and various war trophies (most disgusting) but including a small ceremonial jade blade worth 50 gp. There's also an oval iron disc with two crossed axes painted on it in red dye—any PC with an Orc Lord relationship will know it for a summons from the icon's lieutenants to a council of war. Whoever bears such a token might be given safe passage to and from the council—though it would help to *look* like servants of the Orc Lord instead of adventurers. It might be useful to the PCs or of interest to those watching the Orc Lord's troop movements for signs of the next attack.

Icons

A PC that has relationship advantages with the Orc Lord, Archmage, Dwarf King, Elf Queen, Lich King, or the Three (the Blue) could use one or more of them to remove the curse effect from a PC (from the shaman's *battle curse* attack), perhaps by bringing up a dishonorable action that Tok'rash committed in the past.

A PC with one or more advantages with the High Druid could use them to distract one of the bears for a round or two, whether it's consuming a convenient piece of humanoid flesh the character happens to throw at it, or through other means of communication.

A PC that has an advantage with any icon could use it to break the morale of the orcs before the battle starts, causing them all to take a –1 attack penalty or suffer some other setback (reputation is important to the orcs), at least until at least one PC drops to 0 hit points.

TOK'RASH, ORC SHAMAN

2nd level leader [HUMANOID]
Initiative: +5

Spear +6 vs. AC—6 damage
Dangerous: The crit range of attacks by orcs expands by 3 unless they are staggered.

R: Battle curse +7 vs. MD (1d3 nearby enemies)—4 psychic damage, and for the rest of the battle, melee attacks by orcs deal +1d4 damage against the target (non-cumulative)

AC	18	
PD	12	**HP 36**
MD	16	

CLAWS/FANG, BROWN BEAR

Big, mean, and a taste for humanoid flesh. What's not to hate.

3rd level wrecker [BEAST]
Initiative: +5

Bite +8 vs. AC—10 damage
Natural even hit: The target takes 1d10 extra damage from a claw swipe.

Likes man-flesh: The crit range of the bear's attack against humans expands by 1.

AC	18	
PD	18	**HP 45**
MD	13	

ORCISH ARCHER

It takes patience to be a true archer. Orcs lack that. So they fire as many arrows as possible, hope for the worst, and work themselves toward a frenzy that demands the sword.

2nd level archer [HUMANOID]
Initiative: +5

Scimitar +6 vs. AC—6 damage
R: Short bow +6 vs. AC—7 damage
Natural 1–5: Reroll the attack against a random nearby creature. If the rerolled attack is also a natural 1–5, the orcish archer takes 3 damage from sheer agonized frustration, but it doesn't get to make another attack.

Final frenzy: When the escalation die is 3+, the orcish archer gains a +3 bonus to melee attacks and melee damage.

AC	18	
PD	17	**HP 32**
MD	11	

RAZOREDGE ORC WARRIOR

Most of the ones who survive are fiercer than the rest, not smarter.

2nd level mook [HUMANOID]
Initiative: +6

Spear or axe +7 vs. AC—5 damage

Ferocious: The crit range of the Razoredge orc warrior's melee attacks expand by an amount equal to the escalation die –2.

AC	18	
PD	15	**HP 8 (mook)**
MD	10	

Mook: Kill one Razoredge orc warrior mook for every 8 damage you deal to the mob.

ADDITIONAL REINFORCEMENTS

QUARG, OGRE

Large 3rd level troop [GIANT]

Initiative: +5

Big honkin' club +7 vs. AC—18 damage
> *Miss:* Half damage.

Big shove +9 vs. PD (each enemy engaged with ogre)—1d6
> damage, and the target pops free from the ogre
> *Quick use:* This power only requires a quick action (once per round) instead of a standard action when the escalation die is even.

AC	19	
PD	16	**HP 90 (or 45)**
MD	12	

NEXT STEPS

With the Razoredge orc tribe defeated, the PCs have made it much safer to travel the river, at least until some new threat moves in. If the heroes needed to continue downriver, the gorge ends shortly after the camp and becomes open land, with civilization only a few hours away by raft.

Other story results depend on the opening used; see endings below.

RAFTING RAZOREDGE GORGE STORY ENDINGS

Here are outcomes for each story opening, detailing what success or failure might mean.

If the PCs fought all three battles, remember to give them a full heal-up.

WE NEED TO GET DOWNRIVER QUICK

Success: The PCs reach their destination in time by rafting the river. They accomplish whatever they were trying to do, and word gets out, starting a competition among adventurers to make the Rivergorge Run in under two days. Their fame also brings them interest from the representatives of an icon, who needs to transport something somewhere in a very short amount of time, and they seem like just the heroes to do it.

Failure: The PCs fail to reach their destination in time, probably suffering a campaign loss. They miss whatever opportunity was waiting, or their delay allows their enemies' plans to be set in motion.

A TEST OF COURAGE

Success: The PCs make it through the Gorge unscathed. The spiritcaller seems surprised to see them (or not, because you know, spirits). But he honors his word and gives the PCs the location they seek for showing such great courage. He might also give the heroes some information that will help them in their upcoming endeavor if they're willing to use advantages.

Failure: When the PCs return to the half-orc's camp, it's gone. He's packed up and moved on. They'll have to find what they seek some other way, probably one more dangerous than rafting the river.

INTO THE RAIDER'S DEN

Success: By navigating the river through Razoredge Gorge, the PCs travel quick enough to take out the Razoredge orc tribe leadership before the other raiding groups can rally. Demoralized and without strong leadership, the orcs in the hills fall to infighting and break apart into smaller bands that don't pose as much of a threat to the area. Even better, the mayor of a nearby town had posted a reward for anyone who could solve the problem, so the PCs just have to convince her that they did.

Failure: The PCs' attempt to strike the Razoredge orc tribe leadership directly was bold, but doomed to fail. Now the orcs have increased their defenses in the gorge, and they raze the closest softskin (as they call humans) village to pay for their insolence. A nearby town will surely be next. The town's mayor has connections to one of the PCs' icons and pressures the heroes to help defend the town, to make up for riling the orcs up.

GUARD THE SILVER SHIPMENT

Success: The PCs fend off the attacks of the Razoredge orcs and manage to get the silver shipment to the jeweler for the dwarves, picking up some nice loot along the way. The dwarves gain the contract, pay the heroes well, and some of the PCs make good connections to the Dwarf King's people (gaining an advantage or another opportunity), or to the Emperor (each PC gets a 6 with the Emperor that lasts until they use it or level up).

Failure: The PCs lose the silver somewhere during the ride down the river while fighting and can't find the lockbox again. When the dwarves hear that the PCs aren't dead, but that the shipment is gone, they're not happy. Any future dealings with dwarves or Dwarf King folk until the next level take a −2 penalty to social skill checks, and any 6s the PCs roll with the Orc Lord or Dwarf King are 5s instead as word of their actions/failure gets around.

BATTLE SCENE CONNECTIONS

The stories from this set of battle scenes can lead to scenes in future books:

Temple Reclamation (Priestess): The PCs find a prisoner among the orc camp. It's a priest from the temple of Lasturr. He tells them that a half-orc shaman with a troop of goblinoids came to the Razoredge orcs to see if they would join her in a raid on the temple. They had made the priest tell them of the temple's riches, and then traded him to the orcs to get the meeting.

The King's Tribute (Dwarf King): After the orc battle, the PCs find a magic item among their loot. It's the item that Lord Silveraxe seeks, taken from a thief who was trying to cross orc lands.

ORC LORD: CONQUER & DEFEND

LEVEL RANGE: 4–5

The themes of this set of battles are civilization vs. barbarism, making strategic choices, and being able to protect what you take. This set of battles works best at the borders of civilization where the hordes of the Orc Lord seek to push into the soft underbelly of the Empire.

Tenrock Pass is one of the many low passes among the Giantwalk Mountains (or Frost Range, or another range of hills in the Dragon Empire) that provides passage from the empire to the uncivilized lands beyond. And like most of those other passes, a stronghold guards the pass from unwanted visitors. Some of these holds are Imperial outposts, but others are maintained by the dwarves of Anvil or other forces that wish to keep the barbarians at bay.

Recently, the Orc Lord's forces overran Tenrock Hold, the small stronghold at the top of the pass meant to guard against such forces. For one reason or another, the PCs must travel to the pass and retake the hold and defend it until slow-moving reinforcements (Imperial, dwarven, or other) arrive to refill the garrison.

CONQUER & DEFEND STORY OPENINGS

- **Defeating the Enemy:** One or more PCs with a conflicted or negative relationship with the Orc Lord learns that his forces have taken a nearby stronghold on Tenrock Pass. If those forces are allowed to reinforce it, it could provide a staging point for more trouble. Re-taking the hold would be a serious blow to the Orc Lord's plans in the region.
- **Trial Run:** One or more PCs with a positive or conflicted relationship with the Orc Lord are ordered to take a nearby stronghold of little strategic value and then hold it against determined invaders. The enemies all fly the Orc Lord's flag, but they're expendable or being deliberately targeted by weird Orc Lord politics. The icon wishes to do a trial run to examine strategic weaknesses on a small scale before tacking a similar target, but one that is much larger and more important.
- **A Call for Help:** A rider or other messenger reaches the PCs bearing news that Tenrock Hold, a nearby outpost guarding a pass to the lands beyond the empire is under attack by barbarous creatures of the Orc Lord's horde. If the stronghold falls, the local region will be in danger from raiding barbarians. The PCs are the only ones capable of helping in time. If they go, they'll probably be too late to help the current defenders, but not too late to stem future attacks.
- **Opportunistic Altruism:** Word reaches the PCs that nearby Tenrock Hold has been overrun by Orc Lord forces. A counterattack is being organized by the empire (or local authorities, or whatever lord is responsible for the stronghold), but it will take a few days to reach the pass. There's just enough time for the PCs to get there first, deal with the raiders, and search the place before reinforcements arrive. It just so happens that something one of the PCs is searching for was kept by the former (now deceased) commander of the stronghold. If they hurry, they can acquire the item and hand the place over to the authorities without further losses for the forces of the light, a win-win.

ALTERNATE ICONS

 High Druid: If the empire is at odds with the forces of the wild and it's escalated to barbarian hordes invading civilization, these battles scenes could work for the High Druid's forces. Perhaps the goblins and orcs are forest races of wild humans and bizarrely small elves, and the giants could be elementals or living trees.

 Dwarf King: Instead of a pass into civilization, the stronghold protects a route into the underworld, or a key thoroughfare into the parts of the underworld the Dwarf King truly protects, and these battles should work fine as is with orcs and other evil humanoids. If the PCs are there for an item, the Dwarf King's people might notice its disappearance after the fact and come looking.

ICONS IN PLAY

Characters that have relationships (and story-guide advantages) with the Orc Lord, Emperor, Dwarf King, and maybe the Elf Queen or Crusader should be able to shine in these battle scenes. Moreso than PCs with other icon relationships, feel free to give such PCs extra knowledge about the opposition, make checks to pull off fun actions the players might suggest, and use their advantages to particularly good effect, such as negating or bypassing some of the advantages or abilities of the enemies.

Conquer & Defend Overview

This set of battle scenes occurs in and around a stronghold on Tenrock Pass. In Battle 1, the PCs must find a way to take Tenrock Hold back from the Orc Lord's troops that have invaded it (goblins and orcs). Whether through battle, trickery, or a combination of both, the PCs must get inside the hold and win out over a double-strength set of enemies, many of which are mooks.

Their victory is short-lived, however, because they have little time before reinforcements of troops arrive from the wilds, forcing the PCs to switch from invaders to defenders. Battle 2 is also a double-strength battle, as the Orc Lord's forces throw everything they have in the area against the PCs, including a hill giant, battlecasters, or more orcs.

GM, feel free to expand upon these battles by including fights with additional enemies on the way to the hold, more foes inside the stronghold itself, or encounters with other NPCs in the place that the heroes might not expect (prisoners or trapped diplomats, for example).

The battles outlined here can take place over a few tens of minutes or hours, depending on the setting. Since the Orc Lord is in play, the enemies presented here are the evil humanoids and barbarous creatures that make up his hordes. The location, a hold at the top of a pass, should have sheer cliffs, rock fields, and desolate but beautiful panoramas.

See story endings after the final battle for options on what happens after the PCs finish the last battle.

BATTLE I: TAKING TENROCK HOLD

You followed the winding path back and forth up the mountainous ascent, moving ever closer to the low point between two small peaks—Tenrock Pass. The stronghold is just ahead and above you. A fifteen foot gray stone wall stretches across the narrow V-shaped opening at the top of the ridge, with steep cliffs bordering the path on one side, and a long fall on the other. A single large wooden gate bisects the wall, and goblinoids patrol the battlements along the top of it. There's also a tall stone tower overlooking the path ahead; you can't tell if anyone is up there watching for trouble from your current hiding spot around the bend in the cliff.

Location Description

The stronghold is built into the cliffs of the peak on the left of the path with a 120 x 80 foot courtyard extending away from it to the far side of the pass (see map). The wall facing the PCs is 100 feet long and 15 feet high, with a walkway and battlements across the top (12 feet across). A single 12 x 10 gate of sturdy wood timbers with a heavy beam barring the inside is set near the middle of the wall.

A similar wall, only smaller at 70 feet wide, protects the hold from the opposite side of the pass. There is only an archway there where the path passes through, since the wooden gate was torn off during the previous siege and now lies outside the wall upon the ground. A barricade of timbers and the bodies of dead defenders on spikes now lies in the archway to slow down enemies entering that way.

Finally, a 50-foot tall stone tower with stair encircling the outside rises up near the center of the courtyard. The top is partially enclosed with four archways leading to an open walkway around the outside, allowing sentries to view traffic coming up the passes, as well as giving them an angle for ranged attacks on both gates.

The stronghold itself is a simple structure built into the cliffside and holding seven chambers: barracks, kitchen and larder, dining hall, storage room, natural spring/well, and a commander's quarters. The main door to that structure has been bashed in as well, and now hangs poorly on one hinge keeping out only the cool weather.

The stronghold is currently guarded by the former invaders—a group of elite goblin ground troops, orc heavies and archers, and an orc siege captain.

This is a double-strength battle, but there are a few less mooks than normal since it might take the PCs a round or two to get past the walls.

Terrain & Traps

Outer Wall (PC side): The 100-foot-long outer wall isn't high (15 feet) but it is sheer with few handholds. To make it more difficult for anyone to scale, the invaders have spiked the bodies of the previous defenders (humans) along it, and now the upper half is coated in blood and gore that makes the stone slippery. Climbing to the top requires a DC 23 Strength check with failure meaning the climber slides back down to the ground.

There are battlements at the top and a 3-foot drop to the walkway that provides some protection to those on the wall. Anyone fighting on the top of the wall can attempt to hurl an engaged enemy off the wall. Doing so is a standard action and requires a DC 20 Strength or Dexterity check (or a DC 15 check to avoid being thrown off) or a normal save for the defenders. Anyone falling off takes 2d6 damage.

Due to the bend in the road leading to the hold, once the PCs break cover, they are far away from the gate and wall. It requires two move actions to reach it, and wary defenders will be able to make ranged attacks at that point.

Outer Wall (away from PCs): This wall is 70 feet wide and similar to the opposite one, except instead of blood and gore, old grease coats the upper part of the wall to make it slick.

There is more open space on this side of the hold for seeing approaching enemies, but realistically, ranged attacks against approaching enemies won't be accurate enough to hit until those enemies are far away.

Gates: The gate is made from thick wood and is sturdy on the side the PCs are approaching from. Breaking it down will be difficult, requiring a successful DC 30 Strength check (or DC 20 if the main bar is removed and it is only being held from inside). See **Monsters** for the possibility of having the invaders open it from the inside.

The opposite gate is gone with only a barricade keeping someone from entering (requires an extra move action to push it out of the way or to slide through).

Cliffs: The cliffs to the left of the path are part of the peak on that side and rise steeply near the stronghold. It is possible to scale them and get above the gate and main stronghold, but the cliffs are treacherous and it's windy. It requires two successful DC 22 Strength or Dexterity checks in a row to do so. Failure on either check means a 50-foot or more fall back to the path for 4d8 damage, and a reset of the checks. Once successful, a PC will be on top of the stronghold, 30 feet above the courtyard, and nearly even with the top of the tower; at that point, it's an easier DC 18 check to climb down into the courtyard (2d8 damage on a fall).

The cliffs to the right of the path drop steeply away (between a 80- and 150-foot drop). Scaling the cliffs along the wall is difficult and requires a successful DC 22 Strength or Dexterity check to reach the far peak, then a second check to ascend above the wall. Failure of either check means loss of movement, and failure by 5 or more means a fall of 80 to 100 feet and 5d8 damage. At that point, there are two options to get back up to the path near the outer wall, climb the steep cliffs (DC 22, with failure meaning another fall), or moving back down the pass 1/3 of a mile to ascend at an easier point (out of battle).

Watch Tower: The top of the watch tower is far away from each wall and gate, so it takes two moves from the wall or gate arch to reach the top of the tower. The tower is 10 x 10 and 50 feet high, with exposed stairs ascending it up the outside. If you wish, ranged attackers in the tower could have a +2 attack bonus against enemies on the battlements.

Courtyard: The courtyard is 120 x 80 with the gate to each wall on opposite sides and the entrance to the stronghold on the left (from the approach). The far gate has a barricade set up in the archway since the door is missing. The watch tower rises near the center of the courtyard. There is a set of stairs up to each battlement on the inside. In addition, there's a single partially broken ballista near the base of the tower plus ammunition. Finally, there's a scattering of dead bodies (goblins, orcs, and the former defenders), common weapons, and arrows and bolts in barrels around the area.

Main Stronghold: About half the defenders and the siege captain are inside the stronghold in the dining hall passing time. They will emerge with one move action into the courtyard as soon as any warning is issued. Defenders may flee inside for protection, but those are free-form locations without maps, so battles inside are up to the GM (but it's not a large area unless you want to expand the battles).

MONSTERS

This group of Orc Lord raiders managed to catch the Tenrock Hold's defenders by surprise and gain an entry point at the gate by using destructive magic. Before the defenders realized the threat, half the invading force was in the courtyard. The defenders fought well, and they took out an orc furycaster with the invaders, but their doom was sealed.

How to Get In

Fighting their way in is obviously one option for the PCs. But it's not the only option. Creative players might come up with interesting uses for advantages, or ways to bluff or trick their way past the gate guards. Most likely their ruse is eventually discovered and there'll be a battle, but it could be a lot easier if the melee types aren't stuck outside the walls. Infiltration scenes like this are a great way to test player creativity, and someone usually has an idea that could work, and sort of does, until it fails in some particularly bad way, which is fun for everyone (but mostly the GM).

Whatever the PCs try, go ahead and use a baseline DC of 25 to see if it works, with a great idea possibly being easier (DC 20) and a poor plan or subpar roleplaying being harder (DC 30). Using enough advantages might also bypass the need for a roll.

Currently, the walls are manned by a large group of elite goblin groundpounders (mooks), plus a few orc battlesmashers and crossbow igniters. They are led by an orc siege captain. They all bear the Orc Lord's sign, plus each is also adorned in warpaint that identifies them as the Footpounder band.

Half the groundpounders and the crossbow igniters will start the battle on the walls, with at least one crossbowman in the tower and one battlesmasher in the courtyard keeping an eye on things. The siege captain and a few goblin troops will be in the hold proper, ready to come out at the first sound of trouble. If the PCs try to talk or trick their way in, a battlesmasher will quickly summon captain Urdok to talk to the PCs.

Additional Reinforcements: If you want to challenge the PCs more, include a troll (core rulebook, page 248) among them as their door guard and heavy hitter.

Tactics

The goblins will fight in groups, with each mob focused on one enemy. They will try to use ranged attacks as long as possible, then enter melee to attack an enemy engaged by an orc before popping free back out of range.

The battlesmashers will seek melee combat, though they won't open the gate or go over the wall to do so unless they are staggered from ranged damage and haven't had a chance to deliver a blow.

The crossbow igniters will look for isolated targets with no orcs (and perhaps no goblins, but that's not a real problem) engaged with them to make the best use of their explosive ammunition.

Urdok will move to the walls to help his allies and repel the invaders. Once it comes to full-on battle inside the walls, he'll dive in with gusto, looking to engage the most dangerous enemy that's wiping out the goblin mooks.

As noted above, this battle is designed to have a lot of goblin mooks running around. For ease of running them, you can clump them in groups of 4 and roll one attack for x4 damage if they hit. Or replace 7 mooks with an orc archer, or 10 mooks with an orc battlesmasher.

Loot

The invaders have looted the bodies of the former defenders and come up with a few valuables, most of which are either hidden away on the invader's bodies, or stored in an iron coffer in the commander's office in the hold (where Urdok stays). Urdok has the iron key around his neck.

The troops have a total of 300 gp in loose coins. The iron coffer contains 120 gp in silver (troop pay), plus a small pouch of five 25 gp purple garnets, a +2 magic oil, and a letter to the former commander from someone connected to one of the icons (perhaps a warning about an impending attack, a payoff to be absent during the attack, or some other piece of intrigue).

The orc crossbow igniters may have a few of their explosive bolts remaining after the battle. These bolts were constructed and prepared by the (now dead) furycaster. If the PCs search, there are 1d6 such bolts remaining among the crossbow orcs. Here's how they work: On a natural even roll, the ranged attack deals 5 ongoing damage to the target and to each creature engaged with it, and the target is weakened until the end of its next turn.

If the PCs came here looking for something, it would be kept in the coffer, or perhaps hidden away in a secret wall safe.

#/Level of PCs	Orc Battlesmasher (B)	Orc Crossbow Igniter (C)	Urdok, Siege Captain (U)	Goblin Groundpounder Mook (M)*
4 x 4th level	1	1	1	10 (2 mobs)
5 x 4th level	1	2	1	15 (3 mobs)
6 x 4th level	2	2	1	18 (4 mobs)
4 x 5th level	3	2	1	14 (3 mobs)**
5 x 5th level	4	3	1	18 (3 mobs)**
6 x 5th level	5	4	1	23 (5 mobs)**

* Note, if you don't want to have to roll for every mook, consider clumping them in groups of 4 and multiplying damage by 4 (accounting for double-strength mooks if necessary).

** Make each mook double strength: its *club or mace* attack deals 12 damage, it's *shortbow* attack deals 10 damage, and each one has 24 hp.

Icons

A PC that has icon advantages with the Orc Lord, Dwarf King, Elf Queen, Prince, Diabolist, or maybe the Emperor could use one or more of them to support a convincing story that will help get the PCs in the gate through lies, bluffs, or tricks. Make the DC easier by +5 for each advantage one PC uses (along with a story about why it will work). Any PC who spends three advantages should automatically succeed.

A PC that has icon advantages with the Orc Lord, Dwarf King, Prince of Shadows, or the Three could use one or more of them to help the group scale the cliffs easier (or maybe get a ride), putting them above the courtyard beyond the walls. One option could be to have the PCs possibly find a secret set of handholds that mean it only takes one successful check to access the hold, if you want to keep some drama to the move.

URDOK, ORC SIEGE CAPTAIN

You're sure this orc IS the brute squad, until he stands back for a moment to study the fight and then starts chanting a battle song. Only after the other orcs let out a cheer does he try to murder you.

Double-strength 6th level leader [HUMANOID]
Initiative: +9

Gatebreaker maul +11 vs. AC (2 attacks)—20 damage
Natural odd hit: One nearby mook ally can make an immediate attack as a free action as Urdok orders it to strike.

Natural roll equals escalation die: Urdok can make a third *gatebreaker maul* attack as a free action this turn (but not a fourth).

Battlesong of ruin: As a standard action, Urdok can start an Orc Lord battle song that his troops take up. As a quick action, he can sustain the song. While the song is in effect, each nearby ally gains a bonus to melee damage equal to the escalation die.

Captain's privilege: Once per battle as a free action at the start of his turn, Urdok can cancel one effect on him (including being stunned).

AC	20	
PD	20	**HP 190**
MD	16	

ORC BATTLESMASHER

The big orc's two-handed mace is as long as it is, and twice as deadly. If that makes sense. Math is hard.

6th level troop [HUMANOID]
Initiative: +7

Big friggin' mace +11 vs. AC—21 damage
Miss: Half damage.

Orc smash: When the battlesmasher drops an enemy to 0 hp or below, as a free action it can move and make a *big friggin' mace* attack against a different nearby enemy.

AC	20	
PD	20	**HP 90**
MD	15	

ORC CROSSBOW IGNITER

The orc with the crossbow smiles like it knows a secret you don't as it draws a bead on you. When the bolt explodes at your feet, you get the joke.

5th level archer [HUMANOID]
Initiative: +7

Jagged handaxe +10 vs. AC—15 damage

R: Heavy crossbow +9 vs. AC—16 damage
Natural even hit or miss: The alchemically treated arcane bolt explodes. The target and each creature engaged with it takes 5 ongoing damage, and the target is weakened until the end of its next turn.

Well-aimed shot: Once per battle when the crossbow igniter rolls a natural even *heavy crossbow* attack, it can place the shot so that it sends the target flying. The target must roll a normal save; on a failure, the explosion pushes the target 1d3 x 5 feet in a direction the igniter chooses (like off a wall).

AC	20	
PD	18	**HP 67**
MD	14	

GOBLIN ELITE GROUNDPOUNDER

This goblin is disgustingly vile like most of its kind, but it seems better equipped and looks to have had a little training.

4th level mook [HUMANOID]
Initiative: +7

Club or mace +9 vs. AC—6 damage

Natural 16+: The target must roll an easy save (6+) as the goblin pounds at its legs and feet, knocking if off-balance. On a failure, the target takes 1 extra damage from attacks that hit this turn for each enemy engaged with that target (max +5).

R: Shortbow +9 vs. AC—5 damage

Shifty skirmisher: The goblin gains a +5 bonus to disengage checks, or +10 against a target it hit with an attack this turn.

AC	19	
PD	16	**HP 12 (mook)**
MD	13	

Mook: Kill one goblin groundpounder mook for every 12 damage you deal to the mob.

NEXT STEPS

Once the orc and goblin invaders have been defeated, the PCs will have a short amount of time to catch their breath. If any goblin mooks escaped, have the Orc Lord's reinforcements show up quickly. If not, give the players a few extra minutes warning of approaching enemies (horns, shouts, torches coming up the pass from the back side). A second group of invaders is looking to retake the hold, and the PCs must now defend it.

Depending on how much time they have, the PCs may be able to devise a defensive strategy as this new force hits them from the other side. Remember that the gate is gone on that side and there's only a barricade in the archway. Give the players a chance to be creative with defensive strategies. If they try to build or repair something (like the ballista), use standard DCs for the task. If they're rushed due to the enemy showing up quickly, increase each DC by +5.

Once the PCs have had a chance to develop a plan (or you're ready to hit them with the reinforcements), go to **Battle 2: Defending Tenrock Hold.**

BATTLE 2: DEFENDING TENROCK HOLD

Yells are coming from the far side of the pass. A quick look reveals more trouble coming up the path on that side, and it will be on you soon. The hill giant will definitely be a problem, the orcs riding dire boars will probably be trouble, and the half-orc battlemage and her bugbear flunkies aren't just extras brought along to cheer. This looks like work.

LOCATION DESCRIPTION

The PCs are still at Tenrock Hold, this time playing the part of the defenders. Of course, with the outer gate down, all that stands in the way of the horde is a simple barricade of wood and dead bodies on spikes, unless the PCs have improved the defenses.

Use the descriptions from Battle 1 for this fight too, adjusting for any surprises the PCs had time to prepare. This counterattack by reinforcements is also a double-strength battle.

TERRAIN & TRAPS

Fixed Ballista: If the PCs managed to repair the ballista, it can do some damage. Previously, it was located in the courtyard on a broken tripod. Anyone can make a ranged attack with it as a standard action. Reloading it, however, requires two move actions (but someone else can help). Each time it fires, the attacker must roll a save; on a failure, the ballista breaks again. Make the following attack with the ballista.

> **R: Ballista +9 vs. AC (one nearby or far away enemy at −2 atk)**—2d8 damage per level of the attacker, with no ability modifier damage

Repaired Gate: The hinges on the old gate were trashed, but it's possible to partially repair it, or at least to wedge it in place and prop it up with the barricade or have a PC try to hold it.

If it's a static obstacle, the time it will slow the enemies down depends on the skill check used to repair and place it. DC 25 or less is 1 round, and DC 26+ is 2 rounds. If one or more PCs attempt to hold the door, one of them must roll a DC 20 Strength check each time an enemy uses a standard action to try to bash it in. If the giant is trying to open it, it's a DC 25 check. On a failure, the gate door shatters or is knocked away.

If there's no door, it only takes a move action for one enemy to push the barricade out of the way.

Battlement & Walkway: If you wish you could give small PCs or PCs who are using the walls defensively a +2 bonus to AC and PD.

Improvised Defenses or Traps: If any of the PCs come up with their own defenses or traps, we suggest using the impromptu damage line for champion tier normal obstacles (+10 to attack for 4d6 or 4d8 damage against single enemies, or 2d10 or 2d12 damage against multiple enemies).

Monsters

Approaching the far gate are the Orc Lord's reinforcements. There's a hill giant, orc boar-riders, a half-orc battlemage, and her bugbear honor guards. The boar-riders will move out front, followed by the hill giant. Behind the giant, the battlecaster and the bugbears bring up the rear. This band are called the Skullcrushers.

Note, the boars are not separate monsters in this battle. A killing blow always takes down the orc. The boar either dies also or flees.

Additional Reinforcements: If you want to challenge the PCs more, include an ogre champion in the battle who is effective either with javelins or in melee (see stats). It could be the ogre was out hunting on the other side of the pass and it comes in from the back gate.

#/Level of PCs	Half-orc Battlecaster (H)	Hill Giant (G)	Orc Boar-rider (B)	Bugbear honor guard Mook (M)
4 x 4th level	1	1	1	3 (1 mob)
5 x 4th level	1	1	1	8 (1 mob)
6 x 4th level	1	1	2	10 (1 mob)
4 x 5th level	1	2	2	12 (2 mobs)
5 x 5th level	1	2	3	20 (2 mobs)
6 x 5th level	2	2	4	20 (2 mobs)

Tactics

One of the boar-riders will try to bash in the gate if the PCs put it back up while the other harries them with ranged attacks. The giant will have a boulder ready for anyone on the walls (especially manning a ballista) or in the tower, or use it on the door if a boar-rider couldn't bash it in. The battlecaster and bugbears will focus on defenders on the wall.

Once a path is clear, the boar-riders and bugbears will rush in to secure the courtyard so the others can enter.

The giant will try to bash anyone who hurts him. The riders will charge anyone they can. Some of the bugbears will stay close to the battlecaster to intercept enemies heading for her, while others move out to engage enemies (especially anyone using ranged attacks from the tower).

The battlecaster will either use her *withering burst* attack to strengthen her nearby allies, or use her *sizzling fireblast* attack on ranged enemies attacking her or the boar-riders.

These foes see glory in dying to take the hold in the Orc Lord's name as worthwhile, except for the bugbears, who will flee if the battlecaster and orc riders drop.

Be aware that if you use the *big bully* nastier special on the hill giant, a hit against a staggered PC has a good chance of killing them. You've been warned!

Loot

This group of raiders brought a little wealth with them from a previous raid to the tune of 350 gp in loose coin, jewelry, and small trophies.

The battle caster has a pair of gold nose rings: a plain one worth 20 gp, and one set with a sapphire worth 100 gp. She also carries two champion-tier *healing potions*.

She might also possibly have some sort of written orders from someone called the "Blood General" about another attack due to happen in a few days that the Orc Lord considers tactically important.

Icons

A PC that has icon advantages with the Orc Lord, Dwarf King, Elf Queen, Crusader, Prince, or maybe the Archmage could use one or more of them to recall a nasty trick heroes of old pulled off in just such a situation to give them a one-time benefit or an all-battle benefit. For example, 15 temporary hp each at the start of the battle. Or roll one save for all the mooks each round; on a failure, 1d2 of them flee the battle.

Any PC with an advantage could use it to try to confuse the hill giant during their turn so it makes a free attack against one of its allies (not during its normal turn).

Half-orc Battlecaster

The double boar tusks attached to her staff are coated with the blood of many enemies, and yours will be next.

7th level caster [HUMANOID]
Initiative: +11

Boar-tusk staff +12 vs. AC—20 damage
  Natural 16+: The battlecaster can make a single *withering burst* attack against the target as a free action.

R: Sizzling fireblast +12 vs. PD (one nearby or far away enemy)—23 fire damage, and 5 ongoing fire damage

C: Withering burst +11 vs. PD (1d3 nearby enemies)—10 ongoing damage
  We grow strong, you grow weak: For each target the battlemage hits with the attack, she or one of her nearby allies gains 10 temporary hp as the target's vitality is drained.

Experienced warcaster: When the battlecaster takes damage from an opportunity attack, she takes 7 x the escalation die less damage from that attack.

AC	23	
PD	16	**HP 101**
MD	22	

ORC BOAR-RIDER

The good news is that the orcs are getting better at caring for some animals instead of just killing them and eating them. The bad news is that they're using this advancement to try and kill you.

6th level wrecker [HUMANOID]
Initiative: +8

Spear +11 vs. AC—23 damage
  Miss: 6 damage.

Frenzied charge +10 vs. PD—19 damage, and the target is dazed (save ends).
  Limited use: The orc boar-rider must move before it makes this attack.

R: Shortbow +10 vs. AC (1 nearby or faraway target)—20 damage

Mounted attacker: Once per battle as a free action when an attack hits the boar-rider while it's staggered, the attacker must reroll the attack. If the reroll hits, the boar is killed even if the rider doesn't drop to 0 hp. When this happens, the rider loses its *frenzied charge* attack and its other attacks deal 6 less damage.

AC	21	
PD	19	**HP 95**
MD	15	

HILL GIANT

Hill giants carry their personal goods in massive sacks. The contents of such sacks—shiny rocks, interesting bones, broken keepsakes—bear a disturbing resemblance to the contents of a child's pockets.

Large 6th level troop [GIANT]
Initiative: +8

Massive gnarly club +10 vs. AC—45 damage
  Miss that's a natural 6+: Half damage (sometimes close is good enough).

R: Two-handed boulder throw +8 vs. PD—35 damage

Nastier Specials

Big bully: The giant deals double damage with its attacks against staggered targets.

AC	20	
PD	20	**HP 200**
MD	14	

BUGBEAR HONOR GUARD

The bugbears eye you warily and skulk just beyond reach, waiting to soak their polearms in your blood.

6th level mook [HUMANOID]
Initiative: +10

Polearm +11 vs. AC—12 damage
  Miss: 3 damage.

Extended reach (group ability): For every three bugbear honor guards in a mob, one of them can make a *polearm* attack against a nearby enemy instead of an engaged enemy.

AC	22	
PD	20	**HP 22 (mook)**
MD	16	

Mook: Kill one bugbear honor guard mook for every 22 damage you deal to the mob.

Additional Reinforcements

Ogre Champion

Large 5th level wrecker [HUMANOID]
Initiative: +10

Champion's battle-axe +10 vs. AC—30 damage
  Natural 5, 10, 15, or 20: The ogre champion gains a second standard action this turn, but not a third.
  Miss: Half damage.

R: Heavy javelin +10 vs. AC (one nearby or far away enemy)—26 damage
  Miss: 10 damage.

Orc Lord's enemies: Whenever a nearby dwarf or elf enemy attempts to use their racial power, they must roll a hard save (16+). On a failure, the power fails and has no effect that turn (but they can try again next turn).

Slayer of wizards: Creatures engaged with the ogre champion take opportunity attacks from it when casting close spells as if they were casting ranged spells.

AC	21	
PD	19	**HP 140**
MD	18	

Next Steps

Once this wave of attackers is defeated, no more Orc Lord troops will show up. A few hours later, reinforcements will arrive to defend the stronghold against further attacks. The PCs will be thanked for their effort as cleanup and repair projects get underway. Additional rewards depend on the story endings.

Conquer & Defend Story Endings

Here are outcomes for each story opening, detailing what success or failure might mean.

If the PCs did face both battles, remember to give them a full heal-up.

Defeating the Enemy

Success: The Orc Lord's plans are thwarted by the quick-acting PCs, and now he'll have to find another way to press the region. He and his people also won't forget who ruined his plans. The PCs are recognized for their bravery and valor. The next time the PCs roll icon dice, treat any 5s as 6s.

Failure: The PCs can't hold Tenrock Pass, and the Orc Lord's forces fortify it to use as a staging point for attacks into the empire. The icon wins again, and this time, it means the PCs will soon be facing an orc raiding party who joins in against them sometime soon when they're fighting a normal battle.

Trial Run

Success: The PCs succeed on both phases of the exercise, as planned. They are rewarded for their efforts and each one gains a 6 with the Orc Lord until they use it or level up. They're also told to be ready for a future offensive that should be similar, but larger in scale.

Failure: The PCs inability to complete their mission forces the Orc Lord's generals to have to backtrack on their plans. That doesn't please HIM. Word gets around. The PCs with the Orc Lord relationship treat all 6s as 5s for the next two times they roll icon dice. Enemies of the Orc Lord take notice of the PCs' actions more closely too.

A Call For Help

Success: As Defeating the Enemy.

Failure: The horde takes the hold and pushes into the region. Their presence invigorates local bandits and dangerous humanoids into attacking more openly. The roads aren't safe. The next time the PCs need to get somewhere quick, they'll face a battle that will slow them down, probably ruining plans that required being somewhere quick.

Opportunistic Altruism

Success: The PCs defeat the horde and have just enough time to ransack the hold to find what they seek. The reinforcements rack up its loss to the orcs, none the wiser.

Failure: The PCs can't clear the horde warriors out, and the empire's reinforcements arrive and take the place before the heroes can devise a new strategy. The thing the PCs' seek is delivered to the local lord, to keep it safe. Dealing with her might be tougher than fighting orcs.

Battle Scene Connections

The stories from this set of battle scenes can lead to other scenes:

 Wild Sacrifice (High Druid, page 40): Tenrock Hold isn't far from the frontier village of Thorn, where the PCs head looking to re-equip themselves.

 A Pit of Vipers (The Three, page 153): On their way back from the keep, the PCs are accosted by kobold bandits. One of them has an odd map of the area that notes their lair.

 The Gearwork Dungeon (Dwarf King): The PCs discover a passage into the underworld from Tenrock Hold Keep. It descends to the dwarven town of Stonehelm, and the dwarves are surprised to see anyone coming from that path. Lord Stonehelm invites them to dinner, but then the news of the living dungeon arrives.

ORC LORD:
OLD INJURIES REPAID

LEVEL RANGE: 7–8

The themes of this set of battles are facing giants and their ilk and figuring out who your friends are. This set of battles works best in a location where halflings live, with a forest under the protection of the Elf Queen and wilderness where the Orc Lord's followers raid nearby.

Goodfellow's Day, the annual pipeweed celebration in the small town of Wreath, is a big deal to the locals. While the town falls within the jurisdiction of the empire, it also borders a forest claimed by the Elf Queen (you could also just use Old Town or Burrow next to the Queen's Wood in the Dragon Empire). Besides being a celebration of the many varieties of pipeweed the local halflings grow, the festival is important for another reason. High elf and wood elf delegates of the Elf Queen always come to sign an annual peace accord with the residents of Wreath, a ceremony both of tradition and also power that helps protect the halfling lands.

This year that tradition might be ruined, and it's unclear what it would mean if the accords aren't signed. Always looking for ways to make the Elf Queen pay for past injuries inflicted upon him, the Orc Lord ordered a raid upon the elven ambassadors. Of course, the Orc Lord is cunning and the raid had another purpose—to kidnap the current high elven ambassador, who has knowledge the Orc Lord needs for another plot.

During the raid, half the delegation was killed, but luckily the wood elf ambassador and some of his retinue managed to escape and avoid slaughter. The problem is that the raiding band of giants, ogres, and other enemies captured the high elf ambassador, Nirellwyn Quantiros, and slaughtered the rest of the high elven retinue. Note, the dark elves never send an ambassador to Goodfellow's Day.

The raiders fled with their captive, but two of the wood elf rangers followed, tracking them into a low range of nearby hills. They watched the raiders enter a cave with a secret entrance but dared not follow. So they returned to Wreath to report what they saw.

The raid was carried out by a stone giant named Lars Granum and his band of giants and other allies. They took the ambassador to their hidden (they think) lair at Spire Cavern, where they can wait for the heat to blow over. But there's more to the raid than is obvious, at first.

Lars had inside help. Not only is he working with a dark elf spy from the Queen's Court who provided the time of arrival of the ambassador, but also with a halfling from Wreath named Jivel "Jives" Yellowleaf. When news of the abduction and revelation of the giants' secret lair begins to spread through the town, Jivel will have to improvise to make sure whoever goes after the ambassador fails. To that end, he will offer to travel with the PCs to identify and recover Ambassador Quantiros.

OLD INJURIES REPAID STORY OPENINGS

- **The Orc Lord's Plot:** One or more PCs with a conflicted or negative relationship with the Orc Lord hears about the raid and abduction, plus the fact that the giants bore the Orc Lord's banner. The giants must be made to pay for their brashness, and the Orc Lord thwarted in every attempt to get back at the Elf Queen for old injuries.

- **Returning the Favor:** One of the PCs was in Wreath to see Nirellwyn, who is an old friend or an adventuring companion that had once saved their life. When word of his abduction comes, the PC must go after him to see if he can be saved.

- **The Price of Disloyalty:** One or more PCs with a conflicted or positive relationship with the Orc Lord in the area is contacted shortly after the news breaks about the elven ambassador's capture. It seems the giant Lars Granum has other plans for the ambassador, returning him to the people of Wreath for a tidy ransom from the proceeds of their festival. The Orc Lord wants the elf, and so if Lars will disobey orders, he must be punished. While the townsfolk put together a posse, the PCs must find the giants' hidden lair, destroy all but one of Lars' folk (who can spread word of what happens to those who disobey), and recover the ambassador and deliver him to one of the Orc Lord's lieutenants.

- **For a Fistful of Gold Pieces:** The PCs are in the town of Wreath, enjoying its local pipeweed festival when news of the elven ambassador's abduction begins to spread through town. The town council is busy arguing about calling for Imperial help, sending spies into the cavern, and other options that will only see the elf dead. That's when the PCs interject with their offer—they could go fetch the elf, if the price is right.

ALTERNATE ICONS

Prince: The giants could all be part of a bandit gang, with Jivel being the town facilitator who sends lucrative information their way, and Etsuhli'vis providing information about those in the forest. But this time the bandits weren't careful enough.

Icons in Play

Characters that have relationships (and story-guide advantages) with the Orc Lord, Dwarf King, Elf Queen, Prince, or maybe the Emperor should be able to shine in these battle scenes. Moreso than PCs with other icon relationships, feel free to give such PCs extra knowledge about the opposition, make checks to pull off fun actions the players might suggest, and use their advantages to particularly good effect, such as negating or bypassing some of the advantages or abilities of the enemies.

Old Injuries Repaid Overview

This set of battles has some nuances depending on the PCs' reason for going after Lars and his band. The biggest wildcard is Jivel, who will try very hard to join the group for the mission, and provide some comic relief before his later betrayal.

Thanks to the wood elves' directions, the PCs easily find the "hidden" cave entrance, and the passage beyond is unguarded. The passage eventually passes through a guard outpost where the PCs will have to fight giants, ogres, and a rock troll to continue in Battle 1.

Just beyond the station is Spire Cavern, a huge cave from which a gigantic stalactite descends. The "spire" houses Lars' hideout, accessible by a stone bridge and drawbridge on the far side, with a long fall below. Once the PCs figure out how to get inside, Battle 2 sees them facing more giants and other enemies in a central hall where the raiders lounge.

A stairway up from the hall leads to Lars' personal quarters, where he drinks and plans his next move. During this double-strength battle, the PCs will discover that the giant has powerful allies, including a dark elf sorceress named Etsuhli'vis and their humorous ally, Jives, who isn't so funny anymore.

GM, feel free to expand upon these battles by including more interactions in Wreath with those wishing their help, or arrayed against them. You could also expand the size of the hideout to include more battles with raiders under Lars' command.

The battles outlined here can take place over tens of minutes or hours, depending on how big you want to make the hideout. Since the Orc Lord is in play, the enemies presented here are giants, ogres, and similar enemies, plus some unexpected creatures working with the raiders. The location is a large cavern, but one not truly in the underworld. It could have tunnels to the underworld, however.

See story endings after the final battle for options on what happens after the PCs succeed or fail.

Jivel "Jives" Yellowleaf

Jivel is a short but thin male halfling just out of his teenage years with sandy brown hair, a quick manner of speech, and an odd curved scar on one cheek. He likes living on the edge. As a delinquent, he got into trouble often, ran with the wrong sorts, and spent some time in the local jail for theft. His family, the Yellowleafs, fell on hard times in the last few years as their pipeweed brand fell out of favor due to its bitter taste and little desired color.

Seeing his birthright disappearing, Jivel left Wreath for a time, becoming a bandit and doing unpleasant deeds. During that time, he made some contacts among both the Prince's people and the Orc Lord's unsavory types. He returned recently with a plan for a way to take all his smiling, too-satisfied neighbors for a haul by helping orchestrate a kidnapping and ransom of the elven ambassador who always comes during Goodfellow's Day, when the town is flush with coin thanks to the pipeweed harvest.

Jivel, who's known as "Jives" among his less savory companions, helped put it all in motion, working with Lars on all the details. The only problem is the stupid giant was seen and followed. Now Jives has to figure out how to clean up the mess. He'll do that by discovering the PCs are going after the ambassador and offering to go with them. If questioned about this, use the lie that will work best to convince the PCs:

- He volunteers to go out of a sense of duty to Wreath, to see the peace accords signed and the town protected.

- He has been ordered to go by the Wreath elders to identify the ambassador for them and to make sure the PCs don't harm the elf inadvertently.
- The elven ambassador is an old friend to whom Jivel owes a life debt.
- Jivel wants to be a hero to restore his family's reputation in town.

PCs trying to detect if he's lying or untruthful need to use DC 30 checks, and if caught lying, Jivel will try to inject enough truth to make it seem like he's lying for good reasons. Perhaps he has a couple of lies ready to back him up as needed. If the PCs absolutely won't accept Jives into their group, he'll simply tail them until the final battle.

If the group does accept Jives, he'll stay out of the way in battle, not helping or hurting the team. He will be anxious and should be a good source of comic relief during the first two battles, as only a halfling can be. It's during the final battle with Lars when Jives' true self comes out, as he tries to plunge a blade into the back of one of the PCs.

Alternative Betrayal: If you have a group that won't benefit from having a supposedly trustworthy NPC violently betray them, consider foreshadowing the betrayal. Tell the players that there's a 50/50 chance that Jives is a traitor, but that their PCs don't know that. If they roleplay trusting Jives, and roleplay it well, you'll reduce the chance that Jives is a traitor in the end. Even if Jives does turn traitor, it will be funnier. And not such a betrayal of the GM/player contract.

BATTLE 1: THE OUTER GUARDS

You follow the tunnel beyond the hidden cave for perhaps ten to fifteen minutes steadily downward. It's obviously the right place, judging from the castoff gear and crude graffiti. Eventually, the tunnel begins to level off, and you smell smoke mixed with an acrid rot. The wavering flames of firelight flicker just ahead.

Location Description

Ahead of the PCs is a 70 x 40 L-shaped cave, with a 20 x 30 section forming the extension around the corner to the right. The ceiling is roughly 22 feet high. A small natural spring drips from the ceiling into a natural basin in the wall before flowing across the floor and leaving the chamber through cracks.

Sitting around a fire are Lars' outer guards, a group of ogres and stone giants. Getting past them without being seen will be difficult. In addition, there's another guardian in the chamber that isn't obvious; a rock troll curled up above the entrance.

The guards are a little lax since no one ever bothers them, so stealthy PCs might have a chance to surprise them.

Terrain & Traps

Guards: If the PCs choose to be stealthy, any of them who want to sneak up the tunnel to see where the light is coming from can do so. It requires a successful DC 23 Dexterity check, since the giants and ogres aren't fully paying attention. On a failure, one of the ogres will sniff and tell the others he smells two-legged food as it gets up to look around.

Stealthy PCs surveying the guards will see most of them, but there are a few ogres out of sight around the corner. It takes a DC 30 Wisdom check to notice a telltale sign of the rock troll above the entrance (sounds of slight movement, rough hide grating on rock, a glob of snot dripping, or whatever).

Fresh Water Spring: The spring is what it looks like, and it provides clean water to the guards. The water also leaks across the floor, showing footsteps and splashes of anyone, including invisible creatures, trying to move past (such PCs take a –4 penalty to stealth checks).

Fire Pit: There's a 5-foot diameter fire burning in a rock-ring pit. Coal, animal fat, burnt bones, and half a tree stump one of the giants grabbed is fueling it. The leg of an elf is currently

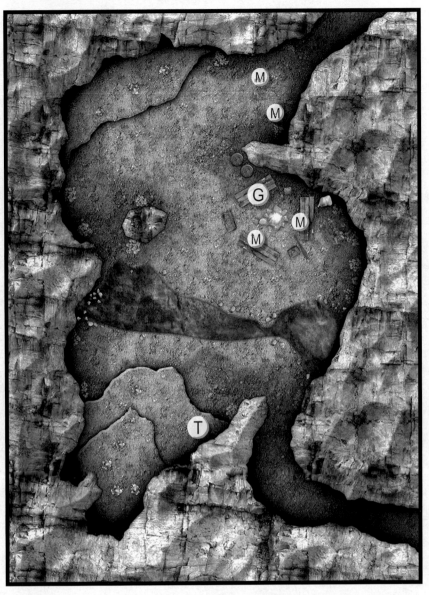

on a spit roasting. A few big logs form the benches for the giants. The smoke fills the cavern and then drifts up the tunnel.

Anyone falling in the fire will take 5 fire damage and 5 ongoing fire damage.

Monsters

The stone giant(s) is garbed in animal hides and has slate-gray skin folded in wrinkles like cracked rock. Each carries a large stone maul.

The ogre minions are garbed like the stone giant, but more rough and even less clean. They are rude, crude, and lumbering.

The rock troll is tall and thin but strong, with wiry, corded muscles and dirty brown flesh that looks like natural stone. It has curled upon itself to take up space on a small shelf above the entrance. It will leap down from above on enemies.

Additional Reinforcements: If you want to challenge the PCs more, add an extra stone giant.

#/Level of PCs	Rock Troll (T)	Stone Giant (G)	Ogre Minion Mook (M)
4 x 7th level	0	1	8 (1 mob)
5 x 7th level	1	1	4 (1 mob)
6 x 7th level	1	1	7 (1 mob)
4 x 8th level	1	1	8 (1 mob)
5 x 8th level	1	2	9 (1 mob)
6 x 8th level	2	2	8 (1 mob)

TACTICS

Other than the hidden rock troll, the giants and ogres use simple tactics: smash the PCs. Unless the PCs' know it's there, when the rock troll leaps down on someone from above, its first attack has a little extra ferocity and you should give it a +2 bonus with both claw attacks.

LOOT

The giants have a few items looted from the elven delegation they attacked, including 40 trines and three pieces of elven-made jewelry worth 50 gp.

ICONS

A PC that has icon advantages with the Orc Lord, Dwarf King, Elf Queen, or maybe the Prince could use one or more of them to scout out the cavern without being detected, including seeing signs of rock trolls, or they could know what types of abilities rock trolls have once it's spotted.

ROCK TROLL

You get a lot more careful around 'motionless boulders' after fighting these monsters.

Large 9th level wrecker [GIANT]
Initiative: +11

Stone-hard claws +14 vs. AC (2 attacks)—40 damage
First natural 14+ each turn: The troll can make a *grinding teeth* attack against the target as a free action.
Miss: 10 damage.

[Special trigger] Grinding teeth +13 vs. AC—30 damage, and the troll grabs the target unless it's already grabbing a creature (+4 attack bonus against grabbed creatures)

Trollish regeneration 30: While a troll is damaged, its rubbery flesh heals 30 hit points at the start of the troll's turn. It can regenerate five times per battle. If it heals to its maximum hit points, then that use of *regeneration* doesn't count against the five-use limit.

When the troll is hit by an attack that deals fire or acid damage, it loses one use of its *regeneration*, and it can't regenerate during its next turn.

Dropping a troll to 0 hp doesn't kill it if it has any uses of *regeneration* left.

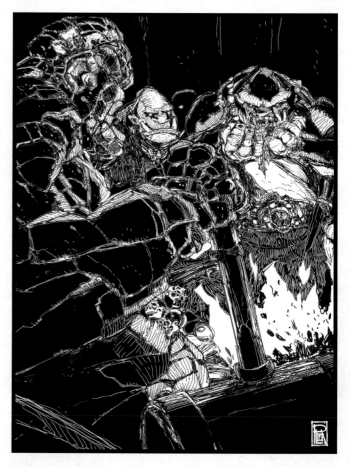

Nastier Specials

Crushing claws: If both *stone-hard claws* attacks hit the same target, the target also takes 20 ongoing damage.

Rocky hide: The troll gains *resist weapons 16+*.

AC	26	
PD	22	**HP 320**
MD	17	

STONE GIANT

"Give me that rib. I need a toothpick."

Large 8th level troop [GIANT]
Initiative: +11

Stone club +13 vs. AC—50 damage
Natural even hit or miss: The stone giant can also make a *stomp* attack against a single target as a free action.

Stomp +13 vs. PD (each smaller enemy engaged with the giant)—30 damage, and the target is dazed (save ends)

R: Thrown boulder +11 vs. PD (one nearby or far away enemy)—40 damage
Natural even miss: 20 damage.

Built of stone: The stone giant has *resist weapons 16+*.

AC	24	
PD	22	**HP 270**
MD	18	

OGRE MINION

Evil masterminds always have a place for minions who are too tough to realize when they are outclassed.

Large 9th level mook [HUMANOID]
Initiative: +11

Ogre-sized chopper +14 vs. AC—35 damage
Miss: Half damage.

R: Ogre-sized javelin +14 vs. AC (one nearby or far away enemy)—20 damage

Incidental damage: When an enemy makes an opportunity attack against the ogre minion, hit or miss, that enemy takes 4d6 damage.

Double-strength mook: The ogre minion mook counts as two 9th level mooks when you're building battles.

Nastier Specials

Punching above its weight: Once per round, the ogre minion mob can take 5d10 damage to reroll an attack (a member of the mob takes one for the team).

AC	24	
PD	23	**HP 80 (mook)**
MD	19	

Mook: Kill one ogre minion mook for every 80 damage you deal to the mob.

PLAYING JIVES

Play up the humorous side of Jives as he asks (in a scared voice) what the PCs think they'll find and if they've faced giants before, etc. He won't give away their position if the party is trying to ambush the guards, but he will stay back in the tunnel so they don't recognize him.

NEXT STEPS

Just beyond this guard post the cave narrows to a short tunnel for about 50 feet, and then it opens onto a wide shelf within a very large cavern. Descending from the roof of the cavern is a gigantic stalactite, whose bottom ends about 80 feet below the lip of the shelf the PCs are standing on. A bridge partially crosses to the spire, with a long fall of a few hundred feet below it to the bottom of the cave. The stalactite holds Lars' hideout.

Once the PCs have had a quick rest and are ready to proceed, go to **Spire Cavern.**

SPIRE CAVERN

The stone shelf you're on overlooks a wide, deep cavern. Descending from above is a thick, massive stalactite that is probably the kidnapper's hideout since there's a drawbridge on the far side in a gap in the spire. A bridge of stone partially extends from your shelf, but comes up about forty feet short, just enough for the drawbridge to span. Thanks to some natural phosphorescence, you spy two other similar bridges forming a triangular pattern around the spire. Each exits the large cave in a different direction.

LOCATION DESCRIPTION

The first test is for the PCs to figure out how to get across the gap from the end of the bridge. Careful study reveals there are ledges on either side of the raised drawbridge carved from the spire stone near eyehooks where ropes are strung, probably to help raise and lower the bridge. There must be a window or other opening there where the ropes go through.

The bridge itself is somewhat crude, being constructed from logs and rope. There are places to hang onto the outside (bottom) of the bridge, though anyone doing so will be over a long fall. It doesn't look like there are any obvious gaps on the edges of the drawbridge.

Guarding the drawbridge from the inside is an ogre minion named Grunch. He's currently asleep, lounging on a chair made from wooden crates.

How the PCs gain entrance should be challenging and interesting.

TERRAIN & TRAPS

Drawbridge & Bridge: The drawbridge covers an opening in the spire 20 feet high and 10 feet wide, with the extra length extending up the spire face. There's a simple winch inside that lets Grunch open the drawbridge in 2 rounds or close it in about half a minute. Anyone clinging to the outside ropes or timbers must make a DC 20 Strength check to grab on, hang there each round, or climb it to the top. When it opens, it generally does so with a loud crash and squeaking of iron hinges on the bottom. No one above really pays attention, however, since guards come and go.

The bridge on the PCs' side is stone and looks dwarven-made. It extends 40 feet out over the cavern, supported by a natural ledge. It's 40 feet from the end of the bridge to the drawbridge (when up).

It's a long way across, so anyone jumping without extra magic must succeed on a DC 30 skill check, or plummet into the cavern. Placing a grappling hook or an arrow rope or line into a secure point is easier, requiring a DC 25 Dexterity check (failure means the connection seems firm but isn't), though anyone crawling across would need to be light. Doing so (or any other checks involving dicey moves) requires a DC 25 check.

Of course, anyone who can fly will be able to easily reach the far side safely.

Ledges & Access Windows: Once the PCs get across, there are two access points beyond the bridge. Near the ledges on top are two openings big enough for a normal-sized humanoid to squeeze through. A large thick rope on either side passes through an eyehook, and then through the opening down to a winch inside. The drop is about 15 feet, though climbing down a rope makes it easy. If PCs crossing the gap, climbing the drawbridge, or sliding

This would be a good time for Jives to help the PCs out if they're stuck on how to get across, proving his value (and that he's not a traitor to suspicious PCs). He'll either suggest fooling the guards, or perhaps be willing to climb across a secured arrow shot line (with another rope tied to him if he falls) to secure a stronger rope for them.

down through the opening wish to do so quietly (and avoid waking Grunch), they must succeed on a second DC 20 Dexterity check.

Grunch: Grunch is an ogre minion and he's sleeping off a bit of drink. Still, loud noises (or yells to open) will wake him. If alerted, he'll groggily get up, grab his spear, and look for trouble. If it sounds like they're being attacked, he'll bang a nearby gong to alert the place, making future battles tougher (no enemies can be surprised, and add a few extra mooks or an extra giant to every battle).

If a PC manages to sneak up on him, they can make a coup de grace attack against him before initiative is rolled. GM, generally you should make him a fairly easy kill unless they bungle it. Use the ogre stats from Battle 1 for Grunch.

If the PCs choose to try to trick Grunch into opening the drawbridge, that's not too hard either, since he's not overly smart. Once they get his attention and wake him up, he'll growl out, "What's the password?" The answer is "By Lar's will, open up Grunch," but at this point he's susceptible to manipulation. It takes a successful DC 20 Charisma or Wisdom check to get him to lower the bridge. On a failure, the next attempt will require a DC 25 check to trick him since he's now suspicious. If that fails, he'll bang his gong. Of course, good roleplaying or use of icon advantages should be rewarded with a lowered bridge.

Spire Cavern & Falling: The cavern is lit by enough phosphorescence that the PCs can generally see what they're doing. Anyone trying to climb the walls to another bridge would need to make too many skill checks for that to be reasonable without magical help, plus the other bridges are up too.

If a PC fails a check and falls into the cavern, it's 180 feet down and 2d10 x 10 damage. Luckily, there are a few pools of water down there. A PC that does fall can roll a d6 (or use an advantage). On a 5 or 6, they land in a pool for half damage. If someone is tied off, they only fall 40 feet before slamming into the cavern wall below for 2d12 damage, and then must climb (or be pulled) up.

Anyone who falls and survives is out of the battle unless they are able to fly back up.

NEXT STEPS

Once inside the spire, the PCs will find that the entrance is a 20-foot wide corridor that leads inward about 50 feet to a long hall/corridor that circles the outer wall of the spire, connecting to each of the other two drawbridges (and 2 more sleeping ogre minions). At two opposite points along the outer hall, a ramp leads upward. Each ramp climbs to a set of double doors that open into a large central chamber above (from opposite sides).

Once the PCs are ready to proceed, go to **Battle 2: The Welcoming Committee.**

BATTLE 2: THE WELCOMING COMMITTEE

You open the doors to reveal a large stone hall supported by four squat, round pillars. A wide set of stairs climbs upward in the center of the wall toward the spire's interior. Scattered about the chamber are a few large wooden tables and a large stack of beer casks. A fire burns in a hearth in the wall opposite the stairs, filling the room with smoke and masking some foul odor. Tied to a set of wood planks that are secured to one of the pillars with ropes is a bleeding high elf with a large hatchet partially sticking into his shin. A giant looks to be practicing throwing hand axes at him. Another giant, this one two-headed, lounges at the table with a mug in each hand, encouraging the game. Finally, a pair of low, vicious growls erupt as something large and low to the ground rises from the shadows.

Location Description

The hall is 70 feet wide, 110 feet long, and 25 feet high, with a set of double doors on either end and the stairway up in the middle of the inside wall. Two long wooden tables with benches fill the center of the place, and the stack of beer casks sits near the fireplace in the wall opposite the stairs.

Anyone listening at the door will hear low, rumbling voices (the giants) and then the "whack" of the hand axe hitting the elf (and planks), followed by the elf's weak scream and more laughter.

Unless the PCs try some sort of subterfuge, when the PCs enter, the giants will grab their weapons and attack, or hurl hand axes or casks of beer. The two-headed giant is the ettin Vorn n' Pog, a massive example of its breed.

The growling creature is Wuggy, Vorn n' Pog's two-headed demon dog.

Terrain & Traps

Tables & Casks: The tables are 4 feet high, 6 feet wide, and 20 feet long. The wood benches have been replaced by stone ones that can support the giants. Moving on top of them is easy enough, with no check needed.

There is a wobbly pile of casks stacked 10 feet high near the fireplace. Anyone attempting to climb it to gain height can do so with a successful DC 20 Dexterity check. Sending the stack tumbling toward an enemy (one time only) requires a DC 25 check as a standard action, with those enemies either being dazed until the end of their next turn or losing their next move action as the get bowled over. Failure means a fall among the casks and being stuck until the end of the next turn.

Pillars & Elf: The pillars are round with rough stone, and climbing one requires a DC 20 Strength check. The elf, Dalinir, is only semi-conscious from pain and blood loss. He was a member

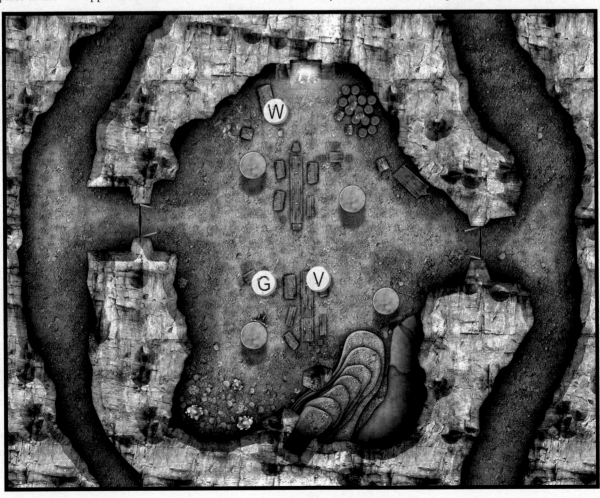

of the delegation. He indicates that the ambassador is upstairs before passing out.

Fireplace: The large hearth is 10 feet wide, and 6 feet high and deep. Empty beer casks burn alongside hot coal. There's also an open cask full of coal chunks next to the hearth. Anyone moving in or thrown in will take 15 fire damage, and 15 ongoing fire damage initially, plus the same damage each round they remain inside.

Refuse Pit: Not immediately visible in one corner of the room is a hole in the ground that's 5 feet in diameter. It goes all the way through the bottom of the spire with a drop to the cavern floor 200 feet down. It's coated with grime and has slick, greasy edges. Anyone falling down it takes damage as per "Falling" in Battle 1, and the giants are willing to give up a standard action attack to try to hurl someone down the pit (giant must hit with attack; PC makes DC 25 Strength or Dexterity check; on a failure they are thrown in; a PC gets one save to stop moving about 20 feet down). Climbing back up the shaft requires a successful DC 20 Strength check.

Monsters

The stone giants are some of Lars' clan brothers. They dress in animal skins similar to the giant in Battle 1.

Vorn n' Pog is a large ettin that the giants like for his hitting power and comedic value (consider giving Vorn a "Laurel" voice, and Pog gets the "Hardy" voice, or some similar duo). Vorn wields a big morning star and Pog uses a large axe.

Wuggy is the ettin's pet, a demon dog they found near a hellhole. During battle they'll order Wuggy to "sik im" on one PC or another. The demon dog has a vaguely canine body but each of its heads is more like a dragon, with poisonous fangs.

Additional Reinforcements: If you want to challenge the PCs more, add 2d4 ogre minions (see Battle 1) that arrive from one of the other bridges exiting the cavern. At the start of the battle, the PCs hear a drawbridge get lowered. When the escalation die is 2+, the ogre minions arrive.

#/Level of PCs	Vorn n' Pog, Ettin (V)	Wuggy, Demon Dog (W)	Stone Giant (G)
4 x 7th level	1	0**	1
5 x 7th level	1	1	1
6 x 7th level	1	1	2
4 x 8th level	1	1	2
5 x 8th level	1*	1	3
6 x 8th level	1*	1	4

* The ettin can use its nastier special.

** Wuggy is a harmless but much loved two-headed poodle instead.

Tactics

This battle should be straightforward with the giants and ettin each facing off against a different PC. Wuggy will attack anyone attacking the ettin, unless they sick it on someone.

The one surprise the giants might have for the PCs is that one of them will give up normal attacks to try to throw a PC into the hearth or down the refuse hole if they move near it (see **Terrain & Traps**).

Loot

The giants have 300 gp in various valuables, most of it elven jewelry. Wuggy has a gold chain collar on each head worth 50 gp each.

The beer is stale but drinkable. There's also some elven bread and cheeses, and some sacks of flour and beans in a few of the casks.

Icons

A PC that has icon advantages with the Orc Lord, Dwarf King, Emperor, Elf Queen, or maybe the Prince could use one or more of them to trick the ettin into setting Wuggy on a giant, or trick the heads into arguing with each other instead of attacking for a round or two (good skill check might also make this happen).

A PC that has icon advantages with any icon could use one or more of them to avoid a fall to the bottom of the cavern via the refuse pit (stuck down the shaft instead, or somehow saved).

Vorn n' Pog, Ettin

This ettin's comedy routine will just kill you.

Large 9th level troop [GIANT]
Initiative: +15

Headchopper axe +14 vs. AC—70 damage, or 80 damage against a stuck enemy

Entangling morningstar +13 vs. PD—30 damage, and the target is stuck until the end of its next turn
Natural odd miss: Pog gets the morning star entangled around his legs and loses his next *morningstar* attack.

Doubly deadly: As a standard action, Vorn n' Pog can make an *entangling morningstar* attack and a *headchopper axe* attack.

Two-headed save: If an ettin's first save against an effect fails, it can roll a second save.

Nastier Specials

Big bully: The ettin deals double damage with its attacks against staggered enemies.

AC	25	
PD	22	**HP 360**
MD	18	

Wuggy, Demon Dog

It looks like a giant hound crossed with a dragon. Two dragons. Two demon-dragons.

Double-strength 8th level spoiler [ABERRATION]
Initiative: +12

Venomous bite +13 vs. AC (2 attacks)—28 damage, and 10 ongoing poison damage
Natural even hit: The attack deals 20 ongoing poison damage instead of 10, and the first time the target fails a save, it's also weakened (save ends both).

Reactive flesh: When a melee attack hits Wuggy, the attacker must roll a save. On a failure, the demon dog's blood and flesh explodes outward in a spray of numbing contact poison and the attacker is dazed (save ends).

AC	24	
PD	23	**HP 250**
MD	17	

Playing Jives

Jives will try to stay back down the ramp during this battle, since he isn't sure if the PCs can take the ettin and his pet. He'll call out things like, *"I hope everyone up there is okay, because if not, then I might be talking to giants, and... gulp... that wouldn't be good."* If given the chance when no one is watching the elven prisoner, he'll inflict an artery wound to let the elf bleed out, just in case he's overheard any names being used by the giants (like his). It will look like the elf's previous wounds finished him off. If this happens, you could give PCs who have a chance of facing that way a DC 35 Wisdom check to spot the move.

Stone Giant

"I told you that ogre was too stupid to run the drawbridge."

Large 8th level troop [GIANT]
Initiative: +11

Stone club +13 vs. AC—50 damage
Natural even hit or miss: The stone giant can also make a *stomp* attack against a single target as a free action.

Stomp +13 vs. PD (each smaller enemy engaged with the giant)—30 damage, and the target is dazed (save ends)

R: Thrown boulder +11 vs. PD (one nearby or far away enemy)—40 damage
Natural even miss: 20 damage.

Built of stone: The stone giant has *resist weapons 16+*.

AC	24	
PD	22	**HP 270**
MD	18	

Next Steps

After a quick rest, the PCs can head up the stairs. It's the only real option, even if the elf tied to the table perishes. On the way up, the stairs pass a gallery with an open face toward the spire cave, showing it in all of its magnificence (and the long fall down).

Once the PCs are ready, go to **Battle 3: Lars' Lair**.

Battle 3: Lars' Lair

The stairs ascend perhaps a hundred feet to a platform then switch back the other way another hundred. Ahead they open into another hall. A low popping or cracking noise echoes off the stone walls of the stairwell, then all goes quiet. Moving upward slowly, you see a good-sized chamber spread out before you. You immediately notice the cage of iron bars hanging by a thick iron chain about 25 feet off the ground to the right, with a pale elven arm extended between the bars. Various furniture and beer casks are strewn about the floor. To the left, up another set of stairs on an upper floor, a stone giant stands by a stone table with two large stone urns. The back side of that balcony holds an open window that overlooks the spire cavern. The giant looks at you and asks, "Who're you, then?"

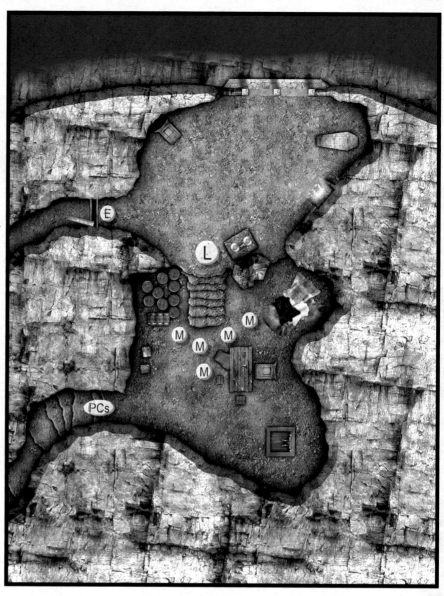

Location Description

If the PCs are stealthy, adjust the descriptive text to fit; they won't see the room's occupants until moving to the top of the stairs. There might be an opportunity to reach the ambassador or try to sneak into the chamber, though Lars is watching. Also, Jives might "accidentally" make a noise to warn the giant.

The hall is 60 feet long, 50 feet wide, and 40 feet high, with the balcony level rising 15 feet above the ground level and framed by two small pillars at the top of the stairs. It extends another 40 feet back. The giant, Lars Granum, stands behind the stone table and urns, which hold a surprise for the PCs. Each is filled with rock scorpions, nasty vermin that Lars has been collecting. He enjoys feeding things to them (the crack was him closing the lid after dropping a rat inside).

The cage holds Nirellwyn Quantiros, the elven ambassador, who's still alive though unconscious. The rest of the main chamber holds a bed of furs, casks of beer, and a chair or two.

Although Lars asked the PCs who they are, he knows their presence isn't good and figures them for the posse. Even if the PCs try to bluff him, he'll just smile and push the two urns over onto the lower floor, sending the scorpions skittering (and mad) between him and his enemies. Lars also has two allies the PCs might not be expecting. The first is Jives, their halfling tagalong, who's been biding his time until this moment. The other is another conspirator in the abduction, Etsuhli'vis, a dark elven sorceress who provided the ambassador's travel plans to Lars; she's staying in a small chamber just above the balcony where Lars is standing with a stairway down to it that's out of sight.

This is a double-strength battle. We've written what follows as if Jives is definitely a traitor. If you decided to tell the PCs that Jives *might* be a traitor from the beginning, to milk the roleplaying for all you could get, sometime during this battle is the time to roll and see if goes traitor. If he turns out to be on the PCs' side, keep him as an ineffective/annoying NPC, and add a few more rock scorpions to the battle. Honestly, that's not as interesting as having him go traitor, but if you cut the deal, you should probably roll for it. If the PCs didn't roleplay it well, make it a lot more likely that he's a traitor!

Terrain & Traps

Stone Urns: The urns are filled with rock scorpions and will fall upon the stone floor and break apart, spilling the creatures everywhere. They are only rubble at that point.

Upper Balcony: The upper level is 15 feet up the stairs, which are wide enough for one giant or a couple of normal-sized PCs. Getting up to that level by climbing or leaping from the stairs for the side ledges requires a DC 20 Strength or Dexterity check.

Hanging Cage: The cage is a 7 x 7 square of iron bars with a solid wood floor and a chain from the top strung through a huge eyebolt in the ceiling. The chain is secured to the wall to the right of the PCs. Climbing the greasy chain to get off the ground or up to the cage requires a DC 25 Strength or Dexterity check. The rock scorpions are capable climbers and willing to scale the thick chain also, however.

Anyone falling from the cage takes 1d12 damage. Opening the locked cage door requires a DC 25 Dexterity (picking it) or Strength (forcing it) check. The key is among Lar's possessions in a trunk near his sleeping furs.

Open Gallery Window: On the upper balcony at the back, the opening to the spire cavern only has a 4-foot lip and is big enough for anyone to move through (or get hurled through). If that happens, the creature can roll a save to try to catch a hold; on a failure, it plummets to the cave bottom (see Battle 1, Falling).

Casks, Furniture, & Bedding: There's some furniture, full beer casks, a pile of furs, and a large stone trunk on the main floor if the PCs want to try to make use of them in some way.

Monsters

At the end of the first round after the rock scorpions spill out and the PCs begin to spread out, Jives will make his play as he attacks whoever he sees as most important and most vulnerable in the group, saying, *"Lars, you idiot. You were followed by the wood elves. Now I have to clean up this mess."* He uses a wicked knife he's been hiding the whole time.

Etsuhli'vis will also arrive at the end of the first round, joining the battle on her initiative in the next round. She yells out something about how she cannot afford to be implicated as she lashes out with her magic. The dark elf wears green silks that flow and move, making her seem fluid like water.

Lars is a large and strong stone giant. He wears a breastplate of carapace made from an umber hulk, an underground monster that he killed when he was younger. He wields a huge maul, though there's a small pile of boulders near the table at his feet that he can hurl (or another jar of scorpions if you prefer).

Additional Reinforcements: If you want to challenge the PCs more, add a drow cavalry (*Bestiary*, page 59) that comes in through the gallery opening (it was guarding that entrance and is Etsuhli'vis's personal bodyguard).

* Jives is double-strength: his *wicked knife* attacks deals 56 damage, or 28 on a miss, and he has 280 hit points.
** The rock scorpions are double strength: their *pincers* attack deals 16 damage, *rock stinger* deals 10 damage and 10 ongoing damage, and each has 60 hp.
*** Add 3 stone giants to the battle; see Battle 2 for stats. Alternately, you could give Etsuhli'vis a pair of double-strength 9th level drow swordmaiden bodyguards (not statted out).

Tactics

Once Lars drops the urns, he'll grab his maul and a boulder, trying to get a ranged attack in as he moves a few steps down the stairs to give himself room to swing (and so only two enemies can come at him at once from the stairs). If an opportunity presents itself, he may try to hurl an enemy out the gallery window, or possibly break free from the fight and flee down the stairs.

Hearing trouble, Etsuhli'vis gathers power (no other effects this time) during the first round and she won't arrive in the upper chamber until the end of the first round. She then goes on her initiative count in the second round. She'll look for targets of opportunity to blast with her *scorching ray*. She can gather power only when the escalation die is even after that.

Jives will act once the PCs have engaged Lars and the rock scorpions, sneaking up on a soft target at the back of the group if possible. His first attack could be deadly if the halfling's target isn't aware of the threat.

The rock scorpions are mad and will rush to attack anything on the same level as them initially.

#/Level of PCs	Lars, Stone Giant (L)	Etsuhli'vis, Dark Elf Sorceress (E)	Jives, Halfling Rogue	Rock Scorpion Mooks (M)
4 x 7th level	1	1	1	3 (1 mob)
5 x 7th level	1	1	1	10 (1 mob)
6 x 7th level	1	1	1*	20 (2 mobs)
4 x 8th level	1	1	1*	22 (2 mobs)
5 x 8th level	1	1	1*	17 (2 mobs)**
6 x 8th level	1***	1	1*	16 (2 mobs)**

LOOT

Lars has the best pieces from the elves stashed in his trunk, along with a few items he previously had. There's 500 gp in trines and other coins, a 500 gp platinum and diamond ring with the Elf Queen's symbol (the ambassador's, but he will give it to them in thanks if they offer it back), and a small pouch of eight 50 gp moonstones. There's also a pair of *+3 runes* with the Elf Queen's symbol on them.

If you like, Lars' umber hulk carapace armor could be a true magic item that resizes down to PC size. If so, it's *+3 umberhulk heavy armor* that gives the wearer the ability to burrow once per day. Quirk: Is confused easily, and thus confuses others around them.

ICONS

A PC that has icon advantages with the Orc Lord, Dwarf King, Elf Queen, High Druid, or the Three could use one or more of them to make some of the rock scorpions attack targets of their choice, using scent or sound.

A PC that has icon advantages with the Elf Queen could use one or more of them to convince Etsuhli'vis to switch allegiance in exchange for promises of not revealing her part in it all, given great roleplaying and maybe a DC 28 Charisma check or two.

A PC that has icon advantages with the Prince of Shadows could use once or more of them to get Jives to betray the giant and dark elf, if the promise of freedom and a decent payoff are part of the deal.

LARS GRANUM, STONE GIANT

Large 11th level troop [GIANT]
Initiative: +14

Massive maul +16 vs. AC—120 damage
  Natural even hit or miss: The stone giant can also make a *stomp* attack against a single target as a free action.

Stomp +16 vs. PD (each smaller enemy engaged with the giant)—50 damage, and the target is dazed (save ends)

R: Thrown boulder +14 vs. PD (one nearby or far away enemy)—80 damage
  Natural even miss: 40 damage.

Built of stone: The stone giant has *resist weapons 16+.*

AC	27	
PD	26	**HP 520**
MD	22	

ETSUHLI'VIS, DROW SORCERESS

The drow woman holds only one value: self-preservation at your expense.

11th level caster [HUMANOID]
Initiative: +15, goes on round 2

Ritually prepared dagger +15 vs. AC—55 damage

R: Scorching ray +16 vs. PD (one nearby or far away enemy)—60 fire damage
  Natural even hit: The target also takes 15 ongoing fire damage.

C: Black dragon breath +15 vs. PD (one nearby enemy, or up to 2 enemies engaged with the sorceress)—36 acid damage against two enemies, or 72 acid damage against a single enemy, and 10 ongoing acid damage
  Limited use: 1/battle, but the spell isn't expended if it misses all targets.

Cruel flames: Once per battle as a free action when *scorching ray* deals ongoing fire damage, she can double that damage and the save becomes hard (16+).

Gather power: As a standard action when the escalation die is even or zero, the sorceress can gather power. When she does, her next attack that battle deals double damage. In addition, each nearby enemy takes 5 fire damage.

Nastier Specials

R: Blistering flames +15 vs. PD (1d3 nearby enemies)—32 fire damage
  Natural 4, 8, 12, 16, 20: The target also takes 5 ongoing fire damage from fiery blisters.

AC	26	
PD	20	**HP 275**
MD	25	

JIVES, HALFLING ROGUE

"Do you think I'm an idiot now?"

8th level spoiler [HUMANOID]
Initiative: +11, end of round

Wicked knife +13 vs. AC—28 damage
  Natural odd hit or miss: Jives can pop free from the target and move somewhere nearby.
  Natural even miss: 14 damage.

Sneaky bastard: When Jives attacks an enemy that isn't aware of him, or that considers him an ally, the attack deals double damage.

Slippery bastard: Twice per battle as a free action when a non-critical attack would hit Jives, it misses him instead.

AC	24	
PD	23	**HP 124**
MD	21	

ROCK SCORPION

Rocks scorpions aren't that big, but their carapaces are hard and that stinger will send you to a whole other world of pain.

8th level mook [BEAST]
Initiative: +15

Pincers +13 vs. AC (2 attacks)—8 damage
Natural 18+: The scorpion can make a *rock stinger* attack against the target as a free action.

[*Special trigger*] **Rock stinger +13 vs. PD**—5 damage, and 5 ongoing damage
First failed save: The target must begin making last gasp saves as it slowly turns to stone, becoming fully petrified after the fourth failed save. Unlike most last gasp saves, the target can continue to act while making these saves.

Agile climber: The scorpion can climb most surfaces. When it attempts to do so, roll an easy save (6+); on a success, it's able to make the climb.

AC	26	
PD	20	**HP 30 (mook)**
MD	17	

NEXT STEPS

Once the battle ends, the PCs discover that ambassador Quantiros is alive thankfully, and happy for the save. In addition, Lars, Etsuhli'vis, or even Jives might have escaped to cause trouble later. The other exits out of the stalactite hideout could go to the underworld or other interesting places nearby. And perhaps there's a simple but direct missive from the Orc Lord's people among Lar's belongings telling him to deliver the elf ambassador intact for questioning, which could open further storylines.

OLD INJURIES REPAID STORY ENDINGS

Here are outcomes for each story opening, detailing what success or failure might mean.

If the PCs did face all three battles, remember to give them a full heal-up.

THE ORC LORD'S PLOT

Success: You save the elf ambassador and return him to Wreath, where the peace accords are signed. The PCs get as much pipeweed as they can each carry. In addition, each PC gains two 6s with the Emperor or the Elf Queen (their choice) that last until they use them or level up.

Failure: The PCs fail to reach the elf ambassador in time, and he's either killed, sent to the Orc Lord, or ransomed back to the town of Wreath at a high cost, which necessitates ending the pipeweed festival.

RETURNING THE FAVOR

Success: See the Orc Lord's plot.

Failure: See the Orc Lord's plot. Another option is that the elf is ransomed back to the PCs at the price of a magic item one of them carries.

THE PRICE OF DISLOYALTY

Success: The PCs defeat Lars, Jives, and Etsuhli'vis and recover the elven ambassador. They manage to sneak him out of there before the posse from Wreath shows up, and they transport him to the Orc Lord's waiting people. For their efforts, each PC is given raid loot of a few hundred gold pieces and each also gains a 6 with the Orc Lord that lasts until they use it or level up.

Failure: The PCs fail to recover the elf ambassador, and he's ransomed back to the town. The Orc Lord is not pleased, not at all. Each PC that rolls a 6 with the Orc Lord the next time they roll icon dice gets a 5 instead. Also, someone (probably Jives) gives the authorities their names to look into about the kidnapping.

FOR A FISTFUL OF GOLD PIECES

Success: See the Orc Lord's plot, plus the PCs gain a few coins in addition to pipeweed.

Failure: The townsfolk come looking for the PCs after they're forced to ransom off half their pipeweed yield to get the elf back, and then someone claims the PCs were in on it the whole time (probably Jives).

BATTLE SCENE CONNECTIONS

The stories from this set of battle scenes can lead to other scenes:

Stonecutter's Axe (Dwarf King): Once the elven ambassador awakes, he is thankful for his rescue. After a time, he relates how he overheard the dark elf woman Etsuhli'vis talk to Lars about how some of her kin were hired to guard the entrance to Lost Garzendahl, the dwarf hold thought long gone. They are trying to get inside, where the mighty artifact Stonecutter's Axe was rumored to be. It's somewhere near Stonehelm in the underworld. The ambassador says that if the axe were to resurface, it would be a mighty boon for the Dwarf King.

The Ritual of Taking (High Druid, page 67): As the PCs escort the ambassador back to Wreath, the elf cries out in pain. He tells the PCs that something foul is happening in the forest to the south. It is crying out in pain. He fears something dark and foul is going on there and worries for the wood, which is under the High Druid's protection. Once they reach town, he suggests they head to Thorn to investigate.

PRINCE OF SHADOWS: BACK-ALLEY POLITICS

LEVEL RANGE: 1–2

The themes of this set of battles are back-alley politics, mechanical traps, and urban skirmishes with thugs, rogues, and others who interact with or are part of the Prince's network.

This set of battle scenes works best while the PCs are in an urban environment, although it could start almost anywhere with a group of bandits or highwaymen and then move to an urban location.

After an easy skirmish with a group of street thugs looking to lighten the heroes' pouches, the PCs are contacted by a member of the local thieves' guild connected to the Prince. That contact either hires them, incites them, tricks them, or blackmails them into doing further violence against a gang crime lord.

Whether the PCs go along, or turn the tables on their contact, they will need to enter the hideout of a local gang leader, fighting their way through the street thugs to the inner sanctum of the leader. Once the job is done, things might get even more complicated.

BACK-ALLEY POLITICS STORY OPENINGS

- **Freedom Comes at a Price:** Shortly after a fight in the streets, one of the PCs with ties to the Prince or another icon discovers a semi-valuable item missing (a non-magic weapon like a dagger is good). Soon after, they are threatened by someone who says the item will be placed at the scene of a high-profile murder, implicating them unless they agree to a job to take out a local crime lord and her thugs.

- **Clearing Their Names:** After being contacted by a rogue trying to blackmail one of the PCs (see Freedom Comes at a Price above), instead of going along with blackmail plan, the PCs ferret out the lair of the blackmailer. They'll need to hit the hideout fast and hard to make sure to get the item back before all the rats flee their bolt hole.

- **Hazard Pay for Dangerous Work:** The PCs are contacted by a shady denizen of the city or town they're currently in. They're willing to pay well for the PCs to take care of a local crime lord and her goons, no questions asked.

- **Help Me Save This Town:** After the skirmish with street thugs, the PCs are approached by someone claiming to represent an icon other than the Prince who the PCs have icon connections with. Claiming he or she has the support of "town leaders" to look the other way, the contact says the icon has need for the PCs to put an end to a local menace—a crime lord whose acts of violence have been harming the city/town and its townsfolk. The contact asks for help putting an end to the crime lord in exchange for something they want.

- **The Price of Doing Business:** After the fight, the PCs are approached by a woman and her "supporters" (basically a gang). She tells them that by attacking/killing her people, they have offended her. As recompense, she's willing to rack the losses up to the price of doing business in exchange for something from them—putting an end to a rival crime lord and her gang. If they don't accept, she threatens that things will go very badly for them in this city/town. The PCs know that they will be strongly overmatched if they take her on directly.

ALTERNATE ICONS

 Diabolist: You can play this set of battle scenes about the same, but the person who contacts them is actually a cultist of the Diabolist. And the crime lord and street thugs are also cultists following a different path that their contact sees as heretical and needs to be eradicated. Or maybe they're holding a fellow cultist in their hideout that needs saving. Add an imp or a few dretches in place of an enforcer or the thugs.

 Emperor or The Three: The PCs will still face off against a crime lord and her goons, but the contact introducing them to this situation will act like someone employed by the Prince of Shadows, but is actually working for the Emperor and making a political strike against a rival Imperial who's gaining funds from the gang. Or is working for the Three (the Black) to fulfill an assassination contract, but wants the Prince's people to blame the PCs instead.

ICONS IN PLAY

Characters that have relationships (and story-guide advantages) with the Prince of Shadows, Emperor, Diabolist, and maybe the Three should be able to shine in these battle scenes. Moreso than PCs with other icon relationships, feel free to give such PCs extra knowledge about the opposition, make checks to pull off fun actions the players might suggest, and use their advantages to particularly good effect, such as negating or bypassing some of the advantages or abilities of the enemies.

BACK-ALLEY POLITICS OVERVIEW

No matter what opening you used, the action starts with the PCs being given or finding the location of the crime lord's headquarters (whether attacking the one blackmailing them or doing the bidding of an agent).

After doing a bit of research, casing the site, and/or studying the movements of those entering and leaving, the PCs have found the "safest" way in, through a warehouse that also is a backdoor into the lair. It should be less-guarded than the main entrances, and allow them to reach the crime lord without going through waves of street muscle.

The warehouse isn't as deserted as it seems and the PCs will have to fight off the warehouse guards to proceed further into the lair. One way or another, they descend below the warehouse into the headquarters' sublevels, entering an underground gladiatorial arena to fight a mix of thugs and enslaved beasts.

After that, they have to face some experienced rogues watching over the heart of the headquarters, thieves who take advantage of the shadows.

Last is a battle against the crime lord and her goons, a group of thugs and murderers who know their business well. But the crime lord controls the terrain, and might be willing to talk her way into a deal.

GM, feel free to expand upon these battles by including battles with more street thugs and gang members to get the information on where the headquarters is located, or additional gang members in more locations within the lair.

The battles outlined here can take place over a few minutes or tens of minutes, depending on how fast the PCs wish to strike. If it takes too long, the crime lord will escape or bring in more troops. Since the Prince is in play, the enemies presented here are shady types and urban warriors who live among the shadows. The locations should exude a sense of seediness and greed.

See story endings after the final battle for options on what happens after the PCs finish the last battle.

BATTLE I: CRATE & BEATSTICK

The warehouse looks normal enough—a one-story brick building with a pair of double loading doors facing an alley and a side door entrance for the workers—but you know the truth of it. It's the backdoor to the headquarters of the Redfangs, a crime gang led by a half-orc named Posk Redfang. The place has no windows and the service doors are barred on the inside. The side door seems like the best option, but it's time to get inside, one way or another.

How the PCs get inside is up to them. The obvious choices are either the service doors or the side entrance for employees. This is a chance for creative problem solving. Whatever method they choose, skill checks will be required: set the DC at 15 (with failure bringing extra trouble but getting them inside). Here's a few options, and we're sure the players will be more creative at finding a way inside.

- A PC picks the lock on the side entrance and subdues the guard (perhaps quietly).
- A PC smashes down the side entrance door, and the others subdue the guard, but it makes noise.
- A PC knocks or gets the attention of the door guard at one of the doors and the group talks their way in.
- A PC knocks or gets the attention of the door guard, then the group physically overcomes the guard, making noise.
- A PC tries the roof and finds the trapdoor there, and maybe the trap too.

LOCATION DESCRIPTION

The warehouse interior is 100 feet by 60 feet, with a 15-foot ceiling. Stacks of wooden crates and barrels of all types are piled all over the place inside, except near the loading doors and within a square space outlined by boxes toward the back of the building. One wall is filled two-thirds high with crates and barrels. Different sections are marked with different seller's brands, and each group contains a different sort of common good: salted fish, sand, dried apples, rice, building materials, etc.

The warehouse seems quiet, too quiet in fact, because the PCs know at least six individuals went inside and only one left while they were watching, not including the door guard. There are actually a number of Redfang thugs inside, plus some gang enforcers.

If the PCs chose an option that made noise, the enemies inside will be ready and waiting for them (possible ambush). If they were quiet about it, the enemies will be lounging around a makeshift table just out of sight of the door. If they talked their way in, some enemies will hide, while others stand watching the interaction.

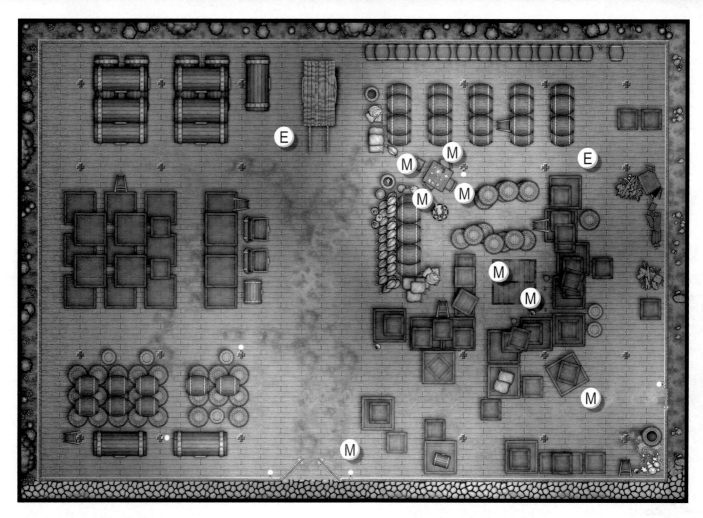

Terrain & Traps

Roof Trapdoor: Getting to the roof of the warehouse from outside isn't hard. It requires a successful DC 12 Strength check to climb it, with failure meaning those inside hear the PC's noisy attempts. Strangely, there aren't any guards on the roof (because that would mean there's something to protect inside, and this place is supposed to be a secret). There is, however, a trapdoor near the center of the roof. While the trapdoor does open to reveal the inside of the warehouse below, it's all part of a cunning trap itself.

The trapdoor, which pulls up and is unlocked, has a catchwire attached to it (DC 20 Wisdom check to notice; DC 15 Dexterity to disable). When tripped, a 10 x 10 section of the roof around the trapdoor suddenly opens and swings down, dropping anyone around the trapdoor into the warehouse (conveniently on top of the trapdoor below). Falling PCs take 1d10 damage and the thugs inside will get a surprise round.

Doors: The service double doors have a thick wooden bar across them on the inside; getting past either one requires a DC 25 Strength (brute force) or Dexterity (moving the bar with a lever) check, or 30 hp in weapon damage.

The side door is sturdy but much more accessible (DC 15 Strength or Dexterity). There's a string tied to a bell just inside the door that the guard can ring if he gets a chance. (Feel free to have any hit drop the guard, or use stats for one thug for him.)

Crates & Barrels: The crates and barrels are stacked anywhere from 3 to 10 feet high around the warehouse. There's a

ripe opportunity for swashbucklers, monks, and dexterous types to have some fun. Moving across this terrain requires a DC 13 Dexterity check for any dicey moves (DC 10 for simple ones), with failure resulting in a loss of the rest of the movement that turn, or possibly even getting stuck (save ends; falling into a barrel of oiled fish, for example).

Using the crates as a weapon or for other means also requires a DC 15 check (failing forward of course), and damage caused this way should be 1d6 to 2d6, depending on the action.

The crates and barrels are positioned such that there is a natural square open on one end near the center of the warehouse where some of the Redfang thugs will try to lure the PCs to fight.

Table: The table the thugs are sitting around is simply a makeshift crate on a half barrel, with crate seats. It holds some cards, dice, and a handful of copper coins, plus a half-empty skin of beer.

Floor Trapdoor The square formed by the crates is actually framing a trapdoor that swings down to a lower storage area. On the right-center of the map, there are two mooks who start the battle on the corners of the trapdoor. A lever near the back right corner of the warehouse will trip it. Anyone standing in the area when it opens will fall below and take 2d6 damage.

There's a ladder on one side of the opening that leads 20 feet down to the floor below. From this square, anyone looking up with notice the outline and hinged doors of the roof trapdoor.

The area below holds only a few barrels of beer stolen from a bar on the other side of town (marked with brand of the

Blue Lizard tavern). A tunnel-corridor leads deeper into the headquarters from here. Climbing back up the ladder requires a move action.

Monsters

The Redfang thugs will either be around a makeshift table gaming when the PCs enter the warehouse, or they'll be hidden behind crates, some waiting to fire crossbows. They wear normal clothing with no signs of gang affiliation on them. Most are human, but there are also a few halflings, half-elves, or half-orcs among them.

The enforcers will stick to the shadows, no matter how the PCs enter. They'll be hidden/out of sight until a battle starts.

There's one additional member of the gang, a young boy of 12 named Fulstin who's in the warehouse. He isn't a combatant, but he will throw the lever to the trapdoor at an opportune time and then try to flee outside to go warn the rest of the gang. He's good at seeming childlike since he's small, but he's one step away from being a ruthless thug himself.

Additional Reinforcements: If you want to challenge the PCs more, have 2d4 Redfang thugs enter the building dressed like town guards and demanding to know what's going on. They were out on a job in disguise and will pretend to help, only to get into a good position to attack the PCs.

#/Level of PCs	Gang Enforcer (E)	Redfang Thug Mook (M)
4 x 1st level	2	7 (1 mob)
5 x 1st level	2	11 (2 mobs)
6 x 1st level	3	10 (2 mobs)
4 x 2nd level	3	10 (1 mob)
5 x 2nd level	4	11 (2 mobs)
6 x 2nd level	5	12 (2 mobs)

Tactics

The thugs will rush the PCs, trying to gang up on one or two of them while they lure their enemies onto the trapdoor. Knowing the price of Redfang's wrath should they fail, the thugs will fight longer than most, but they will flee when down to only one or two with no enforcers around.

A quarter of the thugs will try to stay at range, putting their light crossbows to use.

The enforcers will try to sneak up on ranged attackers or spellcaster and deliver a vicious blow, then remain engaged in melee to try to drop that enemy.

If the thugs can draw at least two PCs onto the trapdoor, the boy will throw the lever, dropping them as the trapdoor swings open.

Loot

Each of the gang members has a few coins on them, though most keep their full stash hidden elsewhere. There's a total of 25 gp in mixed coins among them. One enforcer has a copper locket with the symbol of the Emperor on it; it may have been taken from someone in the Emperor's employ who wants it back badly, or it might be an indicator that the gang member was (or is) an agent for the Emperor.

Icons

A PC that has relationship advantages with the Prince, Diabolist, Emperor, or maybe the Dwarf King or Orc Lord could use one or more of them to help the group get inside without using force (initially) by showing the proper signs, saying the right words, acting like people who belong there, etc.

This could also be a time when multiple advantages with any icon (at least two, probably three) could get the PCs past the entire battle and escorted to the underground arena as participants or gamblers, if the PCs can spin a good story to explain their presence. The warehouse is an entrance only gang members use, so skill checks without advantages should probably only get PCs through the front door at best, and not beyond the warehouse (unless you choose otherwise).

REDFANG THUG

"No one messes with the Redfangs!"

1st level mook [HUMANOID]
Initiative: +3

Beatstick or knife +5 vs. AC—3 damage
  Desperate attackers: Once the mob has been reduced to half its hit points or less, targets hit by this attack take extra damage equal to the escalation die.

R: Light crossbow +6 vs. AC—4 damage

Strength in numbers: For every two allies engaged with the target of a thug's attack, it gains a +1 attack bonus with that attack.

AC	**16**	
PD	**15**	**HP 7 (mook)**
MD	**10**	

Mook: Kill one Redfang thug mook for every 7 damage you deal to the mob.

GANG ENFORCER

This ganger is different than the others. Her confidence in killing shows through.

2nd level spoiler [HUMANOID]
Initiative: +6

Shortsword +7 vs. AC—8 damage
  Natural roll is above target's Wisdom: The target is also dazed (save ends).
  Miss: 2 damage.

Strike from the shadows: If the enforcer is hidden, unengaged, and moves before making a melee attack, it will crit if the attack hits. The target can roll a DC 15 Wisdom check when this happens; on a success, the crit is a hit instead as the target reacts in time.

AC	**17**	
PD	**17**	**HP 33**
MD	**13**	

NEXT STEPS

After the battle, the PCs will find only one exit from the warehouse into the interior of the headquarters—through the room below the trapdoor in the floor. (If they talk their way through this battle, then the thugs will open the trapdoor and one will escort the PCs to the arena.) Go to **Battle 2: Underground Arena**.

BATTLE 2: UNDERGROUND ARENA

The corridor below the trapdoor leads down and deeper toward the gang's headquarters. The way is tight in places, and you take two turns before you see a ramp just ahead leading down to a lighted area. That's when you hear the twang and a click and the floor drops away, spilling you into a large room with a pit-cage in the center. As you recover from the fall, you see cage doors in the sides of the pit open to reveal huge scorpions scuttling toward you. There are yells and movement above the pit as gangers join the fray.

LOCATION DESCRIPTION

Adjust the introductory text if the PCs have managed to avoid the trapdoor or have talked their way to the arena (the thug leading them will point out the tripwire).

Yes, this is *another* trapdoor; see the full explanation in the Terrain & Traps section. The trapdoor in the corridor will probably drop the first rank of PCs 35 feet into the pit, unless there's only one scout. The next rank may go in as well (see **Terrain & Traps**). The corridor also continues past the trapdoor to a ramp that leads into the arena below.

The arena is an 80 x 80-foot room, with a 40 x 40-foot pit at the center. Iron cage walls rise up another 6 feet around the edges of the pit to make it harder for anything inside to get out. Surrounding the pit are three rows of tiered wood benches for viewing the action. A 10-foot walkway leads around the edge of the chamber behind the seats, with stairways down on each side. There are also two exits leading out of the room on that level.

The pit is 15 feet deep. Currently, there's an iron fence splitting it in half that will separate those falling into it (see the Pit in **Terrain**). Each side of the pit has a 5-foot wide exit tunnel covered by a wooden grate that will lift when the trapdoor triggers, allowing the scorpions access.

If the PCs have managed to talk their way into the headquarters this far, it probably stops here. There isn't a pit fight scheduled, and anyone approaching from the warehouse who's not a recognized member of the gang will be scrutinized heavily, and attacked if they don't have REALLY good answers, don't know the passwords, or don't have a token of entrance from Redfang. In this case, add one extra thug to the fight if one escorted them here.

TERRAIN & TRAPS

Trapdoor: There is a thin, black-painted metal tripwire strung across the corridor leading to the arena (most guests come from the other direction). Any PC not searching for traps will trigger it, causing a 5 x 8-foot trapdoor to swing open (though you could give

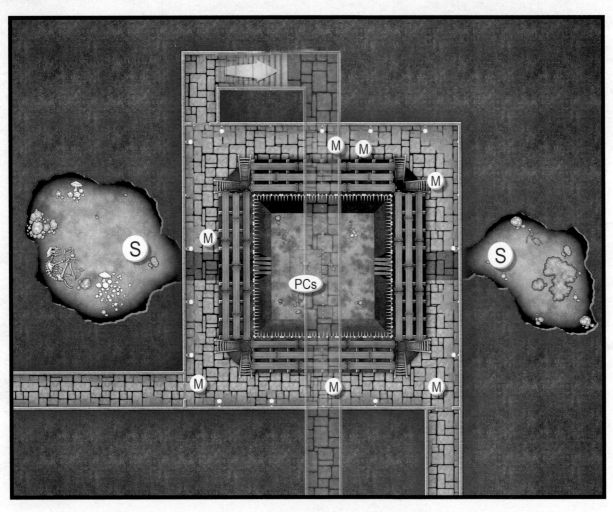

a rogue with Trap Sense who's in front of the group a chance to spot it (DC 18) first). If there's only one PC out in front, that character falls. If the group is together (or don't mention any sort of marching order), the first two fall automatically. Then the next rank of two can roll a save; on a failure, that PC also falls. The first two PCs fall into the pit on opposite sides of the fence. Anyone else falling rolls a d6 (1–3 to the left, 4–6 to the right), but a skill check might let them control their fall to one side or the other (GM's call).

It's a 35-foot drop and any PC that falls takes 3d6 damage. Moving past the trapdoor opening down the ramp into the arena chamber takes one move action, but there is some visibility of the entire chamber from above through the trapdoor opening for PCs who wish to remain there.

Pit: The pit is 15 feet deep. A fence of spiked iron bars also extends 10 feet up from the center of the pit, separating the two sides. To make things interesting, the thugs also greased the bars.

Anyone trying to climb the fence has to succeed on a DC 15 Strength or Dexterity check. The fence is sturdy, but a strong blow might bend or take down a section (DC 22 Strength check or 25 damage). Ranged attacks can be made through the fence, but not melee attacks unless the enemy gets pushed up against it (perhaps as a move action DC 15 Strength check by someone fighting on that side).

There are two wooden panels that lift when the trapdoor swings down, revealing a short corridor that leads to a small bone-filled pen where the scorpions are kept/fed. The thugs will lower them back into place from above during their turn. Breaking the gate requires a DC 20 Strength check.

Anyone falling into the pit from the benches takes 2d6 damage.

Iron Fencing & Benches: Circling the pit is a ring of iron bars spaced six inches apart and extending 4 feet from the top edges of the pit upward, to protect those betting from "escapes." It is possible to climb the center fence and leap to the bars around the edge, but it takes a successful DC 15 Strength check, and then a second such check as a move action for a creature to pull itself up and over. While hanging there, any hit that causes damage also forces a save to avoid falling back into the pit.

The wood benches are low with narrow spaces between them. They're also set on stone tiers that descend 10 feet from the walkway at the back to the edge of the pit. Movement along a row of benches is unhindered, but anyone trying a dicey move up or down them must roll a DC 10 check; on a failure, the move fails.

Monsters

In addition to the giant scorpions in the pit, there's a group of Redfang thugs lounging in this chamber eating, dicing, or taunting the scorpions to make them mad. If there's a second mob of thugs, that group is currently in the adjoining cell room and will enter the battle during the second round. Additional mobs will come from the same way the PCs did on the next round (either finding the warehouse attacked, or coming in through a secret entrance to the street).

Additional Reinforcements: If you want to challenge the PCs more, include a wood elf female gang enforcer (use stats from Battle 1) named Redbelle who's in the stands directing the thugs with some decent tactics.

#/Level of PCs	Giant Scorpions (S)	Redfang Thug Mook (M)*
4 x 1st level	2	9 (1 mob)
5 x 1st level	3	10 (1 mob)
6 x 1st level	4	11 (2 mobs)
4 x 2nd level	3	15 (3 mobs)
5 x 2nd level	4	15 (3 mobs)
6 x 2nd level	3**	16 (3 mobs)

* Add one thug to the battle if the PCs skipped the first battle and were escorted to the arena.

** Make each scorpion double-strength, doubling its hit points and attack damage.

Tactics

The scorpions will attack whatever is nearest to them, and then react to whichever enemy damages them.

The thugs will gang up on those not in the pit, moving up the ramp to attack anyone remaining near the trapdoor above (a great place for thugs to fall and die).

A few thugs will use their crossbows on PCs in the pit while the rest engage them in melee combat (unless all of the PCs fall into the pit, of course).

LOOT

The thugs have 30 gp in coins between them.

Scorpion venom would bring some gold from the right buyer, perhaps 25 gp per dose. Each scorpion has 1d2 doses, and removing the venom is a DC 15 check (one try only per scorpion).

ICONS

A PC that has relationship advantages with the Prince, Dwarf King, or maybe the Three (the Black) could use one or more of them to counteract the trapdoor trap or allow a PC to escape from the pit without a roll somehow if they have a good story about a similar situation.

A PC that has a relationship advantage with High Druid could use it to pacify a giant scorpion for as long as they spend standard actions to focus on it (ala Crocodile Dundee).

GIANT SCORPION

They say the pain of dying from giant scorpion poison competes with the shame of being eaten by an overgrown bug.

1st level wrecker [BEAST]
Initiative: +6

Pincer +6 vs. PD—1 damage, and the scorpion gains a +2 attack bonus against the same target this turn with its *stinger* attack
   Limited use: 2/round, each requiring a quick action. (Hitting the same target twice with *pincer* gives the *stinger* attack a +4 bonus.)

Stinger +6 vs. AC—3 damage, and 3 ongoing poison damage

AC	16	
PD	15	**HP 22**
MD	10	

REDFANG THUG

"No one messes with the Redfangs!"

1st level mook [HUMANOID]
Initiative: +3

Beatstick or knife +5 vs. AC—3 damage
   Desperate attackers: Once the mob has been reduced to half its hit points or less, targets hit by this attack take extra damage equal to the escalation die.

R: Light crossbow +6—4 damage

TALKING TO A PRISONER

There are two exits from the arena: one that leads deeper into the headquarters, and one that leads to a small room filled with cages and cells. In addition to captured beasts, the Redfangs force their captured enemies to fight in the arena to the delight of their invited guests.

After this battle, it might be a good time to rescue a prisoner from one of the cells. It's Rolander Fraye, a half-elf rogue or bard (or someone else that fits your story). He's a member of a rival gang, the Throatslitters, or perhaps a servant of one of the icons. This is a good opportunity to set up the next adventure by getting information from him, or by freeing him and as a thank you, he tells the PCs a secret.

He knows a little about the Redfangs' headquarters, and might be able to impart a bit of information in exchange for his freedom if the PCs don't seem to be interested in freeing him at first (he'll call out to get attention too, if needed).

He doesn't know much, but he can tell the PCs that there are rumors that Redfang is a tricky one who likes to guard her sanctum with traps she can trigger as she fights. "Makes sense of all the trapdoors, doesn't it? Fell in one myself."

Strength in numbers: For every two allies engaged with the target of a thug's attack, it gains a +1 attack bonus with that attack.

AC	16	
PD	15	**HP 7 (mook)**
MD	10	

Mook: Kill one Redfang thug mook for every 7 damage you deal to the mob.

NEXT STEPS

Once the PCs have taken down the thugs and extricated themselves from the pit (if needed), there are two exits to choose from. One leads to a nearby room filled with cells and cages to hold those who will fight in the arena. All but one are empty, if you decide to introduce Rolander. Or they're all empty if you can't be bothered with talkative NPCs.

The other room leads back upward toward a practice facility and the primary point of defense for the Redfang gang. See **Battle 3: Shadow Games**.

BATTLE 3: SHADOW GAMES

After a short walk through a twisting corridor that must follow the foundations of the surrounding buildings, it opens into a larger area ahead. Where there have been occasional lanterns hung along the way, the room beyond is cloaked in shadow. In fact, your light seems to dim as it gets nearer the chamber—shadow magic! Although visibility is poor, you get a sense that the room beyond is large, but also broken up with walls and objects of some type.

Location Description

This chamber is where the Redfang rogues practice their craft: sneaking, stealing, and murdering. They hired a wizard to devise a ritual to cloak the area in shadows, paying him to renew the magic once a week. There is visibility, but it's poor, similar to nighttime outside among the buildings with no moon and distant lanterns.

Currently practicing in the chamber are a group of streetshadow rogues, who play shadow games with each other involving trailing marks, pickpocketing passersby, and getting into position to slip a dagger into a back or across the throat. They are all very familiar with the terrain and know that no one is supposed to interrupt them, so they will recognize the PCs as enemies and begin stalking them.

The chamber is 120 feet long and 80 feet wide, with a 15-foot ceiling. Scattered throughout the area are short false walls to replicate building corners, wooden practice dummies with spikes holding melons to replicate targets, uneven flooring of pockmarked cobblestones to replicate terrain that's tough to move silently over, traps that suddenly attack, and more.

A closed wooden door in the middle of each wall exits the chamber.

Terrain & Traps

Low Visibility: Due to the poor light, any checks to detect objects or people take a –5 penalty, and there's no line of sight to far away enemies.

It is possible to remove the shadow magic laid upon the area, but it's difficult. As a standard action, a divine or arcane caster can attempt to force their will upon the magic while expending a limited power. The DC is 25 (using a primary casting ability), but using a daily power gives the PC a +3 bonus to the check (advantages could increase the bonus, or make it automatic). The shadows will fade for 1d3 + 1 rounds.

Shadowy Obstacles: While the area is covered in shadows, until the escalation die reaches 3+, when a PC moves during their turn, at the end of their movement they must roll a DC 15

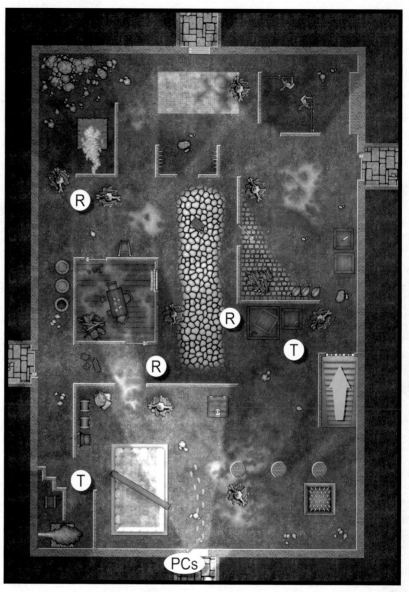

Dexterity check due to the bad footing and unseen obstacles. On a failure, that PC takes a –1 attack penalty to their next attack, and a –2 penalty to all defenses until the start of their next turn. Eventually, the PCs' eyes acclimate to the low light (GM, you can remove this check for PCs who would see well in shadows due to a *unique*, a racial ability, or other ability).

Sudden Attack Traps: When the escalation die is even, each PC must roll an easy save (6+) at the end of their turn. On a failure, they trigger a pressure plate in the ground that causes a trap to attack the area, simulating an ambusher. This represents spinning logs with blades that drop down as they spin, spring-loaded clubs that strike from behind a corner, and hidden crossbows with spring-triggers. When a trap triggers, make an attack against that PC and any PCs next to them.

Sudden attack trap +5 vs. AC—2d6 damage (single target) or 1d10 damage (multiple targets)

A PC can use a move action the turn before to roll a check to spot a trap (DC 15); on a success, they don't have to make a save during their next turn. Also, if a PC doesn't move or attack during a turn (basically standing still), they don't have to roll a save either.

Escalation	Shadowy Obstacles	Sudden traps
1	Yes, DC 15 Dex	No
2	Yes, DC 15 Dex	Yes, easy save 6+
3	No	No
4	No	Yes, easy save 6+
5	No	No
6+	No	Yes, easy save 6+

Monsters

The only enemies in the chamber are streetshadow rogues and trainers. Unless the PCs sneaked up on them somehow, they will be spread out throughout the chamber hiding. Detecting them while hidden requires a DC 20 check since they are geared up for shadow work (dark clothes, face grease, etc.)

Additional Reinforcements: If you want to challenge the PCs more, include sudden attack traps every round, or add an extra rogue or two to the group.

#/Level of PCs	Streetshadow Rogue (R)	Streetshadow Trainer (T)
4 x 1st level	2	1
5 x 1st level	3	1
6 x 1st level	3	2
4 x 2nd level	2	2
5 x 2nd level	3	2
6 x 2nd level	4	2

Tactics

The rogues will practice what they've learned, using a move action to engage an enemy, then using *shadowstrike* to attack and move for free out of engagement. The trainers will do the same, but they will try to silently work around toward any healers or spellcasters being protected, possibly even waiting one round to do so (give the PCs they are sneaking up on a DC 20 Wisdom check to notice the enemy).

At the start of the battle, and when possible during it, they will try to hide in the shadows to gain the advantage of their *hidden attacker* ability.

If the shadows disappear, the rogues will try to hide until the magic returns, or possibly flee if half their number has dropped.

Loot

The rogues and trainer have more wealth than the common thugs in the gang thanks to their skills. Each one carries 20 gp in coins

in a padded, soundproof pouch. They also carry thieves' tools that could bring in another 50 gp total on the black market. Each trainer has a well-made dagger set with a black opal as a sign of rank that's worth 30 gp.

One of them may have stolen something recently that's more valuable than they realize, possibly a piece of jewelry and love letter from a noble or person who's connected to an icon to the spouse of someone else important. That victim will do whatever is required to track down the thief, meaning whoever has the item/letter.

Icons

A PC that has relationship advantages with the Prince, Dwarf King, Elf Queen, the Three (the Black), or maybe the Archmage or High Druid could use one or more of them to help negate the terrain effects of the shadows for themselves (such as gaining twilight sight, or underworld sight, the senses of a bat, etc.)

A PC that has advantages with the Archmage, Elf Queen, Lich King, Priestess, or the Three (the Blue) could use one or more of them to help counteract the shadow magic (see Low Visibility, or gain a bonus to checks to see).

STREETSHADOW ROGUE

All you see is a slight movement in the shadows, and then the flash of a blade.

2nd level spoiler [HUMANOID]
Initiative: +7

Hidden blade +7 vs. AC—6 damage
Shadowstrike: After the attack, the rogue can pop free from the target and move as a free action.
Natural 19+: The attack is a critical hit.

Hidden attacker: When the streetshadow rogue is hidden from the target before it attacks, the target takes 1d8 extra damage from the attack, hit or miss (except natural 1).

AC	18	
PD	17	**HP 33**
MD	11	

STREETSHADOW TRAINER

What looks like a section of the wall suddenly moves, and then you're bleeding... badly.

3rd level spoiler [HUMANOID]
Initiative: +8

Concealed blade +8 vs. AC—9 damage
Shadowstrike: After the attack, the trainer can pop free from the target and move as a free action.
Natural 18+: The attack is a critical hit.

Hidden attacker: When the streetshadow trainer is hidden from the target before it attacks, the target takes 1d8 extra damage from the attack, hit or miss (except natural 1).

Master of the shadows: While in shadowy light, the trainer gains a +5 bonus to disengage checks.

AC	17	
PD	18	**HP 40**
MD	13	

NEXT STEPS

There are three other exits from the training chamber. One of them leads to a barracks-like room of beds with an attached larder and small kitchen where the gang members can congregate and rest. The second leads to a weapons room that holds 100 gp in common, poor quality weapons, including some bows and crossbows, plus plenty of wooden dummy weapons. The last door eventually leads to Redfang, the crime lord leader of the Redfangs. See **Battle 4: Redfang's Sanctum.**

BATTLE 4: REDFANG'S SANCTUM

A set of steep wooden stairs before you leads down to an open archway through which torchlight flickers. As you descend, one of the steps collapses and the entire stairs suddenly flatten into a ramp, spilling you into a medium-sized room full of Redfangs gang members. A big half-orc standing on a raised dais with a pair of long iron levers sticking out of it grins, her red-stained fangs showing through. "So you're the gutter punks sent to snuff Redfang? Not today! Make them hurt, Fangs!"

LOCATION DESCRIPTION

Change the flavor text if the PCs managed to notice and avoid the stair trap (DC 20 for those specifically searching, and note that this trap doesn't do any damage, it just slides you all down to the floor). Unless the PCs have been amazing in their stealth or ability to talk their way through the battles, Redfang will be aware of the PCs' advance from her troops that escaped or fled before the PCs even saw them, and will be ready to spring the trap.

She awaits them in her sanctum—half opulent gang throne room, half chamber of death. The dais where Redfang waits rises only 2 feet off the wooden floor around it, but it's an important location for her as an island of calm in the chaos that's about to start. A slightly worn yet still opulent throne-like chair sits on the dais behind her, and the entire platform is in the center of the far wall from the entrance.

The rectangular chamber is 40 feet wide and 70 feet long, with a 30-foot ceiling. There are two 20-foot-high balconies—one to either side—that look down upon the main chamber, with no sign of stairs to them (reached via a door near Redfang). There is one other exit from the room, a closed door near the dais, and the way back requires climbing the steep stair-ramp.

Some of Redfang's thugs are spread out across the floor and in one of the balconies, and a beautiful, dark-haired and golden-skinned human woman in a flowing silk robe is standing in the other balcony.

GM, if your group likes to talk first and kill enemies after, feel free to have the PCs interact with Redfang before rolling initiative. With good role-playing and roll-playing, plus icon advantages, they might be able to avoid a fight and gain concessions from Redfang, in exchange for doing her a favor....

TERRAIN & TRAPS

Ramp-stair: The ramp is steep and smooth. Anyone who tries to scramble back up it must roll a successful DC 15 Strength check. There's no line of sight from the top back into the chamber except at the base of the ramp. Redfang controls the ramp with the levers.

Dais & Door: The dais is 6 x 10, with the chair taking up some of the space. There's only room for one other creature besides Redfang to fight on it normally. A second PC can attempt to fight while standing on the chair, but takes a −2 penalty to attacks and all defenses while doing so. A PC could probably try

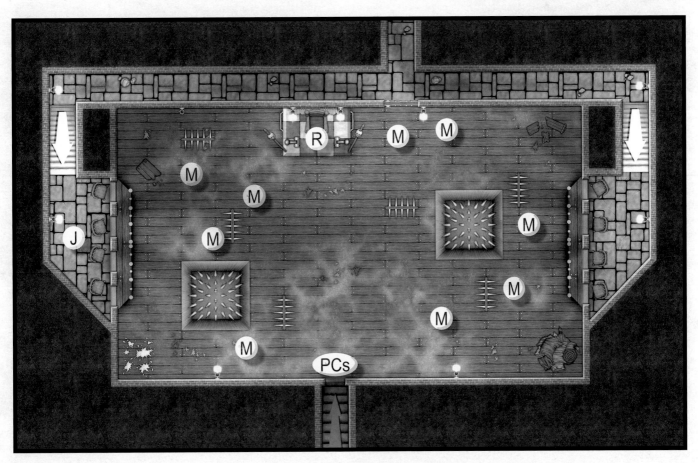

to balance on the edge of the dais, stepping up as a terrain effect triggers, but that would require a DC 15 Dexterity check each time. The chair is nailed to the platform.

The door is currently locked. One of the levers will open it. A DC 15 skill check using Strength (bashing it) or Dexterity (jimmying it) can open it.

Balconies: The balconies are 20 feet up, and the room was designed to make it hard to climb to them (the wood walls are sanded and oiled). Anyone doing so must succeed on a DC 20 Strength check. Each balcony is 15 feet long and 10 feet wide, with an exit to a corridor and stairway that leads down to the door by the dais.

Rapidly Changing Terrain: Redfang will go last each round. During her turn, she will use a quick action to throw a lever if she can. At the start of the next round (when the escalation die advances), the terrain in the room changes according to the value of the escalation die. If the PCs learned of the room's tricks from a prisoner, feel free to give them a +1 or +2 bonus to defenses or saves against these effects. These effects don't affect anyone on the dais, and they must run the full course before resetting. If someone decreases the escalation die, go back to the effect based on that number.

1: **Floor tilt:** The floor tilts downward 2 feet to the right. Each creature (including enemies not on the dais) must roll an immediate save; on a failure, it slides/tumbles 10 feet and loses its move action that turn.

2: **Spikes:** Spikes rise out of the floor, attacking 3 random creatures in the battle. For each spear roll a d6 to determine if it's an enemy (1–5) or an ally (6). Then make the following attack against that creature. A creature can be attacked by more than one spike.

3: **Floor spikes +6 vs. PD**—4 damage, and 3 ongoing damage.

4: **Floor tilt:** The floor tilts downward 4 feet to the left. Each creature must roll an immediate save; on a failure, it slides/tumble 15 feet and loses its move action that turn. The floor is now 2 to 4 feet below the dais, so attempts to move to the dais might require a check.

5: **Spikes:** Spikes rise out of the floor, attacking 3 random creatures in the battle. For each spear roll a d6 to determine if it's an enemy (1–5) or an ally (6). Then make the following attack against that creature. A creature can be attacked by more than one spike.

6: **Floor spikes +6 vs. PD**—4 damage, and 3 ongoing damage.

7: **Floor tilt and Pits:** First the floor tilts 2 foot to the right to become level. Then, two 5 x 5 trapdoor pits open up in the floor. Randomly roll for each creature in the battle standing on the floor (but not the dais, and reroll if you get the same creature twice). The creature must roll an immediate save; on a failure, it's stuck (save ends) in a 4 x 4 x 10 pit (a tight wooden box) and is able to see only targets directly above it. As a move action, someone can move next to the pit and lend a hand to make the save easy. The pits stay open, and creatures can fall or be thrown into them with the same results.

8: **Floor lift:** With grinding gears, counterweights drop and the entire floor rapidly rises 4 feet back to its starting position.

Each PC must roll a DC 12 Dexterity check or become unbalanced and take a −2 penalty that turn to attacks, defenses, and physical skill checks. Each enemy must roll an easy save (6+) or suffer the same effects.

Monsters

Redfang is the leader of this gang, who call themselves "Redfangs" or "fangs." Besides being a capable warrior, Redfang has a trick up her sleeve: she controls the terrain. By throwing one of the levers, she can put obstacles and dangers in the way of anyone on the floor, including her own people. His troops follow her orders almost without question.

The thugs on the floor wait with weapons drawn, ready for what's about to start. The ones in the balcony have crossbows out.

The human woman on the balcony is Redfang's current girlfriend, a gang enforcer named Jalara, who is quite good with her poisoned throwing knives. For larger groups of PCs, include her cousin Jana, and possibly Kohlia. Redfang isn't quite as quick to order Jalara to her death as she is to expend the rest of her thugs, but the gang leader won't die for love. Conversely, if Jalara will did for love, Jana and Kohlia probably won't.

Additional Reinforcements: If you want to challenge the PCs more, include 1d4 human thugs (core rulebook, page 235) already in the chamber. They are members of the Bloody Smashers gang that Redfang captured previously. She tells them they get to live if they can kill the PCs.

#/Level of PCs	Redfang (R)	Jalara (J)	Redfang Thug Mook (M)
4 x 1st level	1	1	3 (1 mob)
5 x 1st level	1	1	5 (1 mob)
6 x 1st level	1	1	9 (1 mob)
4 x 2nd level	1	1	9 (1 mob)
5 x 2nd level	1	2*	10 (2 mobs)
6 x 2nd level	1	3*	11 (2 mobs)

* Redfangs' desires are strong and she has additional girlfriend-enforcers present.

TACTICS

Redfang will remain on the dais, forcing enemies to come to her through her thugs, which also buys her time to throw levers. She is far away from the PCs at the start of the battle. She will look for and taunt the PC who seems to be leading, but will focus attacks on whoever tries to engage her on the dais.

The thugs on the floor will move to attack in groups, but a few will stay back to intercept any PCs trying to get to the boss too quickly. The ones in the balcony have instructions to fire upon spellcasters, especially healers.

Jalara has eyes only for Redfang, and her protection. She will use her throwing knives from the balcony on enemies attacking Redfang (balcony to dais is nearby), unless someone is trying to reach her or engages her. The same goes for any of her cousin-rivals.

LOOT

Redfang wears three gold rings on one hand; each is different but only worth about 20 gp. The thugs have a few coins among them to the tune of 15 gp. Jalara wears a fine silver and jade necklace Redfang gave her worth 50 gp.

In addition, beyond the door by the dais are a number of living quarters and other rooms where the gang members reside. Redfang keeps a stash of 180 gp hidden in his chamber in a cavity behind a fake torch sconce.

There is also a chamber below the floor of the sanctum. It contains wood and metal gears, counterweights, the pit boxes, mechanical beams full of spikes, and a gear-slot system for the room drops of the terrain traps in the sanctum. Most of the equipment is heavy or bulky, but an enterprising PC might be able to find some value in the equipment (up to about 150 gp).

ICONS

A PC that has relationship advantages with the Prince, Dwarf King, Emperor, or maybe the Three could use one or more of them to have some knowledge of the terrain tricks of the sanctum (builder's drawings, former gang members, or whatever). This could mean the ability for them to avoid the terrain dangers altogether (tilt, spikes, or pit) or perhaps a +1 or +2 bonus for all the PCs from those effects.

REDFANG, CRIME LORD

The half-orc strikes an imposing figure with her huge mace and blood-red fangs—she eggs you on to test yourself against her room of death. She'll stop trash-talking when it looks like you might win.

Double-strength 2nd level wrecker [HUMANOID]
Initiative: Goes last each round

Battering strike +7 vs. AC—15 damage
Natural roll is above target's Strength: The target pops free as it gets knocked backward, and it moves into engagement with a nearby enemy.
Miss: 4 damage, and Redfang gains a +2 bonus with her next melee attack this battle.

R: Hurled dagger +7 vs. AC—11 damage
Limited use: 2/battle.

Savvy street fighter: Redfang is used to fighting in tight places and knows how to keep her tactical advantages (like next to the levers). Checks to move her off the dais take a –5 penalty.

AC	18	
PD	17	**HP 75**
MD	14	

JALARA

Her knives coated in asp venom are nearly as deadly as her beauty.

2nd level archer [HUMANOID]
Initiative: +6

Dagger slash +6 vs. AC—5 damage

R: Poisoned throwing knife +7 vs. AC—7 damage
Natural even hit: The target takes 5 ongoing poison damage.
First failed save: The target is also weakened (save ends both).
Second failed save: The save is now hard (16+)

AC	16	
PD	17	**HP 33**
MD	14	

REDFANG THUG

"No one messes with the Redfangs!"

1st level mook [HUMANOID]
Initiative: +3

Beatstick or knife +5 vs. AC—3 damage
Desperate attackers: Once the mob has been reduced to half its hit points or less, targets hit by this attack take extra damage equal to the escalation die.

R: Light crossbow +6—4 damage

Strength in numbers: For every two allies engaged with the target of a thug's attack, it gains a +1 attack bonus with that attack.

AC	16	
PD	15	**HP 7 (mook)**
MD	10	

Mook: Kill one Redfang thug mook for every 7 damage you deal to the mob.

Next Steps

Investigation of the remaining buildings that the gang controls reveals that word about Redfang's demise or capture is out and the other gang members have scattered to the wind, taking as many valuables with them as they could.

As the PCs search the buildings, it would be a perfect time to introduce a letter to Redfang or one of her enforcers from the Prince's people outlining some scheme, or perhaps dropping an item that the gang stole that one of the PCs was searching for. And, of course, there could be links to Redfang's boss, someone up the crime ladder who she made payments to, and who won't be happy that source of income was removed from his or her portfolio.

Back-alley Politics Story Endings

Here are outcomes for each story opening, detailing what success or failure might mean.

If the PCs did face all four battles, remember to give them a full heal-up.

Freedom Comes At a Price

Success: The person blackmailing the PC returns their item in an indirect manner (probably, unless it seems doable to blackmail them again). The PCs take the credit (and blame) for putting down Redfang, and whatever such consequences bring.

Failure: A local noble, member of an icon's organization, or possibly even a high-ranking member of the local thieves' guild is murdered and the PC's item is left at the scene. Arcane or divine magic is used to trace the item to the PC, and the authorities, members of that icon's organization, or possibly guild thieves are now after the PC and their accomplices.

Clearing Their Names

Success: The local crime lord named Redfang was behind the blackmail scheme, hoping the PCs would wipe out a rival gang. Now that she's dead, and the PC's item recovered, that problem is solved. Of course, it's not clear why Redfang targeted the PC; in fact, that seems like a smarter move than Redfang would normally make.

Failure: Redfang has an important person murdered as with the failure with Freedom Comes at a Price. Perhaps to have some other pawn take the fall instead with "new evidence," Redfang blackmails the group into a different job that will help her.

Hazard Pay for Dangerous Work

Success: In addition to whatever the PCs gain from the Redfangs, their contact comes through with payment in the form of a 200 gp blue garnet medallion. Of course, the item is hot and anyone trying to sell or pawn it will run afoul of its owner. Or maybe the payment is another job full of "easy money," or a really quirky magic item.

Failure: Not only do they not get their pay, but they bungle things so badly that Redfang puts a hit out on them, and their contact sets them up to fight his own goons for the reward offered on their heads.

Help Me Save This Town

Success: The PCs end Redfang's menace, but their contact doesn't show up to pay. Investigation reveals there's no such person serving the icon that was supposedly in play. Luckily, no one really seems to care that Redfang is gone, but there is word of a new up-and-comer crime boss who's taking over Redfang's turf.

Failure: Word gets out that the PCs attacked Redfang and her gang in the name of the authorities, or of one of the icons. The repercussions cause trouble for that group, who didn't want to be involved. Now they're looking for the PCs too, to explain things. And the only way they'll let them off the hook is if the PCs do a job for them.

The Price of Doing Business

Success: The PCs hold up their end, taking out Redfang's gang. The rival ganglord holds up her end too. But she also wants to know if the PCs want more work, considering how effective they were.

Failure: Redfang is still alive and looking for them now, plus the other ganglord puts the word out, and now every shopkeeper is overcharging them, no one is willing to talk to them or give them information, and they keep getting targeted by pickpockets and thugs.

Battle Scene Connections

The stories from this set of battle scenes can lead to scenes in future books:

 The King's Tribute (Dwarf King): One of the items the PCs picks up in Redfang's hideout is the item stolen by one of his sneaks that Lord Silveraxe needs.

 Temple Reclamation (Priestess): The PCs find a note among Redfang's possessions from his cousin Grisla, inviting him to join her for a raid on a nearby temple said to have valuable religious relics inside. Her attack will happen in a few days' time, possibly enough time to get there to stop it (but not).

 The Secret Crypt (Lich King): As the PCs finish up the job of taking down Redfang, a strange figure approaches from the shadows of an alley in the wrong part of town. It seeks help with the crypt.

PRINCE OF SHADOWS: MAD WIZARD'S LOOT

LEVEL RANGE: 5–6

The themes of this set of battles are performing under pressure, dealing with strange magic guardians and traps, and navigating the Prince's schemes.

This set of battle scenes works best while the PCs are in an urban environment where they hear about the wizard's vault.

Through one means or another, those in the Prince's employ have convinced (or extracted leverage on) the PCs to perform a job. The PCs need to retrieve an item of importance to the icon (or at least to those requesting it) to have that leverage removed. The catch is that the item or loot they're after is stored in the vault of Soohnei, a mad gnome wizard.

Whether Soohnei still lives is unknown, but his abode is well-known among certain circles for the difficulty of breaching its defenses. Many have tried, and most have failed... horribly. The PCs' new friend thinks they're the heroes for the job.

The PCs need to get in, bypass the obstacles and guardians, find the vault, and get out with the item, keeping anything else they find for themselves. It could be an item that the PCs are looking for as well to add drama, but if not, as a default they are told to retrieve the *Tome of Names*, a book rumored to provide the names of those requested of it (like who stole the Imperial governor's wife's diamond necklace, or what is the name of the merchant in New Port with the Emerald Pin of the Third Emperor).

The wizard's abode is within a small hill on the outskirts of a city, town, or village in the area, and everyone around it knows to avoid the place because of the mad wizard's strange and dangerous ways.

MAD WIZARD'S LOOT STORY OPENINGS

- **Four Days to Live:** The PCs are approached by a shady-looking dark elf after a night spent carousing in one or more taverns in a city or town. He tells them that he's poisoned one or more (or all) of them with a rare and deadly toxin, of which only he can provide the cure. If they want it, they need to do a job for him retrieving something from a wizard's vault. The upset stomachs and chills the PCs begin to have match the symptoms he describes, giving his story some teeth. Luckily, they will be mostly fine until a few hours before the toxin kills them, so they should act quickly.

- **To Catch a Thief:** A local Imperial authority approaches one of the PCs who has a negative or conflicted relationship with the Prince. Someone stole something VERY important to that person's superior. They want the thief's name, but no one is talking (like normal). So they need a workaround. Rumors suggest a mad wizard nearby has a book that can help. If the PCs retrieve it, they will be well-rewarded, and see another member of the Prince's network pay for their crimes.

- **The Test:** One or more of the PCs with a positive or conflicted relationship with the Prince is contacted by his shadowy network. It's time to prove their loyalty if they wish to continue advancing in the ranks. To do this, they must successfully perform a job. There's a mad wizard with a vault nearby, and they need to get into that vault and retrieve something. If successful, their reputations will be secure.

- **The Score:** Word has been cycling among the shadow network that there's a rich target to hit. A mad gnome wizard named Soohnei recently keeled over dead according to eye witnesses. He was rumored to be very wealthy, and his abode must be filled with rich loot. The only problem is, a few who tried it had no luck due to the magical protections the wizard had in place that are still active. Somebody is going to get past them eventually, however, and when they do it will be the score of a lifetime. A contact of the PCs in the Prince's network is willing to tell the PCs where the wizard's abode is located, in exchange for them retrieving one item from the vault for them.

ALTERNATE ICONS

Archmage: The mad wizard instead went rogue from the Archmage's teachings and left with "certain valuable items" that the head wizard's people want returned.

Lich King: The mad wizard was actually trying to become a lich, but the process killed him. The Lich King's lieutenants want certain items the wizard had been given to be returned before any servants of the other icons can get ahold of them. The PCs are either blackmailed into doing it with a death curse, or bribed into doing it with the promise of wealth or magical knowledge.

Icons in Play

Characters that have relationships (and story-guide advantages) with the Prince of Shadows, Archmage, Lich King, the Three (the Black), and maybe the Elf Queen or Dwarf King should be able to shine in these battle scenes. Moreso than PCs with other icon relationships, feel free to give such PCs extra knowledge about the opposition, make checks to pull off fun actions the players might suggest, and use their advantages to particularly good effect, such as negating or bypassing some of the advantages or abilities of the enemies.

Mad Wizard's Loot Overview

This job is more complicated than advertised, of course. In addition to some nasty guardians and tricks the mad gnome wizard Soohnei has in place, there are others who've had the same idea of looting the wizard's home as well, and they found a quicker way in.

Battle 1 involves entering the wizard's abode, a warren of chambers inside a small hill. In addition to the constructs that guard the approach, the PCs will have to be smart enough to bypass the door guardian.

Once inside the wizard's home, the PCs will have to navigate the strange place and deal with one "trap" that forces them to give up valuables in order to proceed. Those who give bad gifts bring Battle 2 to the group in the form of some lightning constructs.

Adding Tension to These Battles

If you used the opening where the PCs are poisoned or cursed, as added tension, you could introduce timed consequences into the game (but it works best if each PC is afflicted). During each quick rest, whenever the PCs dawdle, and when the escalation die reaches 5+ during a battle, something bad happens due to their affliction.

Be aware that adding tension this way will make tough battles even more difficult, but it should also scare the players and add drama to the scenes. Here are a few possible options:

- Each afflicted PC takes damage equal to their recovery dice roll.
- Each afflicted PC takes a –2 cumulative penalty to damage rolls (min 1).
- Each afflicted PC takes a –1 cumulative penalty to saves.
- Each afflicted PC must roll a save. On a failure, they are vulnerable until the next time they roll this save.

The PCs aren't the only ones trying to reach the vault. When they reach the vault door, Battle 3 has the PCs encounter a group of rogues with the same idea who don't want to share.

Battle 4 occurs once the PCs breach the vault if they try to take what they came for. The mad wizard has employed apex zorigami and other clockwork creatures to defend his valuables, and they do it well.

GM, feel free to expand upon these battles by including more fights with constructs and other weird magical creatures within the halls of Soohnei's abode.

The battles outlined here can take place over a few minutes or hours, depending on the PCs' pace and need. The locations should exude a sense of madness, magic, oddities, and the threat of double-crosses.

See story endings after the final battle for options on what happens after the PCs finish the last battle.

Battle 1: The Front Door

Finding Soohnei's lair wasn't easy—few people knew its location, and almost all of them warned you away from the place. Ahead of you a small hill rises from the flat, surrounding land like a blood blister from a smashed thumb. A search reveals only one obvious way in, a large stone door carved with the image of a large ogre-like humanoid on it. Flanking each door is a gnome-faced granite bust carved out of the stone around the door. As you near, one of the gnome faces animates and turns your direction.

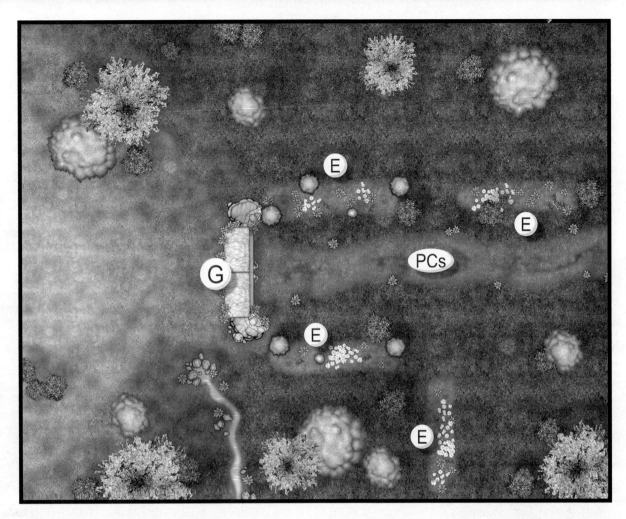

Location Description

The door is 15 feet high and 10 feet wide, but the whole thing isn't a real door, it just looks like one. A smaller door between the ogre's legs can open magically at the order of the gnome bust.

The hill is roughly 80 feet high and hundreds of feet in diameter. The PCs can easily climb it and look around, but there are no signs of any other entrances.

The ground around the door is grass and dirt with a few wildflowers growing around the edges in what once may have been flower beds.

The animated gnome face is a door guardian that will require the PCs to pass its test before it will grant them passage (see Door Guardian below). If any PCs attempt to break or force the door, the ogre golem will emerge from the door and earth elementals will rise from the ground to attack. If any PCs fail to answer the door guardian's question correctly, it will call forth the waiting constructs to deal with them as well.

Terrain & Traps

Door Guardian: Strong magic was used to craft the door guardian, and either gnome face can animate to talk to the PCs (with some crazy attitude). When someone gets near, it will challenge them. It asks, *"What is your name, where do you call home, and who is your master?"*

The answers are unimportant to some extent since Soohnei is no longer around to hear them (and learn about his guests),

except that they help trigger this puzzle and perhaps force PCs to reveal secret information about themselves. The heroes can lie without repercussion (but they won't know that). The name they give is the key here.

In response to their answers, the door guardian will speak two nonsensical sentences (see table below, and feel free to make up your own; you can use both on same row or randomly pick each) to throw the players off, followed by the words *"The answer is X. Why?"* In this case, X is the number of letters in the PC's name (so it's good to know how they spell it ahead of time—GM, if you aren't sure, don't ask the player now since that will give it away, just use your best guess and roll with it). For example, if the PC's name is Golax, then the statue says, "The answer is five. Why?"

The guardian will give the PC a moment to think before demanding an answer (let the players discuss it for no more than a minute). If the PC answers correctly, the guardian will say, *"Very well, you'll be allowed to enter."* If not, it will say, *"If you don't know the count then I have no interest in you. Leave now or pay the price!"* Hopefully using the term "count" is a clue. If they keep failing, feel free to have the gnome face drop other clues mentioning how *"a name is a terrible thing to waste"* and *"reading and math are the basics of any good education."* Don't feel the need to make it too easy though. Each PC gets one shot.

If any PC answers incorrectly, the guardian will summon magical help to send the PCs packing after the last PC answers (no one who failed is allowed in without a fight). But for each correct answer, remove one earth elemental from the battle. If all correct answers are given, feel free to allow the PCs to bypass the door battle freely. Or have only the ogre golem take exception and step out of the door to confront the PCs anyway due to conflicting orders given by the mad wizard (GM choice).

Once the enemies are defeated, or if correct answers were given, the smaller door will unseal and pop open for the PCs to pass.

Nonsensical Sentence 1	Nonsensical Sentence 2
Three for blue, buckle your shoe.	The pearl is in the liver.
Four or more opens the door.	Some old crow, don't you know.
Two by two, they never grew.	Nine and four, not a gold piece more.
One is the loneliest number.	Same as it ever was.
Five, six, seven, eight, that's a wrap.	More from the Prince, what a bunch of wimps.
Three or less, never confess.	Know your role, and never let go.

Doors: The large door is false, although it looks to have seams/cracks like a normal door (part of the intricate carving). A PC investigating it will notice the fact that it's a fake with a DC 25 Wisdom check.

Almost imperceptible is the fact that the archway created by the ogre's legs is a smaller 5-foot door. The seams are nearly perfect, so it will also take a DC 30 Wisdom check to notice this fact.

If you like, feel free to lower the DC by 5 for a dwarf or a PC with a unique or background related to stone, masonry, carving, or doors.

Ground: Anyone investigating the earth around the door will notice that something large and heavy left imprints here and there (the ogre golem). A successful DC 15 Wisdom check reveals they are roughly foot-shaped with no toes and a few days old.

MONSTERS

The ogre golem attacks if any PCs answers incorrectly (after all PCs have answered), if the PCs try to bypass the door without answering the questions, or if the PCs are correct but you want a partial battle anyway. It basically steps directly out of the door, peeling itself away from the stone.

The earth elementals are summoned from the area and appear as they rise up from the soil around the PCs. If some PCs answered correctly and there are less elementals than PCs, those characters won't have an elemental facing them.

Additional Reinforcements: If you want to challenge the PCs more, have two chaos beasts (*Bestiary*, page 39) emerge from the empty door face where the golem came from as they exploit a seam between dimensions through the magic of the door. Of course, they will combine into a chaos brute.

#/Level of PCs	Ogre Golem (G)	Earth Elemental (E)*
4 x 5th level	1	4
5 x 5th level	1	5
6 x 5th level	1	6
4 x 6th level	1	6
5 x 6th level	1	9
6 x 6th level	1	11

* Remove 1 earth elemental for each PC that answers correctly.

TACTICS

The elementals use straightforward tactics and attack until destroyed without disengaging. The ogre golem will focus on any PC not being attacked by elementals. When the golem is destroyed, the magic of this place causes the bits of stone and gravel to begin flowing back into the door (it will be whole again by the time the PCs leave unless they stop the process somehow).

LOOT

Nothing for this battle, unless someone collects elemental dirt and convinces an NPC it's valuable.

ICONS

A PC with a relationship advantage with the Prince, Archmage, Elf Queen, or maybe the Dwarf King could use an advantage to trick the door guardian, convincing it that their answer is correct even when it isn't. That wrong answer should have echoes down the line.

Ogre Golem

It lumbers along without grace, but those granite fists only need to connect once to end you.

Large 7st level wrecker [CONSTRUCT]
Initiative: +7

Granite fists +10 vs. AC (2 attacks)—25 damage
Natural even hit: The target is dazed (save ends).
Natural odd hit: The target is hampered until the end of its next turn.
Miss: 12 damage.

Foot stomp +11 vs. PD (one dazed enemy)—40 damage, and the target is knocked unconscious and helpless (save ends).

Golem immunity: Non-organic golems are immune to effects. They can't be dazed, weakened, confused, made vulnerable, or touched by ongoing damage. You can damage a golem, but that's about it.

Nastier Specials

Vindictive golem: When the golem hits with a *granite fists* attack, it grabs the target. It can grab up to two creatures at the same time. When it attacks with its fists while grabbing an enemy, it will use that grabbed creature to smash new targets. The target takes normal damage and the grabbed enemy takes 12 damage on a hit (4 damage on a miss).

AC	23	
PD	20	**HP 200**
MD	15	

BONUS SCENE – THE WIZARD'S GIFTS

The Wizard's Gift is a short bonus scene which slots between this battle and Facing the Competition. It is included with the downloadable version of **High Magic and Low Cunning**.

Earth Elemental

5th level blocker [ELEMENTAL]
Initiative: +7

Rocky fists +9 vs. AC (2 attacks)—11 damage
Miss: 4 damage.

Boulder up: Roll a d10 at the start of each of the earth elemental's turns. If you roll less than or equal to the escalation die, it shifts into boulder guardian form until the end of the battle. While in this form, it gains a +2 bonus to AC and the *relentless pursuit* ability (and you stop rolling *boulder up* checks).

Relentless pursuit: The elemental must be in boulder guardian form to use this ability. Staggered enemies can't disengage from the earth elemental. (They can pop free, but they can't roll disengage checks.)

Repair damage 10 and below: When the earth elemental is targeted by a natural attack roll of 10 or less, the elemental heals 1d12 damage before taking any damage from the attack.

AC	21	
PD	20	**HP 66**
MD	15	

NEXT STEPS

If the PCs defeat the golem, the door opens once the golem reforms above it while the gnome faces make smalltalk about the prowess of the group and the fact that the wizard is really crazy, so good luck and all that. The hill looks to be filled with a warren of hallways and chambers. After a little exploration, they will move through a few more areas with only common items such as labs and storage rooms before finally following a ramp down into a chamber that holds the vault. Waiting there is a rival group of roguish types who teleported in to access the vault. Not wanting any competition, they will attackt. Go to **Battle 2: Facing the Competition.**

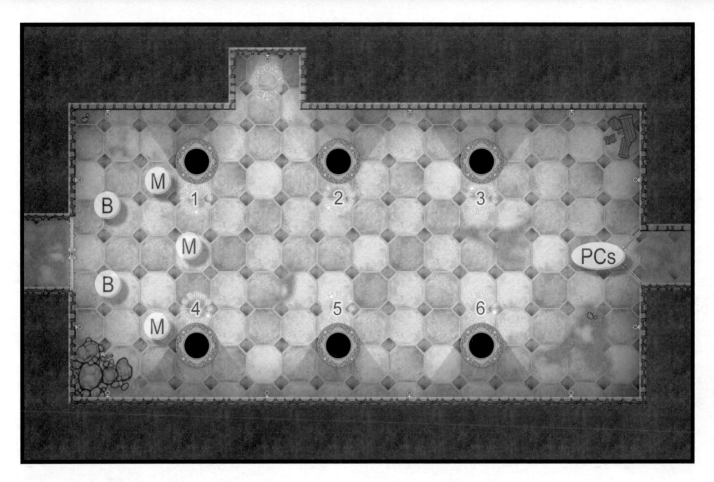

BATTLE 2: FACING THE COMPETITION

The ramp opens up into a large chamber whose roof is supported by six circular marble pillars carved with depictions of magical creatures. A recessed nook in the wall to the right holds a large glowing circle of silver light, and there is a similar but smaller set of glowing silver runes inscribed into the floor near each pillar. Set into an archway on the far wall is a narrow door made of dark metal glowing blue with magical energy. Of more concern, however, are the handful of humanoids arrayed in front of the door. A world-weary looking halfling woman in dark leathers looks you over briefly and then says, "Take care of them boys. We got no room for competitors!"

LOCATION DESCRIPTION

The chamber is 80 x 40 with a 20-foot ceiling supported by the 5-foot diameter pillars. The nook holds a teleportation portal these thieves used to access this chamber. It is also keyed to the six 2-foot diameter circles near the pillars: each is a teleportation circle.

The vault door is still locked and sealed by a magic ward since these rogues haven't yet cracked it. Anyone interacting with the door before bringing the ward down is in for a dangerous surprise.

The chamber holds a mix of halfling burglars and their hired muscle (various races). They are far away, unless someone uses a teleportation circle.

TERRAIN & TRAPS

Teleportation Circles: There are six teleportation circles, plus the large portal in the wall nook. Each one is fully active. Once per turn when someone steps onto a circle, they are teleported to a different circle, which might allow useful positioning. The circles aren't perfectly aligned, however, so there's some randomness to the movement.

When someone steps into a circle by a pillar, roll a d6. On a 1–3, they move to the circle that is one lower in sequence (so from 5 to 4, or 1 to 6). On a 4–6, they move to the circle that is one higher in sequence (so from 2 to 3, or 6 to 1). When someone moves into the portal in the nook, also roll a d6. That creature moves to the circle matching the rolled number.

It is possible to negate the teleportation magic in one of the circles for the duration of the battle, but not the portal in the nook. A PC with a magical background can do so by succeeding on a DC 25 skill check using their primary spellcasting ability. When a circle is inactive, all movement through it goes to the next number upward.

Pillars: Each pillar is circular and 5 feet in diameter. They provide concealment for those trying to hide, and might grant a +2 bonus to AC as cover from ranged attacks if you wish. Climbing one isn't hard due to the carvings and requires a DC 12 Strength or Dexterity check.

Vault Door: If someone touches the vault door (or gets thrown against it), the magic of the ward will flare. Make a *vault blast* attack when that happens.

C: Vault blast +10 vs. PD (one creature touching it, plus the closest 1d3 nearby creatures)—The creature touching it takes 5d8 lightning damage, and each other creature hit by the attack takes half that damage

Getting past the door's ward is what slowed the burglars down. Besides using advantages, there are two ways to bypass the ward. The first method requires a creature to attune itself to the magic through force of will and asking the magic to relent for a time. Doing so requires a successful DC 20 Wisdom check. On a failure, the PC loses a recovery due to the psychic pain of the process and must try again, unless that PC chooses to push through the pain and lose another recovery, bringing down the ward (GM give them the option).

The other method is to negate the magic of the ward for a short time. A PC with a magical background can try it. Doing so requires a successful DC 20 skill check using their primary spellcasting ability. Failure generates a *vault blast* attack.

Monsters

The halfling burglars may already be hidden behind pillars if the PCs were being argumentative or noisy in general. If not, they are closest to the vault door, with the hired muscle arrayed in front of them facing the PCs.

If things go bad, the halflings, part of a burglar gang known as the Ninefingers, may try to flee via the teleportation portal in the nook. It's keyed back to a similar portal in a building elsewhere in the area, and probably guarded by some folk aligned with the Prince or Archmage. It may be that they carry a focus that allows them to use it so PCs can't follow, or not (your choice GM).

Additional Reinforcements: If you want to challenge the PCs more, this group has a dwarf battlemage with them leading the efforts (using the hobgoblin warmage stats from the core rulebook, page 230).

#/Level of PCs	Halfling Burglars (B)	Hired Muscle (M)
4 x 5th level	2	3
5 x 5th level	2*	4
6 x 5th level	3*	4
4 x 6th level	2	3
5 x 6th level	3	3
6 x 6th level	4	3

* The halfling burglar gains its nastier special.

Tactics

Each hired muscle will each try to engage a different enemy, knowing the halflings' preferred attack method. Each burglar will try to lunge in to attack an enemy engaged with an ally, or use a teleportation circle to get their *unexpected attack* advantage. They will try to disengage after attacking whenever possible. They all have a fear of sorcerers and wizards, and will gang up on an enemy spellcaster to try to drop that PC and then threaten a coup de grace against the unconscious individual if the others don't throw down their weapons and surrender.

Loot

The hired muscle has half their pay on them, to the tune of 200 gp. The halflings don't have any loose coin except for the other 200 gp in pay for the muscle. But each has one item of value as part of their gear: a *potion of healing* (champion), *+2 oil*, *+2 rune*, or some other one-shot item of your choice.

Icons

A PC that has relationship points with the Prince of Shadows, Archmage, Elf Queen, or maybe the Priestess or the Three could use an advantage to make a teleportation circle send them to any circle without a roll, or stop working.

A PC with any advantage could use it to gain a +5 bonus to the check to bypass the vault door ward, or give themselves a chance to bypass it even if they don't have a magical background.

A PC with two or more Prince of Shadows advantages could talk the rogues into leaving without a fight, if the PCs paid them well enough (at least 500 gp).

Halfling Burglar

She's smiling at you, but it's a smile that matches her dagger.

7th level troop [HUMANOID]
Initiative: +14

Punching dagger +12 vs. AC—16 damage
Natural 14+: The burglar can make a second *punching dagger* attack against the target this turn as a free action (but not a third one).
Natural 18+: In addition to the second attack, the burglar tries to steal something from the target. The target must roll a DC 22 Wisdom or Dexterity check; on a failure, the burglar gets a random item that isn't armor. GM, decide if the burglar can use the item.

Unexpected attack: The burglar deals 1d4 x the escalation die extra damage when it attacks a target engaged with one of its allies or one that isn't aware of it. It can use this ability when it moves into a teleportation circle if the target is next to the circle it emerges from.

Nastier Specials

Bag of tricks: As a quick action once per round, and twice per battle, the halfling burglar can pull something from its bag to help it during battle. Roll a d4 to see what it gets:
1: A dead snake. One nearby enemy must roll an easy save (6+). On a failure, it is vulnerable until the end of its next turn.
2: Handful of marbles. Each enemy engaged with the halfling must roll a DC 18 Dexterity check. On a failure, the halfling gains a +5 bonus to disengage checks this turn.
3: Sharp tacks in the face. One nearby enemy must roll a save. On a failure, it takes a −2 penalty to attacks during its next turn.
4: Potion of minor vigor (or whiskey). The halfling gains 5 temporary hp.

AC	21	
PD	21	HP 104
MD	20	

Hired Muscle

He's big, strong, not too smart, and... yeah, strong.

6th level troop [HUMANOID]
Initiative: +8

Heavy flail or mace +11 vs. AC—20 damage
Natural 16+: The target takes 10 extra damage as the hired muscle puts some extra strength into the blow.
Miss: The hired muscle's crit range expands by 1 (cumulative) until it crits an enemy.

Close-quarters fighting: Twice per battle as a move action, the hired muscle can get in close with an enemy (momentarily grabbing, shoving then pulling, or whatever). When it does, each of the hired muscle's allies engaged with that enemy can pop free of it.

AC	22	
PD	19	HP 90
MD	14	

Additional Reinforcements

Dwarf Battlemage

5th level caster [HUMANOID]
Initiative: +6

Warstaff +8 vs. AC—15 damage

R: Fireblast +10 vs. PD (up to 2 nearby enemies in a group)—10 fire damage (or 20 if used against a single target), and the target loses its next move action

C: Concussive blast +10 vs. PD (all enemies engaged with the warmage)—10 force damage, and the warmage pops the target off of it
Natural 20: The target is also dazed (save ends).

AC	20	
PD	14	HP 70
MD	19	

Next Steps

Once the vault door is bypassed, there's a short tunnel leading to the vault. But it's not just some box to hold coins. It's a set of chambers with additional guardians. Once the PCs enter the vault, go to **Battle 4: Soohnei's Vault**.

BATTLE 3: SOOHNEI'S VAULT

A short passage beyond the strange door leads to a set of four interconnected chambers. A central room has archways in the far wall connecting to three smaller chambers. Each smaller room looks like it holds shelves, chests, and trunks full of items, many of which are books or other wizardly equipment. Before you can spread out to search the place, you hear a loud clicking noise followed by what sounds like a deep exhalation. Then a strange metal man with a barrel-like wooden chest rolls into view weaving on a great wooden ball instead of legs. Various gears, sprockets, levers, and chains form the thing's body. There are other sounds from the smaller rooms, but the metal man wants to talk, addressing you with a voice that rings like a metal drum, "We weren't expecting guests. I am Ticktockbong. And you are...?"

LOCATION DESCRIPTION

The vault of the mad gnome wizard Soohnei is filled with arcane lore and odd equipment, most of it useless, but not all. The main room is a 30 x 50 rectangle with 15-foot ceilings. Each archway opens into an oddly shaped 20 x 40 (roughly) room filled with containers of stuff.

The construct is an apex zorigami (*13 True Ways*, page 225), a self-aware being constructed from spare parts with its own will. Its name is Ticktockbong, and it wasn't expecting guests. Soohnei has been gone for a while now, however, so while it's cautious, it won't immediately attack. Instead it will talk to the PCs and try to learn about them. It may answer a few questions about itself (it was made by one it calls the Great Zorigami or the Midnight Zorigami at the beginning of the age; it's been here for a few months now). If it learns the PCs are here to take something from the vault without permission from the wizard, it will become wary and aggressive, telling the PCs to leave or suffer the consequences.

Eventually, the PCs will either find a way to convince Ticktockbong to let them search the area and take what they came for, or more likely they'll start a battle with the clockwork creatures in the vault.

In addition to the zorigami, the vault holds some less intelligent constructs the zorigami created to help them called sprocket helpers.

TERRAIN & TRAPS

Debris Pile: The main room is devoid of any interesting terrain at the start of the battle. When any clockwork creature drops to 0 hp, however, that area becomes covered with gears, sprockets, blades, treads, and more. And a lot of the equipment keeps spinning, sawing, gripping, etc.

When a creature moves next to or through a debris pile, it must roll a save. On a failure, some piece of equipment manages to cut, slam, or grab it, causing one of the following issues (roll a d4):

1: 1. The target is stuck (save ends).

2: 2. The target takes 10 damage.

CRANK, THE SPROCKET HELPER

For some fun, have Crank roll out of one of the rooms right after Ticktockbong on a simple tread frame. It has a brass goblin face and two metallic arms: a snapper grip, and a needle poker. It doesn't speak like Ticktockbong, but instead makes whistles and tweets. As Ticktockbong speaks with the PCs, Crank will circle around them like a dog sniffing them and ask the zorigami questions in "machine language." Ticktockbong will repeat the question out loud in the common tongue to the PCs, then relay their answers.

This is a chance for a GM to do some fun riffing. Have the questions be simple and silly. For example, "Why does it smell like that?" Or "Should I poke it?"

Once the fun of questioning is over and the zorigami becomes suspicious, Crank and his friends will likely become more than nuisances.

3: 3. The target is vulnerable until the start of its next turn as it has to deal with a persistent piece of equipment.

4: 4. The takes a −1 penalty to all defenses (save ends) due to an oil slick.

Extra Rooms: The three other rooms attached to main room are cluttered with junk, equipment, books, spare parts, and all sort of strange and mostly useless equipment. If someone needs some type of equipment to pull off a stunt or dicey move, it's probably there. (If a player asks, roll a d6. On a 4–6, what they need is there, within reason.)

Monsters

The zorigami are very intelligent, very curious, and very aggressive once they decide the PCs shouldn't be there. They are alien intelligences in the world, but they have also been around a long time, so they will fully understand some things and be completely naïve about others. They aren't easily tricked, but once they buy into a logic stream (so to speak), they'll roll with it. Other zorigami will roll out if Ticktockbong begins to get agitated; each looks slightly different from the others.

Convincing Ticktockbong to let the PCs take something from the vault shouldn't be easy. The players need to do some great roleplaying to do it, or if you use rolls, they need to succeed on three DC 25 checks each by a different PC (use Charisma or Intelligence; intimidation checks won't work) as different arguments sway the zorigami.

The sprocket helpers will be moving around all over the place, twirping and whistling. Once battle starts, their weapons come out as they try to poke, squeeze, or smash the PCs to pieces.

Additional Reinforcements: If you want to challenge the PCs more, or if you've haven't run the bonus scene (p. 133) there's a black skull in the chamber with them. It's a former wizard who's been trying to convince the apex zorigami on a course of action, but the constructs won't follow it. The skull, named Mortecai, has lost it (more than normal) with trying to have any decent conversation with the zorigami and will be looking to take it out on the PCs.

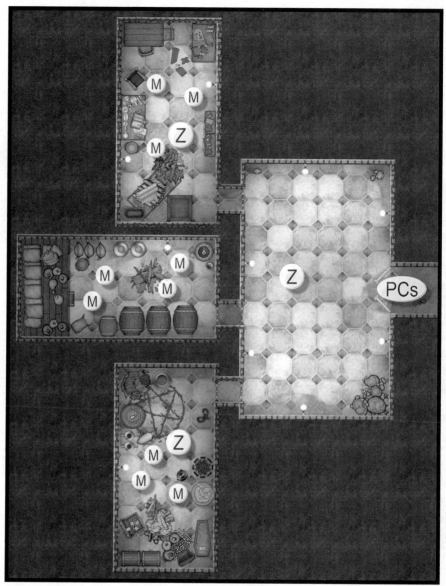

#/Level of PCs	Apex Zorigami (Z)	Sprocket Helper Mook (M)
4 x 5th level	3	10 (2 mobs)
5 x 5th level	3	16 (3 mobs)
6 x 5th level	4	17 (3 mobs)
4 x 6th level	4	15 (3 mobs)
5 x 6th level	5	9 (2 mobs)*
6 x 6th level	5	13 (2 mobs)*

* Each sprocket helper is double-strength: its *grabber* attack deals 16 damage, its *poker or smasher* attack deals 14 damage, and it has 46 hp.

Tactics

Each zorigami will attack a different PC. They are smart enough to identify one enemy who is hurting them badly and change tactics to gang up on that enemy.

Each sprocket helper mob will try to help a different zorigami by ganging up on one enemy engaged with it. They will follow the zorigami's orders.

Loot

Each clockwork has a gemstone "heart" inside it through which the magic of its lifeforce flows. The zorigami use 50 gp rubies. The sprockets have 10 gp chunks of quartz. The metal parts of their bodies have some value for sheer weight, but there's too much to carry out of the vault easily.

In addition, Soohnei has a lot of weird stuff scattered through the other rooms, most of it junk. There are a handful of gemstones and bits of precious metals worth a total of 450 gp. There's also one magic item that one of the PCs could use at the GM's option, plus two *+2 oils*. It's also a great place to store some weird, wondrous item that has something to do with the clockwork creatures but isn't really useful in its own right, or some other story item related to the icons.

Finally, if the PCs are there for a book or other item for the Prince's people, it's sitting on one of the shelves in plain sight.

Icons

A PC that has an icon advantage with the Prince, Archmage, Dwarf King, Orc Lord, Emperor, or maybe Lich King or Elf Queen could use it to gain some benefit over the zorigami. For example, they know a programming password that keeps the zorigami from attacking whoever says it last (one PC only).

Apex Zorigami

The clockwork man moves with a fluidity of motion you've never seen. Every blocked attack offers a perfect chance of reaction. Every cut is precise and deadly. You would weep at the beauty if it weren't trying to kill you.

6th level spoiler [CONSTRUCT]
Initiative: +11

Multi-geared mace +11 vs. AC—20 damage
Natural even hit or miss: The target can't use the bonuses and powers of one of its randomly determined true magic items until the end of the battle.

R: Spray of sharpened gears +11 vs. AC (1d3 nearby enemies or one far away enemy)—15 damage
Miss: 8 damage.

Lethal parries: When an enemy engaged with the apex zorigami misses it with an attack, the apex zorigami rolls a normal save; on a success, it can make a *multi-geared mace* attack as a free action.

Take five: The escalation die does not increase the round after an apex zorigami is staggered or drops to 0 hp.

AC	24	
PD	17	**HP 75**
MD	19	

Sprocket Helper

You're not sure which side is the "front," but every side seems dangerous.

6th level mook [CONSTRUCT]
Initiative: +8

Grabber +11 vs. AC—8 damage, and the helper can make a *poker or smasher* attack as a free action unless it already made that attack this turn.
Natural 16+: The target is stuck (save ends).

Poker or smasher +11—7 damage, and the helper can make a *grabber* attack as a free action unless it already made that attack this turn.

Sprung gear: When the sprocket helper rolls a save, if it fails, that mook stops functioning (the mob takes damage equal to the remaining hp for that mook).

AC	22	
PD	19	**HP 23 (mook)**
MD	15	

Mook: Kill one sprocket helper mook for every 23 damage you deal to the mob.

Additional Reinforcements

Mortecai, Black Skull

Black skulls are urbane conversationalists, and their rich, cultured voices sound like honey made from the dark flowers that grow only where thousands have been massacred. But the Lich King has no fury like a Skull ignored

8th level caster [undead]
Initiative: +13

R: Telekinetic grasp +15 vs. PD (1d3 nearby enemies)—28 force damage
Natural even hit: The target is stuck (save ends).
Telekinetic crush: When the escalation die is even, one enemy of the skull's choice that is stuck from its telekinetic grasp takes 18 force damage at the start of the skull's turn. When the escalation die is odd, one such stuck enemy of its choice is hampered (save ends).

Limited flight: The haunted skull glides and hovers, always within seven or eight feet of the ground. If the skull is incognito, its empty clothing moves around beneath it, held in the shape of a person by telekinesis and it stays closer to the ground to appear normal.

Lost opportunity: This creature can't make opportunity attacks.

AC	23	
PD	15	**HP 110**
MD	23	

NEXT STEPS

After the PCs gain what they need from the vault, they can leave the wizard's lair without further problems. Other issues might arise depending on the story ending, however.

MAD WIZARD'S LOOT STORY ENDINGS

Here are outcomes for each story opening, detailing what success or failure might mean.

If the PCs did face all four battles, remember to give them a full heal-up.

FOUR DAYS TO LIVE

Success: The PCs hand over the item the dark elf asked them to get, and they each get an antidote of vile green liquid. Surprisingly, drinking the stuff doesn't kill them. Their symptoms go away too (or were they gone anyway?). Some of the Prince's people are impressed with their work and make contact about a new job.

Failure: The dark elf lied, sort of. With no item, there's no cure to the toxin. But it doesn't kill them. Instead they slumber deeply and dream. Of course, they wake up somewhere else completely unsure of who they are or where their stuff is, at least at first.

TO CATCH A THIEF

Success: The PCs find the book in Soohnei's lair and their contact gets the name of the thief from it. Their good work gets each one a 6 with an icon of their choice in place of a roll the next time they roll icon dice. Also, one of them peeked in the book and got the name of someone they're looking for.

Failure: Their contact isn't happy with their failure to get the book and that PC's next 6 with the Prince is a 5 instead. In addition, the thief heard about their involvement and starts to stalk the group.

THE TEST

Success: The heroes are successful and the PC proves that they can get the job done. They gain reputation in the organization and are trusted with bigger jobs. Until the PC levels up, each time they roll icon dice for the Prince, they can reroll any of those dice once.

Failure: The PC shows they really aren't ready for the big time yet. The next time they roll icon dice, any 6s with the Prince are 5s instead. In addition, someone tipped off the wizard Soohnei about the PCs' attempt on his abode (no he wasn't dead). Now there's a zorigami and sprocket helper squad after them.

THE SCORE

Success: Word of the PCs' success gets around, impressing certain people. Offers come in to help various parties with "problems." The next time the PCs roll icon dice, each PC can choose to gain one 6 with any icon in place of rolling one die.

Failure: Not only do the PCs fail to score, word of the wizard's demise seemed to be greatly exaggerated. Now there's an apex zorigami and squad of sprocket helpers after them. And someone in the Prince's network keeps telling the constructs where the PCs are at.

BATTLE SCENE CONNECTIONS

The stories from this set of battle scenes can lead to other scenes:

 The Lightning Station (Archmage, page 21): While in the vault, one of the PCs stumbles across a crystal mirror. It reveals the scene of the station filled with lightning from a storm, and then an explosion. They see the cloudbreak begin to fall. Then a cloud giant face shows up. He asks for assistance from the wizard network. When the PCs answer, he says they are the only ones to have heard the call. He will attune the transport so they may come (moving through the mirror, which is a portal). With the station offline, however, the portal delivers them to the edge of the cloud.

 Zephalarius' Nightmares (GGW): The PCs acquire the item from the vault and deliver it. Only later do they realize how powerful the item was, as each time it's used it calls forth a long-lost spirit into the world. Now the spirits have become a public hazard. If the PCs don't fix it, eventually the authorities will blame them. The Lich King's people aren't a viable resource, so the PCs seek out the gold dragon Zephalarius to find out what to do.

PRINCE OF SHADOWS:
THIEF OF DREAMS

LEVEL RANGE: 9–10

The themes of this set of battles are traveling the dreamlands and facing creatures of myth and legend. This set of battle scenes works in almost any environment, since the PCs will travel to the dreamlands. They just need to start someplace where the Prince's people can find them.

The Prince of Shadows is a master of getting into places he shouldn't be able to get to. The latest challenge involves the Elf Queen. It's known that she speaks to elves in their dreams, especially when the moon is full. Often, this happens while an elf is walking the dreamlands, a land of shadow and magic where their minds wander through ancient memories. What many don't know is that the dreamlands are an actual place that even non-elves can visit, given the right magic.

The Prince of Shadows needs to learn something very specific about the Elf Queen's shared dreams with a high elf lord of some authority in the empire. To be able to overhear (oversee?) these dreams, he needs someone who understands the dreamlands well, and the rumors suggest that's the Dreamlord, a powerful entity within that realm. Of course, the Prince won't be handling this himself. He enlists the PCs to travel to the dreamlands via a very special magic item, find the Dreamlord, and enlist his help in spying on the Elf Queen's shared dreams with the high elf lord. Do that, and they'll be richly rewarded... or at least avoid terrible punishment.

THIEF OF DREAMS STORY OPENINGS

- **The Ultimate Score:** One or more PCs with a positive or conflicted relationship with the Prince are contacted through the usual backchannels. The head guy has a job only for the best of the best: he needs someone who can steal a dream, and the PCs are at the top of the list of candidates. Do it, and their names will be spoken of with admiration along with One-armed Jak and Karina the Sly. When they accept, they receive a note detailing the plan and a special mirror that pulls them into the dreamlands.

- **The Worst Kind of Blackmail:** One or more PCs with a negative or conflicted relationship with the Prince is contacted by a go-between. People important to the PC (family, friends, a lover, or whoever) have been taken. The PCs must perform a special job that only they can do, or the loved one will die... horribly. There's no trace of the missing people, so the PCs agree to the job, which involves traveling to the dreamlands to find the Dreamlord via a magical mirror.

- **Guys, Where Are We?:** The PCs suddenly "wake" in a strange dream-like landscape. As they stumble about disoriented, a disembodied voice tells them they are in a drugged sleep, and the speaker could snuff any one of them out in the "real world" with the slightest effort. If they ever want to wake up again, they must traverse the dreamlands (where they're at now) to find the Dreamlord so that they can steal some specific dreams of the Elf Queen. The voice says it shouldn't be that hard, but the choice is theirs.

ALTERNATE ICONS

The Prince of Shadows options for this adventure are manipulative. If your group doesn't respond well to being blackmailed or forced, and are more heroic than shifty, using a story opening from the Elf Queen or the Great Gold Wyrm could work better for you. Unlike many of the other battle scenes adventures, *Thief of Dreams* wouldn't need to be adjusted to fit these other icons—the dreamlands setting offers a lot of wiggle room.

Elf Queen: The Queen needs to reclaim her power over the dreams of elves. The Dreamlord has stolen some of her access to dreams, so she needs the PCs to travel the dreamlands to convince him to let go.

Great Gold Wyrm: The Great Gold Wyrm also speaks to its followers through dreams. Perhaps something has happened in the dreamlands to cause his missives to go to elves, and for the Elf Queen's messages to reach the Wyrm's followers. That's annoying. And a bit embarrassing. The GGW sends the PCs after the Dreamlord to gets things straightened out.

THIEF OF DREAMS OVERVIEW

Once the PCs enter the dreamlands, they must find the Dreamlord. They either received an item (a mirror) that will lead them to his location, discover that they can simply sense his location, or encounter NPC dreamers who help them along

ICONS IN PLAY

Characters that have relationships (and story-guide advantages) with the Prince of Shadows, Diabolist, Elf Queen, Lich King, and maybe the Priestess or Archmage should be able to shine in these battle scenes. Moreso than PCs with other icon relationships, feel free to give such PCs extra knowledge about the opposition, make checks to pull off fun actions the players might suggest, and use their advantages to particularly good effect, such as negating or bypassing some of the advantages or abilities of the enemies.

the way. During their trek they will come to a set of elven ruins upon a lake at twilight. In Battle 1, what they take to be an elven woman kneeling on a dock is actually a medusa archer. She calls upon swarms of blind nightshade pixies to help her add some new trophies to her statue garden.

In Battle 2, the PCs are led to a clearing in the woods that holds a domed dais. Within the building, an elder manafang naga is consuming the psyches of dreamers walking the dreamlands to empower its magic. It doesn't like being disturbed and will use the dreamers' vestiges against the PCs.

Finally, in Battle 3 the PCs are traveling through light forest when they encounter a strange gnome dreamer. The gnome provides information about the location of the Dreamlord, saying that the Huntmaster will know where to find him. Then he summons the Hunt upon the PCs, who must survive to gain what they seek.

GM, feel free to expand upon these battles by including dreamer NPCs, battles with different enemies wandering the dreamlands, and other scenes that fit the mythological setting.

The battles outlined here can take place over a few minutes, hours, days or even weeks, since time within the dreamlands is subjective. The locations should exude a sense of powerful magic, illogical possibilities, and long-forgotten places.

See story endings after the final battle for options on what happens after the PCs finish the last battle.

BATTLE I: MIRROR LAKE

As you walk a path through light woods, you hear the sound of tinkling chimes. Ahead, you see a small lake with ruins of blue-gray marble along the shore. There are a handful of crumbled buildings with fallen marble columns overgrown with vines. The place exudes a sense of great age and sadness. A dock of light-colored wood extends out into the lake, and in the twilight you can just make out a figure sitting there with her back turned toward you. You think it's a "her" due to the fine green silk dress that blows in the breeze and what looks like an elven frame, but a silk cowl covers her head so you can't be sure. You see a handful of small floating wooden platforms out upon the lake around the dock,

and there are many water reeds along the shore. The chimes are coming from somewhere in the reeds.

LOCATION DESCRIPTION

The ruins are mostly broken walls, floors, and toppled pillars, with none of them forming a full structure. The dock extends some 60 feet out into the lake, and there are three additional small, freestanding docks anchored to the lake bottom in a semi-circle around the main dock.

The woman is wood elven in appearance, but she is no longer only an elf. Cursed long ago, Nerelith has been a medusa for longer than an Age, trapped in the dreamlands. She looks into the lake, where the crystal clear water reveals her garden of memories below the surface: statues of those who've come to her and been petrified.

She will keep her back to the PCs, not saying anything at first like she can't hear them, then if they don't come out onto the dock, she will speak to them in a beautiful (and obviously elven) voice, trying to get them close before she whirls around and pulls back the cowl to reveal her curse.

She also has allies in the area. With a whistle, she summons the creatures making the noise of the rippling chimes: swarms of blind nightshade pixies drowsing among the lake reeds, glassy wings clinking lazily like chimes.

WALKING THE DREAMLANDS

Since the PCs are in the dreamlands, you need to decide how deadly they can be. Does what happens there become true in the world too, so for example, those who die in the dreamlands die for real? It seems to us that there should be consequences within this realm, but that's up to each GM.

What should be possible, however, is for the PCs to be able to shape the dream around them to their benefit if they are strong-willed. Icon advantages play perfectly into this idea that help can arrive from anywhere in a dream. But PCs who want to change the rules somewhat should be given the chance, if they can succeed on skill checks to do so, probably Intelligence and Wisdom, and probably with a DC of 30. So that there's a cost to trying, make any effort to change the scene a standard action.

Here's a few ideas for altering the dream, and we're sure players will have many more:

- Increase the escalation die by 1 (once per battle).
- Create a temporary ally who can absorb attacks, or make attacks for a few rounds.
- Create favorable terrain for the PCs that lasts a few rounds.
- Allow someone to heal using a free recovery (once per PC).
- Regain an expended power.

Terrain & Traps

Ruins: The ruins are blue-gray marble of fine elven craftsmanship. There are no full buildings, but some wall corners and other tumbled ruins could provide cover.

Mirror Lake: The lake is crystal clear with only plant growth around the edges (the reeds). It's 10 to 15 feet deep around the end of the main dock, and near each of the smaller floating docks. Set upon the lake floor are perhaps seventy statues of humanoids and beasts that have succumbed to Nerelith's petrifying gaze. It's her personal water garden.

Swimming through the water isn't too difficult for those not in heavy armor. It requires a successful DC 15 Strength check. Those in heavy armor take a −10 penalty, however. The problem is that Nerelith has stocked the lake with eels that will attack anyone in the water.

When a creature ends its turn in the lake, it takes 30 damage from biting eels. Once Nerelith is defeated, the eels will subside, no longer pushed by her dominant will.

Docks: The main dock is 10 feet wide and 60 feet long, ending in a T shape that's 30 feet across. It's very stable, so only dicey moves should risk sending a creature into the lake (but see the nightshade pixies).

There are three 8 x 10 floating docks anchored to the lake in semi-circle around the end of the main dock. Each is 50 feet from that dock. A creature can start a floating dock rocking with a DC 20 Strength check, and must make the check each round to keep it unstable. While rocking, when a creature starts its turn there, it must roll an easy save (6+); on a failure, it takes a −2 penalty to attacks and all defenses until the start of its next turn.

Reeds: The lake reeds are 3 to 6 feet high and can provide concealment to anyone in them. The nightshade pixies are sleeping there at the start of the battle.

Monsters

Nerelith was a wood elf before she was cursed to become a medusa by a powerful enchantress from the Elf Queen's court for stealing her lover. She is still bitter and angry for her punishment and takes it out on those who wander to the lake. She wears green silks and a layered cowl that hides her appearance until she removes it. It's the dreamlands, so the lake reed in hand expands into a short bow when she wishes, though the bow will fall apart as a broken reed when she is defeated.

The nightshade pixie swarms are small blind creatures that look half hummingbird and half miniature gnome, with dark, purple-bruise coloration. Each mook consists of about 20 pixies. They feed on blood, but know better than to attack Nerelith, whose blood is poisonous. Their wings sound like chimes as they fly around the battlefield in swarms crying out where food is located.

Additional Reinforcements: If you want to challenge the PCs more, add a massive mutant chuul (*Bestiary*, page 48) dreamer to the battle. It is trapped in the dream and Nerelith has managed to contain it within the lake by convincing it that it is in a pleasant dream where all non-monstrous humanoids have been

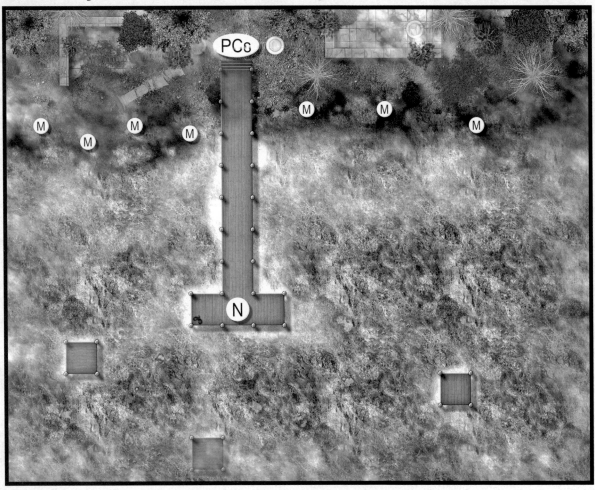

turned into stone. It will lunge out of the water to attack the PCs, but ignore the pixies, since they're providing the soundtrack for its dream.

#/Level of PCs	Nerelith, Dreamland Medusa (N)	Nightshade Pixie Swarm Mook (M)*
4 x 9th level	1	3 (1 mob)
5 x 9th level	1	7 (1 mob)
6 x 9th level	1	11 (2 mobs)
4 x 10th level	1	5 (1 mob)*
5 x 10th level	1	8 (1 mob)*
6 x 10th level	1	11 (2 mobs)*

* Each pixie mook is double-strength: its *bite* attack deals 90 damage and 20 ongoing, and it has 150 hp.

Tactics

Nerelith will try to lure the PCs nearby before revealing her true visage as she begins firing her bow. If there are high elves in the party, they get all her attention, since it was such a one who cursed her. When the PCs engage her, she'll teleport away to a floating dock to continue firing on them.

Once the pixie swarms awake, they'll want blood. They attack the closest enemy, trying to drain it dry. They like the taste of arcane spellcaster blood best, because the consumption of the magic in the blood gives them some resistance to magic.

The good news for the PCs is that they won't attack each other if confused by the pixies' bites; the bad news is that they'll jump into the lake instead, to be eaten by the eels.

Loot

Nerelith has placed a necklace around the necks of three statues to catch the light; she refers to them as her cold friends. She also wears a platinum and emerald ring given to her by her lover long ago; it's worth 500 gp.

Icons

A PC that has relationship advantages with the Prince, Elf Queen, High Druid, or perhaps the Three could use one or more of them

to identify the danger of the eels within the water, and how to make them stop attacking for a couple of rounds.

A PC that has relationship advantages with any icon could use one or more of them to adjust the dreamscape somehow, perhaps allowing them to walk on water or turn to mist and ride the breeze to Nerelith's location.

A PC that has relationship advantages with the Elf Queen could use one or more of them to get Nerelith to stop attacking, if they can convince her they have the pull with the Elf Queen to remove her curse (probably involving a couple DC 30 Charisma checks as well).

NERELITH, DREAMLAND MEDUSA

She seems like a sad wood elven maid, until her ancient anger surfaces and the snakes rise from her head.

Triple-strength 12th level archer [HUMANOID]
Initiative: +19

Snakes and daggers +17 vs. AC (3 attacks)—50 damage, and 20 ongoing poison damage
  Natural 18+: The medusa can make a *petrifying gaze* attack against the target as a free action.

R: Reed bow +17 vs. PD (up to 2 nearby or far away enemies)—90 damage, and 20 ongoing poison damage
  Natural 16+: The medusa can make a *petrifying gaze* attack against the target as a free action.
  Natural even miss: The medusa can reroll the attack.

[Special trigger] **C: Petrifying gaze +17 vs. MD (one enemy)**—50 psychic damage, and the target must start making last gasp saves as it turns to stone

Caught by an eye: Whenever a nearby enemy attacks the medusa noble and rolls a natural 1–5, the medusa can make a *petrifying gaze* attack against that attacker as a free action.

Fey-touched: Twice per battle as a move action, the medusa can teleport somewhere nearby it can see.

Nastier Specials

Serpent wardings: Thrice per battle as a free action, the medusa noble can force an enemy to reroll a spell attack that targeted it. The attacker can't use the escalation die for the reroll.

AC	26	
PD	26	**HP 1000**
MD	26	

NIGHTSHADE PIXIE SWARM

These vicious pixie swarms drain your blood in time with their rippling-chime wingbeats.

12th level mook [HUMANOID]
Initiative: +18

Blood-sucking bite +17 vs. AC—40 damage, and 15 ongoing damage
  Natural 18+: The target is confused until the end of its next turn.
  Miss: 10 damage.

Magic resistance: Arcane magic attacks only deal half damage to the swarm.

Flight: Nightshade pixie swarms fly in unison and maneuver well, even hovering in place like hummingbirds.

Nastier Specials

Nightshade-laced blood: When a creature drops one or more pixie mooks, it must roll an easy save (6+). On a failure, it takes 15 ongoing poison damage and is weakened (save ends both) as it ingests some of the pixies' blood and bits.

AC	27	
PD	27	**HP 75 (mook)**
MD	20	

Mook: Kill one nightshade pixie swarm mook for every 75 damage you deal to the mob.

NEXT STEPS

Once the PCs defeat Nerelith, they will become aware that the Dreamlord lies beyond the lake through whatever means they are using to find him (the mirror, dream senses, a dreamer guide, etc.). After a quick rest, they head in that direction for a while, soon entering a thicker forest.

After a time, they will see someone ahead walking down the same path they are on. It's a halfling girl, but she is wispy and ethereal, the manifestation of a halfling in the world walking the dreamlands. The PCs can talk to her and she'll respond in a dreamy manner, thinking them part of her odd dream brought on by sausages and hard cider. Her name is Maggie.

When the PCs are done talking to her, she will suddenly moan and get pulled ahead of the group in a blur of color. In a clearing ahead, a naga is consuming her lifeforce. See **Battle 2: Dark Dreams.**

BATTLE 2: DARK DREAMS

The halfling girl is ahead of you now, in a large clearing in the forest among the stone ruins of some ancient place. She passes into a structure with a raised dais with three stone pillars supporting a domed roof. There, a strange purple-scaled snakelike creature with a drow's head is swaying rhythmically as eldritch energy circles up and down its body. Suddenly the girl screams as her form is sucked into the snake creature's mouth. The thing licks its mouth and says, "delicious," before turning toward you with golden, glowing eyes. It says, "Ah, dreamers in the flesh. It has been long since I feasted on such. Tasty, and powerful too. I'm so glad you are here!"

LOCATION DESCRIPTION

The clearing is 80 x 100 with thick foliage and trees all around. There are two additional paths exiting it on the far side. The domed dais sits at the center of the clearing, which is open ground otherwise.

The naga, Listeross, has allies in the clearing that aren't immediately discernable: lost dreamers who the naga has stolen lifeforce from. At the start of the battle, when Listeross rolls initiative, it will summon these wraiths forth, and they will rise

from the ground to fight in the first round of battle. Where each rises, it leaves a pool of silvery dreamstuff in its wake that could prove troublesome to the PCs.

TERRAIN & TRAPS

Domed Dais: The round dais sits 5 feet above the ground and is 25 feet in diameter. Three 4-foot-thick round stone columns support the 20-foot high dome, and each is covered with images of the dreamlands (heroes and villains, lost places and long-forgotten beasts, etc.).

Anyone attempting to scale the pillars to the dome must succeed on a DC 25 Strength check. While fighting on top of the dome, a melee attack that hits also forces the target to roll a save; on a failure it gets knocked off. Due to the naga's long body that's coiled around the dome, it doesn't have this problem.

Surrounding Forest: The foliage and trees outside the clearing are thick, providing good concealment and cover. GM, you could give a PC moving/hiding there a +2 bonus to AC and PD (cover), or allow them to hide from sight with a DC 25 skill check.

Dream Pools: Randomly scattered around the domed dais will be 5-foot diameter pools of silvery dreamstuff in each location where a lost dreamer rises. Any PC moving into such a pool, or sent there by a dreamer, becomes lost in a deluge of dreams and memories. Each round, they take no actions as they experience a dream vision or relieve a dark memory (have the

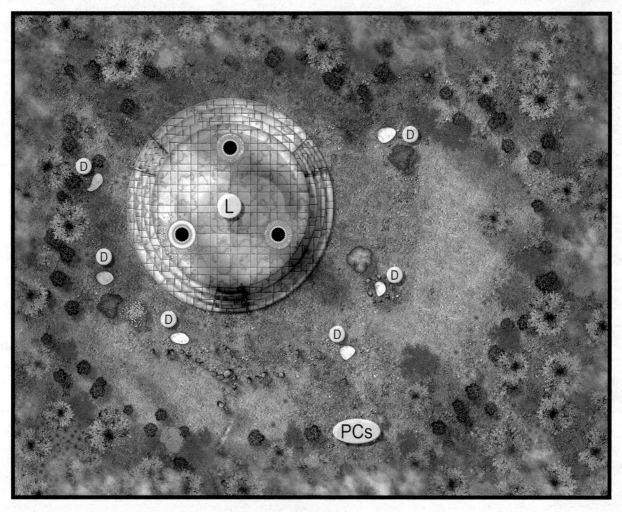

PCs describe the experience) until they succeed on a save (or their confused save) and escape from the pool.

Monsters

The naga has purple scales and magical energy constantly flows around it. It has a high, parched-throat-sounding voice with a hint of music to it that suggests the elven tongue. It is engorged on dreamers, using their nightmares as a way to fuel its own magic.

The lost dreamers are humanoids of all types who encountered Listeross and had their dreams stolen. They are but figments of actual people, who now have trouble sleeping in the real world without having nightmares. But in the dreamlands, these wraithlike dreamers have power, and the naga controls them.

Additional Reinforcements: If you want to challenge the PCs more, a pair of skulls of the beast (*Bestiary*, page 110) rise from the woods outside the glade at Listeross' command. They are figments of nightmare he has chosen to help him from the dreams of those he's consumed.

#/Level of PCs	Listeross, Elder Manafang Naga (L)	Lost Dreamer (D)
4 x 9th level	1	3
5 x 9th level	1	4
6 x 9th level	1	5
4 x 10th level	1*	4
5 x 10th level	1*	5
6 x 10th level	1*	6

* The naga is double-strength: its attacks each deal 90 damage, and it has 420 hp.

Tactics

Listeross summons the dreamers as a free action when it rolls initiative. On its first turn, and whenever it can, the naga will slither up a pillar to the top of the dome to get away from melee attackers. It will try to remain on top of the dome, crawling back there if it's somehow knocked off. It will use *force missiles* as often as it can.

The lost dreamers will intercept PCs trying to reach the naga. The lost dreamers attempt to inhabit the PCs to gain a sense of reality, since each is a piece of a psyche from a dreamer who came to the dreamlands and was consumed by the naga. When they succeed, the confused effect represents the PC's mind being sent to a nearby dream pool while the dreamer controls their body. Until they escape the dream pool (make their save), the lost dreamer gains some understanding that it isn't truly alive, and in denial or fear, it lashes out at the other PCs. Each dreamer will attack a different PC, if able, since sharing a psyche isn't as enticing.

Loot

When defeated, Listeross will begin to fade into a purple haze, leaving behind its eyes—two large amethysts each worth 300 gp.

Icons

A PC that has relationship advantages with the Prince, Archmage, Diabolist, Elf Queen, Lich King, or Priestess can use one or more of them to help a lost dreamer realize it's only a vestige of a real person, giving it peace and allowing it freedom. Convincing it of the fact, however, requires a successful DC 30 Charisma check (reduce DC by 5 for each advantage used).

ELDER MANAFANG NAGA

"Speak to me of these ages, fleshy one. You claim they have come and gone. Those with the First Blood in their veins see them for the illusions they are. Your icons may rise, clash, and fall like children playing at war." —Shakaask Thilsa, manafang naga

10th level leader [BEAST]
Initiative: +18

Bite +15 vs. AC—45 damage
Natural 16+: The naga gains *resist spell damage 16+* against the target's spells until the end of the battle.
Miss: 25 damage.

R: Force missiles (1d4 nearby or far away enemies)—45 force damage
Limited use: 1/battle.

C: Ritual movements +15 vs. MD (one nearby enemy, or one nearby enemy per point of esc. die if *supreme mystic escalator* benefit is active)—45 psychic damage, and the target can't cast spells or use the activated powers of true magic items (save ends)
Miss: 20 psychic damage.

Arcane mirror: Whenever an enemy targets the elder manafang naga with a spell, the naga regains the use of *force missiles* if it's expended. In addition, if that spell is a recharge spell, roll its recharge check immediately after the spell is cast. If the spell is a per-battle or daily spell, roll a hard save (16+) immediately after the spell is cast; on a success, the spellcaster doesn't expend the spell.

Supreme mystic escalator: The naga and each of its nearby allies can use the escalation die unless the naga has been hit by two enemy spells since its last turn.

AC	26	
PD	20	**HP 210**
MD	24	

LOST DREAMER

"This is the strangest dream... ah, no I AM real!"

12th level spoiler [SPIRIT]
Initiative: +17

Dreamer's touch +17 vs. MD—50 psychic damage
Natural even hit: The target is confused (save ends). While confused, the target's body is inhabited by the dreamer, which lashes out in horror as it realizes the truth. The dreamer doesn't make touch attacks while inhabiting a creature.
Miss: 10 ongoing psychic damage.

Dream spirit: The dreamer has resist damage 16+ except against psychic damage.

AC	26	
PD	21	**HP 320**
MD	26	

NEXT STEPS

After the battle with the naga, the halfling girl will "step out of" the naga, saying it was horrible in that place. She will direct the PCs to take the path on the right to get where they need to go. She doesn't know what they seek, or who the Dreamlord is, she only knows that it's the right way to go. If they take her advice, they'll be on track. If they don't, feel free to have them meet more trouble or describe nightmarish scenes of battle and death that they have to pass through (but with no battles unless you want them).

Once they pass through the nightmare, or if they take the right path, they will encounter an old gnome sitting on a log along a riverbank. See **Battle 3: The Wild Hunt**.

BATTLE 3: THE WILD HUNT

You've been traveling for some amount of time, it's hard to know how long in this place, when you come to a small river flowing through the forest. The banks are littered with river stones and logs, and the stones in the water click as they shift in the current. You suddenly spy a gnome in forest garb sitting on a log not far away. He smiles at you and waves you over.

LOCATION DESCRIPTION

The gnome has no name, at least not one that he'll give. He emits a sense of calm and power. He recognizes the PCs as more "solid" than the usual dreamers in this place, so he will ask what they seek in waking form in the dreamlands.

Even if the PCs don't reveal anything to him, he'll make a number of insightful guesses, finally settling on the fact that they must be seeking the Dreamlord. He'll ask if that's why they've come, and offer up that there's only one who can summon the Dreamlord. They must call this creature and defeat it. Only then will it call the Dreamlord for them.

When the PCs ask who this creature is, the gnome smiles at them and says, "*Why the Huntmaster, of course,*" as he gives a long, high-pitched whistle. Then he says, "*The hunt is on. Survive and you can force him to take you to the Dreamlord,*" as he laughs and fades away. In the distance horns sound.

The PCs are now the prey of a Wild Hunt, but if they defeat the Huntmaster and his allies, he will do their bidding. The Huntmaster is an ancient dreamlands creature, who comes at the PCs with satyr archers and fey hounds in a double-strength battle. If the PCs choose, they can try to run and find different terrain than the river. In that case, allow the PCs to dictate the location where the battle takes place (even letting them draw the map out if you use that type of aid). These are the dreamlands, and reality will shift to fit their need.

If the PCs want to fight at the river, bring the Huntsman in from whichever side you like.

TERRAIN & TRAPS

River: The river is 30 feet wide, 5 to 12 feet deep, and fast moving. Jumping or swimming across it requires a DC 25 Strength check. On a failure, the current pulls the PC downstream about 40 feet to the side they don't want to be on, and they are vulnerable to attacks while in the water.

There's a soft sand bank on the PCs' side that gently leads down 10 feet to a 30-foot wide, 120-foot long shore filled with river stones of various sizes with the river forming a natural barrier behind them.

Stones & Logs: The stones make movement in the area slightly difficult. Each time a PC moves, unless they have a means of avoiding the rocks, they must roll a DC 18 Dexterity check or lose that move action. The Huntmaster and his allies have no issues with footing (it's a dream after all).

There are a handful of mid-sized logs in the area that could provide cover, but at most a +2 bonus to AC and PD.

Other Terrain: If the PCs choose to move and find new terrain before the hunt overtakes them, that's fine. Let them describe what they want. Any dicey moves using that terrain should require a DC 25 skill check to succeed.

MONSTERS

The Huntmaster looks like a wood elf with deer horns and lichen-colored skin that's imprinted with strange dark green runes. It stands nearly 10 feet tall and walks on cloven hooves with double-jointed legs. It uses a long spear of white-colored wood inscribed with elvish runes.

The satyr archers wear minimal brown leathers and carry shortbows and quivers, plus hunting knives. Each also carries an ox horn with a silver tip. They say nothing and only laugh as they fight.

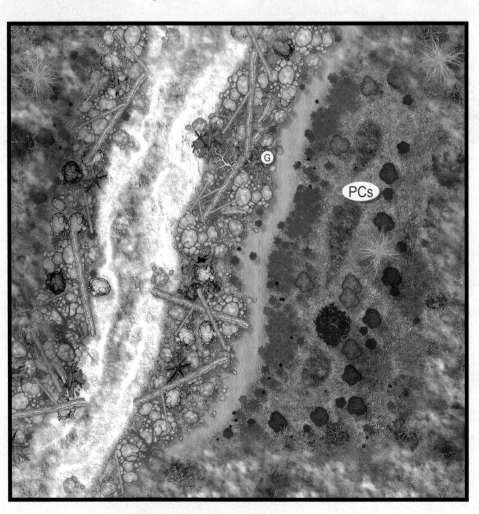

The fey hounds are large white-furred wolves that runs in packs (mobs) alongside the satyrs or out in front of the hunters. They have no collars or leashes.

Additional Reinforcements: If you want to challenge the PCs more, the first time the huntmaster drops to 0 hp, the dreamscape restores him. This time he only has 444 hp and when he would drop to 0 hp again, the battle stops.

#/Level of PCs	Huntmaster (H)	Satyr Archers (S)	Fey Hound Mook (M)
4 x 9th level	1	4	13 (2 mobs)
5 x 9th level	1	5	20 (2 mobs)
6 x 9th level	1	7	25 (3 mobs)
4 x 10th level	1	4*	10 (1 mob)
5 x 10th level	1**	5*	20 (2 mobs)
6 x 10th level	1**	7*	15 (2 mobs)

* Each satyr archer is double-strength: its *knife* and *shortbow* attacks both attack twice instead of once, and it has 560 hp.

** The Huntmaster uses its nastier special.

Tactics

The hounds will engage the PCs while the satyrs try to stay back using ranged attacks. When each satyr drops to 0 hp, it howls or laughs and fades into shadows that streak into the forest.

The Huntmaster will choose its prey and attack that PC no matter what until the PC drops. When the Huntmaster would drop to 0 hp, instead it's defeated and its spear disappears. In a deep but musical voice it will acknowledge that the PCs are not prey and offer them a boon, asking what they wish of it.

Loot

As a boon, the PCs will gain access to the Dreamlord and thus the Elf Queen, which is a big win, and one for which the Prince will reward them (or allow them to live). The Huntmaster gives each PC a 300 gp emerald as a token of the dreamlands. Whether it holds magic or not is up to the GM, but it could be a *+3 rune*.

Icons

A PC that has relationship advantages with the Prince, High Druid, or Elf Queen could use one or more of them to make the Huntmaster choose someone else as prey and ignore them during the battle.

A PC that has relationship advantages with any icon could use one or more of them to give the group a big advantage until the end of the battle with terrain created from the dreamscape, probably +1 to attacks or saves, +2 to defenses and skill checks, or advancing the escalation die by 1.

Huntmaster

A representation of primal elven fear, or only something a deranged dreamlands lord could have conceived? Yes, and yes.

Double-strength 13th level wrecker [HUMANOID]
Initiative: +15

Whitewood spear +18 vs. AC (2 attacks)—80 damage
  Miss: 40 damage
  Natural odd hit or miss: The crit range of the Huntmaster's attacks expands by 1 until the end of the battle or until it scores a critical hit (each time this happens, one of its flesh runes flares with energy so the PCs can see the count).
  Natural 16+: The target is stuck (save ends) as unnatural fear floods its senses.

Designate prey: At the start of the battle, the Huntmaster chooses an enemy as its prey. The prey is vulnerable to its attacks, takes a −2 penalty to all defenses and saves against its attacks, and must use three less recovery dice when it heals using a recovery. When the prey drops to 0 hp or below, the Huntmaster can choose a new prey.

Nastier Specials

Dreamlands lord: At the start of each of the Huntmaster's turns, one condition on it ends (its choice, whether a save ends effect or other duration).

AC	28	
PD	27	**HP 888**
MD	26	

Satyr Archers

The satyr moves nimbly, leaping to the side as it fires its bow again and again.

11th level archer [HUMANOID]
Initiative: +14

Hunting knife +15 vs. AC—50 damage
Natural even hit: The satyr pops free from the target and can move as a free action.

R: Shortbow +16 vs. AC—55 damage
Natural 16+: The satyr can make another *short bow* attack this turn as a free action.

Call of the Hunt: Once per battle as a quick action, the satyr can blow its horn. When it does, 1d2 nearby mook allies can make a basic attack as a free action.

AC	26	
PD	26	**HP 280**
MD	20	

Fey Hounds

The hound is big and strong, has huge jaws full of tearing teeth, and hardly touches the ground as it runs.

10th level mook [BEAST]
Initiative: +16

Tearing jaws +15 vs. AC—35 damage
Natural 16+: The hound grabs the target unless it's already grabbing a creature (attacks against grabbed creatures gain a +4 bonus). It automatically hits with *tearing jaws* attacks against a creature it's grabbing.
Miss: 10 damage.

Fey bloodline: The hound can move over difficult terrain as if it were normal, and can make great leaps and basic dicey moves without a chance of failure unless it's really dicey, in which case it must roll an easy save (6+).

AC	26	
PD	24	**HP 55 (mook)**
MD	21	

Mook: Kill one fey hound mook for every 55 damage you deal to the mob.

Next Steps

When the PCs defeat the Huntmaster, it doesn't die but instead will acknowledge the PCs as not prey, and will grant them a boon, probably delivering them to the Dreamlord simply by willing it if they choose. Whether it's a single boon, or one for each PC, is up to each GM.

Considering their ability to best the Huntmaster, the Dreamlord will deal with them, though agreeing to spy on the Elf Queen's dreams might have its own costs. What the Dreamlord looks like is up to the GM, though the "perfect" version of a male wood elf might be one option. The male version of the Elf Queen is another option, but that would probably raise bigger questions!

Thief of Dreams Story Endings

Here are outcomes for each story opening, detailing what success or failure might mean.

If the PCs did face all three battles, remember to give them a full heal-up.

The Ultimate Score

Success: The PCs travel to the dreamlands and manage to find the Dreamlord, who eventually allows them to spy on the elf lord's dreams with the Elf Queen. The information is juicy, and the PCs return to the world through their mirror to report what they learned. The Prince uses that information to prove yet again that the impossible is routine for him. The PCs are spoken of with awe among the dark alleys and hidden back rooms of the world. Each PCs gains a 6 with the Prince that lasts until they use it. They also still have the mirror…

Failure: The PCs get lost in the dreamlands for weeks but never find the Dreamlord. Eventually it's too late to be of use to the Prince and he writes them off, barely noticing when they finally emerge back into the world a month later. The shadows whisper of their failure, and the PCs must reroll any 6s they get (once) the next two times they roll icon dice.

The Worst Kind of Blackmail

Success: The PCs travel to the dreamlands and manage to find the Dreamlord and even spy on the Elf Queen. Surprisingly, when they hand over the information, their loved ones are returned alive. Honor among thieves and all. But they have no idea who took them. Their loved ones report that they were told they won't be used as leverage again… probably.

Failure: The PCs fail to gain the intelligence they were sent to the dreamlands to collect. Eventually they must return to the world or go mad. Their loved ones aren't returned, though there are rumors that they were given to another icon that the PCs are enemies with in exchange for favors. That icon will probably be contacting them soon, or maybe there's still time for a rescue mission.

Guys, Where Are We?

Success: The PCs do as instructed, and even succeed, relating the details of a certain elf lord's dreams with the Queen through drug-induced lips. When they awake some time later, no one is the worse for wear. A note stuck to the wall by a dagger says, "I reward you with the most valuable gift: your lives."

Failure: The PCs try their best to find the Dreamlord, but ultimately fail. Eventually, they all wake up, but one magic item has been taken from each of them. A note stuck to the wall by a dagger says, "I had to go find some better dreamers, and I'll bribe them with your gear. Come after me and you won't live through it."

BATTLE SCENE CONNECTIONS

The stories from this set of battle scenes can lead to other scenes:

- *The Library of Galwyn* (Elf Queen): While listening in on the Elf Queen's dreams with the Dreamlord, the PCs hear her distress and see visions of destruction at an elven facility. The Dreamlord reveals that it's a place in the real world known as the Library of Galwyn. The dream foreshadows something that will soon happen in the real world. The PCs must quickly travel there if they wish to stop a slaughter.

- *Almost Any Other Battle Scene* (Any): Thanks to the foreshadowing of dreams, the PCs could learn whatever they need to put them on the path of new adventure.

The Three: A Pit of Vipers

LEVEL RANGE: 4–5

The themes of this set of battles are dirty deals, tricky tactics, and deadly dragonic enemies connected to the Three. The enemies include kobolds, dragonics, and a black dragon.

This set of battle scenes works best away from a dense urban environment, where the hill lair of the dragon and her gang can exist without undue notice. It would work fine either in the wilds, near a forest track, or a few miles outside a village or small town in semi-wild lands.

Depending on the story opening, the PCs find themselves infiltrating the lair of a black dragon named Golthrash who's the boss of a gang of dragonics and kobolds who call themselves the Vipers. The opposition is cunning and takes advantage of the terrain in their lair. If the PCs can fight or sneak their way through, they'll face Golthrash herself, who has plans for the local region.

Since this set of battles is connected to the Three, and since there's a dragon involved, the final battle is a double-strength one.

A Pit of Vipers Story Openings

- **The Kobold's Map:** After a well-executed ambush by a band of kobolds that would have worked had they not run into the PCs, the group finds something interesting on the band's leader. The kobold is carrying a crude map that depicts a hill and a cave and the path to reach it. The map also has crude drawings of a dragon, and the words, "Vipers," "Golthrash," "boss," and "big treasure" scrawled on it. The map is easy for the PCs to follow.
- **Rumor to Rumor:** The PCs are on the trail of someone or something and have been following rumors of it from one location to another, talking to one shady denizen after another. The latest rumor suggests that what they seek is hidden in a cave in a hill in the wilds that's guarded by vipers. The PCs have found the cave, and they're ready to clear out the snakes.
- **A Test for Vipers:** Golthrash has set up her lair and its defenses, and the Vipers have been training. But she needs to test things out. Either she's been sending out kobold wannabe Vipers with maps of the lair to draw adventurers in, or she actually sends one of her dragonic sorcerers to hire the PCs for the job. In the latter case, the entire set of battles might be non-lethal... until Golthrash changes her mind for the final battle to make sure the pesky adventurers can't tell anyone else about the lair.
- **Cleansing the Riffraff:** A rogue black dragon named Golthrash has failed to pay proper respect to the Black, and that hasn't gone over well with the icon. The dragon is holed up in her lair with her gang, who call themselves Vipers. A contact in the Black's organization either orders or hires the PCs to put an end to the Vipers and their boss. (The PCs could be aware of who they are working for or not.)
- **Follow Me:** One of the PCs acquires part of a magic item (one glove or boot of a pair, a scabbard missing its sword, a quiver missing its bow, etc.). The item holds enough magic and sentience to direct the PC toward its companion piece, which it can sense. It leads the PCs to a cave in the side of a small hill and tells them its counterpart is inside.

Alternate Icons

 The Three (the Blue): You could switch out which member of the Three the Vipers serve and give the sorcerers and kobolds lightning attacks. Change the black dragon to a blue who likes water and it should play about the same way.

 High Druid: Golthrash is actually a dragon druid and has sworn off service to the Three for the High Druid. She guards an earth node or some other natural wonder (in the small cave), and her Vipers worship her like a nature god. They have all sworn to protect her and that which she watches over, keeping all civilized folk away.

Icons in Play

Characters that have relationships (and story-guide advantages) with the Three, the Prince, the Great Gold Wyrm, and maybe the Emperor or Dwarf King should be able to shine in these battle scenes. Moreso than PCs with other icon relationships, feel free to give such PCs extra knowledge about the opposition, make checks to pull off fun actions the players might suggest, and use their advantages to particularly good effect, such as negating or bypassing some of the advantages or abilities of the enemies.

A Pit of Vipers Overview

This set of battles assumes the PCs have found the large hill hosting Golthrash's lair and are now just outside. The hill rises four or five hundred feet, and the steep back side overlooks a swift moving river. On that side, a small waterfall cascades down the cliff-like slopes into the river. There's only one obvious entrance, a large cave near ground level opposite the river from which a slight track leads away through a dell of large ferns and small trees. There are no obvious guards. (It is possible for PCs who explore to access the hill via the waterfall, allowing them to immediately face the dragon.)

The cave entrance leads to a tall cavern where the Vipers have set up their first defensive system. Kobolds wait hidden in the upper reaches of the cave to put their ingenuity to use as they attack.

Beyond the cavern, there's a warren-like area of tunnels where dragonic servants of Golthrash await the PCs. They will use a combination of stealth and direct force to stop the heroes' advance.

Finally, in a large cavern near the top of the hill, Golthrash waits with her Vipers. She is a deadly enemy in her own right, but with the added support of her gang, the PCs will have a challenge in front of them.

GM, feel free to expand upon these battles by including meetings with shady denizens of nearby population centers, attacks by more kobold wannabee Vipers along the way, battles with beasts roaming the area, and even stealth-based encounters to get past outer-perimeter kobold guards.

The battles outlined here can take place over a few minutes or tens of minutes, depending on how fast the PCs wish to strike. If it takes too long, Golthrash could leave her lair and take it upon herself to trail the PCs and make their lives difficult. Since the Three (the Black) is in play, sprinkle the battle scenes with a sense of hidden enemies, darkness and shadows, sudden attacks, and draconic power.

See story endings after the final battle for options on what happens after the PCs finish the last battle.

Battle I: High-Flying Vipers

The stone and dirt cave mouth is wide and high. It gets dark quickly as it descends gently into the hill. There are some signs of passage in the dirt—small clawed humanoid feet—and an odd, caustic smell to the place. After a turn or two, dirt gives way to stone and you see a long, tall cavern stretched out before you. Flecks of minerals glint in the rock walls, and you can just make out a ramp in the stone at the back of the cavern heading upward. Water drips steadily from that back wall and pools on the cave floor among a bloom of small fungi.

Location Description

The cavern is 100 feet long, 50 feet wide, and 80 feet high. A stone ramp switches back and forth across the back wall up to a ledge 60 feet high, where it exits from the cave (but initially it will be in shadows and the PCs won't see it until they get closer). Water seeps through cracks in the stone to drip down that wall and pool on the ground, before draining through more cracks in the floor.

The cavern is riddled with small stone ledges in the upper reaches that the kobolds have excavated to help them with their attacks. Each ledge is only a few feet across and 2 to 3 feet wide, and most are 30 feet above the ground or more and hidden in the shadows. The kobolds are hiding on those ledges, waiting to swoop down on ropes that they've secured to a series of hooks in the ceiling.

If the PCs tried to be stealthy in their approach to the lair, let them all make Dexterity checks to do so. If more than half succeed (DC 20), then two of kobolds are sipping water unsuspectingly from the pool when the PCs enter, and the PCs will surprise them.

Terrain & Traps

Ledges, Walls, and Ropes: The small ledges range in height between 30 and 60 feet, and there are 10 to 15 of them. The kobolds can swing from the back ledge to any of the wall ledges using the ropes tied off to the ceiling (they've had practice). Any PC attempting this stunt must succeed on a DC 18 Dexterity check; failure means smashing into a wall (3d6 damage) and possibly falling.

Getting to the small ledges requires climbing the walls, which have plenty of handholds. As a move action, a creature can make a DC 15 Strength check to reach a ledge. Some of the ledges also have knotted ropes secured to them for easy climbing (no check if the rope is down, but they have been pulled up by the kobolds).

The ropes the kobolds use to swing on can make it easier to get to the small ledges too. Once a kobold gets knocked off one (or drops), the rope dangles to the ground near the middle of the cave. A PC can climb it (DC 10) as a move action, then use another move action to swing side-to-side to reach a small ledge.

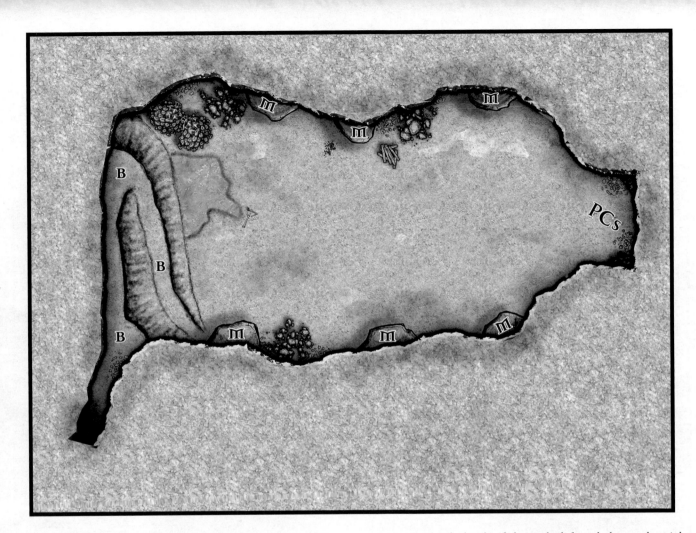

The ropes can also be targeted with attacks, although they are stained dark and not easy to see. Each rope has an AC/PD of 19 and can take 5 damage before severing. A kobold with a severed rope falls to the ground and takes 3d6 damage.

Back ledge/ramp: A ramp leads up the back ledge moving right the first 30 feet, then left up to 60 feet, requiring two move actions to reach the tunnel exiting the cavern. Climbing directly up the wall to the exit as a single move action requires a DC 20 Strength check due to the wet rock.

Pool & Fungi: The pool is only about a foot deep near the center. A lucky kobold (or PC) who falls while on the ledge or on a rope heading toward the back ledge might hit the water and take only half damage (roll a save; success means water).

The fungi are small and harmless, possibly edible for anyone who wants to try them.

Monsters

The kobold ledgedivers will be hiding and waiting in position when the PCs enter the cavern (DC 20 to detect them), unless the heroes were stealthy, in which case two of them will be at the pool.

The bravescales are sitting and resting along the ramp ledges, trying to keep anyone from reaching the exit.

All of them will make strong claims about the worthiness of the Vipers (what they call themselves) and the doom of their enemies during the battle. If obviously defeated, the mooks might beat a hasty retreat for the entrance when down to a few left. If captured, they will extol the virtues of Golthrash and how the PCs are dead meat.

Additional Reinforcements: If you want to challenge the PCs more, when it's clear that the kobolds are losing, one of them will pull a rope opening a wooden cage tied to the ceiling. It releases a thunder bat (*Bestiary*, page 15) that they hope will buy them time to flee.

#/Level of PCs	Kobold Bravescale (B)	Kobold Ledgediver Mook (M)
4 x 4th level	3	7 (1 mob)
5 x 4th level	4	7 (1 mob)
6 x 4th level	5	8 (1 mob)
4 x 5th level	5	8 (1 mob)*
5 x 5th level	7	9 (1 mob)*
6 x 5th level	8	11 (2 mobs)*

* Make each Ledgediver mook double-strength: 32 hp and it deals 16 damage with its *small mace* attack.

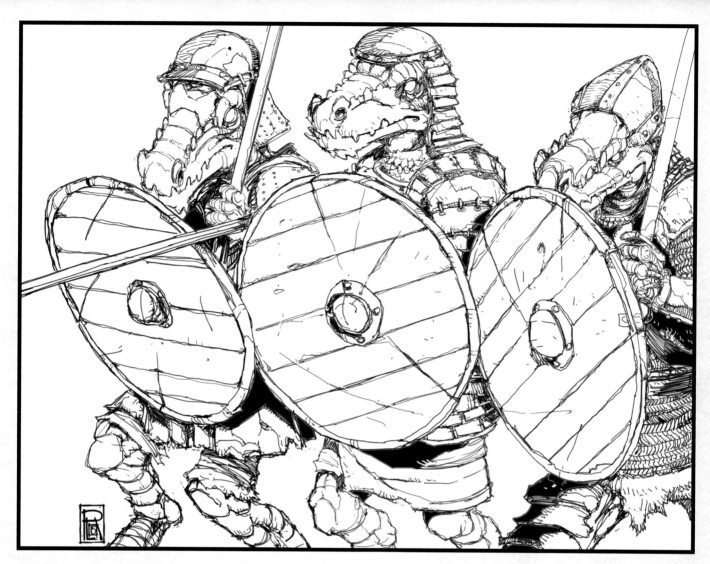

Tactics

The ledgedivers will swing back and forth between the small ledges and the back ledge/top of the ramp as long as possible, making attacks each time. When they drop or fumble an attack, they will crash spectacularly.

Each mob has two nets, and they will time it so two mooks leap off and drop a net as they pass over, trying to entangle some enemies. The nets are large and unwieldy for a single creature to try to use (nearby range, −4 to attack).

The bravescales guard the ramp up to the exit. When one makes a *spear* attack and rolls higher than the target's Wisdom for their *trapster* ability, instead of using a trap as per the Bestiary, the kobold pushes the target off the ledge for 1d4 + escalation die damage.

Loot

There's a scattering of simple jewelry among the kobolds all made from onyx (no flashy bling for these stealthy creeps) worth a total of 50 gp. They also have many weird, odd, or disgusting items lying around on the ledges, such as: extra nets and rope, raven feathers, black silk Viper masks, wood plates with handles with a now-dried sticky substance on the flat side (for climbing to the hooks in the ceiling), and whatever else the PCs might find interesting or disturbing.

Icons

A PC that has relationship advantages with the Three, Elf Queen, Great Gold Wyrm, Orc Lord, or the Prince could use one or more of them to hop a ride from a swinging ledgediver and get someplace fast without climbing, or make some other impressive maneuver without a check.

A PC that has relationship advantages with the Three could attempt to leverage that relationship into bluffing the kobolds to let them pass unhindered as messengers of the icon, though it would require at least one Charisma check.

Kobold Ledgediver

"Dieeeeee.... eeeeeeeeee!"

5th level mook [humanoid]
Initiative: +8

Small mace +10 vs. AC—8 damage
  Natural 18+: The next attack by a ledgediver this battle gains a +4 bonus to damage.

Ledgediver specialist: As a move action and standard action, the ledgediver can launch from a ledge, make a *small mace* attack, and swing back to another ledge. If it hits with the attack, the ledgediver will not take opportunity attacks during that movement. On a miss, the target of its attack can make an opportunity attack against it. On a fumble, the kobold misjudges and that mook dies in a particularly bad way (reduce mob hp to remove one mook from battle), or you can have ropes tangle and two mooks end up sprawled next to the PCs on the ground unhurt.

Net specialist (group ability): Each mob has two nets they can use to make *net hurl* attacks this battle. Choose two nearby mooks in a group to make an attack. As a standard and move action, both will try to drop a net onto enemies as they pass overhead and make the following attack (one roll).
C: Net hurl +9 vs. PD (1d3 nearby enemies in a group)—The target is stuck (save ends).

AC	20	
PD	18	**HP 16 (mook)**
MD	14	

Mook: Kill one kobold ledgediver mook for every 16 damage you deal to the mob.

Kobold Bravescale

These iron-clad woad-painted kobolds don't run away from danger!

4th level blocker [humanoid]
Initiative: +9

Spear +9 vs. AC—13 damage
  Natural roll is above target's Wisdom (trapster): The kobold pushes or trips the target into a trap.

R: Light crossbow +8 vs. AC (one nearby or far away target at −2 atk)—10 damage

Disciplined maneuver: If the escalation die is 3+ and this creature has at least two bravescale allies in the battle, whenever an enemy moves to engage the bravescale, it can make a *spear porcupine* attack against that enemy as a free action.
Spear porcupine +11 vs. AC—10 damage

Lock shields: For each other kobold bravescale next to the bravescale or engaged with a creature that this bravescale is engaged with, the bravescale gains a +2 bonus to AC (maximum of +4), and each enemy engaged with the bravescale takes a −2 penalty (maximum of −4) to disengage checks.

AC	20	
PD	18	**HP 55**
MD	14	

Next Steps

If you want to foreshadow the battle to come, feel free to include some charcoal cave art on the walls of a large black dragon consuming the kobolds' enemies as they watch.

The exit from this cavern passes by two smaller caverns where the kobolds live. Each area contains bedding, food, drink, and debris, but little of true value. The tunnel begins to climb and after a minute enters another cavern and series of tunnels connected to it. See **Battle 2: The Viper's Pit.**

BATTLE 2: BLACK SCALES

Ahead of you, the floor angles downward into a medium-sized cavern with many exits. Six tunnels, three on each side, extend away from the cave out of sight: two in each wall to the right and left, and one on each side of a ramp up directly ahead. The wood ramp leads up to the top of a fifteen-foot ledge that extends back out of sight. There's the smell of vinegar or something similar in the air. Tall figures step forward at the top of the shelf, eyes glowing as one says, "None may pass the Vipers!"

LOCATION DESCRIPTION

Some of the strongest of Golthrash's Vipers are in this cavern and will do their best to halt the PCs' advance. The rough cavern is 80 feet long and 50 feet wide with a 25-foot high ceiling, but the back 30 feet is a shelf 15 feet up from the rest of the cave.

There's a larger tunnel that exits out the far side of the cave on the shelf level (not visible from below). There are also six smaller (humanoid-sized) exits from the lower cave. Each of those exits is interconnected by tunnels, creating a warren of passageways from which the kobold shadow-warriors hiding in them will strike.

Dragonic blackshields and a black sorcerer are on the upper shelf and will work together to keep the PCs from advancing.

TERRAIN & TRAPS

Ramp & Shelf: The heavy wooden ramp is easy enough to move up, except that the blackshields will intercept anyone coming up it to keep the PCs off the sorcerer.

The shelf is not high (15 feet), and the rock wall to it is rough, but anyone trying to climb it is in for a surprise. The black sorcerer has created an alchemical paste out of Golthrash's acidic bile and other elements, which coats all of the ridges and handholds of the rock (that vinegar smell). Anyone attempting to climb the ledge will get the paste on them, exposing them to acid that will burn through flesh and metal. If a PC tries this, they automatically take 10 ongoing acid damage.

The acid paste also makes climbing more difficult (DC 20). Anyone who falls off doesn't take damage, they just have to try again.

Tunnels: The lower tunnels all connect to each other after a short distance. They have lots of nooks and crannies too, making them good places for the shadow-warriors to hide (DC 20 to spot one hiding in a tunnel).

In addition, the sorcerer is a bit of a seer and has laid down various prophecies and mysteries upon the tunnel walls. It would be a good place for a PC to pick up some valuable information on the Three, gain something for a story opening, or to use as a flashback for an icon advantage.

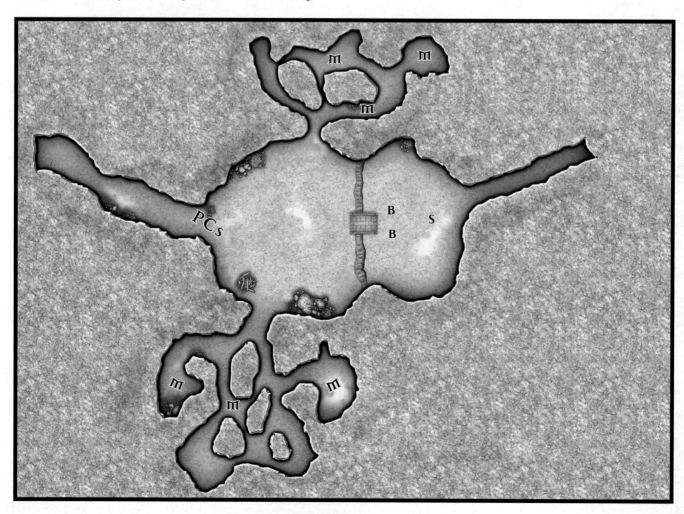

MONSTERS

Waiting at the back of the cave are the dragonic blackshields and a black sorcerer (or two). They will step forward to guard the ramp up to the shelf while their allies, the shadow-warriors, hit the PCs from the shadows of the tunnels. Each blackshield uses an actual scale from Golthrash for its shield.

The dragonics are proud and determined, and don't want to face a black dragon's wrath, so they will fight to the death.

If you don't include dragonics in your game world, reflavor them as lizard men or dragon spawn.

Additional Reinforcements: If you want to challenge the PCs more, make the shadow-warriors double-strength.

#/Level of PCs	Dragonic Black Sorcerer (S)	Dragonic Blackshield (B)	Kobold Shadow-Warrior Mook (M)
4 x 4th level	1	2	5 (1 mob)
5 x 4th level	1	3	6 (1 mob)
6 x 4th level	1	4	7 (1 mob)
4 x 5th level	2	4	10 (1 mob)
5 x 5th level	2	6	12 (2 mobs)
6 x 5th level	3	6	14 (2 mobs)

TACTICS

The black sorcerer will use its *acidic spit* attack on the first round so it can have the chance to use it as a quick action on later rounds. Then it will use *chaotic forcebolt* on any spellcasters or other enemies trying to circumvent the ramp. It will try to disengage if it can, but can fight with claws as needed.

The blackshields will try to hold ground at the top of the ramp, keeping enemies engaged. They can force enemies back down the ramp, or off the shelf with their *shield slam* attack.

The shadow warriors will use their *elusive* ability on the first round if they can and then attack with *elusive strike* on round 2, hitting squishy targets to good effect. The ones that can will keep repeating this sequence.

LOOT

The Vipers only keep a small amount of wealth in the form of jewelry made from onyx, similar to the kobolds in the first chamber. The rest goes to Golthrash. They have a total of 80 gp.

The black sorcerer also has a *potion of acid resistance* and champion-tier *healing potion* in a small satchel around its shoulder.

ICONS

A PC that has relationship advantages with the Three, Crusader, Dwarf King, Great Gold Wyrm, or the Orc Lord could use one or more of them to trick or taunt one of the blackshields to come down the ramp and leave a hole in their defense.

A PC that has a relationship advantage with the Prince could use it to negate a shadow-warrior's *elusive strike* attacks against them. Or maybe that PC and 1d3 of the mooks all move "into the shadows" to play shadow games with only each other. Once the mooks drop, that PC can step back from the shadows anywhere in the cavern (similar to prolonged *shadow walk*).

A PC WITH CONNECTIONS TO A DRAGON

The Vipers will focus attacks when they can (without breaking ranks) on enemies who show obvious signs of supporting the Great Gold Wyrm, or who are known enemies of the Black.

On the other hand, PCs with positive or conflicted relationships with the Three might be able to exert enough influence on the Vipers to get them talking. It probably won't stop a fight, but they may reveal some useful information about "the greatness of Golthrash" that could help in the next battle (attack, damage, or save bonuses, or the right things to say to make the dragon focus attacks on a PC, for example).

DRAGONIC BLACK SORCERER

The wyrm-fervor is strong in this one.

6th level caster [HUMANOID]
Initiative: +8

Sharpened claws +10 vs. AC—17 damage

R: Acidic spit +11 vs. PD—8 acid damage, 5 ongoing acid damage, and the sorcerer can't use this attack again this battle except when it recharges (see below)

Quickened recharge: After the black sorcerer uses this attack, it rolls a save at the start of each of its turns. On a success, it can use *acidic spit* once that turn as a quick action. The save gains a bonus equal to the escalation die.

R: Chaotic forcebolt +11 vs. PD (1d2 nearby or far away enemies)—18 force damage against a single enemy, or 9 force damage if the bolt splits and hits two enemies

Natural 16+: The target pops free from all enemies and is pushed away from its current location (no opportunity attacks). The target must roll a save to avoid falling if it's in a precarious position (like on a ledge).

AC	22	
PD	17	**HP 85**
MD	18	

DRAGONIC BLACKSHIELD

Their black dragon scale shields look as dangerous as the swords they bear.

4th level blocker [HUMANOID]
Initiative: +5

Longsword +9 vs. AC—7 damage

Shield slam +6—4 damage

Natural even hit or miss: The blackshield can choose one: the target is dazed until the end of its next turn; OR the blackshield can try to force the target to move a short distance. When it tries to move a target, the target can make a DC 20 Strength or Dexterity check to resist. On a failure, the target gets shoved out of engagement (and possibly falls off the shelf or ramp) where the blackshield wants it to go.

Slash & slam: As a standard action, the blackshield can make both a *longsword* attack and a *shield slam* attack.

Resist acid 14+: When an acid attack targets this creature, the attacker must roll a natural 14+ on the attack roll or it only deals half damage.

AC	21	
PD	19	**HP 110**
MD	14	

KOBOLD SHADOW-WARRIOR

Stealthy kobolds with color-changing skin, they climb the walls like lizards and strike from the shadows.

4th level mook [HUMANOID]
Initiative: +9

C: Throwing star +9 vs. AC (one nearby enemy)—7 damage

C: Stinging dust +6 vs. PD (up to 2 nearby enemies in a group)—5 damage, and the target takes a –1 penalty to attacks until the end of its next turn

Elusive: If an individual shadow-warrior hasn't been attacked since the end of its last turn, it can spend all of its actions on its turn to disappear from sight (remove it from play as it gets into position). At the start of its next turn, it reappears (dropping down from the ceiling or springing out of cover and re-entering play) and can make an *elusive strike* attack as a standard action.

C: Elusive strike +13 vs. AC (one nearby creature)—18 damage

Evasive: Kobolds take no damage from missed attacks.

Wall-crawler: A kobold shadow-warrior can climb on ceilings and walls as easily as it moves on the ground.

AC	20	
PD	13	**HP 14 (mook)**
MD	17	

Mook: Kill one kobold shadow-warrior mook for every 14 damage you deal to the mob. Apply damage to shadow-warriors using the *elusive* ability last (or ignore that damage).

NEXT STEPS

A tunnel at the back of the shelf exits this cavern and leads up toward the top of the hill where Golthrash waits. GM, if you're feeling kind, you could foreshadow the battle to come with earth tremors, loud, annoyed dragon roars, or other telltale signs of the heavyweight enemy they're about to face if they haven't already figured it out. See **Battle 3: Always Bet on Black**.

BATTLE 3: ALWAYS BET ON BLACK

The large tunnel begins to climb a set of natural stairs worn down the middle by a slow trickle of water. Ahead you hear the sound of splashing, flowing water that rises in volume with each step. At the top of the stairs you can see the source. Daylight weakly streams into a large cavern through a cave opening in the wall, reflecting off of two large linked pools of water. One of the pools appears to be spring-fed, with a channel that leads to the next and then eventually exits the cave opening to spill below as a waterfall. The rest of the cave is cloaked in shadows.

LOCATION DESCRIPTION

This water-filled cavern is Golthrash's current lair. She resides here with her current favorite Vipers, planning their next mission in service to the Black (or for her own gain). If by some chance the PCs choose to explore the terrain around the hill, they might find the cave entrance where the waterfall starts first (although the mist hides it somewhat from below and it's up a cliff). Feel free to reverse the order of the battles if they go in that way first.

The cavern is 80 feet wide and 140 feet long, with a 40-foot ceiling, although there are three large ledges around the edges that are big enough for the dragon to fly to and land on. In addition to the waterfall exit to the outside, there's also a tunnel at the far back of cavern that leads to a small cave—Golthrash's dry lair.

Each bean-shaped pool is somewhat parallel to the other and connected by a shallow channel. Another channel runs from the second pool to the cave opening outside and becomes a waterfall. There's also an out-of-sight underwater tunnel connecting the two pools that Golthrash can use to good effect.

Unless surprised, the dragon will be waiting in the shadows at the back of the cave (having heard the PCs approach, or heard the fight below). The Vipers will also be hiding on ledges and in the shadows around the cave.

Feeling overconfident, as dragons often do, Golthrash is willing to give up a chance for surprise to talk to, learn about, and hopefully intimate those who've intruded upon her (or thank the heroes for their work if they came to test the defenses, right before turning on them). Staying out of sight in the shadows, she will question them about who they work for and why they've come, as well as try to get a sense of their capabilities.

It's possible at this point, either with great roleplaying or copious use of icon advantages, to avoid a battle, probably by giving the dragon a very nice gift and leaving, should the PCs choose that course. Otherwise, once the dragon tires of them or is insulted by them, or they try to move toward her dry lair or the exit, she will pounce.

This is a double-strength battle that should challenge the PCs. With four different types of monsters, it may challenge the GM too. Feel free to remove ten shadow-warriors and add one sorcerer.

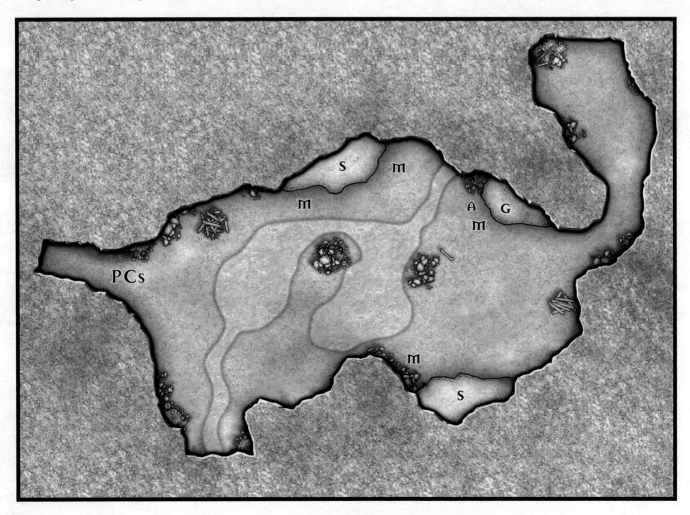

TERRAIN & TRAPS

Dragon Splash: During her first turn, Golthrash will use her move action to rush forward and leap into the pool closest to the PCs, sending a big wave of water at them. When this happens, make the following attack as part of the move action.

> **C: Wave of acidic water +10 vs. PD (1d3 + 1 enemies in a group next to the pool)**—The target is vulnerable until the start of its next turn as slightly burning water gets in their eyes

Pools & Channels: Each pool is roughly 25–30 feet in diameter and 20 to 30 feet deep. The water is cloudy with dragon brine and slightly acidic (but not overly harmful with short-term exposure), making it hard to see more than about 5 feet down. There's a tunnel connecting the pools near the bottom that Golthrash can squeeze through.

The surface channel between pools is only 2 feet wide and 1 foot deep. The channel from the second pool to where the waterfall spills out is 3 feet wide and 2 feet deep. The water pressure isn't strong; only an unconscious PC in the water would be moved by it toward a pool or toward the waterfall.

Ledges & Waterfall: The three ledges vary in height between 10 feet and 30 feet off the ground and are 10 to 15 feet wide. Climbing up to one isn't too difficult and requires only a successful DC 12 Strength check. Each is strong enough to bear the dragon's weight if she chooses to fly to one.

The water spills over the edge of the cave opening, forming a small waterfall down the cliffs to the river below. The cave opening is roughly 10 feet wide and 8 feet high. The ledge drops 50 feet to another shelf; anyone falling to that shelf will take 4d8 damage and have to climb back up (two move actions and a DC 13 check).

Small Cave: The cave is roughly 20 feet in diameter and has no line of sight to the larger cavern. It's where Golthrash keeps some of her dry hoard.

MONSTERS

Golthrash is a dragon, so she's overconfident in her abilities, if not those of the Vipers. She also has an ego, so ploys in that regard might be slightly more likely to work. Any secret information regarding the Three, especially the Black, will get her attention. Her dragon ability mimics a human's *quick to fight* racial power, allowing her to roll initiative twice.

The black sorcerers will stay on the ledges around the room (the ledge at the back is far away), waiting for the dragon to initiate the battle. They will fight to the death, and seeing the dragon drop might cause one or more to enter melee in rage. The black assassins are hiding in the shadows on the ground level near the dragon.

The kobold shadow-warriors wait in the shadows around the edges of the cavern. If the dragon dies, they will probably retreat unless there is a dragonic to lead them or the PCs are close to going down.

Additional Reinforcements: If you want to challenge the PCs more, there's also a wyvern (core rulebook, page 250) just outside the falls that guards golthrash's lair entrance. She's managed to train it for the job, feeding it fresh meat often, and it now serves her.

#/Level of PCs	Golthrash (G)	Black Sorcerer (S)	Black Assassin (A)	Shadow-Warrior Mook (M)
4 x 4th level	1	1	0	10 (1 mob)
5 x 4th level	1	1	1	6 (1 mob)
6 x 4th level	1	2	1	10 (1 mob)
4 x 5th level	1	3	2	10 (1 mob)
5 x 5th level	1*/**	3	3	7 (1 mob)
6 x 5th level	1*/**	4	4	7 (1 mob)

* Golthrash is a huge dragon instead; increase her hit points to 300, her *claws and bite* attack now deals 38 damage on a hit (no increase to ongoing), and her acidic breath attack instead deals 40 damage (no increase to ongoing) and 20 on a miss.

** Golthrash will use her nastier special and move between pools.

TACTICS

Once Golthrash decides to attack, she will surge forward from the shadows and leap into the pool (see **Terrain & Traps**) unless she has two or more PCs engaged with her (then a disengage check to do so). If the PCs were talking to her and she decides to end them, allow her to leap into the pool as the start of the battle without any other actions, then roll initiative.

Golthrash will lead with *acid breath*, then lay into them with her melee attacks, before hitting the group again with her breath when she sees some of them are staggered. Golthrash is smart, so play her that way. She'll make all of her attacks against one enemy to try to drop that PC quickly, and will choose an enemy with weaker defenses when she has an equal choice. When her *draconic grace* triggers, she might be willing to take opportunity attacks to move (not disengage) to a staggered foe to use two sets of *claws and bite* attacks against it.

She'll also use the pool tunnel to her advantage to get close to a squishy spellcaster or other PC who's causing trouble.

The black sorcerers and shadow-warriors will try to stay at range, targeting healers and spellcasters and hoping the PCs ignore them while the dragon wreaks havoc.

The black assassins can either stay at range, or more likely will step into the shadows to suddenly appear behind a melee or ranged attacker to make a *poisoned fang* attack to try to weaken the target for the dragon.

GM, if you want to ratchet up the difficulty of this battle or are using the dragon's nastier special for 5th level battles, after the dragon attacks have her try to disengage. When successful, she will retreat underwater, then use her move action next turn to return to the fight. Treat anyone fighting the dragon underwater as weakened and vulnerable, unless they have magic or a unique that would offset it. Anyone out of the water attacking the dragon while it's in the pool takes a −4 attack penalty and only deals half damage.

Golthrash is not above fleeing a battle once she realizes she's overmatched and reduced below 30 hp. She will make for the waterfall cave and try to fly away, and the PCs will become her hated enemies.

Loot

Golthrash has a small hoard since she and the Vipers have only recently set up shop in this lair. Most of it is in the smaller side cave, though she keeps some of the non-soluble valuables in a nook at the bottom of one of the pools too.

In the cave, there's 300 gp in silver and copper coins in a pile, plus some silver plates and utensils taken from a noble's estate worth 100 gp, and six pieces of jewelry worth another 200 gp. A handful of common weapons and armor from past conquests are also scattered around the room, one suit of armor still holding a skeleton and bearing the symbol of the GGW. The equipment is pitted and worn and mostly of little value. There are also a few magic items: one *potion of acid resistance* (ha!), one champion-tier *healing potion*, one *potion of invisibility* (as the wizard spell's base effect), and a *Belt of Brutal Vigor* (*13TW*, page 234), plus any story items that the PCs might be searching for.

Hidden at the bottom of one of the pools is the rest of the dragon's hoard. Finding it in the murky water requires a successful DC 20 Wisdom or Intelligence check. There's 200 gp in dwarven towers (unstacked), 20 pp, and 40 elven trines, plus 5 pearls worth 25 gp each.

Icons

A PC that has relationship advantages with the Three, Dwarf King, Elf Queen, Emperor, or the Prince could use one or more of them to know the perfect insult to keep the dragon focused on them during combat, or perhaps to convince the dragon that the PCs are protected from acid so it won't use its *acid breath* attack until it's near death.

A PC that has relationship advantages with the Three, Dwarf King, Emperor, Great Gold Wyrm, or the Prince could use one or more of them to have heard rumors that Golthrash keeps a hidden hoard at the bottom of a pool (no check required to find it).

A PC that has two or more advantages with any single icon might be able to talk Golthrash into letting the group go without a campaign loss if they are losing badly and willing to ransom a magic item to her.

Golthrash, Black Dragon

The silky yet dangerous voice rises to a screech of rage as the large reptilian eyes of a predator open fully and a large shadow begins moving toward you.

Large 7th level wrecker [DRAGON]
Initiative: +13, but see dragon ability
Vulnerability: thunder

Claws and bite +12 vs. AC (2 attacks)—25 damage
  Natural 16+: The target also takes 15 ongoing acid damage.

C: Acid breath +11 vs. PD (1d3 nearby enemies)—26 acid damage, and 10 ongoing acid damage
  Miss: 13 acid damage.

Draconic grace: At the start of each of the black dragon's turns, roll a d6 to see if it gets an extra standard action. If the roll is equal to or less than the escalation die, the black dragon can take an extra standard action that turn.

  After the first success, the grace die bumps up to a d8. After the second success, it's a d10, then a d12 after the third success, and finally a d20 after the fourth one.

Dragon ability (Quick to Fight): At the start of each battle, Golthrash rolls initiative twice and takes the best result.

Escalator: A dragon adds the escalation die to its attack rolls.

Flight: A dragon flies reasonably well, powerful and fast in a straight line though not as maneuverable as more agile flyers.

Intermittent breath: Golthrash can use *acid breath* 1d3 + 1 times per battle, but never two turns in a row.

Water-breathing: Black dragons swim well and can breathe underwater.

Resist acid 16+: When an acid attack targets this creature, the attacker must roll a natural 16+ on the attack roll or it only deals half damage.

Nastier Specials

Terrain advantage (water): While in a body of water where Golthrash can submerge herself (like one of the pools), she gains a +5 bonus to disengage checks. After attacking, she will attempt to disengage and submerge.

AC	23	
PD	21	**HP 200**
MD	19	

Dragonic Black Sorcerer

The wyrm-fervor within this black-scaled dragonic is almost as strong as the magic it can call forth.

6th level caster [HUMANOID]
Initiative: +8

Sharpened claws +10 vs. AC—17 damage

R: Acidic spit +11 vs. PD—8 acid damage, 5 ongoing acid damage, and the sorcerer can't use this attack again this battle except when it recharges (see below)
Quickened recharge: After the black sorcerer uses this attack, it rolls a save at the start of each of its turns. On a success, it can use *acidic spit* once that turn as a quick action. The save gains a bonus equal to the escalation die.

R: Chaotic forcebolt +11 vs. PD (1d2 nearby or far away enemies)—18 force damage against a single enemy, or 9 force damage if the bolt splits and hits two enemies
Natural 16+: The target pops free of all enemies and is pushed away from its current location (no opportunity attacks). The target must roll a save to avoid falling if it's in a precarious position (like on a ledge).

AC 22	
PD 17	HP 85
MD 18	

Dragonic Black Assassin

The black-clad dragonic female peels away from the shadows with a dragon fang in hand that holds the promise of a painful death.

Double-strength 5th level spoiler [HUMANOID]
Initiative: +10

Poisoned fang +10 vs. AC (2 attacks)—10 damage and 5 poison damage
Natural 16+: The target takes 5 ongoing poison damage and is vulnerable (save ends both).

R: Acid-coated throwing knife +9—20 damage, and 10 ongoing acid damage

One with the shadows: As a standard action, the assassin can step into the shadows if it's unengaged. While in the shadows, it can't attack or be targeted by an attack or effect. At the start of its next turn, it can reappear from the shadows anywhere nearby as a move action. If it hits with its next attack that turn, the target is also weakened (hard save ends, 16+).

Resist acid 14+: When an acid attack targets this creature, the attacker must roll a natural 14+ on the attack roll or it only deals half damage.

AC 20	
PD 13	HP 130
MD 19	

Kobold Shadow-Warrior

Stealthy kobolds with color-changing skin, they climb the walls like lizards and strike from the shadows.

4th level mook [HUMANOID]
Initiative: +9

C: Throwing star +9 vs. AC (one nearby enemy)—7 damage

C: Stinging dust +6 vs. PD (up to 2 nearby enemies in a group)—5 damage, and the target takes a −1 penalty to attacks until the end of its next turn

Elusive: If an individual shadow-warrior hasn't been attacked since the end of its last turn, it can spend all of its actions on its turn to disappear from sight (remove it from play as it gets into position). At the start of its next turn, it reappears (dropping down from the ceiling or springing out of cover and re-entering play) and can make an *elusive strike* attack as a standard action.
C: Elusive strike +13 vs. AC (one nearby creature)—18 damage

Evasive: Kobolds take no damage from missed attacks.

Wall-crawler: A kobold shadow-warrior can climb on ceilings and walls as easily as it moves on the ground.

AC 20	
PD 13	HP 14 (mook)
MD 17	

Mook: Kill one kobold shadow-warrior mook for every 14 damage you deal to the mob. Apply damage to shadow-warriors using the *elusive* ability last (or ignore that damage).

ADDITIONAL REINFORCEMENTS

Wyvern

Large 5th level wrecker [BEAST]
Initiative: +10

Tearing jaws +10 vs. AC—35 damage
Natural even hit: The wyvern can make a *deadly tail stinger* attack during its next turn.

[Special trigger] **Deadly tail stinger +10 vs. PD**—15 damage, and the target takes 10 ongoing poison damage (difficult save ends, 16+)

Flight: Wyverns are poor fliers in tight spaces, but out in the open, they are more capable.

AC 20	
PD 19	HP 140
MD 14	

NEXT STEPS

If the PCs defeat Golthrash, her remaining followers will flee if they can, and they'll spread word of the PC's treachery in daring to attack Golthrash (a servant of the Black) to those who serve the Three.

it's a major one. (Perhaps the writing on the walls in Battle 2 was instrumental.)

Failure: Facing the Vipers was nothing but a distraction that lead the PCs further from their quarry/the information they want. Now the trail is cold, and picking it up again will take more work, bribes, and probably some outside help.

A Test for Vipers

Success: The truth is, the Vipers failed, but the PCs passed their test. An interested third party who was following the action (or who had orchestrated the whole thing) now knows the PCs live up to their reputations and makes them an offer to go against a "real" threat this time.

Failure: The fight against Golthrash was the final test, and the PCs failed. Maybe the dragon pulled her punches and only knocked them unconscious, or maybe they were forced to flee. Either way, they don't get paid for the job. Also, word seems to be out in the area that the heroes are only posers.

Cleansing the Riffraff

Success: The PCs defeat Golthrash and the Vipers, solving a small problem for the Black. Their contact either pays them well for their service, or each PC gains a 6 with the Three (the Black) that lasts until they use it or level up.

Failure: Not only do the PCs fail to get the job done with Golthrash, but now both the dragon and the servants of the Black are out to get them. One in payback, and the others to make sure the word doesn't get back to their mistress of their failure to "handle" Golthrash.

Follow Me

Success: The PCs find the second piece/part/half of the item and now have a champion-tier magic item. The only issue is that it now seems to have a second quirk that pops up that's very dragon-like (likes to hoard wealth, has acid spit, carries snakes, etc.)

Failure: Seeing the PCs for the losers they are, the item finds a way to get misplaced or stolen, or annoys the PCs so much they ditch it. The problem is, somebody hears that they went into Golthrash's lair and thinks they still have the item—somebody who wants it for their own use.

A Pit of Vipers Story Endings

Here are outcomes for each story opening, detailing what success or failure might mean.

If the PCs did face all three battles, remember to give them a full heal-up.

The Kobold's Map

Success: The PCs followed the map to its source like any good adventurers would, and there they slew the dragon. Living up to such clichés is tougher than advertised, because the heroes' reputation for getting the job done gets them another job offer to rid the area of an even more troublesome foe.

Failure: There was nothing easy about the enemies lairing in the hill, and the PCs now suspect the map was intended to bring them to the Vipers. Now battle tested, the Vipers are confident, have become aggressive, and have already recruited a lot more allies. They also start to hire themselves out as assassins in the region and have been quite effective at it. Putting an end to them will be even more difficult now.

Rumor to Rumor

Success: Not only do the PCs defeat an evil dragon and claim its hoard, but they also find another clue to the thing they seek, and

Battle Scene Connections

The stories from this set of battle scenes can lead to other scenes:

 The Demon Wakes (GGW): Dalyisenes hears about the PCs killing Golthrash. He believes they might just be the heroes for the job and directs Sir Goldenmane to contact them.

 Conquer & Defend (Orc Lord, page 91): The PCs seek an item and they learn a clue to its location on the walls of the Viper lair. What they need is at Tenrock Hold on the edge of the empire.

The Three:
The Blue Sorcerers' Bargain

Level Range: 7–8

The themes of this set of battles are dealing with enemies using necromancy and dragon magic, the corruption of the Blue's servants, and navigating the politics of the Three (the Blue) within the empire.

This set of battle scenes works best in the wilds among the ruins of civilization and where civilization might grow again, preferably near the edge of a swamp or marsh.

The PCs must assault an old, run-down keep that is now the lair of the blue dragon Shirallex and a small group of blue sorcerers sworn to serve her.

As the PCs will learn the hard way, the sorcerer's oaths didn't many of them from falling under the influence of someone worse than the dragon. Seeking power, the sorcerers came into contact with lizardfolk deathcallers in the nearby marsh who serve of the Lich King. These deathcallers revealed secrets of necromancy to the sorcerers. Coveting new magic the Blue had not taught them, the blue sorcerers chose a new path, one at odds with the Three.

Making the situation even more convoluted, Shirallex is a designated envoy of the Blue who was tasked with setting up an embassy in the fortress since civilization will soon expand into the region again. But as part of their deal with the Lich King's people, the sorcerers tricked Shirallex and performed a ritual upon her that has partially brought her under the One-eyed Lord's power as a curse of undeath slowly overcomes her.

Since this set of battles is connected to the Three, and since there's a dragon involved, the final battle is a double-strength one.

The Blue Sorcerers' Bargain Story Openings

- **Hunting Dragons:** One or more PCs with a negative or conflicted relationship with the Three are approached by contacts that provide rumors of a dragon lairing at Falgren Keep near Corpselight Marsh. Those contacts named the beast Shiralex, a large blue wyrm. Time to kill another evil dragon and loot its hoard.

- **Corruption of Noble Power:** One or more PCs with a positive or conflicted relationship with the Three are tasked by high-level representatives of the Three (possibly working through Imperial channels) with a rescue mission. Shockingly, it's a mission to rescue a dragon! Shirallex, an envoy of the Blue has somehow been dominated by a group of traitorous blue sorcerers. The PCs are tasked with cleansing the site, Falgren Keep on the edge of Corpselight Marsh, of all there except the dragon. They are instructed to try to restore the wyrm's self-control, or if it is too far gone, give it a merciful death.

- **A Diplomatic Mission:** The PCs need something from the Three (probably the Blue). They are instructed to go to Falgren Keep, a new embassy of the Blue on the edge of Corpselight Marsh. The blue dragon Shirallex, an envoy of the Three, will provide the information they seek. The PCs are informed that the dragon has Imperial recognition, so they are encouraged not to create a diplomatic incident.

- **Lost Contact:** Agents of the Three contact one or more PCs with a positive or conflicted relationship with that icon. Recently, a new embassy within the empire was started at Falgren Keep, an old ruined stronghold near Corpselight Marsh that the Emperor provided to the Blue's people. But communications from the envoy, a blue dragon named Shirallex, have ceased. The PCs must investigate to determine if the Emperor reneged on the deal, or what may have befallen the envoy.

Alternate Icons

 The Emperor: Relations with the Blue and her status as an Imperial governor in Drakkenhall are always strained. Having a new embassy created by the Blue has caused problems, but when it goes dark, the political implications register on many levels. Some in the empire see the relationship with the Blue as a mistake in the first place. The PCs are tasked by imperial contacts on one side or the other of the political issue to find out what's going on... and possibly to put an end to the problem, however that's defined.

 Priestess: Given the Lich King's necromancers' involvement, PCs connected to the Priestess might be asked to investigate a surge in magic that shouldn't be strong in the Blue's domain.

ICONS IN PLAY

Characters that have relationships (and story-guide advantages) with the Three, the Lich King, the Emperor, the Priestess, and maybe the Great Gold Wyrm should be able to shine in these battle scenes. Moreso than PCs with other icon relationships, feel free to give such PCs extra knowledge about the opposition, make checks to pull off fun actions the players might suggest, and use their advantages to particularly good effect, such as negating or bypassing some of the advantages or abilities of the enemies.

✝HE BLUE SORCERERS' BARGAIN OVERVIEW

As the PCs approach Falgren Keep along the road paralleling the marsh, they are set upon by lizardfolk bog zombies led by lizardfolk deathcallers in Battle 1. It sets the tone. You're only getting out of this adventure covered in mud, or blood. Hopefully not your blood.

Battle 2 requires the PCs to breach the keep's defenses, which include living lizardfolk mooks, swamp trolls, and lizardfolk champions. But since the keep is technically an embassy, other methods could also get them past the gate initially.

Battle 3 is double-strength. The PCs face off against a cabal of corrupted blue sorcerers, their undead lizardfolk minions, and Shirallex, a blue dragon that has been infected with a rotting curse. The curse is slowly turning the dragon into a peat bog mummy, which will fully bring it under the Lich King's control.

GM, feel free to expand upon these battles by including meetings with those interested in sending the PCs to the keep, battles with enemies on the way to the keep, and other dangers from the marsh or within the keep (perhaps there's a dungeon, for example).

The battles outlined here can take place over a few hours or days, depending on how much time you want between the first battle and when the PCs reach the keep. Since the Three (the Blue) is in play, flavor the battle scenes with dark sorcery, dragonic power, and the corruption of undeath.

See story endings after the final battle for options on what happens after the PCs finish the last battle.

BATTLE I: MARSHDWELLER AMBUSH

You've been traveling along the edge of Corpselight Marsh for some hours, following an old dirt track toward Falgren Keep. The stronghold must be close, but the low trees with gnarled roots growing out of the swampy water block visibility. As you cross a rotting bridge over a pool of murky slime, you hear slurping sounds as the muck around you erupts and large reptilian humanoids burst forth. The creatures' flesh is discolored and their eyes only show whites, but they sniff the air and rush toward you. From behind a tree, a cold, hissing voice begins to chant.

LOCATION DESCRIPTION

A band of lizardfolk bog zombies under lizardfolk deathcaller control are trying to ambush the PCs on their way to Falgren Keep. They have chosen a favorable location to attack where the PCs are on a long wooden bridge crossing a pool of swamp water obviously full of muck. A stable dirt path continues on in both directions away from the bridge.

There are a number of cypress trees in the area that provide cover for the deathcallers, who will use ranged attacks. There's also some low vegetation and one pile of rotting logs to the PCs' right off the bridge that might provide some cover.

See Ambush in **Terrain & Traps** for whether the PCs are caught unaware and surprised.

TERRAIN & TRAPS

Ambush: The lizardfolk attackers are in place ahead of the PCs, with the bog zombies hiding in the muck with only their nostrils above water. When the PCs reach the middle of the bridge, have each character roll a DC 25 Wisdom check. More than half have to succeed or the lizardfolk surprise them. In that case, allow two bog zombies to try to knock the PCs off the bridge (see **Tactics**), then roll initiative as normal.

Wood Bridge: The bridge is 70 feet long and 8 feet wide, just enough for creatures to bypass each other. It's fairly stable, but force from below can overturn a section, which the bog zombies will try to do (see **Tactics**). Anyone trying to keep their balance on the bridge when this happens must succeed on a DC 23 Dexterity check. Other balancing maneuvers on the bridge require a DC 20 check. The water is only half a foot below the bridge deck.

Cypress Trees: Clumps of these trees grow both on dry land and out of the marsh in a few feet of water. They have large roots that spread out around the base, providing good cover to anyone hiding behind them. The trees average 35 feet in height, and climbing one requires a DC 20 Strength check.

Pool & Marsh: The pool around the bridge holds 3 feet of mucky water on top of another 2 to 3 feet of mud and slime. The lizardfolk are used to traversing this type of terrain and have little problem moving through it. Normal-size PCs (not halflings or gnomes) in the water will get stuck in the mud. Once stuck, moving through a pool requires a DC 20 Strength or Dexterity check as a move action to reach solid ground (or the bridge). Smaller PCs can swim above the muck.

A PC next to the bridge can attempt to climb out of the muck by succeeding on a DC 15 check (assuming the bridge is intact).

The marsh water is equally thick with muck, but the water grows deeper the farther from shore a creature goes, to a depth of 12 feet once you're 15 feet out, though it gets shallower near trees. Swimming through the water requires a successful DC 15 Strength check or the creature remains in place (hung up on vines, muck, or with a face full of nasty water).

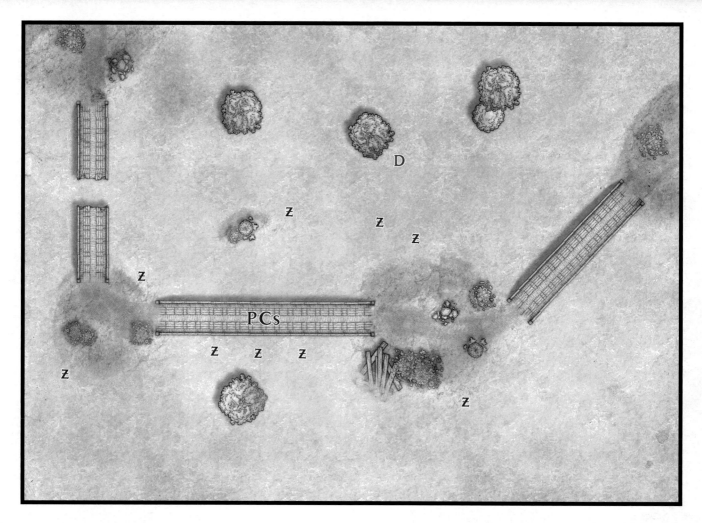

Logs & Vegetation: There are numerous creeper bushes, ferns, and other ground coverings along the path and around the pool up to 3 feet high that could provide some concealment.

The log pile consists of 4 medium-sized cypress trees that are well rotted. The base roots are 7 feet high, providing cover for anyone moving behind them.

Monsters

The lizardfolk bog zombies are being controlled by the lizardfolk deathcaller(s), marsh shamans who study death magic and gain power from association with the Lich King and his magic. They animate the dead flesh of lizardfolk warriors who fall in battle, something not all of the tribes are in favor of, thus making the deathcallers feared outcasts in many circles. They begin the battle hiding behind trees (both in the water and on land). The deathcallers want new bodies to perform their dark rites upon, and the PCs fit the bill. They're also guarding the main approach from this direction to the keep.

The lizardfolk bog zombies are more deadly than they were in life thanks to their high hit points and ability to infect enemies with peat rot. They start the battle submerged in the pool around the bridge and under the bridge. We left the location of the lizardfolk deathcallers off the map; as casters they'll want to be farther away from the bridge, up towards the creeper bushes at the top of the map, out in the water where they're harder to reach.

Additional Reinforcements: If you want to challenge the PCs more, a 7-headed hydra (core rulebook, page 236) hunting in the swamp sneaks into the battle by swimming through the swampy water, emerging closest to the PCs. Go ahead and let it send one attack toward any lizardfolk in range too.

#/Level of PCs	Lizardfolk Bog Zombie (Z)	Lizardfolk Deathcaller (D)
4 x 7th level	5	1
5 x 7th level	8	1
6 x 7th level	5	2
4 x 8th level	6	2
5 x 8th level	8	2
6 x 8th level	9	3

Tactics

If the lizardfolk surprise the PCs, two of the bog zombies will use their surprise action to push up against the bridge from underneath as a standard action, attempting to send PCs flying into the mucky water and bring the tasty flesh closer. If the zombies don't get surprise, they will try to shake the bridge on their first turn.

Any remaining bog zombies will seek out easy prey stuck in the muck. They will target staggered enemies first, even trying to disengage to reach such enemies (but won't take free attacks by moving). If forced to, they will climb up to the bridge to attack.

The deathcallers will emerge from behind their trees after the bog zombies attack (delaying if they have to). They will use ranged attacks as long as possible, either using *draining ray* attacks to damage directly, or *corpselight claws* to create ghostly claws that drag a creature back into the water. If engaged, they will use their *swampgas* attack to try to get away from enemies.

The deathcallers are good swimmers and don't have to make rolls to move through the marsh water freely. The zombies just enter the marsh and walk through the muck on the bottom.

Loot

The bog zombies have nothing of value. The deathcallers carry various necromantic components on them (dead bugs, severed hand, small jar of fetid troll blood, etc.), wield rods (implement) made from cypress root wood, and each has a simple necklace of silver wire and amber with an insect inside worth 100 gp.

Icons

A PC that has relationship advantages with the Three, Elf Queen, Prince, or maybe the GGW could use one or more of them to counteract the surprise round by having knowledge of the tactics used by the lizardfolk of Corpselight Marsh.

A PC that has relationship advantages with the Lich King, Priestess, or the GGW could use one or more of them to distract or scare a bog zombie, forcing it to flee the battle for 1d3 rounds (or leave the battle).

LIZARDFOLK BOG ZOMBIE

Hisssssssssss...

7th level troop [UNDEAD]
Initiative: +8
Vulnerability: holy

Clawed fist +12 vs. AC—20 damage
Natural odd hit: The bog zombie can make a *ripping bite* attack as a free action.

[Special trigger] **Ripping bite +13 vs. AC**—12 damage, and the target is vulnerable until the end of the bog zombie's next turn
Natural even hit or miss: See *bog bite*.

Bog bite: When the bog zombie hits a staggered or vulnerable target with its *ripping bite* attack and gets a natural even roll, the target must roll a save. On a failure, the target is weakened and stuck (save ends) as bog peat quickly covers its flesh and binds its legs together. On a success, the target is weakened until the end of its next turn as peat quickly grows on exposed flesh before sloughing off again.

GM, if you wish, a PC who fails the save could contract *bog bite fever* and need to be cured or face turning into a bog zombie in 1d3 + 1 days. Feel free to come up with symptoms for each day.

AC	21	
PD	21	**HP 135**
MD	14	

LIZARDFOLK DEATHCALLER

"The marsh is death, and it calls your name warmblooded one."

9th level caster [HUMANOID]
Initiative: +12

Knotted root rod +14 vs. AC—40 damage

R: Draining ray +14 vs. PD—45 negative energy damage, and the target is weakened until the end of its next turn

R: Corpselight claws +13 vs. PD (one nearby or far away enemy)—25 damage, 10 ongoing negative energy damage, and the target must succeed on a DC 25 Strength or Constitution check or be dragged somewhere nearby of the deathcaller's choice (allows opportunity attacks) by spectral claws attached to shadowy tendrils.
Natural roll is above both the target's Strength and Constitution: The target doesn't get to roll a check and is automatically dragged somewhere nearby.

C: Swampgas expulsion +13 vs. PD (each enemy engaged with deathcaller)—15 poison damage, the target pops free from the deathcaller, and the target is vulnerable (save ends)
Limited use: 1/battle.

Nastier Specials

Summon bog zombie: Once per battle as a standard action, the deathcaller can summon one lizardfolk bog zombie that acts immediately after the deathcaller's turn in initiative.

AC	25	
PD	18	**HP 170**
MD	24	

NEXT STEPS

If the PCs managed to capture a deathcaller, it may boast how the Marsh Lord (as it calls the Lich King) has claimed the region, including the "scaled god" who rules the keep. Beyond that, it won't be overly helpful except to reveal that some of its brethren now hold the keep.

After the battle ends and the PCs travel a short distance further, they will see the keep in the distance a few minutes' walk away. When they are ready to approach it, see **Battle 2: Entering Falgren Keep**.

BATTLE 2: ENTERING FALGREN KEEP

You stand at the edge of a small copse of trees looking upon Falgren Keep. The stronghold lies next to Corpselight Marsh, whose waters nearly reach the keep's outer wall and carry the strong stench of peat on the breeze. The fortress consists of a rectangular outer wall with a small tower at each corner and a single gate set into a small gatehouse in the center of a long wall. The wall is perhaps 20 feet high with ramparts and broken battlements. Beyond it is a two-story inner keep with a large, round tower on the water side; it looks in poor shape, with obvious places where the stone has crumbled away. You see figures guarding the walls and gate. They are humanoid, more lizardfolk, but not zombies.

LOCATION DESCRIPTION

The outer walls are 20 feet high and made of mortared stone blocks forming a rectangle 300 feet long and 200 feet wide. There's a single 15-foot gate within a small gatehouse that offers cover to those within and on top to guard against attackers.

The doors to the gatehouse are just inside the main gate, giving access to the storerooms and barracks on one side and arrow slits and defensive protections on the other. The outer defenses are generally intact, though there are signs of recent repair in places where the servants of Shirallex began updating the keep.

Other than the marsh water, there are few places to gain cover approaching the keep. The dirt road is open territory except for some small bushes and tree stumps. Mists and fogs do roll in around the keep from time to time, however (and would be a good use of a ritual or an advantage to create one). The marsh does offer more opportunities for concealment, whether under the water or concealed as logs and other things floating on it.

Lizardfolk patrol the gatehouse and ramparts around the top of the outer wall, with guards at each small corner tower. They don't seem to have any ballistae or other large weaponry available for defense (because they have a dragon).

It is possible for the PCs to talk their way inside, since this fort is tentatively a budding embassy (see **Monsters**). The gatehouse and walls are guarded by lizardfolk teethrippers, trolls, and a lizardfolk champion.

TERRAIN & TRAPS

Track, Marsh, & Open Ground: The track and the area around it is mostly wide open. Someone stealthy could use the foliage and stumps to move close to the walls with a successful DC 25 Dexterity check, with failure resulting in that PC being spotted and a call to find out who approaches. Once intruders are seen,

the enemies will rouse and be ready, and further attempts at stealth take a –5 penalty.

Using the marsh water as an approach point might work, but the guards are particularly wary of monsters from that direction. Start with a DC 28 to approach stealthily, but reduce that by up to 8 (DC 20) for creative ideas.

There is a sewage tunnel dug from under the keep about 15 feet out into the marsh. It's hard to see, however, and only PCs actively searching for such an entrance have a chance of finding it (DC 30). It's wide enough for a normal-sized humanoid to move up, and the metal grate rusted away long ago. But anyone doing so has to move through a narrow space filled completely with water and sewage over about 60 feet, requiring a DC 20 Strength and Dexterity check. Failure on either results in the PC making noise and drawing attention at the sewerpipe entrance next to the keep. (A natural 1 fumble might result in drowning and loss of a recovery too.)

Outer Walls: Climbing the walls isn't that hard due to their age and lack of maintenance. Doing so requires a DC 20 Strength check, with failure resulting in the climber getting stuck half way up and being spotted (though a bad failure might result in a fall back to the ground). Creating tunnels under or through the walls would be difficult without strong magic.

Gatehouse & Gate: The guards patrol the gatehouse heavily, and a few will throw javelins from inside against anyone attacking the gate or nearby walls. The gatehouse is a single story but the floor is raised 5 feet higher than the track through the gate, putting most arrow slits about 12 to 15 feet off the ground.

The gate is made from sturdy timbers and has been repaired. Bypassing it through sheer force is difficult during battle due to a large beam kept in place on the inside. With the beam in place, it takes three DC 30 Strength checks as a standard action to bust the gate in. Without the beam, it's one DC 20 check.

The beam is usually put in place by a troll and is large and heavy, requiring a DC 20 Strength check (or possibly another type of check for creative PCs) to lift out of place as a move action. Failure leaves the beam in place and makes noise, drawing attention.

Inner Keep: The inner keep is 130 x 100 with an 80-foot diameter tower on the right side. It has one main entrance on the ground level, a large iron-bound wooden door. The door is locked (DC 25 to bash it or jimmy the lock). A group of lizardfolk bog crawler mooks waits within (part of Battle 3). It's best if the PCs avoid the keep if some of them get inside the walls while the battle against the outer defenses is going on, but if they do try to get inside, feel free to add half of the mooks from Battle 3 to the fight (making it harder). Then remove half from Battle 3 as the PCs face the dragon and sorcerers.

Monsters

Guarding the walls of the keep are lizardfolk teethripper mooks. In the courtyard beyond the gatehouse is one or more swamp troll mercenaries who lounge about, feasting on animal carcasses and making crude jokes until they are needed to defend the fort or open the gate.

Lizardfolk champions walk the walls and oversee the mooks and the trolls. If any PCs approach the gate to talk, one of the champions will interact with them. The champions are cunning, but not overly smart. They have been given orders to keep visitors out, however, while the dragon undergoes the ritual, so they'll tell interested parties that the embassy isn't open to visitors at this time.

A good story, possibly backed by icon advantages, might get a champion to relent. Doing so still requires a successful DC 30 check (Charisma for diplomacy, or Strength for intimidation). At that point, the champion will invite the PCs in but ask them to wait in the courtyard while he talks to a superior to sort it out. The PCs will have about a minute before the champion returns to tell them they must leave or be slain. Of course, if the PCs attack while he's gone, then the waiting troops will retaliate and the champion will return and enter the battle when the escalation die reaches 2+.

Additional Reinforcements: If you want to challenge the PCs more, an iconic chimera (*Bestiary*, page 42) emerges from the swamps to attack the PCs as they are assaulting the keep. Gives nods to Lich King and the Three results over any others.

#/Level of PCs	Swamp Troll (T)	Lizardfolk Champion (C)	Lizardfolk Teethripper Mook (M)
4 x 7th level	1	1	9 (1 mob)
5 x 7th level	1	1	17 (2 mobs)
6 x 7th level	2	1	16 (2 mobs)
4 x 8th level	3	2	15 (2 mobs)
5 x 8th level	4	2	20 (2 mobs)
6 x 8th level	4	3	24 (3 mobs)

Tactics

The teethrippers will use their ranged attacks while the PCs are outside the walls while the trolls wait inside the gate for something to smash. As soon as any PC reaches the top of the walls the champions will move to engage them, as will any nearby mooks.

The remaining mooks will stay spread out on the walls as they use their ranged attacks. They will keep an eye out for other attackers in case the initial assault is a ruse, but being distracted, all DCs are easier by 5.

If all the action is taking place on the ramparts, the trolls will hurl animal carcasses and then ascend to engage enemies there.

Loot

The trolls have a few bags of loot scattered among some debris near the gates, while the lizardfolk have a scattering of simple jewelry. In total, there is 300 gp in valuables.

Icons

A PC that has relationship advantages with the Three, Emperor, Lich King, or maybe the Diabolist could use one or more of them to help convince a champion to let the PCs in the gates as visitors on official embassy business. In that case, reduce the DC to fool the champion by 5 for each advantage used, or let them simply pull it off.

A PC that has relationship advantages with the Dwarf King, Prince of Shadows, Orc Lord, or Crusader could use one or more of them to spot a weakness in the fort's defenses to be exploited, making skill checks to enter the keep easier (+5 to check per advantage).

Lizardfolk Champion

It's as big as an ogre, but with a mean streak.

Large 8th level wrecker [HUMANOID]
Initiative: +10

Giant bone spear +13 vs. AC—45 damage
Hit against a staggered enemy: The target takes 25 extra damage as the champion bites it.
Hit against an unstaggered enemy: The champion can make a *tail swipe* attack against the target as a free action.
Miss: 22 damage.

[*Special trigger*] **Tail swipe +12 vs. PD**—15 damage, and the target is dazed (save ends)

Deadly spear counterattack: When an enemy engaged with the champion makes a melee attack against it, that enemy takes 15 damage if the attack misses. Once per battle, the champion can have a nearby target take damage when it misses the champion with any attack.

AC	23	
PD	23	**HP 290**
MD	17	

Lizardfolk Teethripper

This lizardfolk has a mouthful of oversized teeth that look almost too big for its jaws.

7th level mook [HUMANOID]
Initiative: +9

Ripping teeth +12 vs. AC—15 damage
Natural 16+: The teethripper can make another *ripping teeth* attack this turn as a free action (no limit).

R: Poisoned javelin +12 vs. AC—6 damage and 0 poison damage
Natural odd hit: The target is also dazed and takes 5 ongoing poison damage (save ends both) as the poison sends tremors through its body.

AC	23	
PD	21	**HP 28 (mook)**
MD	15	

Mook: Kill one lizardfolk teethripper mook for every 28 damage you deal to the mob.

SWAMP TROLL

Swamp trolls are larger cousins of their troll brethren and resemble the terrain they live within: dirty, smelly, and unpleasant. They also exude a body oil that makes them reek as bad as the scummiest bog.

Large 7th level troop [GIANT]
Initiative: +9

Iron-hard claws +12 vs. AC (2 attacks)—20 damage
  First natural even hit each turn: The troll can make a *chomping bite* attack as a free action this turn.

[Special trigger] Chomping bite +11 vs. AC—30 damage

R: Hurled animal carcass +12 vs. AC—35 damage, and the target loses its next move action as it unentangles itself
  Limited use: 2/battle.

Troll stench: While engaged with this creature, an enemy must roll a save at the start of its turn. On a failure, it's dazed that turn (–4 penalty to attacks).

Trollish regeneration 15: While a troll is damaged, its rubbery flesh heals 15 hit points at the start of the troll's turn. It can regenerate five times per battle. If it heals to its maximum hit points, then that use of *regeneration* doesn't count against the five-use limit.

When the troll is hit by an attack that deals fire or acid damage, it loses one use of its *regeneration*, and it can't regenerate during its next turn.

Dropping a troll to 0 hp doesn't kill it if it has any uses of *regeneration* left.

Nastier Specials

Rending: If both *claw* attacks hit the same target, the target also takes 10 ongoing damage.

AC	20	
PD	20	**HP 192**
MD	16	

NEXT STEPS

Sounds of battle at the walls or in the courtyard will alert the dragon and corrupted blue sorcerers to trouble. The sorcerers will assemble upon the tower top during the battle with the outer guards as Shirallex is roused. As the PCs make for the main keep, the sorcerers will show themselves atop the tower and curse the PCs' for meddling as they attack. See **Battle 3: The Blue Cabal.**

Battle 3: The Blue Cabal

You overcome the outer guards at the walls but the main keep still waits. There are some narrow upper story windows perhaps a foot wide, but the main entrance into the keep seems to be a large wooden door bound in iron strips. To the right, a round tower rises above the keep and even the walls, overlooking all. That's when you hear the roar of a dragon, a mighty burst of annoyance and... pain? Looking up, you see figures moving on top of the tower along the edge—dragonics! They shout horrible curses upon you. (Seriously. Just hearing them makes you each lose 1d3 hit points. Ouch.)

Location Description

The main door to the two-story keep is currently closed and locked (unless the PCs managed to open during the last battle). It's the main access point into the keep other than upper floor windows that are probably too narrow for anyone to climb through without magic. There's a second access point into the keep, however, because the top of the tower is actually open to the sky except for a narrow wooden walkway around the outer edge. The dragon Shirallex had her servants take the roof off and construct the walkway when they arrived, so that she would have an easy way to access the skies.

The outer wall near the tower is still at least 20 feet away from the tower, and the tower climbs to a height of 60 feet. If the PCs go around to the backside of the keep, there's also a few small storage shacks and a small outer subterranean chamber/cesspool that connects to a sewage pipe out to the marsh, but it doesn't link to the inside of the keep.

The blue cabal, a group of corrupted blue sorcerers who have accessed necromancy to control Shirallex in exchange for magical secrets from the Lich King, are now standing on the walkway on top of the tower. It's far away from the top of the tower to any point on the walls or in the inner courtyard. The dragonics on the tower have line of sight to all below except anyone up against the keep wall opposite the tower. The dragon waits within the tower below the sorcerers, and the lizardfolk bog crawler mooks guard the interior of the keep and inner entrance to the tower.

This is a double-strength battle that should challenge the PCs thanks not only to Shirallex, but also the corrupted blue sorcerers.

Terrain & Traps

Keep & Door: The keep is two-stories high, rising to 30 feet. There are a handful of narrow windows (arrow slits really) on the upper level, but they are probably too small for even a halfling to move through. There are many cracks in the other walls and some vegetation growing upon the building, making climbing not that difficult (DC 20 Strength check) to get to the peaked roof.

The main door is made of thick timber bound in iron. It takes a DC 25 check (Strength or Dexterity) to bash or jimmy it open as a standard action, or 160 points of damage. If the PCs have a battering ram (like the gate beam), they get a +10 bonus to the check, but it takes two PCs to do so as a standard action.

Inside the keep, there are a handful of basic rooms on the ground level (kitchen and larder, dining hall, lounge, trophy room), and bedrooms, a war room, and a study on the upper floor. A stair to the left of the entrance goes to the upper floor. A narrow hallway down the middle of the ground floor to the right connects to the tower stairs, which ascend 10 feet before opening onto the main floor of the tower. Lizardfolk bog crawler mooks guard the entrance.

Tower: The tower is just over 60 feet tall and 80 feet in diameter. On the keep side, it rises 30 feet higher than the roof. Opposite the main entrance from the keep, there's a second set of wooden stairs that ascend up the inside of the tower to the roof. There are no floors other than the ground level, where the dragon waits. The insides have been braced in places with thick beams adding extra support (and places to perch), allowing the dragon to more easily fly out of the tower as she wishes, though that has not been a concern of late for her.

The outer stone walls are crumbled and ill-kept, giving many hand- and footholds. Anyone attempting to climb the tower on the outside must succeed on two DC 20 Strength or Dexterity checks, each requiring a move action. Failure means the PC gains no ground that round, unless the PC fails by more than 5, in which case it's a fall for 3d8 (first check) or 5d8 (second check) damage.

Climbing the interior walls also requires two checks, but the bracing makes it easier, requiring only DC 15 checks (with failure possibly leaving the PC exposed and hanging).

Falls from the walkway at the top deal 5d8 damage.

Courtyard: There is open ground on all four sides of the keep. Only those on the side opposite the tower will be out of view from it, however, due to the tower's height. There's also cover from the tower within the small gatehouse. Anyone on the walls is also visible to those on the tower.

There's a few random items and tools scattered about the courtyard, including shovels, ropes, lumber, a few short chains, and a large wooden gate beam that would be a good ram for the keep door (+10 to any attempts to open, but it requires two PCs to maneuver it as a standard action). If a PC wants to try a dicey move but needs a piece of equipment that would make sense for a keep, give it a 50% chance of being available.

Monsters

Shirallex waits on the main floor of the tower. She is not fully herself, having unwillingly gone through a ritual performed by the corrupted blue sorcerers that have infested her with necrotic peat rot in an attempt to mummify her. Her innate dragon magic has allowed her to partially resist the transformation so far, so she isn't a full undead creature yet and retains much of her dragon nature, but the rot covers her scales and is beginning to work on her mind. She will attack the PCs when they first enter (as the sorcerers tell her to do so), but may be able to indicate her distress and, with the PCs' help, could potentially aid them (or not attack) in exchange for the promise of help.

The corrupted blue sorcerers stand atop the tower walkway. They will attack from above with ranged spells and command the dragon to kill any PCs who enter the tower.

The undead lizardfolk bog crawlers are scattered through the lower floor of the keep by the main door, and are guarding the stairs leading up to the top.

Additional Reinforcements: If you want to challenge the PCs more, include an elder swaysong naga (*Bestiary*, page 144) that is in the dragon's lair, circling the dragon and speaking the ritual words that are slowly converting Shirallex into a mummy. Its name is Ossomer and it will try to move into the stairwell to keep PCs from surrounding it.

#/Level of PCs	Shirallex, Blue Dragon Mummy (S)	Corrupted Blue Sorcerer (B)	Bog Crawler Mook (M)
4 x 7th level	1	1	15 (2 mobs)
5 x 7th level	1	2	12 (2 mobs)
6 x 7th level	1	3	10 (1 mob)
4 x 8th level	1	4	20 (2 mobs)
5 x 8th level	1*	5	15 (2 mobs)
6 x 8th level	1*	6	30 (3 mobs)

* Increase Shirallex by 1 level: +1 to initiative, attacks, and defenses. She has 585 hp instead, her *claws and bite* attack deals 50 damage, and her *lighting breath* attack deals 70 damage. In addition, the threshold on her *mortal terror* nastier is 125 hp.

TACTICS

The corrupted blue sorcerers will use their *necrotic tendrils* ranged attack while the PCs are outside, and then switch between attacks once enemies reach the dragon. They will focus fire on any PC attempting to climb the tower walls to reach them, or who is on the walkway.

The bog crawlers will defend the keep and try to keep anyone from moving into the tower, and especially anyone going up the stairs to the reach the sorcerers. Other than that, they fight whatever is facing them.

At first, Shirallex will attack anyone entering the tower with her, using her breath once at least two enemies are within sight. She isn't above attacking and then trying to disengage, and if successful, leaping 10 or 15 feet upward to an inner support beam to get out of reach. She will then use her breath if possible, only leaping back down when ready to make melee attacks.

The transformation slowly turning her into a peat mummy has weakened some of her innate abilities, but made her more dangerous in other ways. She gets less *lightning breath* attacks and her lightning and magic resistance is weaker, but her physical attacks are laced with corruption.

The transformation overcoming her has also driven her mad with pain, so that initially she will believe the sorcerers' cries that the PCs are there to steal her hoard and attack them. But as she fights, she will act confused and question why she is unable to move as quickly as she once did when she misses with an attack. Her words should open up the possibility to the PCs that she was not a willing participant in her transformation.

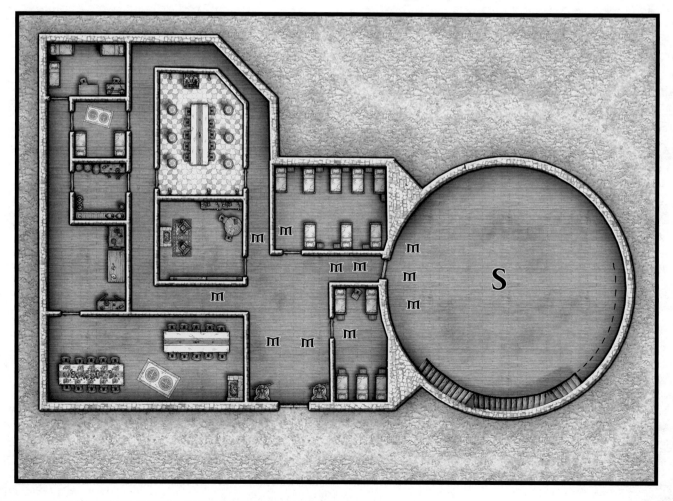

When she's staggered, or when the escalation die reaches 4, she will have a moment of clarity where she demands (in a dragon begging sort of way) for the PCs to release her from the curse those sorcerers put on her. This should give the PCs an opening to consider alternatives to simply killing her. If they ignore her pleas, then the pain will overcome her again and she will fight to the death.

Loot

Shirallex might be slowly changing into a peat mummy, but she's still a dragon and she hasn't let any of the blue sorcerers touch her hoard. Scattered around the tower floor are a pile of coins, some half-heaped into a small wooden chest. There's a total of 4000 cp, 2150 sp, 500 gp, 30 trines, an assortment of gold and silver rings displayed on a wooden plaque worth 350 gp, and a bowl of six large 100 gp topazes.

In addition, Shirallex has displayed the armor of a former "dragonslayer" on the wall of the tower. It's a suit of heavy armor, +3 Armor of the Fallen Hero (daily): The first time each day a melee attack drops you to 0 hp or below, you can heal using a recovery. If the attack would kill you outright, you instead only drop to 1 hp less than half your negative value. Quirk: You like to fill that hero role... too much.

Icons

A PC that has relationship advantages with the Three, Great Gold Wyrm, Lich King, Priestess, or maybe the Elf Queen or Diabolist could use one or more of them to try to help Shirallex break free

> ## Breaking Shirallex's Curse
>
> There's a chance the PCs are here to help the blue dragon, or they may realize that Shirallex has been transformed against her will and choose to try to help her resist the mummifying magic. If the PCs find a way to remove the curse upon her (probably through the use of advantages) or even buy her a short respite from the pain of the transformation to allow her to use her innate dragon magic to shake off the ritual, she will stop attacking them and direct her anger toward the corrupted blue sorcerers. GM, giving her a chance to break the ritual might mean a save each round, a DC 35 check made easier by −5 for each advantage spent, or some other roll that makes sense. Or even automatic success if any PC uses three advantages with the same icon and has a great story.
>
> Of course, once they realize the dragon is against them, unless Shirallex looks to be one hit away from death, the sorcerers will do their best to flee or try to talk their way out of their doom. At that point, Shirallex might grant the PCs a boon for saving her (iconic favors or perhaps the magic armor (see loot), but not her hoard) and then ask them to leave while she "takes care of some administrative matters."

from the magic of the rotting death ritual cast upon her. In this case, allow the PC to inspire the dragon somehow and make a check to help the dragon break the enchantment (see sidebar).

A PC that has relationship advantages with the Lich King, Priestess, or Great Gold Wyrm could use one or more of them to make some of the undead bog crawlers ignore or move away from them for 1d3 rounds as they reveal the power of the icon in some way.

Shirallex, Blue Dragon Mummy

Large 10th level caster [DRAGON]
Initiative: +15
Vulnerability: force

Claws and bite +14 vs. AC (2 attacks)—40 damage
First natural even hit or miss: The dragon can make a third *claws and bite* attack as a free action.
Natural 14+: The target takes 15 ongoing negative energy damage and is affected by peat rot (save ends both).
Each failed save: The target's body is further covered by peat and the ongoing damage increases by +10 (cumulative; saves granted by special powers don't increase the damage).

C: Lightning breath +14 vs. PD (1d3 nearby or far away enemies)—60 lightning damage
Natural even hit: The target is also dazed (save ends).

Intermittent breath: Shirallex can use *lightning breath* 1d3 + 1 times per battle, but never two turns in a row.

Counter-spell: When an enemy targets the blue dragon with a spell, the dragon can roll a save; success means the spell has no effect on the dragon. If the level of the spell is lower than the dragon's level, the save is 13+. Against an equal or higher-level spell, the save is 18+. If the dragon is staggered, the save target increases by +5. Shirallex's saves for this ability take a −2 penalty (already added above) due to her transformation.

Resist lightning 14+: When a lightning attack targets this creature, the attacker must roll a natural 14+ on the attack roll or it only deals half damage.

Nastier Specials

Mortal terror (partial): The presence of a mummy unnerves opponents, giving it an unusual *fear aura*. While engaged with this creature, enemies that have 100 hp or fewer are dazed (−4 attack) and do not add the escalation die to their attacks. Each time an enemy with 100 hp or fewer attacks the mummy, hit or miss, it must roll a save. On a success, it's no longer affected by the *fear aura* effects of any mummy in the battle.

AC	26	
PD	23	**HP 440**
MD	23	

CORRUPTED BLUE SORCERER

Dark power burns within this draconic, even though the flesh that clung to its once-strong frame is now withered and loose.

Double-strength 9th level caster [HUMANOID]
Initiative: +11

Needle-honed claws +13 vs. AC (2 attacks)—40 damage

R: Necrotic tendrils +14 vs. PD (one nearby or far away enemy)—70 negative energy damage as black tendrils of mist suddenly form near the target and lash it
Escalation die is even: The target is also stuck (save ends) as the tendrils hold it in place. It takes 20 negative energy damage each time it fails this save.
Escalation die is odd: The target is also weakened and takes 20 ongoing negative energy damage (save ends both).

R: Chaos pulse +14 vs. PD—70 damage of the following type (roll a d4):
1: *1 Lightning:* The target is also dazed (save ends).
2: *2 Cold:* The target is also stuck (save ends).
3: *3 Force:* The target pops free from each creature it's engaged with as it's flung backward a few feet. If in a precarious position (like near a drop), it must succeed on a save or fall.
4: *4 Thunder:* The target is partially deafened and is vulnerable (save ends) until it regains its hearing.

Dragon's leap: Once per battle as a move action, the sorcerer can make a mighty leap and fly somewhere nearby.

Call of the grave: Once per battle as a quick action, the sorcerer can reanimate two lizardfolk bog crawlers that have dropped this battle. Each has full hit points and acts during the mob's next turn (or immediately after the sorcerer if the mob has been destroyed).

AC	24	
PD	18	**HP 170**
MD	24	

LIZARDFOLK BOG CRAWLER

This muck-covered lizardfolk holds no rage like its brethren, only a cold hunger. You'll do.

8th level mook [UNDEAD]
Initiative: +9
Vulnerability: holy

Scaled fist +13 vs. AC—20 damage
Natural roll is above target's Dexterity and Strength: The bog crawler grabs the target and can make a *ripping teeth* attack against it as a free action.

[Special trigger] **Ripping teeth +13 vs. AC—10 damage**

AC	22	
PD	21	**HP 40 (mook)**
MD	16	

Mook: Kill one lizardfolk bog crawler mook for every 40 damage you deal to the mob.

NEXT STEPS

What happens after the battle depends on the PCs' actions. If they managed to save Shirallex from being fully turned into a peat mummy, she will thank the PCs for their help, perhaps even rewarding them. Then she will ask them to leave as she cleans up her own house and takes some aggression out on the lizardfolk deathcallers in the marsh.

If the dragon is killed, there could be ramifications to the relationship between the Blue and the Emperor.

THE BLUE SORCERERS' BARGAIN STORY ENDINGS

Here are outcomes for each story opening, detailing what success or failure might mean.

If the PCs did face all three battles, remember to give them a full heal-up.

HUNTING DRAGONS

Success: The PCs went to the dragon's lair and slew it, taking its hoard and making themselves even more hated enemies of the Three. Or maybe, seeing Shirallex's plight, they saved her.

In exchange, she reveals the lair of a red dragon whose hoard contains an artifact.

Failure: The PCs fail to slay the dragon, and perhaps worse, the corrupted blue sorcerers. Shirallex fully transforms into a peat mummy and becomes even stronger. With the sorcerers' help, the Lich King gains control of the region, turning the marsh into a breeding ground for undead.

Corruption of Noble Power

Success: The PCs save Shiral
lex, either by helping her throw off the rotting curse upon her, or at least by putting her out of her misery. The PCs tasked to free the dragon are admonished slightly if Shirallex is killed in the process of freeing her, but the Lich King's power can't be allowed to spread. In reparation for her death, they are directed to head into the marsh to put an end to the deathcallers' presence. Each PC gains a 6 with the Three that lasts until they use it or level up.

Failure: Shirallex turns into a peat mummy, and her dragonic power falls into the hands of the Lich King. That icon's power grows in the region, and relations between the Blue and the Emperor become more strained. Until they level up, any PCs with a positive or conflicted relationship with the Three get 5s instead of 6s on icon rolls.

A Diplomatic Mission

Success: The PCs save Shiralex, one way or another. If they are forced to kill her, she reveals what they wish to know as she dies. If not, she tells them in addition to rewarding them in other ways.

Failure: Not only do the PCs not gain the information they need, but now relations are even more strained with the Blue. Her agents are actively seeking the PCs, and because the PCs screwed up, they lose one die on their next icon roll with an icon who wanted to see the mission go well (GM's choice).

Lost Contact

Success: As Corruption of Noble Power.

Failure: The PCs muck up the job and now no one trusts anybody. Agents of both the Three and the Emperor are seeking the PCs to find out what happen, and both sides believe the heroes might be working against them. All 6s with the Three or Emperor are 5s instead until the PCs level up.

Battle Scene Connections

The stories from this set of battle scenes can lead to scenes in this and future books:

 Saving Cedric (GGW): Shirallex is thankful for the PCs save, keeping her from mummydom and a hellish immortality. As a gesture of goodwill (especially since she's now an Imperial official) she mentions a plot she heard about by a group of drow seeking to enslave good dragons. Even now, an assassin has probably enslaved one of the silvers and is headed to their vault in the overworld. She'll fly them to the edge of the upper realm, but no farther.

 Night Hunters (Lich King): While she was being transformed, Shirallex overheard many conversations among the blue sorcerers seeking to become necromancers. Those from the swamp they conversed with talked of a realm that could be reached through the swamp mists. This realm was right under the Emperor's nose, but fully dedicated to the Lich King. Break his things for her, will you? And if not for her, for your Emperor.

 Old Injuries Repaid (Orc Lord, page 101): In thanks for the PCs saving her, Shiralex tells them about news her spies uncovered. There's a plot to kidnap or kill the elvish ambassador on his way to the halfling village of Wreath for the Goodfellow's Day celebration (and the peace accords). The PCs might just be able to get there in time to stop it (no, given that set of battle scenes' plotline), but they can tell everyone that the Blue's ambassador helped warn of the scheme.

The Three: Into the Furnace

LEVEL RANGE: 10

Note, this set of battle scenes is designed to test 10th level characters and might be more challenging than most other battle scenes, depending on the group. The PCs will probably need to rely on some icon advantages to help them get through it, especially the final battle. If it's too taxing for your group, tone down the monsters, terrain effects, and nasty tricks.

The themes of this set of battles are smoke, fire, hit-and-run tactics, and facing an enemy at the top of the food chain in the terrain it fights best in. This set of battle scenes works best in a mountain region or in the wastes containing a semi-active volcano.

The PCs must assault the lair of a huge and ancient red dragon named Vazraka, Scourge of the Wastes, working their way through the multitude of tunnels and caves within a semi-active volcano where the wyrm lives. Not only is the environment dangerous, but the dragon's allies and smoke minions will make life difficult for the PCs. Not to mention that Vazraka fights with guerrilla tactics instead of direct confrontation.

If they survive the final battle and manage to kill Vazraka, a king's ransom awaits them.

Into the Furnace Story Openings

- **Recovering the Golden Egg:** One or more PCs with a positive or conflicted relationship with the Three, and the Blue specifically, are ordered by her directly to undertake a dangerous mission. One of the Red's mates, an ancient red dragon named Vazraka, has possession of a golden dragon egg taken from a past victory. The Blue needs that egg, and the Red can't know about it. She'll reveal the dragon's lair if the PCs recover the egg. The rest of Vazraka's hoard is theirs to keep, a reward beyond imagining.
- **A Blow Against the Red:** One or more PCs with a negative or conflicted relationship with the Three are given the location of the lair of Vazraka, the Scourge of the Wastes, who is one of the Red's mates. She is evil and is prophesized to bring ruin to one of the seven cities. As dragonhunters, this is the ultimate job, and the rewards of her hoard should be mighty too.
- **There Can Be Only One:** One or more PCs with a positive or conflicted relationship with the Three, and the Red specifically,

is tasked with removing one of his rivals by the Black or Blue. Vazraka the Scourge is only a few decades away from challenging the Red, but if she were to win, her tastes would bring her destructive desires immediately to the Empire. The other icons have plans in motion that they don't' want ruined by wanton destruction that comes too soon, and they'd rather keep the current Red in power, embarrassing as that sounds.

- **We Are Dragonslayers!:** The PCs learn the location of the lair of Vazraka, the Scourge of the Wastes, an ancient and powerful red dragon rumored to have an age's worth of hoard. The heroes who slay her would be renowned throughout the empire, and would not want for anything thanks to her hoard. She lives within a volcano in the wild lands.

Alternate Icons

 The Great Gold Wyrm: The dragon hunt could be for an ancient gold dragon instead, possibly one who went insane after exposure to a diabolical artifact. And since golds are resistant to fire too, perhaps the dragon's volcano-lair was an ancient city dedicated to the Great Gold Wyrm, much like Axis.

 Prince: The Prince really wants something in Vazraka's lair, which he'll remove while the PCs are busy distracting the wyrm. Of course, they'll think they were given the location of the mighty hoard as a reward for previous service.

Into the Furnace Overview

After traveling into the wastes to Fireplume peak, a semi-active volcano, the PCs find one entrance to the series of lava tubes and

Icons in Play

Characters that have relationships (and story-guide advantages) with the Three, Dwarf King, Great Gold Wyrm, High Druid, and maybe the Prince of Shadows should be able to shine in these battle scenes. Moreso than PCs with other icon relationships, feel free to give such PCs extra knowledge about the opposition, make checks to pull off fun actions the players might suggest, and use their advantages to particularly good effect, such as negating or bypassing some of the advantages or abilities of the enemies.

caverns forming the dragon's lair. In Battle 1, they must navigate the outer regions of the lair, which are filled with hot smoke and gases, lava streams, and smoke minions that lead them into danger.

Once they've moved further into the volcano near the magma chamber, the PCs enter a side cavern where creatures born of fire wait, efreeti and elemental lava spiders. The dragon has enslaved them to be guardians of her lair, and they will try to slow down the PCs. During the battle, Vazraka will make an appearance, since she's aware of all who enter her lair, and will give them a douse of dragon's breath to test their mettle.

Finally, Battle 3 is a double-strength fight against the dragon, her smoke minions, and her red dragon mate Urgastnir. Yep, two huge red dragons!

GM, feel free to expand upon these battles by including battles on the way to the volcano, encounters with lava terrain and fire creatures in other areas of the lair, and meetings with strange NPCs in the lava-filled chambers such as enslaved azer digging for the volcano's heart gem for the dragon.

The battles outlined here can take place over a few hours or days, if you want to stretch the journey to the volcano out. Since the Three (the Red) is in play, flavor the battle scenes with fire, smoke, destruction, and amazing volcanic environments.

See story endings after the final battle for options on what happens after the PCs finish the last battle.

Knowing Your Enemy

Unless you're a totally cruel GM, the PCs should probably be aware that they're going after a huge red dragon. And with this knowledge, they should be able to load up on potions of fire resistance and healing. If they're not prepared, chances of surviving decrease. If the PCs don't know what they're up against, you'll have to adjust some of the flavor text.

If the PCs don't have fire protection, you could also say that the heat in the volcano makes them sweat heavily and become dehydrated, and that drains 1 recovery per short rest away from each of them. Of course, that's just being mean.

BATTLE 1: ENTERING FIREPLUME PEAK

You're traveling through an old lava tube at the base of Fireplume peak, a semi-active volcano that houses the lair of Vazraka the

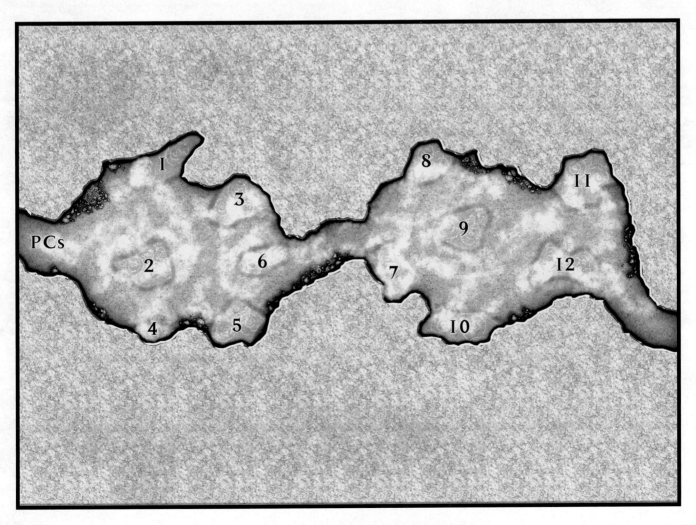

Scourge of the Wastes, an ancient and deadly red wyrm. The dragon's lair is said to be somewhere near the volcano's magma chamber, and this lava tube is heading in the right direction. After a few minutes of travel, you begin to feel the cold stone growing warm and a strong mineral smell hits you. Just ahead, the tunnel opens into a series of larger chambers filled with pools of bubbling water, releasing steam that fills the cavern, making visibility difficult. Off to the side, you think you see movement, but it's only a small geyser of boiling water that suddenly sprays a few feet into the air.

LOCATION DESCRIPTION

There are a pair of natural stone chambers, each roughly 60 feet long, 40 feet wide, and 15 feet high and connected by a natural archway. A number of small pools, between 3 and 6 feet in diameter are scattered throughout both chambers; they seem to be formed from natural springs heated from geothermal activity below that turn them to steam. The steam rises through natural vents in the ceiling, but not before clogging the air and making it difficult to see and breath. The entire place is wet with hot steam.

These chambers are hot but not intolerable as long as the PCs stay to the stone areas between the pools. The problem is that the steam hides enemies. The dragon's smoke minions are here, except they're composed of steam rather than smoke. As the PCs move through the area, they will manifest and attempt to lead the PCs to a boiling death (see Misty Enemies below) as they wear the PCs down.

With just the minions, this battle is a little easier than most, unless they manage to lead the PCs into multiple geyser explosions.

TERRAIN & TRAPS

Misty Enemies: The amount of steam in the area reduces vision significantly. The smoke (steam) minions in the area use that to their advantage, attempting to lure the PCs near pools that are about to geyser. At first, use the minions one at a time to draw the PCs near a pool. The minions will take the rough form of hulking humanoids like ogres or giants, normal sized serpents and drakes, or other enemies to get the PCs to move where they want. With the poor visibility, describe them vaguely (for example, you see a hulking figure half hidden by mists over there). When the PCs move toward the creature, which will be next to a pool, the minion will fade into the mists as the pool sends a geyser spraying (see Boiling Pools & Geysers below).

Once the PCs get wise to this trick, the minions will attack from all directions as they appear out of the mist, but each will try to draw the PCs near a pool by using disengage actions.

Boiling Pools & Geysers: Each pool is boiling hot and steam rises from it. Anyone touching the water or entering the pool takes 15 fire damage, plus 15 fire damage at the end of each turn if they are still in contact with the water. The pools are 3 to 7 feet deep, with a layer of hot gravel at the bottom.

When one or more PCs moves to a pool following a minion, that pool explodes in a geyser of steam and boiling water (the minions can sense which pools are about to do this). Make the following attack.

> **Geyser explosion +15 vs. PD (each PC next to the pool)—** 3d12 fire damage.

Once the minions can no longer draw PCs to pools and are forced to attack, the geysers randomly explode at the end of each round. When this happens, roll a d12 to determine which pool geysers and make a geyser explosion attack against any PCs next to the pool. These attacks don't affect the smoke (steam) minions.

MONSTERS

The smoke minions actually form out of steam. They are semi-independent manifestations of Vazraka's will that help guard her lair. Once the PCs battle the minions, the dragon becomes aware of intruders in her lair.

The minions will take the forms of giants, humanoids, and even small dragons, but only in a rough shape with details seemingly blurred by the steam. Use whatever might draw the PCs to them, such as outlines of hated types of foes among the characters, though not any specific individual.

Additional Reinforcements: If you want to challenge the PCs more, make one of the smoke minion mobs double strength.

#/Level of PCs	Smoke Minion Mook (M)
4 x 10th level	20 (2 mobs)
5 x 10th level	27 (3 mobs)
6 x 10th level	32 (4 mobs)

TACTICS

At first, one minion at a time will try to draw the PCs to a pool before fading into mist (either nothing to attack, or you can let the PCs who move there get an attack in, but no damage will spill over to the rest of the mob).

Once the minions attack, each mob will swarm a couple of PCs, trying to boil their lungs with superheated steam. If the PCs flee past the area, the minions will follow for a few rounds before losing... steam.

LOOT

One of the pools holds a calcified skeleton of a dwarf adventurer who died here. His chainmail is mostly rusted away, but the skull and part of his ribcage have become fossilized and stuck in the side of the pool. Around the skeleton's neck is a golden medallion with a sapphire worth 150 gp, but prying it out of the wall will take 1d3 rounds of exposure to the boiling water.

ICONS

A PC that has relationship advantages with the Three, Crusader, Dwarf King, Great Gold Wyrm, or High Druid could use one or more of them to recognize the smoke minions for what they are after seeing the first one, or possibly to disrupt the dragon's control over them, making some dissipate, others attack their allies, and a few impart images of Vazraka to the PC.

Smoke Minions

12th level mook [CONSTRUCT]
Initiative: +13

Invasive gases +17 vs. AC—55 damage
> *Natural 16+:* The target is hampered from burning eyes and gases in its lungs until the end of its next turn.

AC	26	
PD	20	**HP 80 (mook)**
MD	24	

Mook: Kill one smoke minion mook for every 80 damage you deal to the mob.

Next Steps

Once the PCs defeat the smoke minions or flee the area, the lava tube tunnel continues a short distance. Then it starts intersecting many small caves and more lava tubes in a maze of chambers filled with heat, smoke, and occasionally lava. These locations are a good option for adding additional battles, if the GM chooses to.

Eventually, the PCs will find the correct lava tube that leads toward the volcano's magma chamber. Once the PCs approach it, go to **Battle 2: Servants of Fireplume.**

BATTLE 2: SERVANTS OF FIREPLUME

You travel deeper into the volcano known as Fireplume, steadily getting closer to the mountain's heart where you believe the dragon lairs. The heat has been steady and draining, and its intensity is fierce. You stand at the edge of a huge cavern just off the hollow conduit that leads up to the surface crater, which you can see through a large opening in the far side of the cavern. A large pool of lava pours in through a wall, forms a pool, and then flows to a smaller pool near the opening before draining over the edge to the magma chamber below. There is a path between the pool and lava falls that crosses a short, arched, stone bridge over the lava and climbs to an opening in the opposite wall. What has your attention, however, is the huge statue of black volcanic glass carved from the wall over the large pool that depicts a mighty dragon. It's impressive. Wonder who made it?

Location Description

This cavern borders the lava conduit up to the caldera, but sits some hundreds of feet above the primary magma chamber. A secondary chamber produces the lava filling the cave. The chamber is 90 feet wide and 120 feet long, with a high 70 foot ceiling that keeps the hot gases from filling the lower regions. The main pool is 30 to 40 feet in diameter, with the secondary pool only 15 feet in diameter, but effectively blocking the open ledge to the conduit.

The statue was crafted to honor Vazraka by her efreeti servants, who inhabited this volcano before the dragon arrived but now serve her as guardians of her lair when she leaves to hunt. They retreat to their own pocket dimension when not needed, but keep tabs on the lair constantly and will seem to suddenly appear out of a flaming hole in the wall.

In addition to the efreeti, there are additional guardians in this chamber—giant fire spiders. The efreeti have created these creatures through imagination and will. The elementals wrap the molten rock around them into the form imprinted upon them by the genies, in this case spiders. At the start of the battle, they are below the lava pool out of sight.

In addition, there's one surprise for the PCs once the battle starts: Vazraka will make a sudden appearance to breath fire on the PCs, landing on the ledge amid the lava. But this is only a hit-and-run tactic to test them. On her next turn, she flies away out of sight into the conduit (see Dragon Attack, below).

Terrain & Traps

Lava Pools & Channel: Each lava pool is filled with molten rock that flows from one to another and then over the edge. Anyone

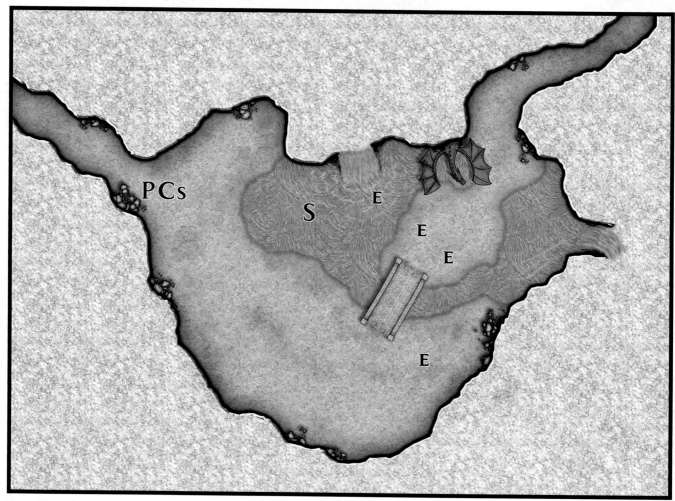

who enters a lava pool takes 25 fire damage and 25 ongoing fire damage each round they remain in the lava.

The channel is 30 feet long and 15 feet wide. The bridge crosses it safely. A PC can leap over the channel with a DC 15 Strength check, but doing so requires and easy save (6+). On a failure, gases bubble and pop at the wrong time and the PC takes 25 ongoing fire damage.

Opening to the Conduit: The opening to the conduit is 20 feet wide and 15 feet high, with the channel of flowing lava falling over the edge to the magma chamber hundreds of feet below. It's just big enough for Vazraka to fly into and land for her surprise attack.

The conduit is a few hundred yards in diameter, with a 300-foot drop to the magma chamber below. It's very hot and anyone going over the edge is probably dead (give them a save to manage to grab the conduit wall about 40 feet down, plus 4d12 fire damage). If you want to roll for it, call it 3d10 x 10 falling damage, plus 25 fire damage and 25 ongoing fire damage each round they spend in the chamber or conduit. Unless a PC moves to the edge, however, it's unlikely any enemy will be able to force them over.

Glass Idol: The volcanic glass idol of the dragon holds no special value. It's simply a nod to the dragon from the efreeti. While Vazraka is in the chamber, however, if she sees anyone harming the statue, they will be her number one target when she faces them with her full strength in Battle 3.

Dragon Attack: At the end of the second round of battle, Vazraka will swoop in from the conduit and land on the ledge among the lava pool there (so anyone who wants to engage her will have to move into the pool). Then she'll use her *primal fire breath* (against a single staggered enemy if she sees one, or against the group if not). To keep the PCs from wasting attacks on her, and because she's cunning, as a free action after the first two PCs act in the next round, she will step off the ledge and fly away into the conduit. This is purely a hit and run affair.

If the PCs damage her before she flees, that damage can remain for the next battle if you're feeling nice. Or you can say that during the time it takes for the PCs to reach her, she bathes in fiery pools and restores herself.

Here's the dragon's *primal fire breath* attack for easy reference. Her full stats are in the next battle.

C: Primal fire breath +17 vs. PD (1d4 + 1 nearby enemies, or one enemy)—60 fire damage, and 15 ongoing fire damage; OR 180 fire damage, and 30 ongoing fire damage and the target is weakened (save ends both) if used against a single enemy

Natural 18+: If the breath targeted multiple enemies, the target takes 25 ongoing fire damage instead of 15. If the breath targeted a single enemy, the target takes 60 ongoing fire damage instead of 30.

Monsters

The efreeti are crimson-skinned giants standing 12 feet tall with ornate brass bracers, greaves, and jewelry that pierces their flesh, pants and jerkin of some black material that doesn't burn, and large scimitars of black volcanic glass. They will step out of their pocket dimension as the PCs begin to cross the cavern, saying that the characters have trespassed into the lair of Vazraka the Scourge and must die for their transgressions. This honorable act of a declaration of intent means they don't get a surprise attack—make sure the PCs understand the efreet chose honorable battle instead of an ambush.

The fire spiders are huge constructs of lava with fire elemental spirits that stand well over 15 feet tall on their long legs. Each rises from the main lava pool.

Additional Reinforcements: If you want to challenge the PCs more, have the dragon return for a second blast of *primal fire breath* on round four. She then flees again and heals all damage.

#/Level of PCs	Efreet (E)	Fire Spider (S)
4 x 10th level	2	1
5 x 10th level	4	1
6 x 10th level	3	2

Tactics

The efreet will focus attacks on those not engaged with the spider(s). At least one will simply fly around the chamber near the ceiling using its ranged attack and avoiding melee damage. The others will attack in pairs against one worthy opponent (worthy being a melee type). Each will laugh deeply when the dragon appears, then yell, "*All praise the Scourge!*"

The fire spiders rise from the pool and start battle by throwing *fire webs* against the closest enemies to stop their prey from fleeing, then reel in those who become stuck, dragging them into the pool for melee attacks. Anyone wishing to make a melee attack against a spider must enter the primary pool to do so (taking fire damage), unless they find a way around that (perhaps leaping onto the creatures). The elemental spirits aren't cunning, however, and the spiders might be lured out of the pools if no enemies are engaged with them.

The efreeti will follow PCs moving out of the chamber, but the fire spiders won't.

Loot

The efreeti's scimitars could be a nice trophy piece, but the real treasure comes from defeating them due to the "wishes" they grant, which should be particularly useful in the battle to come.

Icons

A PC that has relationship advantages with the Three, Archmage, High Druid, or maybe the Lich King could use one or more of them to disrupt the elemental spirit within the fire spider form. Doing so could cause the creature to not attack for a round or two, attack an efreet, or perform some other action.

A PC that has relationship advantages with the Three or High Druid could use one or more of them to tap into the elemental energy running through the volcano, causing the lava to harden in places, flow where they want, or have some other interesting effect.

Efreet

It's customary to speak of the efreet as brutal and callous in comparison to the supposedly more urbane djinn, but it's not true. It's just that people are more afraid of being burned alive than torn limb from limb by screaming winds.

Large 10th level wrecker [GIANT]

Initiative: +15

Vulnerability: cold (only while staggered)

Blade of the perfect warrior +15 vs. AC (3 attacks)—35 damage
Natural 5, 10, 15, 20: Each nearby enemy takes 20 fire damage.

R: Jet of absolute conflagration +15 vs. PD (one random nearby conscious enemy)—110 fire damage
Natural 5, 10, 15, 20: The target loses all fire resistance until the end of the battle and is hampered (save ends).

Flight: Efreeti don't fly as well or as quickly as djinn, but they are able to get around okay.

Grant-a-wish: A PC whose attack drops an efreet to 0 hp gains the equivalent of an extremely favorable roll of 6 with an icon relationship die with an icon of the PC's choice that the PC already has a positive or conflicted relationship with. Treat this advantage as if it came from a positive relationship. The GM is encouraged to treat this result with the utmost benevolence and compassion.

Resist fire 18+: When a fire attack targets this creature, the attacker must roll a natural 18+ on the attack roll or it only deals half damage.

Energy transformation: The efreet can choose to deal lightning damage instead of fire damage with its attacks.

AC	25	
PD	24	**HP 420**
MD	23	

Fire Spider

Fire spiders are creatures of fire and elemental spirit in spider form. Two things that most people hate.

Huge 11th level spoiler [ELEMENTAL]

Initiative: +12

Vulnerability: cold

Flaming bite and piercing claw +16 vs. AC (2 attacks)—50 damage, and 40 fire damage

R: Fire web +16 vs. PD—70 fire damage, and 25 ongoing fire damage (hard save ends, 16+)
Natural even hit: The target is also stuck (save ends both). While stuck this way, as a move action the spider can reel it in and engage it.
Limited use: 2/battle.

Melee burn: When an enemy makes a natural odd melee attack roll against the spider, that attacker takes 3d12 fire damage.

Resist fire 18+: When a fire attack targets this creature, the attacker must roll a natural 18+ on the attack roll or it only deals half damage.

AC	26	
PD	26	**HP 840**
MD	20	

Next Steps

If the PCs have some way of flying into the volcano's conduit and protecting themselves from fire for an extended period, they can approach Vazraka's lair from an unexpected direction. Otherwise, there is only one viable exit from this chamber—the tunnel on the far side of the cavern. It circles around to the far side of the conduit as it descends a few hundred feet, before entering the dragon's sanctum.

Vazraka's lair actually rests a little ways from the magma chamber, with a long, wide tunnel from the conduit to it that she can close off if she senses the volcano coming alive (to save her hoard). That route also provides an escape route for her to fly out through the caldera if she ever needs it.

She'll be waiting for the PCs, however, and ready to spring her tricks upon them. When they're ready for the final showdown, go to **Battle 3: Vazraka the Scourge**.

BATTLE 3: VAZRAKA THE SCOURGE

You follow the wide tunnel down away from the chamber with the dragon statue. The roar of flowing lava gets loud as you near an opening to the conduit and magma chamber, and then recedes as you move away again, though the heat is intense. Finally the tunnel empties into a large cavern filled with smoke from flowing lava as a sense of ancient and immense power washes over you; this must be Vazraka's lair. A waterfall of lava pours into a pool on your right, flows in a channel across the chamber to second smaller pool, and then flows out a large tunnel on the far side of the cavern. There's also a section of the cave that bends away out of sight. A few natural stone pillars stretch to the high ceiling, offering some cover. There's no sign of the wyrm, however.

LOCATION DESCRIPTION

Note, if the PCs managed to travel through the conduit, they enter from the large exit on the far side of the cave and you should adjust the description accordingly. The cavern is 200 feet long, 130 feet wide, and 50 feet high. A 20-foot wide channel of lava flows between the two pools. The pool on the right is roughly 40 feet in diameter, and the one on the left is narrow (20 feet wide) and long (70 feet), with a natural peninsula on the far side. There's also a ledge high up a wall at the back of the chamber that one of the dragons can use as needed.

Vazraka has a surprise for the PCs. Her current mate, Urgastnir the Cruel is currently with her. Vazraka is hiding below the larger lava pool, while Urgastnir waits in the smaller pool. Both look forward to the surprise these would-be heroes (meals) are about to experience. They will wait until the PCs get close to one of the pools before bursting forth in a spray of lava and majesty to end the interlopers.

This is a double-strength battle, and also one that should be deadly for the PCs, even if they bring fire protection, and if they go in without any icon advantages, it might be a TPK. But hey, it's an end of campaign type of battle, so don't hold back.

TERRAIN & TRAPS

Lava Pools & Channel: Each pool is 20 to 40 feet across and deep and remains liquid-molten thanks to the dragon's presence. The small stream of lava that falls into the cavern provides a low but steady glurping sound that mutes sounds slightly. It flows from one pool to the next, and then out the back tunnel to the conduit, where the lava drains into the magma chamber.

Any PC that touches the lava or goes into a pool or channel takes 25 fire damage, and 25 ongoing fire damage each round they remain in the lava.

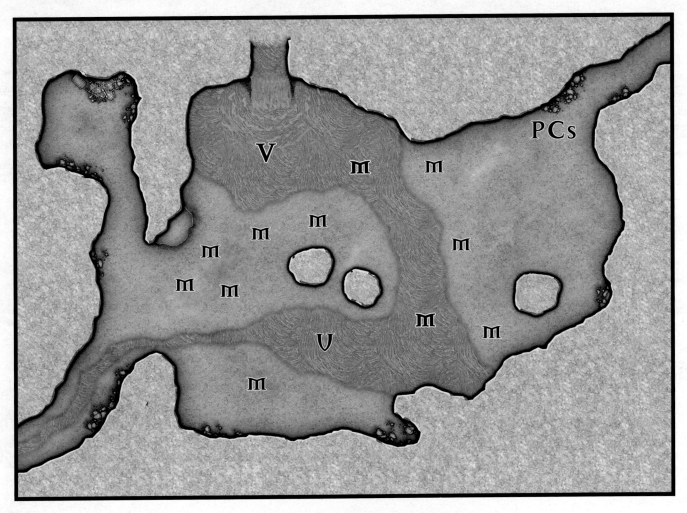

If you're feel particularly vicious, when the dragons burst forth, they could spray lava on each nearby creature (give them a save to avoid it, or make it a PD attack).

The channel is 20 feet wide and 10 feet deep with no obvious way over. Jumping it requires a DC 20 Strength check.

Stone Columns: There are three natural columns of stone that extend from floor to ceiling. They are big enough to provide some cover for PCs, and can take a few hits from a dragon before collapsing, though they make a good set piece for a dragon tail to slam to pieces during the battle.

Climbing a pillar is a little tough since the stone is hot to the touch. Doing so requires a DC 25 Strength check.

Side Cavern: The alcove/side cavern at the back of the chamber bends out of sight from the main area. It's more than far away from the PCs initially (so two full moves to reach the entrance, and another move to go into it). It will only be far away, however, once the PCs move into the cavern near the pools. It provides cover and holds Vazraka's hoard. Anyone moving into that area will draw her attention.

High Ledge: Not obvious at first, between the larger lava pool and side cavern is a 20-foot wide ledge 30 feet up. It's just big enough for a huge red dragon to fly to and perch on, in case one of them wants to use its breath while avoiding melee attacks.

Climbing to the ledge requires a DC 25 Strength check.

Monsters

Vazraka is a huge, ancient red dragon, one that would be in line to replace the Red if he ever perished. Her scales are large and hard as adamantine, colored ruby to deep crimson. Her very presence inspires fear and awe, and her ego is huge to match. It may be one weakness the PCs could exploit, since she may toy with the heroes while not staggered, not finishing PCs who drop unconscious.

Urgastnir is a fell opponent in his own right, but has standard stats for a flamewreathed dragon. While proud in his own right, he chose not to pass up an opportunity to mate with Vazraka, and thus produce younglings that would one day rule the world (in his view). Being proud, he will attack enemies not engaged with Vazraka, at least until only one or two are left. But knowing what's good for him, he'll let her have the final kill.

The smoke minions swirl around the smoke near the ceiling of the chamber. They will descend, taking on forms of small winged drakes, as they attack the PCs. Once on the ground, they aren't capable of flight. Note, Vazraka doesn't have the smoke minions' nastier special, but she can create them outside of combat.

Additional Reinforcements: If you want to challenge the PCs more, you must love your players very much. Use this: when Vazraka drops (unless she flees), she will roar in pain and fury, bringing the roof of the cave down in many places. Lava begins to pour into the chamber. Each round the PCs remain in the cavern, they must roll a save. On a failure, they take 25 fire damage, and ongoing 25 fire damage.

#/Level of PCs	Vazraka, Flamewreathed Dragon (V)	Urgastnir, Flamewreathed Dragon (U)	Smoke Minion Mook (M)
4 x 10th level	1	1	5 (1 mob)
5 x 10th level	1	1	15 (1 mob)
6 x 10th level	1	1*	15 (1 mob)

* Use Vazraka's stats for Urgastnir too.

Tactics

When one of the PCs nears a pool, the dragons will burst forth looking to put fear into their enemies, but they won't immediately attack as they showboat, so there's no surprise.

During their first round, each dragon will use its *primal fire breath*, depending on when it goes in initiative order. Urgastnir will spread his breath around, targeting as many PCs as he can. Vazraka will focus on one enemy to try to drop it quickly (an undamaged one if you want to be nice to the PCs). GM, you might want to be nice and have one of the dragon's go latter in the round to give the heroes time to heal between attacks.

After that each will use melee attacks, or another breath attack if targets were missed by it previously, plus use *whirling inferno* if some PCs are on fire.

These are smart and old dragons, so go ahead and use good tactics like having them disengage and fly to the ledge up above, or to the spur of land on the far side of the small pool, or just remain in a lava pool to make the PCs come to them.

Each dragon will try to flee when reduced to 100 hp or less.

EXTREME MEASURES

Fireplume peak is only a semi-active volcano, meaning it hasn't erupted in about a century, but does spew ash and gases, and occasionally large, molten boulders out the top. If things become dire for the PCs and it's looking like a TPK, it wouldn't be impossible for one of them to expend a strong advantage with one of the icons to have received an item with a powerful ritual stored within (or just become connected with the volcano somehow). When triggered, the volcano wakes, sending an explosion of magma into the many chambers and lava tubes through the mountain.

It might be a fiery death worthy of heroes. Or just maybe, it buys the PCs time to gather their wounded and dead and escape while the dragon tries to protect her hoard. And maybe a wish from an efreet could result in the PCs being carried away on a stone disk out of the volcano, protected from gases and molten rock by a pack of elemental servants. Now there's a retirement story!

LOOT

So this should be one of the final confrontations for the PCs before they retire into legend. Feel free to make Vazraka's hoard huge, containing far more wealth than normal for their level. There should be at least one magic item for each PC, perhaps even an artifact.

If the PCs came for a gold dragon egg, it's buried in a pile of coins among the dragon's hoard.

Here's one item left behind from a previous dragonslayer who wasn't so lucky. Perhaps one of the PCs discovers it during the battle.

+3 *Dragonslaying [weapon] (Daily):* You ignore all damage from a dragon's breath weapon attack this battle. In addition, dragons are vulnerable to your attacks using this weapon.
Quirk: Compelled to seek out and kill all dragons.

ICONS

A PC that has relationship advantages with the Three, Archmage, Diabolist, Great Gold Wyrm, High Druid, or Lich King could use one or more of them to ignore any terrain effects during the battle (from the dragon's *elemental control* or from a lava pool for example).

A PC that has relationship advantages with the Three, Great Gold Wyrm, or Prince could use one or more of them to convince Urgastnir to leave after he is staggered, along with a great story and a few successful skill checks. Or if the story is really good, to attack Vazraka to take her hoard.

A PC that has relationship advantages with any icon could use one or more of them to have an item that helps them against Vazraka specifically, perhaps giving expanded crit range, resistance to fire, or something similar.

Remember, each dragon has the two following abilities:

Escalator: A dragon adds the escalation die to its attack rolls.

Flight: A dragon flies reasonably well, powerful and fast in a straight line though not as maneuverable as more agile flyers.

VAZRAKA, FLAMEWREATHED DRAGON

"You dare come here? Then you seek incineration."

Huge 14th level spoiler [DRAGON]
Initiative: +17

Fangs and claws +19 vs. AC (3 attacks)—105 damage
Natural 16+: The target takes 25 ongoing fire damage.

C: Primal fire breath +19 vs. PD (1d4 + 2 nearby enemies, or one enemy)—80 fire damage, and 20 ongoing fire damage; OR 200 fire damage, and 40 ongoing fire damage and the target is weakened (hard save ends both) if used against a single enemy
Natural 18+: If the breath targeted multiple enemies, the target takes 30 ongoing fire damage instead of 20. If the breath targeted a single enemy, the target takes 70 ongoing fire damage instead of 40.

C: Whirling inferno +19 vs. PD (each nearby enemy taking ongoing fire damage)—The target's ongoing fire damage increases by 10 and becomes hard save ends (16+) as the dragon fans the flames
Limited use: 2/battle, as a quick action (once per round).

Draconic fire: The dragon's will and magic are so powerful that it ignores the fire resistance of creatures battling it.

Intermittent breath: A flamewreathed dragon can use *primal fire breath* 1d4 + 2 times per battle, but never two turns in a row.

Resist fire 18+: When a fire attack targets this creature, the attacker must roll a natural 18+ on the attack roll or it only deals half damage.

Elemental control, fire (dragon ability): The dragon can assert control over fire, lava, boiling liquid, and hot gases in its lair. Twice per battle as a quick action (once per round), it can create an obstacle for an enemy (stuck), cause an explosion of flames near an enemy (dazed), or send hot gases swirling around an enemy (vulnerable). This effect lasts until the end of the enemy's next turn. The target can avoid the condition by making a DC 30 skill check.

Wyrm of fear and flame: While engaged with this creature, enemies with 192 hp or fewer are dazed (−4 attacks), do not add the escalation die to their attacks, and take 4d20 fire damage at the start of their turn.

AC	30	
PD	23	HP 1760
MD	29	

SMOKE MINIONS

12th level mook [CONSTRUCT]
Initiative: +13

Invasive gases +17 vs. AC—55 damage
Natural 16+: The target is hampered from burning eyes and gases in its lungs until the end of its next turn.

AC	26	
PD	20	HP 80
MD	24	

URGASTNIR, FLAMEWREATHED DRAGON

Now you know fire. A final lesson.

Huge 12th level spoiler [DRAGON]
Initiative: +15

Fangs and claws +17 vs. AC (3 attacks)—75 damage
Natural 16+: The target takes 20 ongoing fire damage.

C: Primal fire breath +17 vs. PD (1d4 + 1 nearby enemies, or one enemy)—60 fire damage, and 15 ongoing fire damage; OR 180 fire damage, and 30 ongoing fire damage and the target is weakened (save ends both) if used against a single enemy
Natural 18+: If the breath targeted multiple enemies, the target takes 25 ongoing fire damage instead of 15. If the breath targeted a single enemy, the target takes 60 ongoing fire damage instead of 30.

C: Whirling inferno +17 vs. PD (each nearby enemy taking ongoing fire damage)—The target's ongoing fire damage increases by 5 and becomes hard save ends (16+) as the dragon fans the flames
Limited use: 2/battle, as a quick action (once per round).

Intermittent breath: A flamewreathed dragon can use *primal fire breath* 1d4 + 2 times per battle, but never two turns in a row.

Resist fire 18+: When a fire attack targets this creature, the attacker must roll a natural 18+ on the attack roll or it only deals half damage.

Tough hide (dragon ability): Urgastnir gains a +1 bonus to AC as his dragon ability (included).

Wyrm of fear and flame: While engaged with this creature, enemies with 120 hp or fewer are dazed (−4 attacks), do not add the escalation die to their attacks, and take 4d20 fire damage at the start of their turn.

AC	29	
PD	21	**HP 1100**
MD	27	

NEXT STEPS

Should the PCs survive, they will stand among the greatest heroes of the empire, having slain two of the strongest red dragons behind the Red himself. That should make a good story.

INTO THE FURNACE STORY ENDINGS

Here are outcomes for each story opening, detailing what success or failure might mean.

If the PCs did face all three battles, remember to give them a full heal-up.

RECOVERING THE GOLDEN EGG

Success: The PCs manage to defeat Vazraka and recover the golden egg, delivering it to the Blue. Besides acquiring the red dragon's hoard, each PC gains a 6 with the Three that lasts until they use it. In addition, the PCs with positive relationships with the Blue gain important positions within her Imperial agency.

Failure: The egg is missing or destroyed, or the PCs fail to beat Vazraka. Whatever the case, the Blue is displeased with failure, so this time she sends the PCs on real suicide mission.

A BLOW AGAINST THE RED

Success: The PCs find Vazraka and put her down, another evil dragon dead. Her loss, plus that of her mate, is a big hit to the power of red dragons in the region. Enough even to make the Red himself have a sliver of a doubt. Each PC gets two 6s with one of their icons that lasts until they use it.

Failure: Vazraka the Scourge was too much for them. The PCs take a hit to their reputation and are forced to seek lesser dragon opponents for a while. Their normal contacts don't seem to have time for them either. The next time each PC rolls icon dice, each 6 is a 5 instead.

THERE CAN BE ONLY ONE

Success: Vazraka is destroyed and the Blue and Black can continue with their plots. All is well, and the Red no wiser. Each PC with a relationship to the Three gains two 6s that last until used.

Failure: The PCs fail to put down Vazraka, and worse, it stokes her anger. She and her consort travel to the empire to take their anger out on the world.

WE ARE DRAGONSLAYERS!

Success: The PCs are victorious and hailed as the greatest dragonslayers of the Age. All doors are open to them and all drinks are free.

Failure: The PCs join the list of failed heroes who Vazraka defeated, but at least most of them lived to retire.

BATTLE SCENE CONNECTIONS

The stories from this set of battle scenes can lead to at least on future scene:

Playing With Fire (Diabolist): After the PCs defeat the dragons, they will discover Vazraka's hoard in the back chamber. Among that hoard is an elemental fire node in the form of a huge fire opal embedded in the wall that glows hot with fire and magic. They soon realize that the dragon used it as a scrying device, and that it is cycling between two images that she must have been following. The first is a familiar city, and an entrance to the undercity. The second is a group of robed cultists that seem to be able to summon demons into the world without using the Diabolist's power. If true, it could be very bad, since the demons would have fewer limits and destruction is imminent. The PCs should follow up on the images.